THE FUTURE OF

THE CITY OF INTELLECT

The Future of

THE CITY OF INTELLECT

The Changing American University

EDITED BY STEVEN BRINT

STANFORD UNIVERSITY PRESS

Stanford, California   2002

Stanford University Press
Stanford, California
©2002 by the Board of Trustees of the
Leland Stanford Junior University
Printed in the United States of America

Library of Congress Cataloging-in-Publication Data

Brint, Steven

    The future of the city of intellect : the changing American university / edited by Steven Brint.
      p. cm.
    Includes bibliographical references and index.
    ISBN 0-8047-4420-3 (cloth : alk. paper) —
    ISBN 0-8047-4531-5 (paper : alk. paper)
    1. Universities and colleges—United States. 2. Education, Higher—Aims and objectives—United States. I. Brint, Steven G.

LA227.4 .F92   2002
378.73—dc21   2002001560

This book is printed on acid-free, archival-quality paper.

Original printing 2002

Last figure below indicates year of this printing:
11   10   09   08   07   06   05   04   03   02

Typeset at Stanford University Press in 10/13 Galliard

Contents

Acknowledgments

This volume grew out of a conference held at the University of California, Riverside, in February 2000. During the three days of the conference, participants heard of many things: bean bag curricula, investments in technological fool's gold, amoebas in baskets, fox princes and their snail cousins, and higher education's journey from Williamstown to Las Vegas. The conference will be remembered not only for vivid metaphors but also for the festival of stimulating conversation it produced. Papers presented at the conference have been substantially revised for this volume. I would like to thank the authors for their good humor in the face of my many queries and editorial suggestions. In addition to the contributors to this volume, a number of other distinguished scholars and social critics presented papers at the conference. They included Troy Duster, David John Frank, Thomas L. Haskell, Zachary Karabell, L. Scott Miller, Masao Miyoshi, Thomas Mortenson, Guy Neave, Cary Nelson, David Noble, Mary Poovey, Sheldon Rothblatt, Jack H. Schuster, James Sheehan, Lee S. Shulman, Keith F. Widaman, and Longxi Zhang. These people contributed greatly, not only to the success of the conference but also to the quality of this volume.

Financial support for the conference was provided by the William and Flora Hewlett Foundation, the University of California Humanities Research Institute, the University of California Office of the President, the University of California, Riverside Center for Ideas and Society, and the University of California, Riverside Office of the Dean of the College of Humanities, Arts, and Social Sciences. I am grateful for the support of these institutions. I would also like to thank Georgia Elliott for her help with fund-raising. Trudy Cohen, Marilyn Davis, Antonette Toney, and, especially, the magnificently calm and competent Laura Lara helped to make the conference a success through their organizational wizardry. Bob Clark, Clark Kerr, Woody Powell, Sheldon Rothblatt, and Jack Schuster deserve thanks for advice that contributed to the liveliness of the conference and, ultimately, to the quality of this volume.

Claremont, CA

Preface

In *The Uses of the University*, Clark Kerr introduced a now-familiar term, the "multiversity," and he offered a metaphor to help explain its meaning. The university, wrote Kerr, is becoming "a *city* of infinite variety." He went on to contrast the multiversity with two other images from the past: the one-industry towns of the early research universities, with their intellectual oligarchies, and the villages of the nineteenth-century colleges with their priestlike masters.

> "The Idea of a Multiversity" is a city of infinite variety. Some get lost in the city; some rise to the top within it; most fashion their lives within one of its many subcultures. There is less sense of community than in the village but also less sense of confinement. There is less sense of purpose than within the town but there are more ways to excel. . . . As against the village and the town, the "city" is more like the totality of civilization as it has evolved and more an integral part of it; and movement to and from the surrounding society has been greatly accelerated.

When he wrote of these "cities of intellect," Kerr was thinking of research universities, like his own University of California and other large institutions such as the University of Michigan, the Massachusetts Institute of Technology, and Stanford University. In the generation since Kerr's book was published, the number of these cities of intellect has grown. By the estimate of the Carnegie Foundation, some 125 institutions can be categorized as research universities—perhaps 80 to 90 would qualify by their size and range of activities as true multiversities, or cities of intellect.

The metaphor of the City of Intellect resonates beyond the illustrations that Kerr used to convey his point. As in urban neighborhoods, intellectual enclaves abut one another but may have little or no interaction among their members. New activities grow up at the outskirts of the city, eventually growing strong enough to form new economic centers. As the city spreads out and becomes more complex, regulatory mechanisms grow larger and more formalized. New technologies come in to change how business in the city is conducted. The amenities of city life become important to consumers, and the upgrading of recreational and consumer areas becomes a priority for administrators. The city becomes both a major employer and a major influence in its surrounding area.

Kerr marveled at the scale of the City of Intellect as an enterprise in the early 1960s:

> The University of California last year had operating expenditures from all sources of nearly half a billion dollars, with almost another 100 million for construction; a total employment of over 40,000 people, more than IBM and in a far greater variety of endeavors; operations in over a hundred locations, counting campuses, experiment stations, agricultural and urban extension centers, and projects abroad involving more than fifty countries; nearly 10,000 courses in its catalogues; some form of contact with nearly every industry, nearly every level of government, nearly every person in its region.

Today, the activities of even a single institution may outstrip those of Kerr's seven-campus UC system of the early 1960s. The provost of Columbia University, Jonathan Cole, reported an operating budget of $1.1 billion in the mid-1990s—a budget one hundred times greater than it had at the end of World War II, fifty years before. And Columbia is not even the largest or most complex of universities. Harvard University's operating budget will soon top $2 billion.

Over the last several decades, universities have become more important than ever before in American economic and social life. We hear often of the importance of the "knowledge economy" as the center of the country's economic growth, and empirical studies do confirm the greater dynamism of industries employing large numbers of highly educated workers. As an elevator up the class structure, advanced degrees have replaced shop-floor promotion and up-by-the-bootstraps entrepreneurial activity in nearly every field. Because of their importance for adult careers, college degrees are no longer rare. Nearly one in four adults in the United States now has a baccalaureate or higher level degree. Universities are also expected to generate research and policy ideas that help to solve problems of the larger society. Many of the important cultural conflicts and status tensions in society—from conflicts over multicultural curricula and gay rights to the ethics of cloning and the human implications of new technologies—are expressed first and debated most passionately on university campuses.

As their importance grows, so do criticisms of today's universities. Michael Berubé, a leading critic, offers, for example, a satiric set of proposals to complete the transformation of universities into big business. It is true, he writes, that "American colleges and universities have adopted some of the most constructive developments of the business world, such as boosting the pay of their dynamic executive officers to over half a million dollars per annum and insisting on a flexible, 'as-needed' work force for . . . tasks like maintaining the physical plant and teaching freshman composition." But, he notes, they have not done everything in their power to topple the remaining barriers between themselves and the rest of corporate America. They have, he observes, been slow to register their names as commercial trademarks, to attach the names of corporate sponsors to their stadiums and academic chairs, to raise tuition to a market-clearing price, and to consolidate departments that make no discernible contribution to the task of preparing students for the labor market. Other critics find universities becoming the playthings of corporate sponsors, adapting their programs to fit business needs and increasingly at the service of corporate sponsors of research. These portraits give rise to the uneasy sense of a transition from public-serving social institutions to industrial institutions, and from collegial to corporate enterprises.

And yet for every portrait of a wayward Goliath, sloughing off its commitments to the progress of all, competing narratives have been written of the necessity of evolutionary change, of the inexorable logic of altered circumstances. Indeed, it is difficult to contest a central theme of this competing narrative: that the university has been asked to do many things for many people, and that the scope of its activities has consequently multiplied over the last thirty years without, however, being accompanied by a comparable increase in the traditional revenue streams that have supported those activities. Many proponents of this competing narrative argue that the new university is not just inevitably more entrepreneurial than the old but also more responsive and stronger because of it.

The authors in this volume tend to question these two familiar story lines, because they find the reality of the changing American university at once more complex and more interesting than either allows. The authors do, however, focus on a common set of forces for change—and also on a common set of structures that can restrain and shape those forces.

A number of the challenges currently faced by universities are consequences of their unprecedented opportunities following World War II. Continuing high demand for educational credentials in an ever-expanding number of fields has opened up new training markets for universities in such far-flung fields as nuclear medicine, leisure and fitness, protective services, film studies, and financial engineering. Opportunities for involvement in ancillary activities have also expanded, including alumni and student services, provision of continuing professional education courses, university extension, and university-industry research collaborations. Universities require funds to operate in these new markets and to engage in these new activities. With the relative decline of state support for universities, the institutions have been forced to develop new revenue streams, primarily by raising tuition and fees and working hard to obtain gifts and grants from private sources. Sale of educational services—from computing and printing services to tickets for cultural events—have also become more important sources of revenues. To recruit top students and faculty, the university must spend money on student services and campus amenities and continuing improvements in instructional technology. The self-generating pressures of credentials inflation and knowledge expansion lead to strong pressures for growth, while the costs of attracting students and faculty and supporting their educational activities lead to equally strong pressures to cut back on less "profitable" activities. The result has been much larger enterprises under constant pressure of rising costs and competing priorities.

Under these circumstances, competitive pressures to attract top faculty and students are very intense. The reasons are clear: Top faculty bring in government and corporate research funds, foundation support, and raise prestige through their achievements. Top students reinforce the standing of their universities and eventually contribute through their donations as alumni to their economic well-being. Other forms of competition have also become keen, because they are connected to retaining high-quality faculty and attracting high-quality students. Competitive pressures have encouraged relaxation of restrictions on corporate involvement in sponsored research and efforts by university lobbyists to earmark government research funds for particular institutions (thereby bypassing the peer-review system). They have also led in some cases to hard times for arts and sciences departments that do not appear to "pay their own way," lax requirements in many academic and professional programs eager to attract students, and a shift toward maximizing consumer satisfaction rather than students' academic preparation. Funds have been poured into recreation centers, food courts, student services, and amenities in the campus and commercial areas surrounding the campus.

Another major source of change originates in the profit potential of intellectual breakthroughs in a few disciplines. Scientific and engineering knowledge has, of course, always been a source of profit for private firms, but the previous division of labor between universities as centers of discovery and firms as centers of profitable application has now broken down because of public policy emphasizing American competitiveness and the rights of universities to profit from new discoveries. Today, the university has become increasingly close to industry in a few fields in which: (a) applications are potentially very profitable, (b) knowledge changes very quickly, and (c) top experts are distributed between academe and industry and collaborate without regard for the nominal divisions between the two spheres. The life sciences and biotechnology firms are the leading edge of change in this new world of integrated research organization, but similar circumstances can be found in computer science, engineering, and, to a degree, also in finance. These disciplines exist in a very unusual resource-space, but they nevertheless represent a model of the future for some university and business leaders. These new developments in the "knowledge economy" raise ethical issues about the future of academic oversight and free exchange of research findings under circumstances of proprietary sponsorship. Do the life sciences show the university the way into the future, or do they threaten to diminish the autonomy and distort the priorities of universities as knowledge-producing and knowledge-conserving institutions?

A final major source of change (one whose potential is not yet known) comes from the new means of production available to instructors through the Internet and other digital media. Earlier technologies, such as film and television, were also hailed as revolutionary forces in their time, but they developed as supplements to conventional instruction. The Internet, however, appears already to have sunk roots deeper into the culture and practices of teaching and learning than those previous technologies. No force has a greater potential to transform higher education. In an immediate sense, the new technology allows for far more creative teaching through a mix of visual, aural, and verbal information.

But more dramatic outcomes are also easy to imagine. What, other than inertia and institutional legitimacy, prevents large parts of lower-division education from being absorbed by "all-star" faculties offering courses on the Internet and CDs? If accompanied by e-mail question-and-answer sessions, would such an outcome lead to distinctively lower-quality undergraduate education than the lecture courses now commonplace at many universities that seat six to eight hundred students? How, indeed, will the ever-increasing number of students seeking higher-education credentials be taught, if not, at least in part, through these alternative media?

The major theme of the book can be expressed in this way: Universities today are responding simultaneously to several important forces of change. They are *demographic:* the growth of near-universal attendance of postsecondary institutions by high school graduates and the concurrent development of a market also among midcareer adults; *economic:* the increasing wealth of selective private universities and the resulting increases in inequality between these and other universities; the increasing involvement of private firms in the research and service activities of universities; the rise of market-consciousness among university administrators and students alike; and competition in some spheres of activity from for-profit enterprises; and *technological:* the development of the Internet and other distance media as teaching and research tools. These forces of change will have important consequences for the organization and purposes of universities of the future.

The authors in this volume adopt one of two major positions. In some cases, they accept that a significant transformation is occurring, and they show how the new world of academe works. This position is characteristic of the chapters by Randall Collins, Patricia Gumport, Walter Powell and Jason Owen-Smith, Richard Lanham, David Collis, and Richard Chait. In other cases, the authors raise questions about the extent of the transformation. That more skeptical outlook is characteristic of the chapters by Roger Geiger, Carol Tomlinson-Keasey, Andrew Abbott, Steven Brint, and Sheila Slaughter. Although these latter authors are careful to challenge misleading images of change, they do tend to agree that forces outside the university present exceptional challenges to the traditional priorities and levels of autonomy enjoyed by universities. That is another important theme of the book; both the introductory chapter by Clark Kerr and the concluding chapters by Richard Chait and Burton Clark focus on threats to university autonomy and what universities can do to preserve their autonomy against the influence of powerful external forces, be they markets or governments.

Universities have developed a complex organizational structure to allow them to pursue their (substantially) self-regulated activities in teaching, research, and service while remaining responsive to external sources of resources and legitimacy. This structure involves a dual organization of knowledge authority and administrative authority. Some academic structures, such as the department, the major, the academic ranks, and lifetime tenure create very significant resistances to change. Others, such as administrators' responsibility for managing and enhancing revenue streams, create significant incentives to change. The challenges of new markets, unrelenting cost pressures, fierce competition, weaker insulation from industry, and new instructional technologies guarantee that the future of the City of Intellect will involve significant strains on existing structures and particularly on traditions of shared governance. If universities wish to maintain high levels of autonomy in the face of these pressures, they will need somehow to find ways to build consensus about shared commitments among key internal constituencies, while continuing to broaden the revenue streams available to support their still-growing operations.

Organization of the Chapters

In a bracing introductory essay, Clark Kerr contrasts two periods of exceptional challenge to American universities. During the 1960s, universities were rocked by the simultaneous shocks of rapidly increasing enrollments, student protest, and new responsibilities for large-scale scientific inquiry. In the near future, Kerr argues, universities will encounter equally momentous forces: the development of new markets for higher education and the rise of private-sector competitors, the Internet as a potentially transforming instructional tool, the explosive potential of the biological sciences and corporate interest in them, and relative declines in government funding. Kerr argues that a strong economy and university leaders' clear vision of the major forces at work helped universities adapt to the conditions of the 1960s. He is not as sanguine about universities' ability to create a "golden age" out of the storms of the twenty-first century. Productivity gains, he argues, are not as assured, and competition for resources will for this and other reasons remain fierce. Kerr provides not only an acute analysis of the major forces at work in the City of Intellect today but also the outlines of a prescription for successful adaptation to those forces. This prescription involves a new kind of leadership and mechanisms for strengthening the position of the major decision-making parties: boards of trustees, presidents, and faculty senates.

The four chapters in Part One look in greater detail at the demographic and economic forces of change. Where Kerr examines a number of forces that will influence the future development of the City of Intellect, Randall Collins adopts a steadfastly "hedgehog" perspective, focusing on a single key force for change: the ever-increasing demand for credentials as an inherent feature of mass higher education. In Collins's view, credential inflation is the skeleton key that unlocks many of the perplexing developments of late-twentieth-century higher education: the dominance of vocational curricula, declining academic intensity in the midst of ever-fiercer competition for access to selective institutions, and a record in many disciplines of exceptional intellectual progress in the midst of declining conditions for the majority of faculty.

Patricia Gumport focuses on a second inherently dynamic factor: the constant expansion of knowledge. She argues that the inability of universities to keep pace with knowledge production during periods of economic constraint has led to a new dominant conceptual understanding of the university. This new conception has become particularly popular among public sector university administrators and higher-education policy-makers. Drawing on case studies of three major public research universities, Gumport argues that a new "industrial logic" has begun to replace the earlier "social institution logic" that once animated both discourse and practice in these institutions. This new logic focuses on applied research, contributions to economic development, and selective investment in disciplines closely related to growth industries. Many universities are attempting to develop a hybrid vision, composed of elements of both logics, but the strains of doing so are evident. She concludes by raising a key question: Will tomorrow's research universities provide as safe a home for intellect as they do for marketable expertise?

Roger Geiger concentrates on the competition among universities for high-ability students, because, in his view, this market drives many other forms of competition. High-ability students attract highly productive faculty and create unusual opportunities for fund-raising once these students graduate. Compared with their private counterparts, public universities should be at a disadvantage in the competition for these students because they can offer neither the concentration of high-ability peers nor comparable levels of educational expenditure. However, Geiger finds that they have not fared as badly as might be expected. Although larger concentrations of high-ability students are found in the private sector, many top students continue to decide that state universities have much to offer intellectually and culturally and at more attractive prices. For that reason, a hierarchical system dominated by a small number of private universities has not come to pass, in spite of resource conditions that greatly favored the private sector between the mid-1970s and the mid-1990s.

Walter Powell and Jason Owen-Smith focus on the blurring boundaries between the life sciences and private firms, another face of "industrial logic" and one that many predict will come to affect disciplines outside of the life sciences as well. Leading experts in these fields are as likely to work in profit-making firms as in the university, and research teams are likely to include many people employed in both sectors. Powell and Owen-Smith cast doubt on assumptions about the research superiority of universities over corporations and about the meaningfulness of the line separating these two spheres. Instead of universities supplying the knowledge and corporations supplying the practical applications, what will the world look like if knowledge production moves toward the private sector and universities no longer enjoy a relative monopoly over cutting-edge research? For Powell and Owen-Smith, the new world promises to be more dynamic and the universities more integrated into the for-profit sector, but a number of problems may also emerge. These include blocks on the free flow of information and much higher levels of inequality between institutions and disciplines. This chapter raises a number of questions: How many fields have the potential for moving in this direction? Will those that have the potential do so? Will the new world of knowledge production in the life sciences prove enduring or transitory? Powell and Owen-Smith provide reasons to believe that the transformation will be less extensive and long-lasting than many believe.

The chapters in Part Two examine technological forces of change. Nearly everyone agrees that the Internet and digital media have enriched the research environment for scientists and scholars. Questions remain, however, about the value of these media as instructional technology. Will Internet- and CD-based courses favor visually and aurally attractive content without stimulating the deeper engagement possible through face-to-face interaction and immersion in printed texts? Will the private sector take over a significant share of undergraduate teaching, just as it has begun to attract educational consumers in the markets for continuing professional and recreational education? Will large numbers of professors be made technologically obsolete by these new media?

Carol Tomlinson-Keasey is optimistic about the ability of universities to adapt the new technologies to enduring purposes while fending off potential competitors. She describes several creative applications of the Internet, showing its potential for creating learning communities and more individualized learning environments, both on campus and, literally, in global villages of students. She shows how both the teaching and the learning role change with the new technology. Teachers spend less time in direct student contact, in course administration, and lecturing; they spend more time on lab hours, answering e-mail, and in generating instructional materials. In the best of the new experiments, Tomlinson-Keasey argues, students are required to take a more active and independent role in learning, an orientation that does not come easily to many. Tomlinson-Keasey shows some of the exciting possibilities of the new technology. Whether most institutions will have the imagination and resources to take advantage of these possibilities is a question she leaves open.

In an unusually provocative chapter, Richard Lanham critiques the traditional "campus-based operating system" from the perspective of the new information technologies, finding the latter superior in many ways. He argues that the impersonal, loosely bounded, free-flowing, efficiency-conscious world of the Internet provides a sharp challenge to each one of ten assumptions about the advantages of universities as protected and sequestered worlds in which educationally productive inefficiencies are cultivated. Lanham suggests that the organizational structure of universities prevents them from taking advantage of the shift from an economy based on commodities to an economy based on attention. "The university's stock should rise (in the economy of attention), but only when it realizes that its business is not renting seats in classrooms but constructing attention-structures deep inside the world of work."

In the 1990s, the management expert Peter Drucker predicted that higher education would soon be rationalized through the utilization of the Internet for basic undergraduate and professional courses. Many colleges and universities, he predicted, would fail in the wake of the new forces of production. Although Drucker's prediction was at a minimum premature, it is clear that both universities and private firms have moved aggressively into the market for online courses. In the final chapter of this section, David Collis examines the strategies of for-profit firms for increasing their share of the market for online courses and degrees. The chapter surveys the activities of more than one hundred firms, analyzes their business strategies, discusses their strengths and weaknesses in comparison to universities, and provides the most persuasive investigation thus far of the Drucker thesis. Collis's conclusions will provide short-term comfort to those who consider the corporate threat to universities overblown, while suggesting reasons for long-term concern.

The chapters in Part Three examine how demographic and economic forces of change have influenced the rise and fall of fields of knowledge in the university. In a chapter distinguished by dry wit and sociological acumen, Andrew Abbott focuses on research and scholarship in the humanities and social sciences. Abbott argues that the structural foundations of the university are the undergraduate major and the department. So long as these structures exist, very little change in the distribution of fields can be expected. These two structures stabilize faculty appointments and therefore the specific set of topics and analytical devices characteristic of the disciplines. The structure requires a complement of interdisciplinary research for issues and topics that necessarily crosscut disciplinary lines. Abbott shows that interdisciplinary research developed at almost the same time as the disciplines themselves, and he suggests that the proportion of interdisciplinary work has been relatively constant since that beginning. Abbott's structural analysis allows him to explore a number of other processes linked to the system of disciplines, such as faculty poaching on the analytical devices of more advanced disciplines as a means for status advancement within less advanced disciplines, the inevitability of fractal distinctions within the disciplines reproducing themselves in every topic the field assays, and the routine creation of orthodox and heterodox careers. Looking toward the future, Abbott anticipates an erosion of the disciplines in the nonelite sector caused by commercial competition, but he argues that "it is quite hard to imagine the disciplinary system coming apart in the elite universities."

My own chapter discusses the implications of the rise of occupational and professional programs as a growing part of the curriculum in American universities. Where Abbott's focus on the disciplinary context of research leads him to emphasize powerful forces of inertia, my focus on the movement of student enrollments leads me to emphasize the shrinking role of the traditional center of the university, the arts and sciences disciplines, and the rise of the "practical arts." I discuss the dimensions of this change and its consequences both for the university at large and the arts and sciences in particular. I agree with Abbott that the consequences are more profound in the nonelite sector, where in many cases general education requirements alone stand in the way of a sharp reduction in the size of the arts and sciences faculty. Nevertheless, throughout the university system, the rise of the practical arts has helped to support significant changes, including the migrations of faculty and even whole disciplines toward professional identities, increased vulnerability of small liberal arts disciplines, and a rapidly rising interest in interdisciplinary curricula for economic, as much as intellectual, reasons.

Sheila Slaughter's chapter provides the outlines of a full-blown theory of curricular formation. Slaughter criticizes theories of curriculum-formation that emphasize single causes—whether they be demographic change, market forces, or professorial paradigm shifts. Instead, she shows that three major forces shape the curriculum: (a) disciplinary developments influencing professors' research interests, (b) social movements, such as those that fought for women's and ethnic studies programs in the 1960s, and (c) powerful organizations in the political economy. Each of these forces, Slaughter argues, has been at work at least since the Progressive Era. Of these forces, Slaughter is inclined to emphasize the significance of powerful external organizations as suppliers of jobs and research directions. She concludes: "Only if curricula planners are able to ensure that curricula will lead to prestige and resources for faculty and professional careers for students are new curricula likely to be institutionalized."

In the final section of the book, Richard Chait and Burton Clark consider the changing conditions of academic work and institutional governance. Both chapters are based on a reconsideration of the "academic revolution" proclaimed by Christopher Jencks and David Riesman in the late 1960s. Jencks and Riesman argued that the increasing importance of knowledge and expertise in American society, combined with the institutional acceptance of faculty prerogatives, had led to unprecedented power for the faculty. Professors controlled curriculum, course content, selection of colleagues and senior administrators, and standards for student admissions and graduation.

In a masterful review of the period following Jencks and Riesman, Richard Chait argues that the influence of the faculty remains great only at selective institutions. By contrast, heightened managerial control, often combined with faculty unionism, has taken root below the top tier. Even in selective institutions, the faculty's influence is precarious. Here, Chait argues, power is shifting not toward the administration or the board but toward off-campus agents who provide resources to the university—that is, toward student consumers, state legislators and executives, individual benefactors, and corporate sponsors. There is less total power to go around on campus, and neither the faculty nor the administration nor the board feels able to shape the future direction of their institutions. Thus, Chait concludes, the single most dramatic shift from the days of the academic revolution "may not be that the professorate has lost power, but rather that the university has lost control. . . . If the board, the administration, and the faculty do not coalesce and, maybe even if they do, the 'market revolution' will supplant the 'academic revolution.'"

Surrounded by external forces threatening to overwhelm its traditional values and forms of self-governance, it is no wonder that universities are increasingly aware of threats to their prized record of intellectual progress combined with high levels of self-governance. In the concluding chapter of the volume, the distinguished scholar Burton Clark provides suggestions, based on his research in Europe and the United States, concerning how universities can maintain high levels of achievement and autonomy in the face of the growing power of groups external to the university. He does so by commending a collegial form of "entrepreneurship" as a model for future programmatic development and institutional governance. For Clark, this new form of collegial entrepreneurship involves the self-conscious strengthening of planning units involving both faculty and administrators; enhancement of units on the periphery of the academic disciplines that are involved in service to the surrounding community and practical problem-solving involving researchers from several disciplines; a funding base that is less dependent on any single revenue stream; and the creation of an entrepreneurial spirit and some money-making educational activities even in the "academic heartland" of the arts and sciences. Opposed in principle to a radical distinction between the university as a social institution and the university as an industrial organization, Clark suggests that universities can selectively borrow elements from the latter model to become stronger in their primary purposes. Of course, not everyone will agree with Clark's recommendations, but, like so many of the chapters in this book, it is instantly recognizable as an important vision of the future of the City of Intellect.

Contributors

ANDREW ABBOTT is the Gustavus F. and Ann M. Swift Distinguished Service Professor in Sociology at the College at the University of Chicago. His work falls into three main streams: substantive study of professions and disciplines, methodological development in the area of sequence analysis, and theoretical writings on social structure and temporality. The professions and disciplines work was early synthesized in *The System of Professions* (1988), an ecological and dynamic theorizing of the comparative histories of professions. His historical writing on the Chicago School of Sociology, summarized in *Department and Discipline* (1999), advanced both his theories of disciplines and his ideas about temporality. In *Chaos of Disciplines* (2001) he offered a novel "fractal" theory of intellectual change, broadening that theory gradually into a more general analysis of cultural and social structure. *Time Matters* (2001) brought together his work on the foundations of social science methodologies, linking it to his theoretical stance with its focus on structures in process. In methodological and substantive analyses in a variety of areas, he has pioneered the application of dynamic programming to the analysis of social sequence data like careers and comparative histories.

STEVEN BRINT is Professor of Sociology at the University of California, Riverside and Director of the *Colleges and Universities 2000 Study*. He received a B.A. with highest honors in sociology from the University of California, Berkeley, and an M.A. and Ph.D. from Harvard University. His work focuses on the professional middle class and the institutions of intellectual and professional life. He is the author of *The Diverted Dream* (with Jerome Karabel, 1989), *In an Age of Experts* (1994), and *Schools and Societies* (1998). *The Diverted Dream* won the American Educational Research Association's Distinguished Publication Award in 1991. His articles have appeared in *The American Journal of Sociology*, *Sociological Theory*, *Work and Occupations*, *Sociology of Education*, and other journals. He is currently at work on an NSF-supported study of continuity and change in American colleges and universities, 1970–2000, in collaboration with the American Council on Education.

RICHARD CHAIT is Professor of Higher Education at the Harvard Graduate School of Education. He received his B.A. in history from Rutgers University and his M.A. in history and Ph.D. in higher education from the University of Wisconsin. His research has focused on two areas: academic administration and governance. His publications on academic administration include *The Question of Tenure* (ed., 2002) and *Beyond Traditional Tenure* (with A. Ford, 1993). In the area of governance he has co-authored *Improving the Performance of Governing Boards* (1996) and *The Effective Board of Trustees* (1991). His work has also appeared in *The Harvard Business Review* and many other periodicals. He directs the Project on Faculty Appointments, a four-year, $2-million research effort funded by the Pew Charitable Trusts. In 2001 he began a study of "Governance Futures" funded primarily by the Packard Foundation.

BURTON R. CLARK is Allan M. Cartter Professor Emeritus of Higher Education and Sociology, University of California, Los Angeles. He has taught in departments of sociology and graduate schools of education at Stanford, Harvard, the University of California, Berkeley, Yale, and UCLA. His major books include *The Distinctive College* (1970), *The Higher Education System* (1983), *The Academic Life* (1987), *Places of Inquiry* (1995), and *Creating Entrepreneurial Universities* (1998), and, as co-editor, *The Encyclopedia of Higher Education* (1992).

RANDALL COLLINS is Professor of Sociology at the University of Pennsylvania, where he is also a member of the Graduate Group in Comparative Literature; in Religious Studies; and in History and Sociology of Science. He is the author of more than a dozen books, including *The Sociology of Philosophies* (1998), which won the American Sociological Association's Distinguished Publication award in 1999. His research includes the topics of long-term historical change in economic institutions and in culture; states and geopolitical power; and the micro-sociology of face-to-face interaction. He is currently completing a collection of essays on the micro-sociological theory of interaction rituals and is working on a book on the sociological theory of violent conflict.

DAVID J. COLLIS is the Frederick Frank adjunct Professor of International Business Administration at the Yale School of Management, where he has been a top-rated teacher since 1998. For the previous eleven years he was an associate professor in the Business, Government, and Competition area at the Harvard Graduate School of Business Administration, where he continues to teach and chair Executive Education programs. He is an expert on corporate strategy and global competition and is the author of the recent books *Corporate Strategy* (with Cynthia Montgomery, 1997) and *Corporate Headquarters* (with Michael Goold and David Young, 2000). His work has been published in the *Harvard Business Review, Academy of Management Journal, Strategic Management Journal*, and *European Management Journal*, and in many books, including *Managing the Multibusiness Company, International Competitiveness,* and *Beyond Free Trade.* The more than fifty cases he has authored have sold over 400,000 copies worldwide. Collis received an M.A. (1976) with a Double First from Cambridge University, where he was the Wrenbury Scholar of the University. He graduated as a Baker Scholar from Harvard Business School, MBA (1978) and received a Ph.D. (1986) in Business Economics at Harvard University, where he was a Dean's Doctoral Fellow.

ROGER L. GEIGER is professor and former head (1997–2000), Higher Education Program, Pennsylvania State University, where he has taught since 1987. A historian, he has written two volumes on the evolution of research universities in the United States: *To Advance Knowledge: the Growth of American Research Universities, 1900–1940* (1986) and *Research and Relevant Knowledge: American Research Universities Since World War II* (1986 and 1993). He is writing a study of current developments at these institutions, "American Universities in the Marketplace." Since 1993 he has edited the *History of Higher Education Annual*, and in 2000 he published *The American College in the Nineteenth Century.* "The Reformation of the Colleges, 1800–1820" appeared in *History of Universities* (2001). He has also written on comparative higher education: *Private Sectors in Higher Education: Structure, Function and Change in Eight Countries* (1986).

PATRICIA J. GUMPORT is an associate professor in the School of Education at Stanford University and serves concurrently as the director of the Stanford Institute for Higher Education Research (SIHER) as well as the executive director and principal investigator of the National Center for Postsecondary Improvement (NCPI). She earned a Ph.D. in education and two master's degrees (education, sociology) from Stanford University. Her research addresses several critical issues for higher education—from the management of academic change and organizational restructuring, to the interdependence between graduate education and knowledge production, to reconciling the tensions between management and governance in contemporary academic workplaces. Her current research examines academic restructuring in public higher education.

CLARK KERR, A.B., Swarthmore (1932), M.A., Stanford (1933), Ph.D. Economics, University of California, Berkeley (1939), is Professor Emeritus of Economics and Industrial Relations, UC Berkeley. He has served as Chancellor of UC Berkeley (1952–58), as President of the university (1958–67), and as Chair of the Carnegie Commission on Higher Education (1967–73) and the Carnegie Council on Higher Education (1974–79). He was the architect of the California Master Plan for Higher Education of 1960 and has served as adviser on national goals, labor management policy, and railroads to five U.S. presidents. He has worked as an arbitrator for machinists, meat packers, longshoremen and warehousemen, utility, transportation, automobile, aircraft, and postal workers, and he is the author of many articles, chapters, and books on labor economics and higher education, most notably *The Uses of the University* (5th ed., 2001). His two-volume memoir, *The Gold and the Blue*, is being published by the University of California Press.

RICHARD A. LANHAM is President of Rhetorica, Inc., a Los Angeles consulting and educational services company. He is professor emeritus of English at UCLA. He holds A.B., M.A. and Ph.D. degrees in English from Yale University. He is the author of *The Motives of Eloquence* (1976), *Literacy and the Survival of Humanism* (1983), and eight other books of literary criticism and prose stylistics. His latest book, *The Electronic Word: Democracy, Technology, and the Arts*, was published in both print and electronic form by the University of Chicago Press in 1993. Since 1971 he has also acted as a literary consultant and expert witness in copyright disputes in the television and motion picture industry.

JASON OWEN-SMITH is completing two years of post-doctoral research in the Stanford University School of Education. He received his Ph.D. in Sociology from the University of Arizona in 2000. His current research focuses on the intersection of science, formal organization, and the economy, with particular emphasis on the dynamics of scientific collaboration, the effects of increased patenting on research universities, and the role of publicly funded research organizations in regional and industrial development. In 2002 he joins the faculty of the University of Michigan as Assistant Professor of Sociology and Organization Studies.

WALTER W. POWELL is Professor of Education and affiliated professor of Public Policy and Sociology at Stanford University, where he directs the Scandinavian Consortium on Organizational Research. He has previously taught at the University of Arizona, MIT, and Yale. He works in the areas of organization theory and economic sociology, with a current focus on forms of collaboration and competition in high tech industries. He is particularly interested in the processes through which knowledge is transferred from research universities into commercial development by startup firms. He is currently working on various studies of the evolving organizational and network structure of the life sciences field.

SHEILA SLAUGHTER is Professor of Education at the University of Arizona. Her research areas are academic freedom, science and technology policy, political economy of higher education, and women in higher education. Her most recent book is *Academic Capitalism: Politics, Policies, and the Entrepreneurial University* (with Larry Leslie, 1999). Her recent articles have appeared in *Science, Technology, and Human Values, Higher Education, Organizations*, and *The Journal of Higher Education*. Her most recent National Science Foundation grant is with Jennifer Croissant and Gary Rhodes, a study of changing work, organizations, and values in academic science and engineering. She received the Association for the Study of Higher Education Research Achievement Award in 1998 and the American Educational Research Association Award for Research in 2001.

CAROL TOMLINSON-KEASEY is the Chancellor of the tenth campus of the University of California, UC Merced. In developing this campus, she is examining the many ways technology can be used to facilitate teaching, research, and administrative activities. She received her Ph.D. in Psychology from UC Berkeley. Her academic interests and her books and scholarly publications have focused on developing cognitive potential in adolescents and following the intellectual development of women. As a teacher, she received the Distinguished Teaching Award from UC Riverside in 1985. Prior to being named Chancellor of UC Merced, she held a series of administrative posts at UC Riverside, UC Davis, and the UC Office of the President.

THE FUTURE OF

THE CITY OF INTELLECT

Shock Wave II: An Introduction to the Twenty-First Century

CLARK KERR

Over the course of three and one-half centuries, higher education in the United States has met many challenges and adapted to many powerful forces—mostly one at a time. These include:

—Accommodating the English and Scottish models of the college to the circumstances of a frontier society, beginning with the founding of Harvard in 1636.

—Introducing the German model of the research university after 1800 and abandoning the Bible as the main source of knowledge.

—Accepting the land-grant model of providing service to the nation and all its people after the Morrill Act of 1862, starting with agriculture and later extending to the legal, medical, and engineering professions, to business and industry and the military, and other segments of society.

—Moving from education for only the elite to mass access, again after 1862, and later moving to universal access with the development of community colleges after 1900, with the G.I. Bill of Rights after World War II, and especially with the passage of the Master Plan for Higher Education in California in 1960.

—Accepting assignment of responsibility by the leading universities for advances in science rather than by government laboratories or by industry, during and after World War II.

—Adapting to the student movements in the 1960s, including responding to the tactics of civil disobedience and to the themes of the counterculture.

Shock Wave I

The above were great developments in the history of American higher education. These major challenges arrived, for the most part, one at a time, and they unfolded over a lengthy period of adaptation. The first major exception to this pattern was the period from 1940 to 1970, when higher education had to respond to several powerful forces all at once. These included the following: acceptance of responsibility for scientific research and development; universal access for all high school graduates, a force greatly expanded by the high birth rates after World War II; and the demands of politically restless students. I will call this period "Shock Wave I." It turned out to be a period of unprecedented success for American higher education, although there were many casualties among college and university presidents whose terms of office became shorter and shorter, and much reduction in attention to undergraduate students in the large universities.

Shock Wave I left American higher education greatly changed. The number of students enrolled in colleges and universities vastly increased. A new type of institution, the research university, was created and came to lead the world in scientific research. Community colleges spread across the nation and came to include a quarter of all enrollments. Teachers' colleges became "comprehensive" colleges of an increasingly polytechnic nature. American society, once organized around agriculture and industry, became increasingly organized around its technological and informational and service economies, and around higher education. American higher education became a model for the world.

Shock Wave II

Now a new and even more numerous set of powerful forces are hard upon us. Over the next thirty years (2000–2030), and perhaps beyond, they may lead to extensive changes in higher education. These forces include the following:

The New Electronic Technology. The last technological invention affecting higher education came five and one-half centuries ago, with Gutenberg's printing press. Higher education moved out of the monasteries, and literacy spread to entire populations. In the meantime, new technologies have revolutionized agriculture, industry, transportation, and the military. Now it is the turn once again of higher education. Some even predict that campus-based higher education as we have known it will disappear, as did the horse and buggy before it (Levine, 2000). Peter Drucker, who has been so right so many times in his appraisal of future possibilities, has written that "long distance learning . . . may well make obsolete in 25 years that unique American institution, the free-standing . . . college" (Drucker, 1998). This would leave mostly the universities, which Drucker, however, ominously calls "a failure" (Normile, 1997: 311).

The DNA Revolution. Unraveling the secrets of DNA may turn out to have been the scientific discovery of all time. It may lead to changes in many forms of life, with many consequent ethical dilemmas. The atomic bomb made it possible to extinguish all life; the manipulation of DNA makes it possible, even likely, to transform many forms of life. The biological sciences are already spearheading the invasion of industry into the campus, as physics did the invasion of government and the military over half a century ago. This invasion will bring new opportunities for better research, but also for potential interference with academic integrity. But above all the pursuit of the secrets of DNA will raise many ethical issues within the general public—a new Pandora's Box enclosing all forms of life subject to change. Does the future of human life, even all forms of life, belong with God, the creator; or with nature's process—Darwin's survival of the fittest; or with the scientists—with mankind itself? The concerns and anxieties of the public about the new potential of science to save some and not others and to create new forms of life may even exceed the fears that accompanied the explosion of atomic bombs over Hiroshima and Nagasaki.

New Demographic Realities. The first demographic reality is the rise in the proportion of historically disadvantaged racial and ethnic groups. In some larger states, these groups will soon be a majority of the labor force. Non-Hispanic whites just lost their majority status in California. What educational opportunities will these minorities be given to advance their skills and their chances for upward mobility? The second demographic reality is the population's changing age distribution. By 2030, for every retired person there will be only two persons in the labor force. When Social Security was introduced in the 1930s, the ratio was 20:1. Great conflicts will result over the distribution of earned and unearned income. The young and the aged, and the institutions and policies that serve them, will be placed in opposition.

Episodes of both significant ethnic and generational conflict are very possible. How will higher education come out of the battles for support?

Competition for Public Sector Resources. Public institutions of higher education in the United States recently experienced twenty years of restricted resources—1970 to 1990—for two reasons. One was the decline in the rate of productivity growth per man-hour after 1970. The rate of increase in the 1960s had been 3 percent per year, falling to 2 percent in the 1970s and 1980s, and to 1 percent in the early 1990s. Now it has risen again to 3 percent or more, but future rates are not foreseeable and may not be as high. The second reason was the rising competition for state funds. Higher education generally has been losing in this competition as state legislatures have increased financial support for health and other care for an aging population, and for the criminal justice system. In the years between 1970 and 1990, the result was a 16 percent reduction, in real dollar terms, in state and local government financial support per student in public colleges and universities—a reversal of long-term trends.

The recent past has been disappointing. The future is uncertain.

Competition for Students from the For-Profit Sector. A new market that I have called Market II (Kerr, 2001: chap. 9) has developed among adult re-entry students who are interested in moving up in their jobs. Market II, composed of students in the twenty-five to sixty-five age group, already constitutes 40 percent of all enrollments on a head-count basis. In this market, education for the sake of a job has replaced education for the sake of one's total life experience. Traditional nonprofit colleges and universities and for-profits, such as the University of Phoenix, now compete for students in this market.

Responsibility for Improving Primary and Secondary Education. The United States has entered a period of sustained efforts to reform K–12 education marked by higher standards for achievement, high-stakes testing, and the introduction of new information technology. Colleges and universities are the principal preparers for K–12 teachers, and they also have better personnel and facilities than do school districts to offer information technology courses, which may become vital to the improvement of primary and secondary schools. Schools of education are already being asked to assume new responsibilities for the improvement of K–12 education, and the pressures to assume these responsibilities will likely grow in the near future.

Globalization of the Economy. The globalization of the economy pits nation against nation, as never before, in the quality of their scientific research and the skill levels of their labor forces. No nation can afford to neglect either form of competition. This process compels each nation to pressure its colleges and universities for high performance, as is so well illustrated currently by the United Kingdom.

The performance of all levels and forms of education is more central to national influence around the world than in any prior time.

Contention over Models of the University. The dominant current model of the university is based on the eighteenth-century Enlightenment. This model replaced the religion-based model in northern Europe subsequent to the Reformation of the sixteenth century. Its key values are rationality, scientific processes of thought, the search for truth, objectivity, and knowledge both for its own sake and for its practical applications. This dominant model is now being challenged in some of the humanities and social sciences by what can be termed a "postmodern" model. To quote John Searle, the traditional university "attempts to be apolitical or at least politically neutral. The university of postmodernism thinks that all discourse is political . . . and it seeks to use the university for beneficial rather than repressive ends. . . . The postmodernists are attempting to challenge certain traditional assumptions about the nature of truth, objectivity, rationality, reality, and intellectual quality" (Searle, 1993: 56). This conflict, which is just beginning, has the potential to tear apart some of the humanities and some of the social sciences — and to create a gulf between adherents of the postmodern university and those of the university of the Enlightenment.

Higher Education in the New Century

These several developments will create a new period of destabilization stretching at least through the next thirty years. I call this new period "Shock Wave II." Each element taken by itself and given time might be subject to piecemeal adaptation, but taken together they promise much conflict and impressive changes — impressive even compared with the results of Shock Wave I.

Yet, with all these new developments, I do think there are some certainties on which to base plans for the future, along with some wild cards that can be built into possible future scenarios. I also think that some of the likely outcomes of Shock Wave II can be described. In addition, some institutional adjustments in governance need to be made to raise the probability that higher education will successfully survive Shock

Wave II. Let me now catalogue these certainties and wild cards, discuss their likely outcomes, and outline the institutional adjustments that I believe should be made.

CERTAINTIES AND WILD CARDS

Even in a chaotic world, there are some certainties on which to build. Many of these reflect the new realities of Shock Wave II, and some involve completing unfinished business from the twentieth century.

Electronic Technology Will Become a More Widely and Better-Used Element in Teaching and Learning. I expect that the new video- and Internet-based learning technologies will be mainly an add-on and not a low-cost total replacement, as some seem to hope in their plans for "virtual universities." The big test of electronic technology will be quality, not cost alone, and quality is very costly. I realize that with interactive technology, people can have fairly satisfactory human contact at some distance from one another. They can see, hear, and converse with one another, and among groups, from separate locations. Also, e-mail has sometimes encouraged debate and increased faculty accessibility. But education has long been a hands-on enterprise. Like the other ancient professions, such as medicine, law, and theology, education deals with many different individuals with many different needs not subject to standardized treatment.

I do nevertheless see a vast expansion of local learning campuses using the video lecture or computer-based program, for example, as the basis for subsequent direct discussions among students under the guidance of seminar chairpersons. Discussion leaders, "coaches," or "mentors" may replace subject matter lecturers, particularly in large-scale and standardized courses for lower-division students. The one-room primary school may be replaced by the one-room university and the drive-in university. The best example of this new approach that has come to my attention is the University of the Highlands and Islands in Scotland. It combines the textbooks and the computer and video programs of the Open University in England with student-to-student discussions on local campuses under the guidance of trained discussion leaders.

If the electronic revolution, however, should turn out to be a total replacement instead of primarily an add-on, it would become the great theme of the next century. That indeed would be a grand vision that dwarfs anything we saw during Shock Wave I.

The Biological Sciences Are Becoming the New Center for the Sciences. With the ability to manipulate the genetic code, the biological sciences will replace physics and chemistry as the center for all the sciences, a process that is already well under way. They will continue to draw into their area of influence medicine, engineering, physics, chemistry, and much else. The biological sciences have already become the greatest university fields for federal, philanthropic, and industrial support, and they are becoming the greatest source of change in the surrounding society, and the biggest source of ethical conflicts in the new world being born. Leadership in the biological sciences will be necessary for any research university that aspires to greatness in the twenty-first century. Here is another possible great theme for the coming century.

Two New Markets for Higher Education Will Become Increasingly Important. Much of higher education in the United States began as an effort at moral uplift. It continues as an effort mostly at getting a good or better job. This extends now into preparation for midcareer promotions, leading to the rise of a whole new level of higher education (Market II). The market for adult re-entry students interested in midcareer advancement is bound to become more important as advanced training is required for every move up the ladder. Corporate classrooms and the University of Phoenix have led the way. I am sure there is much more to follow, perhaps particularly in the area of medical care, where so many new skills at the highest levels of competence are so desperately needed. Higher education, so enlarged, will become even more of an appendage to the labor market.

Another rising market, which we can call Market III, is for retired persons wanting education for consumption purposes. Higher education, work, and leisure are being scrambled according to many new recipes. Higher education is less an institution apart and more a part of all economic and social life. Markets II and III may be particularly subject to service by electronic means.

Underrepresented Minorities Will Continue to Make Persuasive Claims for Improved Opportunities through Higher Education. In an age of universal access and demographic shifts toward traditionally underrepresented minorities, one certainty is that issues involving equality of opportunity for all will continue to be important. In California, there have been backward movements since the Master Plan of 1960, and some have increased inequality of opportunity. These include enormous discrepancies between low-income and high-income neighborhoods in the availability of advanced placement courses in high schools and transfer programs in community colleges (Kerr, 1999).

Higher Education Will Be Increasingly Called to Aid Primary and Secondary Education. I know of no college of education that has distinguished itself in this endeavor, although some have tried valiantly. The calls for closer involvement between higher education and primary and secondary education will not abate, and new mechanisms for strengthening these links will need to be found. One possibility would be for these colleges to adopt more completely a land grant rather than a letters and science approach, with experiment stations and extension services rather than affiliation with departments such as history, philosophy, and psychology.

Wild Cards. Each of these certainties has embedded within it a number of uncertainties. And there may be "wild cards" ahead, such as wars and depressions, that no one can today foresee, although we are fearful that some may occur. Let me mention a few other wild cards that could alter the scope of higher education or the direction it takes in the future. One is what will happen to increases in productivity. Will productivity increases per annum remain at the current 3 percent rate, retreat to the lower rates of the 1980s and early 1990s, or even increase? The resources that higher education has to work with depend greatly on this. Another wild card is how well the United States will fare in the global economy as other nations or unions of nations, such as the European Union, attempt to catch up with or even surpass it. And perhaps new episodes of student protest may occur.

NEWER AND SHARPER FORMS OF SEGMENTATION

Leaders in higher education worked out the solutions to Shock Wave I in large measure through the differentiation of missions and functions among the institutions of higher education. One result was the rise to prominence of two types of institutions: community colleges and research universities. Another result was a higher degree of segmentation in higher education as a whole. I expect that the conditions of the twenty-first century will advance this process of segmentation. There will be more distinctive segments and more variation in their fates. This may mean the end of "higher education" as a unified element of society.

The Carnegie classification system of 1973 recognized the differentiation of missions and of students that had taken place over prior years (Carnegie Commission, 1973a). Some institutions had come to concentrate on research (the research universities), others on universal access (the community colleges), still others on advanced occupational training of a polytechnic nature (the comprehensive colleges), and still others on professional training (doctorate-granting institutions). The several categories were identified as Research Universities (I and II), Doctorate-Granting Institutions (I and II), Comprehensive Universities and Colleges (I and II), Liberal Arts Colleges (I and II), Two-Year Colleges and Institutes, and Professional Schools and Other Specialized Institutions (such as seminaries, free-standing law schools, and business colleges). The distinction between public and private institutions was kept.

This classification system no longer reflects the current reality and is now being revised by The Carnegie Foundation for the Advancement of Teaching (Basinger, 2000). The new system, in turn, may need subsequent further revision to reflect the changing realities of the twenty-first century. This third system will need to reflect the key developments discussed in this essay, notably the educational technology revolution, the reorganization of research around the "new biology," the further extension of service to Markets II and III, the growth of the for-profit sector servicing Markets II and III, and the forced movement of higher education into primary and secondary education.

The new developments will continue to leave the Liberal Arts Colleges I largely untouched. They have loyal alumni who give them assured financial support. They service a special group of youth: those looking for a well-rounded introduction to life and not just a good job, for lifetime sports and cultural interests, and lifelong friends. These colleges also serve as feeder schools to the research universities and to the most prestigious professional schools. They are the institutions with the longest histories, some tracing back to before the Civil War. Secure and respected, they serve an important role in an increasingly affluent society.

The other segment most assured of its future is the research university. But it is also assured of substantial change. The change may come, in large part, from the biological revolution. In the course of responding to the new biology, these institutions may gradually remove themselves from their less research-oriented professional activities, such as social work, education, architecture, criminology, and the arts, to make way for their primary interest. Rockefeller University and MIT represent what the new research university might look like. Professional school universities (growing out of today's doctorate-granting institutions) may pick up the leadership in the relinquished areas.

Regardless of the institutional setting in which they are found, the part of higher education that will change most will likely be schools of education. They will, I believe, be placed under enormous pressures from state governments to take more responsibility for the performance of primary and secondary education—to develop new models and new policies for the schools. They may truly become an "arm of the state." Schools of agriculture may become the model.

The newest institutions may be those devoted to raising and expanding labor force skills for Market II and catering to educational interests of retirees in Market III. These institutions will be both nonprofit and for-profit, and they will often rely on the new information technology. In addition, new publishing houses are concentrating on creating IT programs for these markets. They may become the most vital centers of activity below the research level.

As to the political emphases of the "postmodern" model of the university, I see no chance that they will find substantial public support. Rather, I see groups of faculty members capturing little islands within the archipelago of the multiversity—a counterorientation inserted quietly into a university largely directed to other purposes. The humanities, in particular, will need to work their way through this confusion. Will their faculty members become mostly lost souls, huddling together but ignored by the larger society?

In sum, it may become increasingly difficult and misleading to talk about the future of "higher education." There will be many quite different segments, each with its own future. We will see many different institutions with many different markets, many diverse forms of governance, more contrasting production methods. Institutions in the different segments will not know or care much about each other. If segmentation continues along the lines I have outlined, I see a new classification of institutions of higher education emerging:

> Research universities
> Professional school universities
> Liberal arts colleges (holistic education)
> Market I colleges (polytechnic)
> Market II colleges (special job advancement)
> Market III colleges (retirees)
> Community colleges

A new term may be necessary to describe this constellation of endeavors. The term "further education" is now used in England to describe that part of higher education most closely connected to job advancement. This term will be more relevant to this new structure than the term "higher education" because it more accurately denotes the coming lateral movement into more diverse forms of teaching and learning—more diverse missions, clienteles, and methods of instruction. Historically, the movement has been more vertical; more movement of students into higher levels. Now it is becoming more lateral.

Can Higher Education Respond Effectively?

Leaders in higher education were able to respond effectively to the challenges of Shock Wave I because the major transforming forces were well understood and because the country had the resources to organize a response to them. By the early 1960s, it was well known that the two great forces affecting higher education would be universal access to higher education and the decision made by the federal government at the beginning of World War II to base scientific research in the universities. Along with these two enormous impacts on higher education came an unprecedented period of high prosperity. Increases in productivity per man-hour rose to 3 percent a year on a cumulative basis, creating the possibility of doubling the per capita flow of goods and services in a single generation and thus resulting in rapid advances in affluence. It made possible a flow of resources to more than triple the size of the higher-education establishment and increase many times over support for university science. It also helped, in addition, to create good jobs for college graduates.

Because leaders in higher education understood the great forces at work and had the resources to harness their power, they were in a position to master the challenges of Shock Wave I. Indeed, these forces resulted in a golden age for higher education in the United States and, in particular, the rise in eminence of the research university. Universal access, a greatly increased emphasis on scientific research, and high prosperity together lifted American higher education to the very center of human progress, where it remained, although in diminished degree, for the rest of the century. And these three forces also lifted American research universities to the forefront of higher education around the world.

The success of that period was built on investments in access and in science. These investments took a differentiated form, as anticipated by the California Master Plan for Higher Education. Community colleges, which opened nationwide at a rate of one a week in the last years of the 1960s, became the preferred option for fulfilling the goal of universal access. Students who succeeded in their studies at a community college could then transfer to a four-year college. Those who were less successful or less interested in continuing could, in any event, gain job-relevant skills. Through a competitive, peer-reviewed system of funding, the federal government helped to underwrite the facilities and research apprenticeships that were essential for continuous progress in scientific research.

In the 1960s, higher education leaders were confident that progress would continue. Plans were made for twenty, thirty, forty years ahead with confidence that they would be realized. Now the time horizon for planning is three or five or ten years—no longer.

There are, it seems to me, several reasons why it is harder today than in 1960 to develop an assured vision of the future. To begin with, there are no three so dominating and so welcome forces at work as universal access, responsibility for scientific progress, and unprecedented prosperity. The recent return to a 3 percent productivity increase may not prove to be a long-term development, but only a one-time shot in the arm. However this may turn out, increasingly competitive demands for public resources will continue unabated, as prisons, health care and retirement income, and improved facilities for transportation all make politically popular claims on resources. Therefore, the effective use of resources will become a more dominant concern within higher education, and a natural concern, in particular, of trustees and governors but not of faculties. Moreover, in making plans for the future, authority within the university is now more circumscribed than ever before. There are more checks and balances by governments, by the courts, by faculty members, and by students. In sum, there are more contradictory variables, more uncertainties, more checks and balances, and more possibly unwelcome developments. This situation makes successful adjustment much less certain. Above all, a period of fundamental but uncertain technological change makes advance planning difficult and possibly even unwise. It could create rigidities in responses where flexibility is needed.

In the 1960s, many of us had a clear view of the big forces at work, and we were correct. But we also had blinders on and looked straight ahead. We too often ignored the pathologies of the institutions we were building. And we seldom saw the rise of the student rebellion until too late and then treated it too often as an interference with the urgent pursuit of our visions. Academic leaders of this new century, or at least of its early decades, may be able to identify no great visions to guide them or great and compatible forces to dominate them. They may need to look around in more directions, to be sensitive to many diverse opportunities and to many threats. In Isaiah Berlin's terminology, they may be foxes who know many little things rather than hedgehogs who know a few big things (Berlin, 1953). With no great visions to lure them on, they will mostly be concerned with survival—for themselves and for their institutions.

THE NEED FOR STRENGTHENED GOVERNANCE

Fortunately, not all segments of further and higher education must face the full range of challenges I have outlined. The DNA revolution poses challenges primarily for the research universities, and the information technology revolution will have its largest repercussions on standardized courses for undergraduates and for job seekers. But all segments will face serious and continuing conflicts over resources, creating and exacerbating tensions on campus and between campuses and the larger society:

—More students will be attending colleges and universities but the physical facilities and faculty members to accommodate them may be insufficient. In light of this imbalance, some very sensitive decisions will have to be made. As enrollments run ahead of resources, faculty and trustees will come into conflict over issues involving the efficient use of resources. Efficiency does not rank high on faculty scales of virtue, but it does for trustees.

—Faculty will confront one another over a number of issues related to resource constraints and competing values: Which fields will grow? Should salaries be set in terms of internal criteria of productivity and prominence or should they be set by the markets outside the university for different forms of professional expertise? How should admissions opportunities for students be distributed, relative to absolute standards or taking into account academic and cultural backgrounds?

—Campus administrators will confront governmental and other external authorities in a more elaborate system of checks and balances. Trustees, state coordinating boards, the courts, the legislatures, the governors, accrediting agencies, and community leaders—all seek to influence developments in the City of Intellect. Each decision will therefore take more time to make and each campus leader will run the risk of making more enemies when a decision is finally made. As higher educational attainment becomes more central to the lives of individual students and to the general economic and political welfare of society, the public will scrutinize the performance of colleges and universities more closely. This process will be energized by more intrusive investigative journalism.

To meet the conflicts of the new century, further and higher education institutions will need to find ways to strengthen the capacity for effective action of three key sets of actors involved in governance: boards of trustees, presidents, and faculties.

The Trustees. The first and greatest stress point in governance, I believe, will be the board of trustees. Many of the new and intensified problems that institutions will face will come to rest particularly on the trustees' shoulders. These include:

—Ensuring that cooperation with industry does not intrude on the basic science activities and the integrity of research universities.

—Developing admissions and tuition policies to serve the vastly expanded numbers of potential students.

—Improving the performance of schools of education in training teachers and in recommending educational policies for primary and secondary education.

—Finding sufficient resources and monitoring their efficient use.

—Selecting and supporting able presidents.

In light of these increasing demands, let me suggest that attention be given to the following recommendations for strengthening boards of trustees: (1) Move toward longer terms of service for trustees. Institutions of higher education are very complex, and it takes time to understand and appreciate them, and to change them. (2) Higher education also needs more sources of trustee appointments in public institutions and thus less gubernatorial control of appointments. Additional appointments might come from alumni organizations; from educational authorities such as superintendents of public instruction who are interested in the performance of all types of education; and perhaps by means of faculty members choosing persons from other similar institutions. (3) Additionally, the work of the boards should be reduced in the area of administrative decision-making and enhanced in the area of providing direction for future institutional movement. More concentration should also be devoted to audit, both fiscal and program, of established activities. Above all, trustees are needed who will give wise and loving care to their institutions.

The Presidents. The second stress point is the presidency. Shock Wave I put greatest pressure on the presidents of colleges and universities. One indication of that pressure was the turnover of presidents, ostensibly appointed "for life" but serving, in fact, for five to seven years until "burn out" and "turn out" caught up with them. The length of presidents' terms should really be measured by the number of tough decisions they have to make, not by the number of years they serve. Now in the midst of Shock Wave II, the same phenomenon will occur as presidents make more and harder decisions while facing a more formidable array of external interests and internal critics.

Changes will have to be made to enhance the position of presidents in this new environment: (1) Terms of service have become too short to deal with the many long-term problems lying ahead. (2) Decision-making has become too encumbered with barriers to quick and decisive responses. (3) Perhaps most important, the rewards of the position are too meager to balance the pain involved (Association of Governing Boards, 1996; Commission on Strengthening Presidential Leadership, 1984; Kerr and Gade, 1986). And, as I have argued, (4) the conditions of the future encourage a shift from selection of "hedgehog"-type presidents to the choice of "fox" types (Kerr, 2001: chap. 9).

The Faculties. The third stress point is faculty governance. It is now too often centered on internal issues and moves too slowly. Some changes in the institutions of faculty governance are therefore also advisable. (1) I suggest that faculty senates elect executive committees to exercise ongoing total oversight of the institution, meeting frequently with the president and having authority to act quickly. (2) I also recommend that faculty governing bodies establish external affairs committees concentrating on relations with government agencies and industry. These two committees might be combined. (3) External guidelines can also assist in making faculty participation in governance more effective. The American Association of University Professors might work on a new code of trustee and faculty ethics. The last one came at the time of World War I and concentrated on internal concerns. A new code might be more oriented to external concerns—in particular on how to protect the university's function as an independent critic of society, on how to guard the integrity of its role as a conscience of society.

A new age has arrived. Its consequences will depend both on the major challenges that characterize it and on how institutions of higher education respond to them. Leaders in higher and further education of the twenty-first century will have many opportunities to explore and create solutions. If they are resourceful, they can turn these challenges into triumphs. In any event, higher education in America will not emerge from Shock Wave II the same as before.

A fond farewell to Shock Wave I and apprehensive greetings to Shock Wave II! "Apprehensive" because Shock Wave II may prove to include some of the greatest but also some of the most uncertain impacts on higher education of all time.

The very way that instruction is delivered may change completely for many undergraduate students. The instructional process for undergraduates has centered around the lecturer in the large classroom. This may turn out to be no longer the most efficient and effective way of transferring standardized knowledge. Two decades ago, I conducted a survey that found that "eighty-five institutions in the Western world established by 1520 still exist in recognizable forms, and with similar functions and with unbroken histories." Seventy of those were universities "still in the same locations with some of the same buildings, with professors and students doing much the same things, and with governance carried on in much the same ways." One reason was that "universities have not been subject to any major technological change." Now it is the turn of higher education to go the way of agriculture, industry, transportation, and military endeavors—and those all went a long way. Professors and undergraduate students may no longer continue doing the same things in the same ways. I then said that "kings that rule, feudal lords with vassals, and guilds with monopolies are all gone" (ibid.: 115; Kerr, 1987). Some future scholar may come to add "and professors that lecture in large auditoria"—all gone.

Also important, the new era threatens some long-standing purposes of the university in American society. The Carnegie Commission on Higher Education (1973b) set forth the following list of major purposes of higher education in the United States:

The provision of opportunities for the intellectual, aesthetic, ethical, and skill development of individual students, and the provision of campus environments which can constructively assist students in their more general developmental growth

The advancement of human capability in society at large

The enlargement of educational justice for the postsecondary age group

The transmission and advancement of learning and wisdom

The critical evaluation of society—through individual thought and persuasion—for the sake of society's self-renewal.

I should like to comment on the last of these purposes. I list the appropriate characteristics of this "evaluative" role of higher education as being:

"Independent"—based on careful analysis of the facts and of what improves public welfare, and not just based on the profit of some specific group.

"Constructive"—measures intended to improve, not to destroy, performance for the sake of general public welfare.

"Persuasive"—based on an effort to convince other citizens and not to coerce them to yield to pressure.

In the 1960s, I was concerned that too much of the "evaluative" role was aimed more at destruction than at reform and made more use of compulsion than of persuasion. Now I think there is more of a threat to "independent" appraisals aimed at improving public welfare as opposed to adding to private profit. In a highly competitive global economy, where success and even survival depend so much on access to new knowledge, it is tempting for industry to move inside the decision-making processes of institutions that produce the new knowledge in order to encourage diversion of resources to projects that have a prospective monetary payoff and to provide early capture, through patents, of ownership of the new knowledge.

This is an area of possible gross exploitation and deserves the most careful consideration.[1] A new code of academic ethics should include control of the selection of scholarly endeavors by scholars alone. Further, the results of scholarly endeavors should be available to the public at large and not just to single profit-making enterprises.

Academic researchers might well adopt the stated goal of the Rockefeller Foundation as the guiding theme for their work: "the welfare of mankind around the world."

Note

1. The Novartis contract with the University of California, Berkeley, is an illustration of these problems. The $25 million project is under the guidance of an "oversight" committee composed of two members from the Novartis company, a biotechnology firm, and three from UC Berkeley. The committee in charge of distribution of research funds has two of its five members from Novartis. Novartis has "first rights" to license new discoveries made in the university's Department of Plant and Microbial Biology, which its funds help support. These "first rights" apply to discoveries based on funding by state and federal agencies as well as by Novartis. Novartis can "delay" publication of research findings, and Novartis staff can work in university laboratories. There are protective provisions for withdrawal from the contract, and advice was sought and presumably will be sought from the Academic Senate at Berkeley. There are other somewhat similar cooperative arrangements involving Monsanto with Washington University and Sandoz with Scripps Research Institution, among others. Let me note that I have full confidence in those who negotiated the Novartis-UCB contract. But I think its operation needs close continuing supervision by the Berkeley Academic Senate.

References

Association of Governing Boards of Universities and Colleges (AGB). 1996. *Renewing the Academic Presidency: Stronger Leadership for Tougher Times*. Washington, DC: Association of Governing Boards of Universities and Colleges.

Basinger, Julianne. 2000. "A New Way of Classifying Colleges Elates Some and Perturbs Others." *Chronicle of Higher Education* 46 (Aug. 11): A31ff.

Berlin, Isaiah. 1953. *The Hedgehog and the Fox*. New York: Simon and Schuster.

Carnegie Commission on Higher Education. 1973a. *A Classification of Institutions of Higher Education*. Berkeley: Carnegie Commission on Higher Education.

———. 1973b. *The Purposes and Performance of Higher Education in the United States*. New York: McGraw-Hill.

Commission on Strengthening Presidential Leadership in Colleges and Universities (Clark Kerr, chair). 1984. *Presidents Make a Difference: Strengthening Leadership in Colleges and Universities*. Washington, DC: Association of Governing Boards of Universities and Colleges.

Drucker, Peter F. 1998. "The Next Information Revolution." *Forbes ASAP* (Aug. 14).

Kerr, Clark. 1987. "A Critical Age in the University World: Accumulated Heritage versus Modern Imperatives." *European Journal of Education* 22 (2): 183–93.

———. 1999. Testimony before the Joint Committee to Develop a Master Plan for Education, Kindergarten through University (Senator Deidre Alpert, chair). The California Legislature, Sacramento, CA, Aug. 24.

————. 2001. *The Uses of the University.* 5th ed. Cambridge: Harvard University Press.

Kerr, Clark, and Marian L. Gade. 1986. *The Many Lives of Academic Presidents: Time, Place & Character.* Washington, DC: Association of Governing Boards of Universities and Colleges.

Levine, Arthur. 2000. "The Soul of a New University." *New York Times,* op-ed (Mar. 13): A21.

Normile, Dennis. 1997. "Schools Ponder New Global Landscape." *Science* 227 (July 18): 310–11.

Searle, John R. 1993. "Rationality and Realism: What Is at Stake?" *Daedalus* 122 (4): 55–83.

PART I

Demographic and Economic Forces of Change

CHAPTER ONE

Credential Inflation and the Future of Universities

RANDALL COLLINS

Most problems of contemporary universities are connected to the process of credential inflation. The inflation in educational credentials that drove university expansion throughout the twentieth century shaped the internal structure of universities as well, and thus the conditions of academic work. We will need this broad viewpoint to capture the main dynamics that have driven the development of disciplines, including their internal divisions into specialty areas and their compulsion to continuous research. If the fundamental versus applied character of the disciplines are at issue in today's university, as well as the growing distance between a highly paid elite of noted researchers and a professorial underclass of temporary lecturers, the causes are in the economic strains of a system whose mass production of educational credentials for employment has become extremely expensive.

Educational Credential Inflation and the Expansion of the University System

The expansion of higher education has been driven primarily by the changing value of educational degrees in the job market. As the number of persons with academic degrees has gone up, the occupational level for which they have provided qualifications has declined. At the turn of the nineteenth century, when high school degrees were held by less than 10 percent of the population, they were badges of substantial middle-class respectability, and until midcentury they conferred access even to managerial level jobs. By the last quarter of the twentieth century, when a large majority had graduated from high school, the degree barely qualified for manual or menial service work. Similarly, college degrees went from possessions of a tiny elite of professionals and the wealthy at the beginning of the twentieth century, to being held by over a fifth of the U.S. population today; in enrollments and, above all, the aspirations of the youngest cohorts, now more than one-half the population is on the path to a B.A. level degree. Under these circumstances, the occupational value of the degree has declined. Higher-level occupations require increasingly higher and more specialized academic credentials. Lower degrees have not lost all value, but their value is increasingly within the educational system, as a way station toward acquiring yet higher levels of education. A high school degree has become little more than a ticket into a lottery where one can buy a chance at a college degree, and that in turn is becoming a ticket to a yet higher level lottery. Most degrees have little substantive value in themselves; they are bureaucratic markers channeling access to the point at which they are cashed in, and guaranteeing nothing about their value at the point at which they are cashed.

The process of credential inflation is largely self-driven; it feeds on itself. A given level of education at one time gave access to elite jobs. As educational attainment has expanded, the social distinctiveness of that degree and its value on the occupational marketplace have declined; this in turn has expanded demand for still higher levels of education. That is the main dynamic, although other factors have played into it.

Education is valued not only as an occupational credential. At one time it indicated social status, or admission into elite or at least polite middle-class circles; in the first half of the twentieth century, a considerable portion of female students, being excluded from the job market (except as teachers) attended college as a social experience and marriage market. This socially elite quality of higher education has largely disappeared, except perhaps in a few enclaves within (but not coextensive with) expensive private colleges. On the social-consumption side more broadly, college for many students was a place for sociability and carousing; that aspect has lost its Scott Fitzgerald tone, but the same kind of activities are carried on by the entertainment side of higher education as a scene of sports spectacles and drinking parties. The former have grown essential to the public recognition and revenues of many universities, while today's administrators tend to carry on a moralistic crusade against the latter, perhaps confident that the university is so firmly ensconced in the necessities of occupational credentialing that it need no longer appeal to students as a place to have a good time. All these are auxiliary features of the social attractiveness of higher education in America, and they all have their antecedents—remember Doctor Faustus carousing in the wine cellars of Leipzig University. They also contain some aspects of inflation as well, such as the spiral of revenue and expense in big-time college athletics.

On a very different side of university culture, higher education still has significance to some unknown proportion of people who treat it as cultural consumption for its own sake; but it may well be the case that the pool of generally cultivated persons who enjoy the accumulated fruits of learning has been winnowed down to high-level intellectuals who cultivate esoteric specialties mainly because they are professors of them. Ramirez and Boli's (1982) argument that higher education spreads as a mark of modernity does not apply to the United States, at least at the institutional rather than individual level; for it was the United States that originated the model of mass higher education as characteristic of a modern society, the model that other societies have emulated.[1]

At the lowest level, some rise in education has been due also to compulsion, motivated by campaigns to assimilate immigrants, inculcate nationalism, religion, or moral respectability. This was important largely in nineteenth- and early-twentieth-century primary and secondary schooling; it has become largely irrelevant to higher education, which has been sustained by its own economic compulsion of credentialing students for careers. Nevertheless, there is a vestige of nineteenth-century community control campaigns in the stay-in-school propaganda aimed at teenagers disillusioned with being at the tail end of the competition for credentials; increasingly this campaign is switching toward the academic low end of the colleges, such as the finish-your-degree campaign aimed at athletes. One can foresee more of the same at successively higher levels in the future. Thirty years from now we may have "don't drop out of college" campaigns.

All these processes play into and reinforce the cycle of rising educational attainment and rising occupational requirements; whatever the reasons for more people finishing a given level of schooling, they all ratcheted job requirements upward, and that in turn has increased pressure for educational attainment. If job access may have been a less important part of schooling in the early twentieth century and before, with rising credential inflation it steadily has come to overwhelm all other considerations.

Credential inflation is largely supply driven, not demand driven; it is driven by the expansion of schooling, like a government printing more paper money, not from demand by the economy for an increasingly educated labor force. The opposing theory, that rising educational requirements have been determined by the functional requirements of jobs in the modern economy, does not hold up under the evidence. I summarized that evidence twenty years ago (Collins, 1979; Dore, 1976; see also Brown, 1995) and have seen nothing since then that leads me to believe that educational requirements are any more demand-driven in our era of educational hyperinflation than they were in late-midcentury educational inflation. Even in our "high-tech" era, the value of educational credentials is still mainly determined by the fact that the U.S. educational system has built up continuously widening access to each successive level of degree; it has been able to flood the market for educated labor at virtually any level.

Many people have been mesmerized by the high-tech sector and easily fall into the rhetoric that makes it a justification of massive educational expansion. I will not repeat the analyses given elsewhere (Collins, 1979) but only note that the skills of the cutting-edge high-tech industries, such as computers, are generally learned on the job or through personal experience rather than in the formal bureaucratic setting of schooling. Advanced computer skills are generally learned by teenage boys, in much the same way that men who operate heavy machines and other well-paid skilled laborers learn their job skills through family and other early personal connections. Technical schooling has always been a way of trying to catch up with the informal networks that produce the self-trained elite of the technical world. Compare the financial success of the youthful founders of Apple or Microsoft (some of them school dropouts) with the more modest careers of graduates of computer schools. Spence's (1974) economic theory of market signaling admits that education may not provide job skills but is taken by employers as a signal that might be correlated with desirable employees; what is missing is the dynamic nature of credential inflation over time, and the recognition that it is driven from the side of public pressures to expand access to schooling, not from the side of employers with a constant interest in signaling.

Let us be clear about what this means. A high-tech society does not mean that a high proportion of the labor force consists of experts. A more likely pattern, and the one we see emerging today, is a bifurcation of the labor force into an expert sector (perhaps 20 percent) and a large proportion of routine or even menial service jobs. Indeed, with future computerization and automation, it may well be the case that routine middle-class jobs will gradually disappear (just as skilled and semiskilled manual jobs have greatly diminished), leaving an even bigger gap between a small technical/managerial/financial elite and everyone else. For this reason, we may expect that the most vexing social problem of the future will be not race or gender, but class. In a largely automated economy further on in the twenty-first century, the majority of the labor force may be kept employed mainly because their wages are lower than the costs of maintaining robots—especially if the production of robots changes as faddishly as the production of computer systems.

Under such conditions, credential inflation processes will continue, indeed at even higher pressure. First: with few good jobs, there is extremely high competition for access to them, hence driving up educational requirements to very high levels. Second: the educational system comes to play an important role in dealing with the displaced part of the labor force, warehousing people and keeping them temporarily off the job market (and thus keeping down the unemployment rate); it may even serve as a hidden welfare system, doling out social support in the form of student loans and subsidizing WPA-style make-work. Education is politically acceptable as welfare because it is not defined as such. But the warehousing also keeps up the supply of education credentials, reinforcing the first process.

The development of the high-tech economy has also been affected by educational credential inflation. For example, as the competition for managerial positions increased among B.A. holders in the 1960s and 1970s, M.B.A. degrees became increasingly popular and eventually the new standard for access to corporate business jobs. Holders of these degrees have attempted to justify the credential by introducing new techniques of management; often of a faddish quality, they nevertheless have given a technical veneer to their activities. Credentialed workers tend to redefine their jobs and to eliminate noncredentialed jobs around them. Thus the spiral of competition for education and the rising credential requirements for jobs tend to be irreversible.

Credential inflation has been driven to unprecedented levels in the United States during the twentieth century because the United States has a uniquely open educational market. Schools of all kinds have been founded by religions, state jurisdictions at virtually all levels (with the notable exception of the federal government), and commercial entrepreneurs. Educational overexpansion has been common in some periods, and many institutions have been financially strapped or have failed. But with the long-term inroads made by credentialing throughout the job market, reinforcing a large popular demand for degrees, the market has largely been an expansive one. The flattening of enrollments in the 1970s, especially of male students, was one of those temporary checks when the inflation in the occupational value of the currency, in relation to the rising personal costs of acquiring education, brought a readjustment of goals; but the inflationary cycle took off again by the 1990s. This proliferation of educational institutions has continued in recent times, with new institutions—community colleges, commercial schools—pointedly oriented to providing practical job credentials and discarding older cultural justifications for education. There has also been a renewed educational expansion on the part of religious sectarianism in the form of Christian schools, or, in the black community, Muslim schools. According to Jencks and Riesman's (1968) model of the "academic procession," self-consciously alternative forms of education all end up emulating the credentialed pattern of mainstream education, and thus the window of distinctiveness of these forms of education may not be open very long. They may all be seen as an effort to get a head start, away from the palpably alienated and defeatist atmosphere of the struggle for credentials in public high schools.[2]

The growing split between high-tech, high-paying jobs and all the others is already upon us; as downsizing (generally imposed by new M.B.A.'s applying their economic rationality) has displaced traditional managerial and white-collar jobs, the surplus has flowed into increasing the number of educational entrepreneurs (just as it increases the number of consulting firms). Our popular ideology celebrates this, by lionizing the few who are most successful; what is overlooked is the overall change in the structure and the increase of stratification within it.

The dynamics of credential inflation and what is has been doing to educational careers and educational organization have not been much recognized; credential inflation is conspicuously alien to official pronouncements. In a concrete way, of course, inflationary dynamics are understood by many people and discussed in backstage, private contexts, where they are usually described with humor or cynicism. Education for high-tech is a legitimating ideology; it is a quarter-truth, at best, insofar as some percentage of persons who make it through the educational system acquire skills relevant to their jobs, and may even apply them at some part of their careers. Education is also legitimated as democratic equality of opportunity; here is another quarter-truth, since the massive expansion of educational access through the twentieth century has not reduced the association between occupational attainment and family background, and sociologists have extensively documented how educational advantage and disadvantage are passed along through family culture and economic means. We all know these latter points. Yet it is striking how virtually all ideological factions in the United States embrace education as the favored solution to social problems. It is a kind of secular religion, keeping alive the ideology of equality because we go through the motions of having our children in public schools in which they are superficially treated as equal.

The combination of ideologies favoring education—technological progress plus democratic opportunity—also operates as a protective ideology for those who make their livings in the educational system. If that focuses on a crass material aspect of academic lives that professors prefer to keep discretely hidden (like salary negotiations), one can add that the high-tech/democratic opportunity ideology supports not only professors' jobs but also the material base of intellectual life; it helps professors obtain the sponsorship that allows for concern with the production of knowledge and the enjoyment of high culture. Credential inflation is the dirty secret of modern education; if everyone admitted it publicly—worse yet, if it became a topic for political discussion—it would force us to face head-on the issue of class inequality and indeed growing class inequality, in part directly tied to the expansion of credentialing. By several routes, the continual expansion of an inflationary educational credential system palliates the problem of class conflict in the United States: both by holding out prospects for mobility somewhere down the line, while putting the connection in a remote enough form to cover all failures of the system to deliver; and by hidden transfer payments to the un- or underemployed, the Keynesian or WPA aspect of the educational system.

Cost Limits on Inflationary Minting of Credentials

In principle, educational expansion and credential inflation could go on endlessly, until janitors need Ph.D.s, and household workers and babysitters will be required to hold advanced degrees in household appliances and childcare. Persons could be kept in school at increasing ages, up through their thirties and forties—perhaps in the distant future of the later twenty-first century even longer. This is not without precedent for a limited segment of the population; in the late Chinese dynasties, massive competition over official degrees kept the gentry studying for exams into their forties (Chaffee, 1985). In principle, since this is a self-feeding process, any amount of education could become the endpoint required by rising credential inflation. It may even happen in some distant future that a species of socialism will come about in which virtually the entire population is on stipend in school, or working for the school system, while the material work of society is done by computers and robots.

In reality the spiraling pathway of school expansion and credential inflation does not unfold smoothly. So far, my discussion of credential inflation has neglected the question of cost. In the case the monetary inflation on which it is modeled, the costs of printing more currency are negligible. Educational credentials, however, are generally costly to mint; they include the costs of teachers, staff, physical plant, instructional materials, and student living expenses. Historically there have been instances in which universities have straightforwardly printed (or inscribed) and sold degrees, such as moribund French universities in the eighteenth century (Collins, 1981). In the modern United States, accrediting agencies try to eliminate diploma mills, ensuring that all educational credentials are as costly as the prevailing standard. It is not possible, after all, for credential requirements to rise to any level at all—the "Ph.D.s for janitors" level; the limit is set by what percentage of the GNP can go into producing educational credentials as compared to other work. More precisely, let us break suppliers of educational credentials into public and private sectors (which may be analytically overlapping). For the public sector, the limit is how much of the government budget (and of public taxation) can be devoted to education; for privately produced education, the limit is how much students (or their parents) can afford to spend. As credential inflation rises (that is, as it takes more years to produce the educational degree currency usable on the job market), costs of either private investment or public subvention in supporting the production of educational currency rise, to some point at which counterpressures slow down, stop, or even reverse the expansion of education.

Several kinds of adjustments are possible. Individuals can drop out of the contest for credentials, caught between the cost of education and the payoff they can receive (or expect to receive) on the job market. This happens to a varying extent in all periods and is part of the trail of dropping out that shapes the hierarchy of educational attainment. Another kind of adjustment takes place on a collective level; public willingness to pay for education may decrease. Instances of public reactions against education are documented in Collins (1998: 515–20, 581–82); educational hyperinflation in Spain during the 1500s brought a wave of disillusionment with schooling and the collapse of many schools; in Germany and France during the late eighteenth century, there were widespread movements to abolish the university, an action which was actually carried out in France. In the contemporary United States, education continues to have strong ideological legitimacy; politicians on both sides of the political spectrum generally favor educational spending. There is a third form of adjustment: to cut the costs of producing educational credentials. Teachers and staff can be cut back; and "superfluous activities" can be eliminated, allowing schools to concentrate on the allegedly practical content of school that is supposed to result in negotiable credentials. The latter is to a certain extent artificial, given that the value of the degree is its symbolic legitimacy in relation to the prevailing standard of education in the population. Nevertheless if one is in a cost-cutting, get-down-to-business mode, that is reflected in the way in which the content of degrees is defined. These various forms of adjustment may all go on at the same time, in varying proportions; all are part of the environment in which academics operate today.

Historical Expansion of the Social Sciences in the Context of an Inflationary Credential Market

I will examine the growth of the social sciences as an example of how disciplines have been shaped by the process of credential inflation. The existence of the social sciences historically has depended largely upon expansion of the university system.[3] The universities of medieval Christendom were designed to produce theologians, lawyers, and medical doctors; they developed internal degree credentials—originally the Master of Arts—as entry requirement into the guild of teachers of the preparatory subjects within the university leading up to the advanced professional faculties. The second phase of credential production, and of change in university organization, came with the foundation of the German research university in 1810. The German university model was adopted by most other Western educational systems later in the nineteenth century. Reform of the German universities was carried out in the context of establishing educational credential requirements for positions in government administration, and for the expanding system of free and compulsory public schooling, also pioneered in German states. The key internal development was that the credential for professors—entry into the guild of higher teachers—became the publication of original research. The expansion of research, and indeed the very idea that the professor should be an innovative scholar, was thus tied to the creation and expansion of credentialing of modern occupations. The development of laboratory sciences flourished in the nineteenth-century German university; so did historical disciplines, and eventually the humanities as well.

The social sciences branched off as specialized professorships were established. This came about in part because universities competed among themselves in prestige according to the new ethos of scholarly innovation and discovery; in part because as university enrollments grew, the increasing numbers of faculty pressed to create specialized niches as distinct fields of intellectual competition. Many of the social sciences had precursors outside the university, such as the amateur explorers who did archaeology and anthropology, or the political reform movements of various kinds that fed into sociology and economics. Disciplinary identities and self-conscious focus upon systematic theory and research, however, generally came about with the establishment of university positions and degrees. Psychology based on laboratory experiment developed in the 1870s in Germany as underemployed physiologists colonized more abundant positions in the older field of philosophy. Economics developed into a technical field using mathematical tools above all in the British universities of the 1860s and 1870s, newly reformed on the German model, as mathematicians like Jevons migrated into older chairs in moral philosophy. Anthropology grew partly out of medical and biological professionals, partly as an intellectual rejuvenation of long-standing professorships in classics or newer research professorships in languages. Sociology obtained its academic niche through several routes; its most militant disciplinary statement was produced in France during the educational reforms of the Third Republic. During that period Emile Durkheim used a chair in pedagogy as a platform from which to organize sociology, a discipline whose claims to autonomy were based in its aspirations as a science of human organization.

It was above all in American universities that the range of social sciences became most fully institutionalized and set on the path toward expansive research enterprises. This came about in part because the American universities from the late nineteenth century onward, building upon an earlier proliferation of religious and state colleges, rapidly became the world's largest pool of institutions of higher education, and contained the largest student enrollments. Both conditions favored internal differentiation. Underlying this was the larger dynamic. The era of credentialing, initially for the classic professions at the turn of the twentieth century, and subsequently for all higher occupations, was the era of differentiation of the social sciences as an array of research specialties. The social sciences did not become research disciplines merely in order to carry out practical work at the behest of commercial interests; some of this pressure existed, and perhaps even more for a covering ideology put forward by university statesmen extolling the practical benefits their research faculty were producing. But this was public relations, and in fact the expanding credential system made the professors much more autonomous from outside commercial concerns. Credential inflation has been good to scholars, because it gave scholars a material base and insulated them from other pressures; as long as the numbers of students seeking job credentials went up, and those numbers were able to pay for themselves, academic specialists could go their own way. The snide phraseology of "publish or perish" hides a subjectively much more favorable atmosphere of the revolution of the professors, what I have called the intellectuals, for the first time in history, taking control of their own material base (Collins, 1998: chap. 12).

In a favorably expanding credential-producing market like the United States during most of the twentieth century, differentiation of specialties took place on two levels. One was the separation of disciplines. The positive side of this has been obscured by our current habit of disparaging disciplines and extolling the ideal of interdisciplinary studies. What the creation of disciplines did was to give specific groups of scholars the power to recruit their own members according to their own criteria; thus the founding period of disciplines is also the founding period of systematic theories. Theories, or our conceptions of distinctive methods and ways of framing subject matters, are what give disciplines the rationale to reserve a set of salaried positions for persons who operate in a particular network of discourse. Disciplinary theories and methodologies operate as frameworks for credentialing colleagues and students. Theories are the cultural expression of scholars' guilds.

The second kind of differentiation takes place within disciplines, which is to say within departments. The United States has been in the forefront here for organizational reasons. Unlike German, French, and

British universities, U.S. universities have created entire departments for specialties rather than individual chairs, and allowed multiple chairs (that is, full professorships) within the same department, thus promoting specialization within disciplines. Here again we have a circularly self-reinforcing process; expansion in numbers of teachers within a department (or the prospects of successfully making arguments to university administrators for such positions) promotes differentiation of specialties; and the ethos of creating new research specialties, by hybrids or other forms of research entrepreneurship, keeps up the pressure to establish new teaching positions. Intellectual substance and material considerations reinforce one another; the competition for prestige among universities, and among departments across universities, focuses attention on the departments that carry out research in the prestigious newer specialties; administrators, in turn, encouraged by the idea (not always unrealistic) that greater prestige will bring more funding (from increased numbers of students, more successful alumni, and more grants and subventions), tend to go along where they can with the forefront of research specializations.

Empirical studies provide more room for differentiation into research specialties than do synthetic theories; this is one reason why the huge American university system during the twentieth century became the world leader in empirical research throughout the social sciences, whereas the smaller European systems often have maintained some eminence in the more theoretical areas. The growth of empirical research in U.S. universities has had other causes as well: the distinctively American pattern of funding by philanthropic foundations, by governments, earlier in the century by religions, and sometimes by business and other organizations seeking practical applications. But all these promoted the growth of massive empirical research because they played into an organizational structure of disciplines based on university careers into which the research dissertation was the credential of admission. University ranks initially consisted of assistant, associate, and full professor (modeled on the German *Privatdozen*, *Extraordinarius*, and *Ordinarius*). With the development of internal ranks and elaborate salary step systems in highly bureaucratic universities like the University of California, the emphasis has shifted to a lifetime of publishing. Again the ideal and the material aspects of the process mesh; research professors are supposed to be (and indeed many are) dedicated to making an endless succession of discoveries which are publicized by publications; this is also structurally demanded by the intermittent routine of reviews that faculty impose on each other, making careers by accumulating publications between previous and current reviews.

Contemporary Pressures

What happens to this system under conditions of economic strain within the entire credential-producing system—that is, the system of higher education as a whole? Universities are under pressure to credential more students at lower cost; they also face an ideological problem of convincing students, politicians, and others who pay the bills, that the ideals of the system are meaningful even though the strains of credential inflation are felt in daily practice. Different levels of the credential-producing sector provide parts of the machinery, and comprise parts of the cost, of minting credentials that are used at other levels of the educational system. Research faculty at the universities prefer to concentrate their energies, and derive their prestige from their research and the kind of teaching that is closest to it, apprenticing graduate students to carry on their kinds of research. But only some of their students will become full-scale productive researchers; even among the relatively successful, many of them will primarily teach undergraduates. The same division holds analytically within a particular individual professor's allocation of work time; part is devoted to shepherding undergraduates through the process that will get them job credentials or intermediate credentials within the academic progression. Whether the division occurs within a single professor's time or between graduate and undergraduate-oriented specialists, the several areas of credential production depend upon each other; as is well known in academic budgeting, undergraduate enrollments are needed to support graduate students; and indirectly research professors depend upon academic credentials having enough value on nonacademic job markets (such as those pursued by most undergraduates) in order for their own jobs to exist.

High-level research professors often identify only with the intellectual parts of their disciplines; very often their main consideration of material conditions is to issue complaints about the level of academic support and the intellectual unworthiness of students. In reality, research lives depend upon large numbers of undergraduates being attracted to academic fields, for whatever reasons, whether purely intellectual or not.

Structurally it does not matter whether students like sociology (or some other field) because they are genuinely interested in its ideas and discoveries, or for ideological attraction, or because they think it will give them a practical skill, or just for the sake of an easy course to fill out requirements on the way to a degree. Teaching nonintellectual students and indeed undedicated or even alienated students is the price professors pay for the material infrastructure of life on the research frontier. Each professor can pay the price by sharing the burden; or the burden can be shouldered by a lower class of instructors. Structurally either way will work; but the decision has consequences for the ethos of a discipline, especially in an era when ideals of many social science disciplines are democratic.[4]

All this suggests another reason why the disciplinary organization of departments is useful to professors working in specialized research fields that do not attract many students. Because they all belong to a larger department that receives funds as a unit, the more popular courses in attracting students pay the way for the esoteric or elite specialties. Smaller specializations, including the various interdisciplinary mixtures that are continually being constructed, are not usually viable inside the budgetary economy of the university. And there is a strain on the individual level: professors in small, specialized departments find less opportunity to work in their preferred area. Thus traditional departments usually end up surviving, even though frontier-area researchers like to complain about them.

My analysis has concentrated on the pattern in which popular demand for credentials is met by allowing students to push through to higher and higher amounts of education, making each level successively more massive. There is another way in which inflationary pressures can be met: by restricting the numbers who get through each credential bottleneck. That is done in some contemporary professions, for example, by making state bar examinations harder in order to limit the number of lawyers. The Chinese government examination of the Ming and Ch'ing dynasties responded to massive increases in the numbers of students for the most part by setting smaller and smaller quotas of those passing exams; this was mitigated by some adjustment over the centuries by adding more levels of exams, and giving some social privileges to those who passed intermediate levels of exams, even though they had not yet passed the very highest exam, which gave access to government appointment (Chaffee, 1985).

Within American universities, our current period of credential inflation has gone along with several other kinds of inflation: grade inflation, admissions inflation (students multiplying the number of schools to which they apply), recommendation inflation (as increasingly glowing rhetoric is used to extol the merits of students and job candidates), c.v. inflation (as academic job candidates add more and more details to their official accomplishments). Our prevailing cultural ethos is for teachers to treat students sympathetically, to try to get them through what they recognize as a competitive grind. The ethos of democracy and equality fits with the structure of self-reinforcing inflation. The opposite pattern, found in some other historical circumstances (and found more often today within some fields like premedical science courses than in the social sciences or humanities) is to deal with massive competition by raising standards; here an elitist or hierarchical cultural ethos goes along with a deflationary or at least inflation-resisting dynamic. The alternatives fit the pattern that Pareto proposed for political and economic cycles, alternating between democracy-cum-inflationary-market-expansion, and authoritarianism-cum-deflationary-economic-retrenchment.

What we mean by "pressures" affecting the academic system is a matter of perspective. If we are committed to continuing the ethos that prevailed during the relatively smooth expansion of the research disciplines throughout the middle twentieth century, when the price of minting educational credentials seemed reasonable to those concerned, then the readjustments looming in a period when minting credentials is becoming to seem too costly look like intolerable pressures. But adjustments are not necessarily crises; they are largely a matter of how big a proportion of the whole the research-oriented faculty will be, and how privileged they are in their work lives at the expense of teachers of nonintellectual students. Short of some truly apocalyptic crisis, it is not likely that research faculty will disappear but only will become fewer, and hence more aspiring professors (and graduate students thinking of their careers) will have to face their reduced chances for such a position.

The rub comes on the ideological level, in the cultural terms professors define for themselves, and also in the ways they define themselves and their students to the outside world. This is a difficult ideological problem; for many reasons, professors lack the vocabulary to talk about it in language they are willing to have overheard. The reasons are scattered through what I have been arguing: a general unwillingness to see that the educational system, and research careers within it, are based upon a credentialing mechanism subject to inflationary pressures; preferences for idealized ways of describing what universities and academic disciplines do; somewhat contradictory legitimating arguments of high-tech combined with democratic opportunity; and especially in the social sciences oriented toward liberal social reform, the inability to talk about inequality inside professorial ranks as something that is structurally built into the very system of conducting research and teaching about its discoveries. I make no claim to solve that ideological problem; sticking to my trade as a research sociologist, I will only give the most realistic picture I can of the social dynamics that create the problem.

It is an easy, and glib, rhetoric to declare that we are working for greater equality. The structural realities work in the other direction. Consider differentials in pay within departments. Well-known research professors are paid more than teachers, even at schools that attract academically elite students. The prestige of a department depends primarily on its biggest names and their research-based reputations; hence the competition among the many upper-tier universities today drives up the salaries of the star professors, and leaves proportionately less for the mass of teachers and lesser-known researchers. Universities are one of the few established sectors of the twenty-first-century economy in which oligopoly does not prevail, and concentration of market share has even been decreasing. Financially, universities would be better off if there were a more stable hierarchy of prestige among them, since the labor costs would be lower for the same level of professorial prestige; hence the entire credential-producing sector would be less costly. If universities were merely profit-oriented enterprises, they would not be a good investment. But the credential-producing economy is a prestige economy, closer to the structure of the potlatch than that of a classical laissez-faire market.

This is one basis for the increasing split between the elite research professors and everyone else, and the especially apparent growth of an academic underclass of temporary employees at very low salaries. This structural split is papered over on the ideological level by identification through disciplinary membership. We are all sociologists (or economists or psychologists), the hundred thousand dollar annual salaried research professor and the acting instructor paid a few thousand dollars per course. The ideological identification is strong too because the latter may well be pupils of the former, or at least connected in a chain of teachers and pupils; and because such low-paid temporary positions may seem like another extension of the genteel poverty of graduate student years before landing a tenure-track job. And the gap is papered over because we teach the same things; indeed the academic underclass may teach the very research produced by the elite professor. Since much of that research in a field like sociology (and elsewhere as well in the social sciences and humanities) has a leftist slant both in theory and topic, the content of what they think and lecture about makes them comrades in liberal reform or radical emancipation at the same time that the practical realities of their lives put one of them in the stock-market playing upper-middle class and the other at the level of the working poor.

Is There a Crisis in Intellectual Quality?

What effects do such pressures have on the contents of research disciplines? We have little in the way of systematic empirical analysis here, which would call for comparative studies of the quantity and quality of intellectual production under various conditions of credential inflation and credential system cost. What follows are crude estimates, guesses, and theoretical suggestions.

Credential inflation manifests itself in heightened pressure for publication, all the more so because competition concentrates on a diminishing proportion of tenure-track jobs. At the same time, the financial rewards for the highest research reputations may also foster competition over the kind of innovativeness that makes big reputations; it may well be the case that the quality of intellectual work at the top level increases under these conditions. This example warns us against assuming that a situation of crisis or difficulty within some levels of the academic community is necessarily bad for other levels or aspects of the system.

In some ways the increased pressure for publication throughout academia has favored the social sciences in relation to the humanities. The same pressures exist inside the humanities, where scholars during the last century have had to concentrate on more and more minutely detailed materials within canonical literature and the conventional topics of history. Publication pressures have been in part responsible for the shift toward social history and literary theory. The latter is a good example of a theoretical framework that legitimates a new subject matter. The various text analysis movements—which have gone under the names of "structuralism," "poststructuralism," "deconstruction," or just "literary theory"—have all worked in the same way to legitimate humanistic scholars working on a widened terrain, one that discerns textlike or semiotic features in all areas of culture. The upsurge of these movements occurred in the French academic system during the time when it was undergoing the rapid expansion of higher education in the 1960s, from a closed elite system to a U.S.-style mass system; the alienation of students and young degree-holders of the late 1960s and the following decades was related to the shortage of academic jobs resulting from a bulge of overproduction of high-level degrees. (On this period, see Bourdieu [1988].) This shift toward the study of texts tends to make the research field of the literary and aesthetic disciplines coextensive with the topics of the social sciences. The movement away from the canon of high-culture writers is not merely a result of insurgent political/ideological movements (feminism, racial/ethnic nationalisms, gay liberation) but a way of opening up fresh materials for publications. This has been favorable to the social sciences, especially anthropology and sociology, since sociological models and researches have acquired a wider audience; and there has been fruitful cross-fertilization especially in the area of the sociology of cultural production. Indeed, one can say that the sociology of culture has been in a golden age because of this crisis-induced rearrangement of disciplinary definitions.

At the same time, there is an atmosphere of disillusionment, in part reflecting the career difficulties in a severe competition over positions; these difficulties have been especially acute in the French academic system, where recent decades have seen massive unemployment and underemployment of credentialed intellectuals. More generally, it has been the case throughout world history of intellectual communities that when there is a proliferation of schools and hence the formulation of a very large number of intellectual positions, a skeptical epistemology becomes prominent. Given a cacophony of positions (what I have called a violation of the upper limit of the law of small numbers, the number of teacher-pupil networks can reproduce themselves coherently across the generations; see Collins, 1998: chaps. 3 and 9), the argument becomes widely accepted that apprehending truth is impossible. The periods of skepticism in ancient Greek and in late medieval Christian philosophies occurred under these structural conditions; the skeptical strain in deconstruction or postmodernism fits the same pattern. We need not take this metaskepticism at face value. Under the umbrella of these forms of semiotic/textual theory, a great deal of work has confidently gone on exploring the production, historical valuation, and audience consumption of culture, work that is not skeptical about its own projects. Epistemologies only frame the intellectual field at a high level of aggregation; they are so to speak foreign policy statements about the relations among disciplines (in this case, denigrating the older, traditional, or safely funded fields as positivist, naive, or illegitimately privileged), while inside the disciplinary boundary work goes ahead that yields publications whose truth value is not questioned by peers.

Let us return to the established core of the social sciences. Here, despite various conditions of strain in the university base and movements of ideological self-questioning, I would judge that intellectual advance has been moderate to good. In sociology, the field I know best, there are a number of research areas that in recent years have produced empirical studies and theoretical formulations that are the high-water mark of those fields; these fields include historical sociology, especially dealing with state-building, state-breakdown and revolution, and global/world-system processes; ethnographic and micro-sociological studies of street codes, violence, and emotion; network analysis, and overlapping with it, a burgeoning field of economic sociology that formulates an alternative to idealized neoclassical economic conceptions of how markets operate; and as already mentioned, the sociology of culture. A good deal of sociology also operates on the level of what Kuhn called "normal science," elaborating details within well-established paradigms. I am less able to judge the proportion of cutting-edge or outstanding "normal science" work in anthropology, psychology, economics, and political science; my impression is of a good deal of normal science in these disciplines, with hot areas here and there as well. In a condition of credential inflation and hence massive publication pressure, the large majority of publications will be relatively detailed and not attract attention outside of narrow subspecialties. Because academics judge a field by its best results—those that make the biggest splash in the intellectual attention space—not by its average publications, there may be a growing split in quality between top and middle, without a sense that the field as a whole is doing badly intellectually.

Pressures for Practicality

There are two main ways in which crisis pressures of credential production can affect intellectual content. One, just reviewed, is via the publication explosion; the second, which we now consider, is increased pressure to be practical. This arises in part because researchers in a cost-cutting university system seek sources of funding from clients seeking practical payoffs; another source of emphasis on practicality can come from the desire to convince students that a credential in a social science does indeed carry practical work skills. The shift to practicality is easier in some social sciences than others. Some social sciences, like anthropology, have generally had a pure-knowledge appeal, although they have had the advantage that some of their researches (for example, in archaeology) have a considerable audience as popular entertainment. Others, like sociology, have a practical side that is largely oriented toward "social problems," and therefore that have a strong politically partisan position. (On the ramifications of this point, see Turner and Turner, 1990.)

Sociology's application is generally from the point of view of liberal reformers or leftist social critics; hence support for applied sociology largely depends upon leftward political swings in the surrounding society and partisan government patronage. It needs to be added, too, that the contribution of liberal social science to applied problems is largely in providing descriptions (for example, documenting how much racial segregation exists, gender discrimination, and so forth); there is relatively little well-established theory of what kinds of interventions produce what kinds of ameliorative results. One can hire a team of sociologists, or economists, anthropologists, and so forth, to show the extent of a social problem; but there is little they can reliably offer as to what to do that will change that condition, based on social science knowledge per se. Such social scientists, of course, are quite willing to offer prescriptions, but these are usually identical with those of liberal political programs, and meet with the same kind of political struggle as any other political ideology. This is another way in which the politicized character of social science limits its salability as practical skills. There are some other areas in which the social problem is not necessarily approached from a liberal side; criminology and criminal justice studies may take a conservative or merely administrative stance. But here too the social problem itself is framed by social interests and conflicts (see Black, 1993); and thus actual interventions are strongly shaped by political partisanship. There are other fields as well that move in and out of favor depending on political winds. In political science, security studies (that is, the military aspect of international relations) experienced a sharp drop in interest and funding with the end of the Cold War; today, they can retrench toward other problems of security (for example, ethno-nationalist conflict, terrorism).

The social sciences that have had the easiest time in expanding their applied offerings have been those that have had large specialty areas operating below the level of ideological controversy. These are psychology and economics, the two fields that did best in the competition for student enrollments (Waller and Collins, 1994) when the cost crisis of credential inflation first hit in the 1970s and 1980s. Economics prospers by producing analyses for business, investment bankers, and government; it did especially well with the investment boom of the 1990s and its call for detailed economic information about particular sectors and firms. Credential inflation for business careers, bringing about the proliferation of business-school programs and the requirement of M.B.A.'s for higher-level business jobs, has been a major source of support for economists. Psychology has prospered on a side that was once quite low on the totem pole of its disciplinary subspecialties: counseling and clinical psychology. Beginning in the 1970s, with the creation of credential programs leading into professional licensing in clinical psychology, applied psychology has boomed, making big inroads in the professional practice once controlled by psychiatrists credentialed by medical degrees; alongside the strictly licensed clinical psychologists, there have proliferated a variety of "soft" credentialed psychologists offering various kinds of counseling and self-help programs on a commercial market. Psychology and sociology, before the 1970s, had approximately equal numbers of undergraduate students (ibid.). The former has boomed while the latter has not, above all because psychologists have been able to sell a practical service directly to individual customers in any part of the ideological spectrum; for example, there are now conservative Christian psychologists, and many rightist religious groups have adopted psychological group dynamics techniques. In contrast, sociologists generally have had to find institutional patronage on the liberal philanthropic or welfare side.

Even in the successful applied social sciences, there is a split between a pure research-oriented sector and the applied sector. Among economists, there is a prestigious elite that commands high salaries in the leading economics departments and competes for the Nobel Prize, by formulating esoteric mathematical theories remote from the mass of applied economists tracking the performance of particular firms and industries. The split is especially severe in psychology, where the professional association split in the 1980s, as the applied/counseling psychologists became a majority, whereupon many of the leading research-oriented experimental psychologists seceded to form their own association. Such splits, whether institutionalized or not, and indeed whether publicized or ignored, exist in all the social sciences.

Conclusion

Inside each academic discipline is a highly differentiated community: differentiated by specialties, and even more importantly, differentiated by rank and resources. The top of the research elite does rather well under current conditions of costly credential inflation production; they do well not merely materially but also intellectually; in general, the research forefront of the social sciences has been making at least normal progress, and some specialty areas are experiencing golden ages. At the other end of the professorat, there is a growing and increasingly beleaguered teaching proletariat; the material conditions of their lives are poor, and the strains of making their careers are severe. Not least of the severity is the uncertainty about where they are heading in the career spectrum; most start out struggling for tenure-track jobs, and they are produced in the same graduate programs that include the privileged ones who will follow the normally defined career of academic promotion through publication. Between the top and bottom is a middle mass, where strains are probably increasing because of the publication pressures that go along with increased competition over a declining proportion of research/ teaching jobs. Proposals for greater accountability or even abolition of tenure strike mainly at this middle mass. It is entirely possible for the intellectual condition of the system, determined by what is done by the research elite, to be flourishing, while there is pressure, alienation, and misery at the levels below.

Will there be a revolt of the professorial proletariat? Framing the issue in those terms makes it seem at least hypothetically possible. Theory of social conflict, on the other hand, suggests that it is not very likely. Mobilization of an unprivileged stratum depends upon formulation of a self-conscious ideology of group identity, and upon organizational conditions for mobilization; such conflict would be further complicated by the existence of middle strata in the academic hierarchy, who have their own latent interests (and even more cross-pressures regarding their identity). Mobilization at the bottom alone does not change a system of power; such changes start with breakdown at the top, and struggle among competing elites over how to fix it. All this is very remote from conditions of academic life today. Professors still define themselves primarily in terms of the intellectual content of their disciplines, and this gives enormous implicit power to the research elite. The strains that are palpable today for many scholars lower in the hierarchy seem likely to remain merely localized, personal troubles. It seems likely that there will be little overt resistance as the disciplines become much more severely stratified.

Notes

1. Meyer and Rowan (1977) provided the institutional theory on which Ramirez and Boli drew. They used schools as a prominent example of institutions whose prestige is based on a myth of what they actually do. Credentialing indeed is a manifestation of organizational myth, and it has come to define the respectable culture of modernity: but the dynamics of credential inflation in the expansionary U.S. higher educational market created this culture.

2. Home schooling might seem a genuine break with formal credentialing; it remains to be seen how this will work out. There are suggestions (Bills, personal communication) that pressures to make home schooling conform to official patterns of credentialing are already under way.

3. On these processes, and for sources on historical comparisons in what follows, see Collins 1998, 2000.

4. Indeed, this may be an especially hard problem within my own discipline of sociology, precisely because the self-image of the generation of sociologists now occupying top professorial positions is that of egalitarian social reformers, and this disciplinary self-presentation is a major factor in inducing students to join the field.

References

Black, Donald. 1993. *The Social Structure of Right and Wrong*. San Diego: Academic Press.

Bourdieu, Pierre. 1988. *Homo Academicus*. Stanford: Stanford University Press.

Brown, David K. 1995. *Degrees of Control: A Sociology of Educational Expansion and Occupational Credentialism*. New York: Columbia Teachers College Press.

Chaffee, John W. 1985. *The Thorny Gates of Learning in Sung China*. Cambridge: Cambridge University Press.

Collins, Randall. 1979. *The Credential Society: An Historical Sociology of Education and Stratification*. New York: Academic Press.

———. 1981. "Crises and Declines in Credential Systems." Pp. 191–215 in Randall Collins, *Sociology since Mid-century: Essays in Theory Cumulation*. New York: Academic Press.

———. 1998. *The Sociology of Philosophies: A Global Theory of Intellectual Change*. Cambridge: Harvard University Press.

———. 2000. "Comparative and Historical Patterns of Education." Pp. 213–39 in Maureen T. Hallinan (ed.), *Handbook of the Sociology of Education*. New York: Kluwer Academic/Plenum Publishers.

Dore, Ronald P. 1976. *The Diploma Disease: Education, Qualification, and Development*. Berkeley: University of California Press.

Jencks, Christopher, and David Riesman. 1968. *The Academic Revolution*. New York: Doubleday.

Meyer, John W., and Brian Rowan. 1977. "Institutionalized Organizations: Formal Structure as Myth and Ceremony." *American Sociological Review* 83: 340–63.

Ramirez, Francisco, and John Boli-Bennett. 1982. "Global Patterns of Educational Institutionalization." Pp. 15–36 in Philip Altbach (ed.), *Comparative Education*. New York: Macmillan.

Spence, A. Michael. 1974. *Market Signaling: Informational Transfer in Hiring and Related Screening Processes*. Cambridge: Harvard University Press.

Turner, Stephen P., and Jonathan H. Turner. 1990. *The Impossible Science: An Institutional Analysis of American Sociology*. Newbury Park, CA: Sage Publications.

Waller, David V., and Randall Collins. 1994. "Did Social Science Break Down in the 1970s?" Pp. 15–40 in Jerald Hage (ed.), *Formal Theory in Sociology: Opportunity or Pitfall?* Albany: State University of New York Press.

CHAPTER TWO

Universities and Knowledge: Restructuring the City of Intellect

PATRICIA J. GUMPORT

During the past century American research universities have been challenged to modify their practices in response to fluctuations in enrollment, state and federal funding, and wider economic conditions. It is commonly acknowledged that universities have demonstrated a remarkable adaptive capacity—to expand, to pause, and more rarely to contract. However, at the dawn of the twenty-first century, there is talk of even more pressure to respond to heightened market competition, advanced communications technologies, and unprecedented public scrutiny. For the most part, scholars of higher education emphasize continuity in such enduring features as the departmental organization of knowledge, the guild mentality of faculty, and the guiding influence of the disciplines (for example, Clark, 1993; Kerr, 1995; Rothblatt, 1997). Yet even these scholars herald imminent change. The concern is whether universities can continue to respond to a formidable mix of changing environmental demands.

For universities, keeping pace with knowledge change is of utmost importance. It is a perennial issue with high-stakes consequences. For well over a century, the historical interdependence between research universities and knowledge has brought a predictable albeit daunting set of challenges: campuses and their faculty are expected to be at the forefront of knowledge change, to move fields forward with new discoveries or at least to stay current with new developments. In both research activities and educational programs, research universities are expected to modify their academic structures, practices, and resource allocations appropriately. Such decisions are of great consequence, not only for the effects on personnel but also because dismantling them may be shortsighted given years of prior investment.

Keeping pace with knowledge change in the contemporary era is compounded by changes in knowledge creation and dissemination practices. Worldwide, there is an increased societal demand for specialist knowledge that transcends disciplinary modes of problem-solving, a proliferation of knowledge producers at nonuniversity sites, and a diffusion of technological applications that make possible new patterns of communication and collaboration (Gibbons et al., 1994). As these forces are realized, they not only alter the competitive arena for research universities but also force reconsideration of the very categories that anchor academic work, student learning, and professional expertise recognized in the wider society.

The academic organization of knowledge has an inherent dynamism shaped by historical circumstances and contested at several levels. For public research universities in particular, the challenge to keep pace with knowledge change is evident in relations with state legislatures, statewide coordinating agencies, systemwide offices, and across campus subunits. Issues range from abstract intellectual matters to concrete requirements for facilities and space, from scrutiny of numerical projections and proposed budgets to disputes over domains of authority. The questions are at once intellectual, organizational, economic, and professional. The management of academic knowledge and its organizational structure warrant attention from postsecondary leaders and stakeholders as well as researchers. In this chapter I offer a conceptual and empirical contribution that examines the rationales underlying academic restructuring.

University Responses to Changing Conditions

The academic landscape of universities is expected to reflect both continuity and change in what counts as knowledge. In the post–World War II era, universities acquired and sustained academic legitimacy through expansion. They kept up with the growth and specialization of knowledge by expanding and differentiating their organizational structures. The creation of new academic departments, programs, and faculty positions conveyed to competitors and constituencies a willingness and a capacity to shift resources to new lines of inquiry. Maintaining existing units was equally important, as it signified that universities could fulfill societal expectations to preserve and transmit knowledge in enduring fields.

Upon entering the last quarter of the twentieth century, however, expansion was no longer viable as a widely taken-for-granted operating principle. Various resource constraints along with imperfect enrollment projections prompted universities to develop alternative structural responses and rationales. In the 1970s, universities were challenged by state fiscal crises and steady-state presumptions. In the 1980s, although resource flows improved in some states, universities were criticized for spiraling costs. Admonished to downsize and streamline along with organizations in industry and government, universities faced cost-cutting mandates from legislatures, state coordinating agencies, and their own systemwide offices. Both the mandates and the management prescriptions met resistance from those who prized academic self-determination (Gumport, 1993; Gumport and Pusser, 1997, 1999). Keeping pace with knowledge change came to mean structural consolidation and selective elimination of the programs, activities, and people that were deemed unproductive, duplicative, or irrelevant.

By the 1990s expectations for universities to develop priorities were amplified. The proportion of state budgets allocated to higher education declined in many states, under strain from a weakened economy and a devolution of federal responsibilities to state levels. This resulted in budget shortfalls for many public universities along with the stark realization that higher levels of state support could not be presumed.[1] While some campus leaders characterized the state's posture as abandonment and hoped to translate it into increased autonomy, such a silver lining was not forthcoming. Instead, mediated by coordinating agencies, state policy-makers fortified their accountability demands with efforts to assess institutional performance.

Simultaneously, there was a decline in the relative share of revenue from state sources within public research university budgets. Attempting to reduce vulnerability, university leaders adopted strategies to cultivate additional revenue from nonstate sources, such as students, alumni, and private companies.[2] This enabled some public research universities to amass discretionary resources in spite of state budgetary constraints. Keeping pace with knowledge change was accomplished by identifying revenue-generating opportunities, continued monitoring of academic units for potential consolidation, and selective investment in promising academic programs. Academic commitments came to be cast in terms of prospective markets, comparative advantage, and projected costs and revenues. Cumulatively, these changes reconstituted the scaffolding for the stage upon which universities would be judged for their performance and upon which academic programs would be deemed either cutting edge or dispensable.

The strategy to restructure for selective excellence has not been without dissenters. One chorus of voices has warned of likely—and perhaps dire—consequences of this shift, particularly for the educational character of the enterprise. The fundamental concern is that market forces have become the most prominent influence in reshaping academic structures and practices to their detriment.[3] The fear is that cumulatively such forces will redefine public higher education as a private economic benefit rather than a public good.

Another chorus of voices has embraced the shift in planning assumptions for its radicalizing potential, arguing that it may result in a much-needed remaking of universities that includes better alignment with labor market demands and economic development opportunities. Those who seek gains in academic self-determination are among the champions of this shift in planning assumptions. Through savvy academic management and entrepreneurial initiatives, these advocates hope universities will be able to protect their own interests. Two strategies for improving their resource base have been most visible. For teaching, incentives have been developed to cultivate among faculty an ethos of quality in educational "service delivery" (Meyerson and Massy, 1994). For research, incentives have been refined to encourage faculty to seek revenue from nonstate sources through activities such as private fundraising and commercialization (Powell and Owen-Smith, 1998; Slaughter and Leslie, 1997).

In summary, during the last quarter of the twentieth century, public research universities have been challenged to keep pace with knowledge change within changing economic and political conditions that call on them to generate nonstate revenue and demonstrate their direct contributions to the economy. Although universities have shown some similar responses to these expectations, they have also exhibited different patterns that correspond to their distinct legacies and inherited structures. In this respect, they provide an ideal opportunity for conceptual development and case study research.

Understanding Institutional Legitimacy: Conceptual Anchors

Before presenting the case studies, I want to identify the multidimensional basis upon which the legitimacy of public research universities has been socially constructed. Both a legacy of service and the centrality of knowledge have been critical touchstones to which universities refer as they seek legitimacy for their academic programs and activities.

The legacy of service entails responding to short-term exigencies as well as longer-term societal interests that are independent of the marketplace. Universities have struggled to serve both simultaneously, which heightens the ambiguity implicit in this basic social charter. Moreover, universities have also claimed some degree of autonomy as an essential precondition to fulfilling societal expectations, even though in the past few decades university leaders have been less inclined to articulate a rationale for this presumption (Geiger, 1993; Rothblatt, 1997).

Regarding the centrality of knowledge, public research universities have come to play several roles beyond the initial land grant idea, as producers, wholesalers, and retailers of knowledge (Kerr, 1995: 86). Aside from this diversification of knowledge functions, it is essential to note that the academic structure itself plays a critical societal role by representing an evolving map of knowledge, constituting the categories of ideas that society values in the past, present, and foreseeable future (Gumport, 2000). The basic organization of academic knowledge has been slow to change—whether because of inertia, tenure and entrenched professional interests, or expectations for universities to preserve enduring fields. Yet some dynamism has also been permitted, as intellectual advances have led to new joint or interdisciplinary appointments, experimental degree programs, and incremental refinements to courses, majors, and departments. The potential ripple effect of such academic initiatives is noteworthy when one considers that campuses tend to emulate those that are highly regarded (DiMaggio and Powell, 1983).

The most significant feature of a university's academic structure is its scope. Comprehensive field coverage is a long-standing ideal, although what constitutes field coverage has changed over time. Historically, public research universities have sought to provide learning and inquiry in all fields of knowledge and to serve as gateways to the universal reservoir of knowledge. The prospect of an ever-expanding knowledge base—particularly with an ever-accelerating pace of change—poses obvious challenges to universities that seek to cover the full range of fields. They must also determine the appropriate form of their commitments to each knowledge area: a course or set of courses; a minor, major, graduate specialization, or degree program; tenure-track or nontenured faculty positions; program or departmental status. Sustaining comprehensive field coverage is easier than establishing it, as inherited structures carry their own momentum. In contrast, broadening the scope of academic offerings is difficult amid resource constraints, except in those areas that have currency.[4] Thus, the ability of a university to keep pace with knowledge change depends in part upon its structural legacies.

Both the legacy of service and the centrality of knowledge provide sufficient breadth and ambiguity for universities to legitimately recast their missions and academic priorities.

THE FUNCTIONS OF INSTITUTIONAL LOGICS

Rationales that support the academic structure and its reorganization are commonplace in universities. The concept of institutional logic, drawn from neo-institutional theory, provides a powerful lens for us to conceptualize how such beliefs and values are anchored in the wider environment and enacted locally within organizations to obtain legitimacy. As defined by Friedland and Alford (1991: 248) and developed by Scott et al. (2000), "institutional logic" refers to "a set of material practices and symbolic constructions—which constitutes its organizing principles and which is available to organizations and individuals to elaborate."

An institutional logic may have historical limits and thus potential for change, such that a new logic may come to dominate, supplementing or overtaking an old logic, either gradually or abruptly. Certain factors may facilitate a change. Within public research universities over the last quarter of the twentieth century, a gradual devaluing of bureaucracy and professional competence has made room for managerial authority and entrepreneurial initiatives to move into the foreground as suitable solutions to changing political and economic conditions.

Multiple logics may be in use at any point in time, and their relative sustainability under varying conditions is an important issue for analysis. Tensions among logics or within a logic can form the bases of political conflict. When such conflict is played out in postsecondary organizations, strain *between* logics can be evident. For example, faculty may appeal to professional prerogatives of academic self-governance in opposition to state mandated and centrally steered academic program reduction. Strain *within* a logic may also be evident. For instance, the expectation for public research university faculty to become more accountable may include demands for them to both spend more instructional time with students and increase their research productivity. The conceptual point is twofold: institutional logics do not entirely determine behavior; and even a dominant logic may be weakened by persistent strain that is either inherent or in tension with a coexisting logic.

The analysis of institutional logics can make evident the presence of several value sets, their convergence or divergence, as well as the extent to which they are institutionalized as a logic-in-use (a constellation of beliefs already underlying an accepted set of practices or symbols) or a logic-invoked (a shared ideal to which actors may aspire or a rationale to which actors may refer). While the theory conceptualizes logics as embedded in determinative taken-for-granted constructs, it is also worthwhile to consider the potential for organizational actors to embrace and articulate a logic strategically in order to accrue legitimacy for themselves or their organization. That is, there may exist both conscious and unconscious manifestations of institutional logics.

TWO INSTITUTIONAL LOGICS

My analysis of case study archival data on academic restructuring provides evidence of institutional logics that contemporary public research universities have drawn upon for legitimacy. Simply stated, an "industry" logic has gained momentum at the macro level in the last quarter of the twentieth century to the extent that it has supplemented and in some circumstances become a viable alternative to the logic of "social institution." A number of factors have contributed to the ascendance of an industry logic in public research universities: the rise of accountability demands from political actors and the wider public, reinterpreting the service legacy to make skill training and economic development priorities, the prominence of management science as an ideology, a recognition of knowledge's proprietary value, and a declining regard for professions that corresponded to a rise in market forces as a legitimate compass for decision-making. Before presenting the case study data, I briefly contrast the two logics, their presumed goals, and the appropriate means for achieving them.

TABLE 2.1

Dominant Institutional Logics in University Restructuring

	Social Institution	Industry
Wider Context	Societal expectations	Market forces
Legacy of Service to Society	Multiple, including educational, citizenship, knowledge preservation & advancement	Contribute to economic development via skill training & research applications
Appropriate Response to Changing Demands	Pause and discuss	Scan and re-position
Central Value of Knowledge	Inherent worth of ideas, original scholarship	Revenue-generating, commercialization potential
Time Horizon	Long-term	Short-term
Dominant Rationale from Funder's Perspective	Invest in inquiry, including basic & applied research; invest in future generations	Procure applied research or educational services
Shapers of Knowledge	Disciplines, faculty-driven	Markets, demand-driven
Ideal Academic Structure	Comprehensive; continuity and change are faculty-governed	Selective and flexible; modified by managers
Ongoing Academic Challenges	Sustain comprehensive academic landscape within resource constraints; internal disharmony; loss of public confidence	Fixed costs in the face of change; imperfect information; lack of alignment between discourse and structure

Historically, the logic of social institution has encompassed a wide array of educational and social functions, from instruction and credentialing, to enhancing social mobility and socializing citizens. Over time, this logic has been elaborated into expectations that universities would fulfill a multiplicity of social goals, aims tied closely to those of the nation-state with a distinctive utilitarian cast. The logic has also included some traditional academic ideals. Foremost among them were beliefs that the university would promote liberal education, protect freedom of inquiry, foster the preservation and advancement of knowledge, and cultivate intellectual pluralism by providing a social space for intelligent conversation, social criticism, and dissent. Even though the "multiversity" has been championed as an extraordinary achievement, an inherent weakness lies in the tension among some of its ideals and aims. Thus, within the social institution logic itself, what it means to serve the public interest, and how, has been open to alternative interpretations.

While the social institution logic seemed infinitely elastic in its ability to justify expanded societal expectations, the likelihood that universities could deliver on all dimensions seemed increasingly slim. Moreover, under resource constraint, it is unclear which purposes are priorities and who decides. Strain has long been evident within faculty ranks. For example, as Smelser (1974: 111) observed in his study of systemic change in California public higher education, a discrepancy between academic ideals and resource-based realities has had a negative impact on faculty morale, "feelings of relative deprivation, generalized dissatisfaction, diminished loyalty, and proneness to attack the university and one another." This situation has only worsened over the past few decades of economic fluctuations, increased public distrust of professional competence, and widespread disaffection for bureaucracy (Gumport, 1997). The cumulative effect has been to weaken the foundation of the social institution logic and to call into question whether several academic ideals can be sustained. These include the pursuit of disinterested inquiry and universal knowledge, the authority of faculty to self-govern, as well as egalitarianism and collegiality within the academic community.

In contrast to such liberal ideals, the industry logic has focused upon vital resources and dynamic markets. The term "industry" in this context is meant to emphasize the activities of universities as actors in a competitive enterprise.[5] Primary goals for public research universities include providing skill training that corresponds to labor market needs and developing knowledge applications that enhance the economy. In their management, universities are expected to attend to harsh realities of market forces and adopt strategies such as scanning their competitive environments, planning, cutting costs, and re-engineering for efficiency and flexibility. Appropriate adjustments include changing product lines, substituting technology for labor, and reducing fixed costs through such means as outsourcing and privatizing as well as increasing the proportion of part-time and temporary personnel. Students tend to be viewed as consumers rather than as members of a campus community. The major responsibility for managers is to read the market for constraints and opportunities, and attempt to reposition accordingly. A university's decision to add an academic unit or program could be seen as a strategy to expand enrollments and thereby increase revenue. Hence structural changes are cast as necessary and prudent market corrections.

Signs that this industry logic has been moving to the foreground in public research universities can be traced back to visible financial and ideological support from the government. In World War II, the government involved universities in national defense and the advancement of science and technology, and dramatically expanded its investment in academic R&D in the postwar period. By the last quarter of the twentieth century, the federal government modified the incentives for industry to expand its partnerships with academic researchers and enabled universities to profit from federally funded R&D projects.[6] State governments also supported university-industry collaboration. As one set of observers appraised the change: "Universities, once wary beneficiaries of corporate largess, have become eager co-capitalists, embracing market values as never before" (Press and Washburn, 2000).

Pursuing an industry logic as a basis for university legitimacy has entailed several challenges. The biggest impediment to flexibility is the underlying academic structure itself, which is not easily tractable, especially in older universities. Thus, university leaders may be caught in a tension between the discourse they put forward and the results they can demonstrate. Neither swift restructuring nor results-oriented performance measures are easily achieved within or imposed upon universities. As my case studies will show, the use of an industry logic has been in tension with a social institution logic insofar as the values of the former unduly narrow public research university purposes and redefine the appropriate strategies for achieving them.

These two logics have much diagnostic potential for understanding the dynamics of academic restructuring in contemporary universities. The contrast between the two logics for public research universities is profound. The industry logic has great momentum in the contemporary era, even cross-nationally (Clark, 1998). It is strengthened by the belief that the unwillingness or inability of universities to adapt will result in a loss of centrality and perhaps ultimately a loss of viability for universities to compete as the major providers of education and new knowledge. In contrast, the social institution logic is supported by a concern that adaptation to market forces gives primacy to short-term economic demands at the neglect of a wider range of societal responsibilities, thereby jeopardizing democratizing functions and the long-term public interest. For any given campus, the ways in which either of the two logics are evident in the organizational discourse or prevail in structural modifications depend upon a mix of historical legacies, inherited structures, and perceptions of resource needs and constraints.

Studying the Academic Landscape: Empirical Anchors

The remainder of this chapter examines the coexistence of these two dominant logics as they are manifest in three public research universities: the University of California, Berkeley (UC Berkeley), the State University of New York (SUNY) Stony Brook, and the University of Illinois at Chicago (UIC). The case study sites are drawn from a larger research project on academic restructuring in public higher education.[7]

The three research universities are appropriate for a comparative case study analysis because they have many features in common. They are all public, located in metropolitan areas, and classified by the Carnegie Foundation as *Research Universities I*. State budget data suggest a similar pattern of fiscal constraint, especially from 1980 to 1994 when the proportion of the state tax revenue allocated to public higher education declined in California from 12.0 percent to 6.7 percent, in New York from 5.4 percent to 3.6 percent, and in Illinois from 7.1 percent to 6.2 percent (Halstead, 1998). Over the same time period, all three universities also show a marked decline in the relative share of their revenue coming from the state: the revenue from state appropriations, grants, and contracts as a proportion of total adjusted revenue declined from 1980 to 1994 for UC Berkeley from 52 percent to 39 percent, for SUNY Stony Brook from 69 percent to 34 percent, for UIC from 51 percent to 33 percent.[8] Together, these measures suggest that each campus faced a state context of resource turbulence that would figure prominently in their organizational responses. Yet the universities varied substantially in age, size, and academic landscape, which would suggest some differences in their strategies and rationales.

A rich array of archival documents serves as an empirical anchor for examining the institutional logics that each public research university drew upon for legitimacy in the last quarter of the twentieth century. Documents were coded systematically for statements about each university's responses to changing conditions and the justification for continuity or change in the array of academic programs offered. The evidence suggests increased efforts by all three universities to align their organizational discourse with an industry logic, although their responses differ in many particulars.

UC BERKELEY

The University of California at Berkeley, founded in 1868 as the land grant university of the state, has a long-standing reputation for excellence as one of the world's leading intellectual centers.[9] A founding member of the prestigious Association of American Universities, UC Berkeley has maintained its elite standing and its status as flagship of the state system. The ideal of comprehensive field coverage was established at its founding, with expected curricula in agriculture and mechanical arts and secondarily in classical and scientific studies. Over the next century, however, the ideal was expanded to include knowledge in all avenues of inquiry and learning. This wide scope was justified as the university's commitment to "the people of California," which was reiterated in several catalogs along with a prominently placed quotation from President Lyndon B. Johnson: "The cost of knowledge—whatever its price—is small against the price the world has already paid throughout its history of human ignorance."

Particularly in research, UC Berkeley kept pace with knowledge change by positioning itself at the forefront of new lines of inquiry. As the prototypical post–World War II "multiversity," UC Berkeley demonstrated this commitment through hiring faculty engaged in pioneering research and establishing organized research units staffed by nonfaculty research personnel. Both symbolically and materially, the ongoing expansion and differentiation of the organizational structure demonstrated that the university was eager to pursue opportunities in new research areas. During the last quarter of the twentieth century, federal R&D funding remained a sustaining component and a signal of the university's achievement. In recent years, however, the university did lose some ground, dropping in national rankings of federally financed R&D expenditures from eighth in 1974 to twenty-third in 1998. UC Berkeley's track record in federally financed research is all the more impressive considering that it has no hospital or medical school.

Although UC Berkeley has often been referred to as the nation's preeminent public research university, campus leaders worked actively to maintain its reputation for excellence through changing fiscal conditions. Keeping pace with knowledge change in educational programs was more difficult when the rapid expansion and resource abundance of the 1960s ceased. Documents indicate that campus leaders foresaw the resource constraints that would crystallize in the 1970s (for example, steady state enrollment and the post–Proposition 13 state fiscal crisis), and they shifted their planning assumptions accordingly. Although the first campus academic plan was developed in the late 1950s, the revised plan for 1969–75 was more significant. Three and a half years in the making, this revised plan identified a trajectory that differed markedly from the years of continuous and rapid expansion. Emphasizing constraints imposed by "an inelastic resource base," the plan set out "a blueprint to designate educational priorities and resource allocations." The new operating principle was succinct and dramatic: "Growth or improvement in one area will mean retrenchment in another."

The revised plan also indicated that the viability of the departmental structure had been considered in light of a growing interest in interdisciplinary fields and a concern as to whether traditional departments could accommodate the dynamic intellectual pursuits of faculty. The plan ended up reaffirming it as "a known and tested structure" that did not impede instruction in new areas and had already won the university its reputation: "The departments have 'made' Berkeley. They are strong. And they are here now." New departments could still be added as needed. As an example of departmental expansion, the plan stated that a Department of Ethnic Studies was to open in 1970. The plan also said that they had considered "optimal departmental size." Rather than identifying a planning principle in this regard, the document simply warns of imminent resource constraints, foreshadowing the possible consolidation of academic units and elimination of degree programs.

Consistent with these stated intentions, catalog data for the 1970s show a marked decline in the number of degree programs offered at the undergraduate level. From 1969 to 1977 the number of undergraduate degree programs offered declined by 38 percent, from 159 to 98. The biggest changes were seen in the reduction of the number of interdisciplinary programs by two-thirds, and social sciences and engineering/computer science/math by half. This reduction of undergraduate offerings is the largest change during the decades under study, and the closest correspondence between degree program data and the plan's warning of the need to adapt to resource constraints. Notably during this same period, the number of graduate program offerings increased from 1969–77, primarily in the humanities where the graduate programs grew from forty-six to fifty-six.

The theme of imminent resource constraint persisted through the documents of the 1970s and into the late 1980s. However, the number of degree programs expanded. The basic intention evident in the documents was resilience in a context of limited resources. Along with Berkeley's distinguished track record, the sheer magnitude of the existing university structure enabled coverage of a full range of academic subjects and specializations. The colleges of letters and sciences alone had over forty departments and twenty budgeted research institutes. The university envisioned its overall academic structure as a core of "fundamental disciplines" surrounded by "a group of professional units dedicated to integrated application of the disciplines to identifiable areas of human interest." Yet the premise that these areas of knowledge were open to all interested learners was explicitly challenged in this era. "Ceilings" were established for academic units so that student enrollments in courses and majors would be controlled to match departmental capabilities. The university conceded that this policy departed from an age-old ideal: "the tradition of free student choice . . . is warmly cherished by students and faculty alike . . . [but] it is clearly untenable as a public commitment."

In its catalogs during the late 1970s and well into the 1980s, the university still advertised a full range of departments and an expanding menu of academic programs, especially at the graduate level. In fact, the overall number of degree programs offered increased from 299 in 1977 to 344 in 1987. The number of master's degree programs increased from 101 to 127, with the largest expansion seen in interdisciplinary master's programs, from 16 to 36. Doctoral degree programs also increased from 98 to 112, also showing an expansion of interdisciplinary doctoral programs, from 15 to 24. At the undergraduate level, there were increases in the number of degree programs in engineering/computer science/math (from 11 to 17) and in interdisciplinary studies (from 13 to 26). The only counter to this trend at the undergraduate level was a decline in the total number of humanities degree programs from 31 to 22, which can be attributed to the renaming of several foreign language degree programs as interdisciplinary studies, which are coded separately. The basic trend of expansion came to a halt in the subsequent decade. From 1987 to 1999, there was some consolidation of master's programs and, to a lesser degree, doctoral programs. Overall the total number of degree programs offered declined by about 10 percent, from the 1987 high of 344 down to 316 in 1999, with the biggest changes seen in consolidation of the biological sciences (a 46 percent decline, from 48 degree programs to 26). Offsetting this was a modest expansion of the number of engineering/computer science/math degree programs at all three levels, reflecting new disciplinary specializations in those fields.

These data on degree program trends suggest that the university was able to maintain continuity in offering a core set of programs in each knowledge area and when necessary make incremental adjustments in the number of programs offered. In terms of program type, when expansion occurred it was concentrated in new graduate degree programs and in new areas of specialization, both in traditional areas like humanities and in the engineering/computer science/math and interdisciplinary areas. The degree program data can be interpreted as consistent with the planning intention to maintain continuity in comprehensive field coverage across knowledge areas while keeping pace with change. This could be due to the fact that catalogs are notorious for portraying continuity in universities' symbolic commitments to academic areas without regard for whether there are consistent resource allocations and faculty lines associated with those programs.[10]

When juxtaposed with earned degree data, there is greater correspondence between the data and the stated intentions in the planning documents to respond to resource constraints. When the documents said expansion would be curtailed, the data show fluctuations in degree production (although there is some lag time, as would be expected since the data are degree completions). First, there was a dramatic 28 percent increase in total number of degrees granted from 1966 to 1976, the largest increases coming in social sciences and "other professions," which include law, architecture and environmental design, and social services. Then, early in the next decade, the total number of degrees granted dropped by 11 percent, with notable declines in humanities, life sciences, and degrees in "other professions." Finally, there were small increases in the following decade (with gains for social sciences and life sciences), but total degree production did not reach its 1976 peak of 9,294. Earned degree data, though it should not be taken as a proxy for institutional commitment, can be interpreted as evidence of purposeful adjustments of educational output to market forces, albeit with some lag time.

By the 1980s and into the 1990s, planning documents indicate that the university wanted to prepare for projected enrollment increases and engage in long-range planning to accommodate them. The major concern was that the state legislature would not provide the necessary budget increases to accommodate expansion. Representatives of the university indicated that a possibility existed that they would adjust offerings to keep only those programs that were "first class" and certainly should not curtail degree production in programs producing the country's most talented graduates. However, the data suggest that the university did not depart from the principle of comprehensive field coverage, particularly in knowledge areas deemed "core," such as history. By the 1990s academic planning documents show university leaders calling for expanded investment in areas deemed "vital," for example in developmental biology and bioengineering. They made it clear that faculty recruitment efforts were needed in these areas as well as in other knowledge areas, where three waves of a voluntary early retirement initiative left some academic specializations without enough faculty to meet instructional demand. Overall the number of full-time-equivalent (FTE) faculty declined by 11 percent between 1987 and 1997. In this era the university's ability of the campus to sustain comprehensive field coverage at a high level of excellence became questionable, and there was concern that the Regents' 1995 policy to eliminate affirmative action along with the state's Proposition 209 would impede faculty recruitment. Moreover, documents acknowledge that the state budget continued to be seriously strained, and thus remained an unlikely source of unexpected revenue.

The university's fundraising activities have had excellent results and continue to be a promising strategy for bolstering faculty recruitment efforts and selective academic expansion. In the decade of the 1980s resources from the private sector increased fivefold, from $19.7 million in 1980 to $100 million by 1989, and corporate support increased from $7.2 million to $29.4 million over that same period. In 1990 a capital campaign, "Keeping the Promise," raised over $470 million, more than any previous campaign by a public university. These ambitions were extended, as another major campaign was launched in 1996, "Campaign for the New Century," which sought to raise $1.1 billion over the following five years.

In addition to fundraising, there have been visible initiatives to commercialize knowledge. One example is the 1998 strategic alliance between the Department of Plant and Microbial Biology and Novartis, a Swiss pharmaceutical company and producer of genetically engineered crops. While the contractual agreement was considered praiseworthy by some observers, it engendered controversy among others who were apprehensive about the blurring of boundaries between public and private entities, specifically whether the university was conducting research for the public good or for profit (Press and Washburn, 2000). The UC Berkeley–Novartis agreement enabled critics to assert that the university was not committed to disinterested inquiry. It also provided fodder for dissension among faculty, with deliberations over whether the process or outcome violated faculty governance norms. This initiative was even more remarkable because the dean of the College of Natural Resources circulated a request for proposals (RFP) among private companies. Moreover, he did so on behalf of an entire department and conveyed a willingness to negotiate some terms for the conduct of research and the graduate program.

UC Berkeley leaders have considered additional revenue-generating activities in the 1990s, such as the increased marketing of logos and university paraphernalia, income from royalties and licensing of technology, renting of conference facilities, and establishing fee-based distance learning programs for corporations. The aim was clear: to develop more discretionary resources and to decrease dependence on state revenues. Acknowledging that this approach departs from old ways, university leaders urged that they would proceed with caution: "The campus must be willing to do business in new and different ways. In developing new ways of generating revenue, we must decide whether the means justify the effects on our academic programs." The tight coupling of academic and fiscal concerns was evident in an elaborate data-gathering system, "Cal Profiles." Created in the mid-1990s to monitor cost-effectiveness and productivity of academic units, Cal Profiles was refined and then made available on-line to the university community in 1998, with the hope that such measures would decrease faculty complacency and raise awareness about wider accountability demands for enhanced efficiency and productivity.

Of the three case studies, UC Berkeley most consistently abided by the social institution legacy of comprehensive excellence during the changing resource conditions of the last quarter of the twentieth century. By the late 1980s, documents show the university using an industry logic as a supplementary discourse, urging cost-cutting alongside selective academic expansion in graduate degree programs and in new specializations to remain competitive. Yet this use of an industry logic was not accompanied by a marked restructuring in the overall array of academic programs offered, only incremental adjustments to keep pace with new fields and to take advantage of revenue-generating opportunities alongside ongoing efforts to fortify the enduring academic structure.

In contrast, the other two case studies show strong evidence of an industry logic in both their official discourse and in their structural development. While UC Berkeley's goal was to sustain legitimacy, the other two universities sought to acquire legitimacy. Aspiring to grow and to become regarded as among the finest public research universities in the country, SUNY Stony Brook and UIC more closely aligned their university discourse and developing structures with an industry logic and justified their strategy as appropriately opportunistic. Details on these two cases indicate that they pursued slightly different paths while following this same general strategy.

SUNY STONY BROOK

SUNY Stony Brook's trajectory is the story of a "rising" university whose rapid ascent was achieved through external funding.[11] A new campus developed in the 1960s, SUNY Stony Brook was to be, from the outset, "a University Center" committed to conducting research. The research profile was a priority, and the university made strides quickly. In federally financed R&D spending, Stony Brook moved from seventy-third in 1975 to sixtieth in 1982, up slightly to fifty-second in 1998. The university was designated "Research Universities I" within the Carnegie Foundation's 1987 classification.

SUNY Stony Brook found opportunities to improve its competitive position during successive periods of resource strain from the 1970s through the 1990s. The competitive lever that facilitated their rise was research funding for academic medicine and health sciences and the expanding capacity of a medical school and hospital. According to Graham and Diamond (1997: 122), in the 1970s an infusion of funds from the National Institutes of Health (NIH) set the stage for substantial subsidies and profits in the health sciences. SUNY Stony Brook was one of the major recipients of healthcare revenues generated by federal legislation creating Medicare and Medicaid. Over the next two decades, the university was able to ride this success through fluctuations in federal and state funding.

In contrast to UC Berkeley's long-standing comprehensiveness, SUNY Stony Brook struggled from the outset to develop an academic structure that was broad in scope. By 1977 the campus mission statement reported that fiscal uncertainty would not dissuade the university from its goal: "to match, and perhaps eventually to surpass, the distinguished public universities in other parts of the nation." The university's stated goal at the time was "a level of selectively comprehensive excellence," an oxymoron that reflects the ambition of university leaders to have the best of both. Campus leaders defined "comprehensiveness" as a full array of traditional liberal arts and sciences disciplines along with professional programs and applied sciences, while the term "selective" conveyed their intention to be flexible "to current needs and opportunities without being exhaustive."

Like UC Berkeley, the university stated that it was committed to serving the people of the state. For SUNY Stony Brook, embracing this commitment in the 1970s meant focusing on knowledge areas oriented to the economy. As one planning document stated: "Since the strategic resource base of the post-industrial economy is basic knowledge, and the skill base is the ability to apply that knowledge," the university's should grow in selected areas: "High technology and industries such as electronics, aerospace, defense, communications, media services, publishing, computing and data management, health care and educational materials."

The authors of the planning documents acknowledged that these fields had "high costs as well as high anticipated returns," a somewhat risky strategy given that the state economy was in the throes of a series of fiscal crises. These realizations prompted the university leadership to focus on generating discretionary resources. The major strategy was "strategic resource reallocation." The university stated it would pursue retrenchment in all parts of the campus, making "difficult and painful choices for budgetary reductions." The criteria for program reduction and elimination included quality, need, and productivity. The protected areas were those that demonstrated immediate economic impact and contributed to economic development. Yet the documents also indicate the university still aimed to expand its array of degree programs. They identified several "unmet needs," including management science, bioengineering, and interdisciplinary programs in ethnic studies, such as Puerto Rican Studies. Some documents also acknowledged the need for resources in humanities and social sciences.

University leaders into the 1980s wrote that they were hurt by the state's fiscal stringency and ensuing cuts: "We are still bleeding profusely from the old wounds, but circulation has been improved in a few extremities." In the better times of the mid-1990s, the university declared they were strong enough to embark on "a highly selective expansion of physical plant facilities and programs with an emphasis on quality." They referred to this as a "Decade of Refinement" to "move ahead carefully in identified areas." One specific priority was to expand doctoral programs, even as university leaders were admonished to do so only in accordance with market demand.

In addition to changes in resource reallocation, university leaders also focused on generating external funding. In the 1970s, the emphasis had been on federal funds, symbolized by the creation of a new position, vice president for research, in 1978. In the late 1970s, they also turned to industry directly, seeking funds for research projects as well as offering to develop continuing education programs for corporate employees. The ensuing partnerships with industry took several structural forms: contractual agreements for collaborative research and technology transfer, as well as customized instruction. The university's success was also exemplified by its bid in 1997 to lead a coalition in the management of the Brookhaven National Laboratory, a $2 billion, five-year contract from the Department of Energy to conduct research in physics, the life sciences, and nuclear medicine. Obtaining this contract was a visible accomplishment for SUNY Stony Brook, even though Brookhaven had been plagued by environmental and safety problems.

By the late 1990s the documents reflect campus leaders' pride in the university's many contributions to the local economy and in the establishment of structural units dedicated to this continuing effort. As the provost enumerated in a speech, "The Entrepreneurial University": "At Stony Brook we provide direct research support for local industry through our Strategic Partnership for Industrial Resurgence (SPIR). SPIR has resulted in the retention and creation of many jobs on Long Island and brings millions of dollars to the local economy. The university also helps to manage the Long Island High Technology Incubator on the Stony Brook campus. The incubator provides a nurturing environment within the university community for new businesses." The university also established a Small Business Development Center and a Center for Advanced Technology to contribute to the business community. In articulating the rationale behind this overall strategy, the provost cited the need to keep up with the taken-for-granted assumptions of the wider society: "The future of higher education is likely to be tied to the development of capitalist economies. . . . This will require significant change in the culture of institutions and will radically alter the relationships among students, faculty and the administration."[12]

From the 1970s through the 1990s, changes in the academic degree programs at Stony Brook were justified with a similar rationale, growth to meet labor market demands, to support the economy, and to correspond to areas that were strong in funded research. Catalog data offer evidence that is basically consistent with the university's resource fluctuations, with periods of successive growth in numbers of programs offered and dramatic increases in new graduate (especially master's degree programs). From 1969 to 1977 for example, the total number of undergraduate degree programs increased dramatically from 49 to 105, with the largest concentration of new programs in engineering, health sciences, and interdisciplinary. (This was the only period of growth for undergraduate programs in humanities, which increased from 9 to 14 and remained at that number through 1999.) The interval from 1977 to 1987 reflected no growth overall and modest expansion of the number of master's degree programs offered, which increased from 33 to 38 with gains for health sciences, applied social sciences, and new specialized humanities programs. By the interval from 1987 to 1997, the total number of degree programs offered saw another wave of expansion similar to the 1970s, with an increase from 109 to 164. The biggest increases were in master's programs (from 38 to 66) and in doctoral programs (from 24 to 42), with the largest numbers of new graduate programs in biological sciences, health sciences, and interdisciplinary fields.

Earned degree data suggest some corresponding trends in total number of degrees awarded: growth from the 1960s to the 1970s, and some growth spurts through the 1970s and 1980s because of increases in master's degrees awarded. By 1996 the university's total annual degree production reached a peak of 3,950, with the largest gains seen in biological sciences and engineering/computer science. The degree data correspond more directly with the ebb and flow of resources, as expected lagging a few years behind conditions stated in the documents. In the leaner years of the 1980s there were reductions in degree production. In times of abundance, particularly in the 1990s as the university intended to expand selectively, it reached unprecedented levels of expansion both in degree production and in the number of degree programs offered.

Thus, with much optimism, the university's president in 1998 declared: "We can indeed celebrate what lies ahead for having endured the bad years of debt, deficit, and budget cuts. We have before us a year teeming with possibilities for building, growing, and creating the structures of Stony Brook's future." The stated intention was to do so selectively, even though some major academic areas remained "underfunded." For example, the social sciences had a 25 percent decline in FTE faculty between 1977 and 1997, and the humanities disciplines still lacked their own building at the end of the 1990s. Affirming the president's optimism, in May of 2001, the university achieved a much-sought-after goal in receiving an invitation to become the sixty-second member of the prestigious Association of American Universities (AAU).

UNIVERSITY OF ILLINOIS AT CHICAGO (UIC)

The University of Illinois at Chicago's story is similar to Stony Brook's rapid gain in national reputation from federal R&D funding, specifically in health science fields.[13] UIC had a different legacy, though, and a later start. It was founded in 1982 from the merger of the University of Illinois at Chicago Circle (UICC) and the University of Illinois Medical Center. Before the merger, UICC had had its own aspirations for upward mobility. Although located in an urban setting and pursuing an urban mission, campus leaders thought the best way to serve their citizens was to become "a university of the first rank . . . [b]eing not only a conveyor of knowledge but a producer of knowledge as well." In the mid-1970s their "high priority" was to expand research activities, a commitment that was symbolized in a new Office of Sponsored Research. Characterizing its achievements to date and its intended trajectory, UICC referred to itself as "the flagship of public higher education in the Chicago metropolitan area," and accordingly aspired to establish an academic structure "similar in programmatic range and quality to the Urbana-Champaign campus and other fine public institutions in the nation."

UICC struggled and failed to realize this goal. As a commuter campus, it reflected the demographics of the city and admitted "far too many students who have virtually no chance of graduating." However, degree production in the ten-year period from 1966 to 1976 did increase more than fivefold, from eight hundred degrees to forty-five hundred. Life sciences accounted for one-third of the total. By 1979, UICC documents have a prominent cost-effectiveness discourse, stating that the university was committed to seeing that "resources are utilized in the most effective, efficient ways possible. . . . The campus must be prepared to experience major retrenchments in some areas and reallocation to others. . . . Priorities will be set by targeting units that with the addition of resources can be more responsive to external demand and/or can make a quantum jump in programmatic quality and performance." Like UC Berkeley and

SUNY Stony Brook, UICC identified revenue-generating as the solution to resource constraints: "[to] bring in dollars from external non-State agencies to finance many of [the] research, instructional, and public service programs." Campus leaders urged faculty to step up efforts to obtain research funds and other income-generating possibilities.

By the time of the merger in 1982, UICC had brought an inventory of degree program offerings that matched the scope of Stony Brook's of the same era, although none of the programs were nationally recognized. The inherited educational mission was decidedly local, enrolling undergraduates who were largely working class and the first in their families to attend college. University leaders attributed the lack of national reputation to "the failure of the campus to pursue internally consistent strategies in terms of academic programming." When the merger occurred, the new University of Illinois at Chicago (UIC) had a number of well-developed health sciences programs inherited from the medical center, but clearly had a long way to go to establish a full range of subjects in the liberal arts, let alone a national reputation for quality in those fields. The university aspired to broader academic excellence nonetheless, particularly in the sciences and applied sciences.

Remarkably, UIC quickly grew into a research university with a national reputation. The university developed a strategy similar to Stony Brook's: securing federal research funds, especially in the health sciences. UIC's federal R&D ranking improved from ninety-fifth in 1975 to sixty-fifth in 1982. (It did not advance in the rankings between 1982 and 1998.) Like Stony Brook, UIC was designated "Research Universities I" by the Carnegie Foundation in 1987. A UIC planning document underscored the very competitive context and their desire to keep up: "Everyone wants to be Research I"; we are "in competition for the research dollars, stellar faculty, and top graduate students. Have we the ingenuity and resources to successfully compete?"

UIC's competitive strategy remained consistent: to "expand our commitment to research," noting that "the surrounding metropolitan area and the state indicate a ready audience for research results," specifically nearby pharmaceutical and other health-related companies. University leaders saw potential for "immediate opportunities for technology transfer. . . . The existence of other major institutions in the city provided easy access to collaborations which can foster both expansion and dissemination of knowledge."

In addition, the 1987 documents show that university leaders foresaw expansion opportunities in academic programs, especially in doctoral programs that could be linked with research. One planning document stated the goal clearly: "*Goal*: Develop Ph.D. programs of distinction which reflect the interdisciplinary nature of modern inquiry, and which parallel the growth of UIC research activity. The rapid growth of our research enterprise and our potential to develop new programs suggest that we set a goal of developing one to two Ph.D. programs per year over the next ten years." Remarkably, from 1987 to 1999, the number of doctoral programs nearly doubled, from twenty-five to forty-nine, with new programs established in entirely new areas (six in business, four in humanities) and expanded programs in areas where the university already had some offerings (from three to eight in engineering/computer science/ math, and six to nine health sciences).

Simultaneously, the university adopted another explicit goal, to develop a centralized capacity for academic management: "a coordinated program/unit evaluation linked with budgeting and other planning processes. . . . Further we recommend that a system be put in place to measure and recognize contributions (or lack of contributions) of various programs and activities to our goals. It is important to keep a scorecard, track progress and make changes when necessary." The criteria for academic units were clearly stated: centrality, quality in terms of "value-added to students," projected demand for the program, and "comparative advantage the program has relative to other programs in the metropolitan area, the state and the country." They also hoped their evaluation system would become an exemplary model for other universities that sought to improve campuswide coordination.

By 1991, UIC's academic organization had become complex: fifteen colleges and schools with over 160 degree program offerings, and granting annually just under five thousand degrees. Compared to UC Berkeley's size and scope, UIC offered half the number of degree programs and granted about two-thirds of the annual degree production. The UIC chancellor established a Standing Campus Priorities Committee (SCPC) whose charge was to oversee long-range academic planning and to articulate fully "the land grant mission in an urban setting." In 1991, UIC's first Master Plan was produced. It focused on improving its current assets to lay a foundation for future growth. Outreach to the surrounding community was a priority, through activities such as "the Great Cities Initiative" for urban research and service projects and "the Neighborhoods Initiative," collaborative efforts between the university and community groups to strengthen the quality of life for nearby residents and businesses.

The intention of campus administrators to modify the university's array of academic program offerings was a prominent theme in the documents of the 1990s. Academic units faced a clear imperative: to earn their keep or else face consolidation or elimination. As *Preparing UIC for the 21st Century* warned: "It cannot be assumed that all programs currently in operation at UIC will be continued, or continued at the current level of support. . . . Central campus goals require that some resources must be freed up to support new programmatic initiatives." Reminiscent of UC Berkeley's growth-by-retrenchment principle and Stony Brook's strategic resource reallocation, the university's stated intention to centrally oversee academic unit performance coincided with the Illinois Board of Higher Education's (IBHE) "Priorities, Quality and Productivity Initiative," a 1992 statewide mandate for public colleges and universities to measure all units based upon student demand, degree production, cost, and centrality. Reported to the IBHE, campus data were to be used as a basis for academic program reduction and elimination justified at the state level as financial savings.

In the 1990s, the university expanded the number of degree programs offered at all levels, especially doctorates. Between 1987 and 1999 undergraduate degree programs increased from seventy-two to eighty-one particularly in humanities and education, while master's degree programs increased from sixty-seven to seventy-six, with increases in applied social sciences, engineering/computer science/math, and interdisciplinary fields. The number of doctoral programs expanded even more considerably than the other programmatic levels, from twenty-five to forty-nine, with large increases in business, education, engineering/computer science/math, health sciences and interdisciplinary studies. Thus, looking back over two decades, degree program offerings expanded dramatically, from sixty-one to eighty-one undergraduate programs, from forty-four to seventy-six master's programs, and from nineteen to forty-nine doctoral programs. It is only in the second decade, between 1987 and 1997, where we see new faculty positions created, overall a 10 percent increase in the number of FTE faculty which included a 15 percent increase in faculty located in the professions as well as a 19 percent increase in the humanities. By the end of the decade approximately 70 percent of the university's FTE faculty were located in professional fields. This corresponds with the major areas of degree production: the health sciences, engineering, and business.

The university leadership then made a bold move. Since UIC had ascended quickly to a national reputation and amassed a base of discretionary resources, they were in a position to make a symbolic and material commitment to liberal arts and sciences. In 1999 they hired a new dean for the College of Liberal Arts and Sciences, Stanley Fish, a high-profile humanities scholar, who aspired to raise UIC's national profile by recruiting scholars from some of the most elite universities in the country. With the provost providing the funds to enable UIC to compete for designated "star scholars" with generous six-figure salaries, Fish quickly succeeded, hiring several nationally known scholars with academic specializations in fields that were considered "hot," such as gay and lesbian studies, disabilities studies, and feminist economics, as well as in political science and English. Several of the new hires were brought in to develop new programs and were given joint appointments across two or more academic units. This suggested flexibility in the university's academic structure and willingness to support cutting-edge interdisciplinary pursuits. It also served as an effective strategy for positioning the university to take the lead in small but visible academic niches, such as disability studies and gay studies.

This strategy had two possible justifications given the prevailing institutional logics. One is that the university was attempting to fill in gaps in humanities and social sciences, thereby seeking to widen its span of quality program offerings that are usually found at older nationally eminent universities. From this perspective, UIC was reflecting a social institution logic in seeking to redress the programmatic imbalance by building up previously neglected fields. On the other hand, this strategy can be seen as further pursuit of an industry logic without looking back, with more selective investment and a gamble to invest resources in academic superstars and "hot" knowledge areas that may yield big gains in prestige. In either case, the consequence is not yet clear. As UIC aspires to be the state's "second flagship," this recruitment strategy has proven risky. Although it earned the university national news coverage, it also drew vocal criticism from conservatives in the state legislature and the Chicago area who were decidedly unenthusiastic about the new dean and the expertise of some of his new hires. Then again, such public criticism could be interpreted as a signal that UIC had truly arrived, as stories like these are grist for the media mill's coverage of today's great research universities.

Conclusion

In this chapter, I proposed that the basis for legitimacy of American public research universities has been in transition during the last quarter of the twentieth century. Data from three case studies point to the role of resource scarcity—both actual and perceived—in meeting the challenge to keep pace with knowledge change. My analysis of archival documents suggests that organizational discourse about goals and solutions came to be cast in an industry logic. Beyond this general pattern, the differences in academic restructuring across the cases offer three insights about the legacy of service, the centrality of knowledge, and the dynamic nature of institutional logics.

First, the ascendance of an industry logic was facilitated not only by resource turbulence but also by ambiguity inherent in the legacy of service. A multitude of university initiatives were justified in the name of service— service to the people of the state, the surrounding neighborhoods, and the local economy. By invoking the service legacy, campus leaders sought to satisfy external constituencies while simultaneously furthering each university's own interests. For UC Berkeley, economic development initiatives went hand-in-hand with fundraising and commercialization activities, essentially as a supplementary layer of activities alongside the comprehensive array of educational, research, and service activities that had already been established via a social institution logic. SUNY Stony Brook and UIC invoked the legacy of service in a different way: by contributing to economic development and committing to knowledge areas with the greatest currency, they established the scaffolding and funding upon which their academic organizations were built. It is unlikely that either Stony Brook or UIC could have achieved such rapid ascents had they sought to climb in the 1990s; changes in the organization of health services and the healthcare economy suggested grim prospects for the revenue-generating capabilities of university hospitals (Cohen, 1998).

Second, the case studies affirm the proposition that multiple logics may coexist, with some variation in how logics are enacted in different organizational settings. UC Berkeley as a long-standing elite university had fully institutionalized a social institution logic in its academic structure, and that logic continued to be in use by some faculty and in some quarters of the wider society. Later in the university's development, an industry logic was adopted in its discourse as a supplementary rationale. It was accompanied by minor structural adjustments in the number of academic programs, changes that even some traditionalists may have accepted as appropriate pruning after more than a century of knowledge growth and specialization. Even though campus leaders changed some academic management practices, at UC Berkeley an industry logic has not supplanted the social institution logic, nor has it narrowed the scope of knowledge offered or destabilized the academic structure.

In contrast, SUNY Stony Brook and UIC embraced an industry logic in their discourse and structural commitments throughout the last quarter of the twentieth century. They did so early in their organizations' development, and the logic was linked with the pursuit of research funding and selective investment in health sciences and "other professions," leaving underfunded or neglected some fields of instruction and inquiry historically considered an integral part of the academic core. At Stony Brook, while there was an initial attempt to draw upon a social institution logic, stating an early goal of "selective comprehensiveness," the university did not make material commitments to comprehensiveness. Through the 1990s, Stony Brook continued to invest selectively in the fields drawing research funding and develop new areas that were of interest to local industry. By 2001, the university's inclusion in the AAU signals the achievement of a much-sought-after goal, the recognition for excellence as one of the country's most prestigious universities. In contrast, UIC still appeared to labor in the shadow of the elite and the legacy of the comprehensive ideal. For UIC, in the late 1990s, initiatives to expand academic offerings, especially new doctoral programs in the College of Liberal Arts and Sciences, were launched to make the university more attractive to the "star scholars" it sought to recruit. While clearly an attempt to raise the university's national profile, it is not yet clear how to interpret the logic underlying the initiatives—whether they are evidence of further selective investment in "hot" new fields or possibly a signal that the university seeks to accrue legitimacy by invoking a social institution logic by attempting to develop a more comprehensive academic landscape.

Third, and finally, the case studies suggest that university rationales and behaviors can contribute to wider institutional logics, either by reproducing or weakening them. In this sense, institutional logics not only coexist but also coevolve. Logics are constituted and potentially reconstituted both through symbolic constructions and material practices, an interdependence that warrants analysis. Symbolic and material commitments can remain decoupled from one another, especially for organizations that lack inspection at lower levels (Meyer and Rowan, 1977). Without material investment or structural change, the talk of change has an entirely symbolic function. Indeed, official discourse can function symbolically, while the structure has embedded in it a different value set. In this study, such a decoupling was most evident at UC Berkeley, the oldest organization. This would account for why there is much talk of academic restructuring yet little actual change within more established university settings.

Symbolic constructions gain credibility when aligned with material practices. Stated intentions can be reinforced when accompanied by even small-scale material investments or self-contained structural initiatives that signal a willingness and capacity to respond. As universities establish new research centers, contractual agreements with industry partners, and data-gathering or academic performance monitoring systems, they send powerful signals to the environment that they are aligned with an industry logic. The converse may also be true, that the lack of alignment between symbolic commitments and material resources can potentially weaken a logic. The failure to change the structure to correspond with the discourse may ultimately cause credibility problems for a university or its leaders. This scenario is more problematic if a university has been under fire from its external constituents, but it is less problematic if a university's stock of legitimacy is high.

From this perspective, it is also apparent that long-existing structures reflect the institutionalization of an old social institution logic and as such carry their own momentum. The existing structure can be a reproductive force for itself or a source of strain as a new logic takes hold. During times of transition, an existing structure can be a referent for organizational actors who align themselves with different logics. Subject to alternative interpretations by interested actors, the structure can either be celebrated for retaining values that are not currently dominant or it can be discredited as a holdover from the past. The spin may be used to the organization's benefit or detriment. In the first case, the existing structure can be invoked to signal the enduring vitality of an old logic and to align with values of a long-established knowledge constituency whose legitimacy is still sought. In the second, the existing structure can be invoked to assert that leaders continue to invest in fields that are irrelevant or obsolete. This can weaken the competitive position of the university, foster internal disharmony, and threaten the basis of legitimacy for knowledge workers in those areas.

These matters are of great consequence for the university and for society. At issue is not only organizational viability but institutional integrity. As Kerr (1995: 94) reminded us in his essay on the future of the City of Intellect: "[T]he intellect, and the university as its most happy home, can have great potential roles to play in the reconciliation of the war between the future and the past." As tensions between institutional logics become evident within universities, the structure of the academic landscape itself is implicated in the struggle. It is worth considering how reconciliation can be effectively and justly managed so that the intellect does not need to search for a happier home.

Notes

1. It could be argued that public research universities made unrealistically high projections for budget increases. A shortfall in projected budget increases is a different matter from an actual decline in state funding. To examine one measure of the latter, from 1977 to 1996, the level of state appropriations, grants, and contracts per FTE student for *all* public research universities did not decline; rather it increased by 5 percent. State appropriations alone per FTE student increased by 0.73 percent. This measure does not capture variation across states. Calculations were based upon HEGIS and IPEDS data for two financial variables: State Appropriations (adjusted for changes in hospital reporting after 1986) and State Grants and Contracts (which cannot be adjusted for the change in hospital revenue reporting for 1987–96 because of the aggregating of all gifts, grants, and contracts to hospitals regardless of the source, resulting in possible understated values and change over time). Financial data were deflated to constant 1997 dollars using HEPI. FTE students were calculated by adding one-third of part-time enrollment to full-time.

2. While the conventional wisdom is that public research universities became entrepreneurial in response to declines in state funding, a decline in the relative share of revenue from state sources can also result from relative increases in other revenue categories. A direct cause-effect relationship should not be presumed; rather it must be examined for each university.

3. Some research argues that market considerations have for some time been factored into programmatic decisions (Slaughter, 1993), and increased in the past two decades by national initiatives and changes in the global economy (Slaughter and Leslie, 1997).

4. Engell and Dangerfield (1998) state it succinctly: those academic fields most likely to be supported have clear links to money, either the promise of money (for example, graduates' earnings), the knowledge of money (for example, economics), or as a source of money (revenue for the university).

5. The use of the term "industry" has changed over time. Although the meaning of industry as factory production is still common, since 1945 "industry" has

come to signify a generalized domain of activity in nonindustrial kinds of service and work, such as the holiday industry, the leisure industry, and the entertainment industry (Williams, 1983: 176).

6. Two key initiatives illustrate the point and the eagerness with which universities responded. One is the set of programs launched by the National Science Foundation in the 1980s in order to stimulate collaboration between universities and industry: Engineering Research Centers, Industry-University Cooperative Research Centers, and Science and Technology Centers. A second is landmark legislation, the Bayh-Dole Act of 1980, which permitted universities to retain the title and thus profit from inventions generated from federal R&D projects (Geiger, 1993: 315–16).

7. The larger research project consists of a stratified set of public universities clustered in three metropolitan areas. Collected from 1997 to 2000, the case study data include: HEGIS and IPEDS data, archival documents (for example, catalogs, academic plans, self-studies, speeches), and two hundred interviews with administrators and faculty. Data were analyzed using the conceptual framework developed in this chapter, allowing for emerging themes and disconfirming examples. Data on degree programs were also gathered for selected years of *The College Blue Book*, 13th, 16th, 21st and 27th editions. This chapter reflects an abbreviated version of the conceptual framework and document analysis used in the larger project.

8. However, such changes in the revenue mix should not be interpreted as a decline in state support, since universities simultaneously generated additional revenue from nonstate sources. As a more direct measure of state support, state revenue per FTE enrollment during this period did fluctuate for the three universities: overall SUNY Stony Brook had an increase ($1,689 per FTE), while UC Berkeley had a slight decline ($350 per FTE) and UIC a larger decline ($1,587 per FTE). The measure was calculated using two IPEDS variables, state appropriations and state grants and contracts. The total revenue from state appropriations, grants, and contracts was divided by FTE students, the latter calculated by adding one-third of the part-time enrollment to the total for full-time. Financial data were deflated to constant 1997 dollars using HEPI. The lower revenue for UCB can be linked to the lack of a medical center and hospital.

9. In chronological order, the following University of California, Berkeley, documents were analyzed:

Academic Plan Steering Committee. 1969. *Revised Academic Plan 1969–1975*. University of California, Berkeley.

Academic Planning and Program Review Board. 1974. *University of California Academic Plan 1974–1978*. University of California, Berkeley.

University of California, Berkeley. 1977, 1987, 1997. *General Catalog*.

Self-Study Steering Committee. 1979. *Report Submitted to the Accreditation Commission for Senior Colleges and Universities of the Western Association of Schools and Colleges for Reaffirmation of Accreditation*. University of California, Berkeley.

University of California, Berkeley. 1980. *Long-Range Academic Plan 1980–1985*.

Office of the Chancellor. 1984. *Fifth Year Report Submitted to the Accrediting Commission for Senior Colleges and Universities of the Western Association of Schools and Colleges*. University of California, Berkeley.

Steering Committee for WASC Accreditation. 1990. *Change: The '90s at Berkeley—Self-Study Prepared for the Western Association of Schools and Colleges*. University of California, Berkeley.

Office of the Vice Chancellor and Provost. 1995. *Mid-Term Accreditation Report*. University of California, Berkeley.

Berdahl, Robert M. 1998. "On the Threshold of the Twenty-First Century." Chancellor's Inaugural address. University of California, Berkeley.

Department of Plant and Microbial Biology. 1998. *Invitation letter to various companies*. University of California, Berkeley.

Rausser, Gordon. 1998. *Strategic Alliance Time Line*. University of California, Berkeley.

Rausser, Gordon. 1999. *Private/Public Research: The Case of Agricultural Biotechnology*. University of California, Berkeley.

10. There are two additional possibilities. First, data on degree programs do not reflect the elimination or reallocation of faculty lines. Second, change-by-substitution may occur within the same knowledge area. This would not be reflected as a change in the aggregate number of degree programs offered by broad field.

11. In chronological order, the following SUNY Stony Brook documents were analyzed:

State University of New York–Stony Brook. 1976, 1986, 1996. *Graduate Bulletin*.

State University of New York–Stony Brook. 1977, 1986, 1997. *Undergraduate Bulletin*.

State University of New York–Stony Brook. 1977. *Campus Mission Statement*.

Middle States Steering Committee, Office of the Academic Vice President. 1978. *Stony Brook in Transition: 1978 Interim Report—A Report to the Commission on Higher Education—Middle States Association of Colleges and Schools*. State University of New York–Stony Brook.

Marburger, John H. 1982. *Preliminary Planning Proposal 1982–86*. Planning information with budget request. State University of New York–Stony Brook.

Self-Study Steering Committee, Office of the Provost. 1984. *Stony Brook's Unfinished Agenda—A Report to the Commission on Higher Education—Middle States Association of Colleges and Schools*. University of New York–Stony Brook.

State University of New York–Stony Brook. 1988. *Into the Fourth Decade*.

Middle States Steering Committee. 1994. *Education, Research, Public Service: A Model for the Research University of the Future—A Report to the Commission on Higher Education—Middle States Association of Colleges and Schools*. University of New York–Stony Brook.

Five Year Plan Coordinating Committee. 1995. *Five Year Plan 1995–2000*. University of New York–Stony Brook.

Kenny, Shirley Strum. 1998. *State of the University Address*. Presidential address. University of New York–Stony Brook.

Mission Review Task Force. 1998. *Mission Review*. University of New York–Stony Brook.

Richmond, Rollin C. 1998. "The Entrepreneurial University." Speech at Kyung Hee University Executive Vice President's Conference. Provost's Address. University of New York–Stony Brook.

Richmond, Rollin C. 1998. *A Student-Centered Research University—Academic Plan*. State University of New York–Stony Brook.

12. In a striking juxtaposition, this statement came just after Stony Brook's president finished chairing a Carnegie-funded national commission to study undergraduate education in research universities. Among other things, a visible result of the commission's work was the widespread promotion of the phrase "the student-centered research university," which she herself intended to emphasize at Stony Brook. Simultaneously, the SUNY trustees indicated that SUNY campuses would increasingly need to rely on revenue from students. This also prompted Stony Brook leaders to state explicitly their commitment to improve the quality and quantity of undergraduate degree programs.

13. In chronological order, the following UICC and UIC documents were analyzed:

Committee on Self-Study. 1970. *University of Illinois at Chicago Circle: A Report for the North Central Association*. University of Illinois at Chicago Circle.

University of Illinois at Chicago Circle. 1975. *The Second Decade*.

University of Illinois at Chicago Circle. 1977. *Graduate Study*.

University of Illinois at Chicago Circle. 1977. *Undergraduate Study*.

Office of Academic Affairs. 1979. *UICC Planning and Development for the 1980's*. University of Illinois at Chicago Circle.

University of Illinois at Chicago. 1986, 1996. *Graduate Study*.

Strategic Planning Committee. 1987. *A Look to the Future: Strategic Plans for UIC*. University of Illinois at Chicago.

University of Illinois at Chicago. 1987, 1997. *Undergraduate Catalog*.

University of Illinois at Chicago. 1991. *Master Plan—University of Illinois at Chicago*.

Standing Campus Priorities Committee. 1993. *Preparing UIC for the 21st Century*. University of Illinois at Chicago.

University of Illinois at Chicago. 1997. *Institutional Self Study Report*. A report to the North Central Association of Colleges and Secondary Schools Evaluation Team.

References

Clark, Burton. 1983. *The Higher Education System: Academic Organization in Cross-national Perspective*. Berkeley: University of California Press.

———. 1993. "The Problem of Complexity in Modern Higher Education." In Sheldon Rothblatt and Bjourn Wittrock (eds.), *The European and American University since 1800*. Cambridge: Cambridge University Press.

———. 1998. *Creating Entrepreneurial Universities: Organizational Pathways of Transformation*. Surrey: Pergamon Press.

Cohen, Linda. 1998. "Soft Money, Hard Choices: Research Universities and University Hospitals." In Roger Noll (ed.), *Challenges to Research Universities*. Washington, DC: Brookings Institution Press.

DiMaggio, Paul, and Walter Powell. 1983. "The Iron Cage Revisited: Institutional Isomorphism and Collective Rationality in Organizational Fields." *American Sociological Review* 48: 147–60.

Engell, James, and Anthony Dangerfield. 1998. "The Market-Model University: Humanities in the Age of Money." *Harvard Magazine* (May–June): 48–55, 111.

Friedland, Roger, and Robert Alford. 1991. "Bringing Society Back In: Symbols, Practices and Institutional Contradictions." In Walter Powell and Paul DiMaggio (eds.), *The New Institutionalism in Organizational Analysis*. Chicago: University of Chicago Press.

Geiger, Roger. 1993. *Research and Relevant Knowledge*. New York and Oxford: Oxford University Press.

Gibbons, Michael, Camille Limoges, Helga Nowotny, Simon Schwartzman, Peter Scott, and Martin Trow. 1994. *The New Production of Knowledge*. London and Thousand Oaks, CA: Sage.

Graham, Hugh, and Nancy Diamond. 1997. *The Rise of American Research Universities*. Baltimore: Johns Hopkins University Press.

Gumport, Patricia J. 1993. "The Contested Terrain of Academic Program Reduction." *Journal of Higher Education* 64 (3): 283–311.

———. 1997. "Public Universities as Academic Workplaces." *Daedalus* 126 (4): 113–36.

———. 2000. "Academic Restructuring: Organizational and Institutional Imperatives." *Higher Education* 39: 67–91.

Gumport, Patricia J., and Brian Pusser. 1997. "Restructuring the Academic Environment." In Marvin Peterson, David Dill, and Lisa Mets (eds.), *Planning and Management for a Changing Environment*. San Francisco: Jossey-Bass.

Gumport, Patricia J., and Brian Pusser. 1999. "University Restructuring: The Role of Economic and Political Contexts." In John Smart (ed.), *Higher Education: Handbook of Theory and Research* 14: 146–200. Bronx, NY: Agathon Press.

Halstead, Kent. 1998. *State Profiles: Financing Public Higher Education 1978 to 1998 Trend Data*. Washington, DC: Research Associates of Washington.

Kerr, Clark. 1995 [1963]. *The Uses of the University*. 4th ed. Cambridge: Harvard University Press.

Meyer, John, and Brian Rowan. 1977. "Institutionalized Organizations: Structure as Myth and Ceremony." *American Journal of Sociology* 83: 340–63.

Meyerson, Joel, and William Massy (eds.). 1994. *Measuring Institutional Performance in Higher Education*. Princeton: Peterson's.

Powell, Walter, and Jason Owen-Smith. 1998. "Universities and the Market for Intellectual Property in the Life Sciences." *Journal of Policy Analysis and Management* 17 (2): 253–77.

Press, Eyal, and Jennifer Washburn. 2000. "The Kept University." *Atlantic Monthly* 285 (3): 39–54.

Rothblatt, Sheldon. 1997. *The Modern University and Its Discontents*. Cambridge: Cambridge University Press.

Scott, W. Richard, Martin Ruef, Peter Mendel, and Carol Caronna. 2000. *Institutional Change and Healthcare Organizations*. Chicago: University of Chicago Press.

Slaughter, Sheila. 1993. "Retrenchment in the 1980s: The Politics of Prestige and Gender." *Journal of Higher Education* 64 (3): 250–82.

Slaughter, Sheila, and Larry Leslie. 1997. *Academic Capitalism: Politics, Policies, and the Entrepreneurial University*. Baltimore: Johns Hopkins University Press.

Smelser, Neil. 1974. "Growth, Structural Change, and Conflict in California Public Higher Education, 1950–1970." In Neil Smelser and Gabriel Almond (eds.), *Public Higher Education in California*. Berkeley: University of California Press.

Williams, Raymond. 1983. *Keywords: A Vocabulary of Culture and Society*. Rev. ed. New York: Oxford University Press.

CHAPTER THREE

The Competition for High-Ability Students: Universities in a Key Marketplace

ROGER L. GEIGER

Undergraduate education in four-year colleges and universities has been traditionally the core task of colleges and universities. Despite the tumult that often seems to surround this endeavor, the overall market for this core activity has been in some ways quite stable. The number of freshmen entering four-year institutions has fluctuated within just a narrow range since the mid-1970s. The total number of full-time students in those institutions has grown by only 1 percent per year (NCES, 1999).[1] Important demographic shifts have occurred, but the dimensions of this core activity have remained remarkably constant. Yet within this relatively static setting some important changes have occurred. From outward indications at least, the competition among students to gain entrance to the most desirable colleges and universities seems to have intensified, as has the competition among institutions to enroll the most desirable students (Crenshaw, 1999).

Competition and markets have long been present in the decentralized American system of higher education. But in all likelihood American colleges and universities have become more market-driven in the last two decades. Why this has occurred is an intriguing question. At least five historical factors would seem to have played a role.

Privatization has powerfully affected higher education since 1980, in part by condoning involvement in commercial activities. Most conspicuously, universities formed linkages with industry for purposes of technology transfer and engaged directly in such commercial activities as patenting, providing venture capital, and creating business incubators. The opposition of traditionalists was fierce at the outset of this period, but largely exhausted by decade's end. As old inhibitions were forgotten, universities sold their logos with abandon, signed exclusive agreements with soft drink companies, and privatized operations. Collectively, these commercial activities represented a different way of thinking about what was or was not appropriate behavior or suitable spheres of university endeavor (Geiger, forthcoming; Geiger, 1993).

A managerial revolution occurred in higher education over the last generation, prompted in part by fiscal pressure, regulatory burdens, and the sheer availability of managerial expertise. By the 1980s universities had rationalized many of their operations and were engaged in forward-looking exercises like strategic planning. Administrative efficiency took a place among older values. The new managerialism facilitated adaptation to privatization and reduced the purview of academic governance. University activities became increasingly subject to the discipline of the budget (Birnbaum, 2000; Keller, 1983).

Revenue sources shifted significantly in the public sector. State support was reduced in relative and absolute terms at the start of the 1990s. Even as cuts were gradually restored, state funding was hedged with restrictive conditions. Public institutions compensated chiefly by raising tuition. Such revenues doubled in relative weight—from 29 percent of state appropriations in 1980 to 58 percent in 1996. Universities also moved aggressively to increase other sources of private revenue (gifts, endowment, sale of services). Commercial activities account for only a tiny proportion of these revenues. Student tuition, overwhelmingly from undergraduates, provides the largest source of variable private income. For public Research I universities, private gifts, which are substantially linked with undergraduate education, have been an increasingly important source of revenue.

Geographical market integration is the most encompassing secular trend. Huge improvements in the communications infrastructure have decreased the time and cost of moving people and information. But these changes were only a precondition. Institutions quite consciously extended their purview, often throughout the nation, in an effort to gain access to more students and resources (Geiger, 2000; Hoxby, 1997).

Student financial aid was transformed in its role and scope, especially in the private sector. Prior to the Educational Amendments of 1972, financial aid was the exception. Today it is the rule, with 63 percent of students in the public sector and 80 percent of private students receiving some form of aid. The two chief components of this revolution have been federal student loans and institutional financial aid by private institutions. The former increased fivefold in real terms from 1980 to 1995; the latter almost fourfold. Beginning in the 1980s in the private sector, tuition revenues became intertwined with financial aid through a highly sophisticated system of tuition discounting. This phenomenon worsened in the 1990s, making private institutions far more market sensitive than ever before (McPherson and Schapiro, 1998).

The market for undergraduate students is clearly important to universities. However, that market and, indeed, most markets affecting universities are described with terms like peculiar, awkward, or curious (Clotfelter, 1999; Winston, 1999).

Market Forces in Higher Education

In a market economy the allocation of resources is largely determined by prices set by voluntary exchanges between producers and consumers. Universities operate in competitive markets for undergraduate students, graduate students, faculty, research support, and gifts, but these markets differ greatly from classical free markets in the way that each of these factors is allocated. They are influenced nevertheless by the sway of *market forces*. Conditions of relative supply and demand have material effects on outcomes.

The principal "distortion" in the markets of higher education derives from their hierarchical nature. The behavior of universities is frequently described as competition for prestige to achieve or maintain status. This process is ambiguous, to say the least. Prestige is both the cause and the result of getting or having good students, good faculty, and ample financial support. This situation is most confusing in the case of students, who are both consumers demanding the product and inputs to the quality of the product. In addition, higher education markets are highly segmented—by student abilities, cultural preferences, and academic programs. The higher education market in fact is a segmented hierarchy, in which head-to-head competition occurs chiefly among roughly comparable institutions (Garvin, 1980; Winston, 1999; Zemsky et al., 1999). Still, near the top, recognized national markets exist for students, faculty, and research support.

Table 3.1 illustrates conditions in some of these markets in a simplified way.

TABLE 3.1

Market Forces Affecting Universities in the 1990

Factor	Supply : Demand	Consequences
High-ability under-graduates	<	Pressure on admissions and marketing Manipulation of financial aid (merit aid)
Student financial aid	≥	Students' capacity to pay increased Allows institutions to raise tuition
Doctoral students	<	Improving support packages Recruitment 25 percent of Ph.D.s awarded to noncitizens
Ph.D.s, scientists	>	Increase in the number of postdocs Improvement in the number of weaker departments Dispersion of academic research
Candidates for junior faculty	>	Increased use of part-time faculty Disincentives to add tenured faculty High-quality Ph.D.s to low-rated universities
Senior, "star" faculty	<	Private advantage in salaries and ratings Creation of professorial chairs
Funds for academic research	<	Growth of precommercial research Increased use of centers/institutes University research relationships

All of these markets have a bearing on prestige in higher education, and hence on markets and hierarchy. Although each of these factors deserves study, this paper will concern itself only with the competition for high-ability students. It argues, first, that competition for these undergraduates is in the forefront of the multiple priorities of American universities. Put differently, insofar as these institutions are market driven, this market is doing much of the driving. Second, this market operates differently for public and private universities. Third, despite the greater financial resources of private universities, their advantage in this market is less than conventionally assumed. And fourth, prestige in research plays a much larger role in this market than has been hitherto recognized. The argument begins by examining the nature of prestige in American higher education.

Students, Faculty, and Prestige

Two basic factors have the greatest influence on the prestige hierarchy—an institution's selectivity of undergraduate students and the scholarly reputation of its faculty. Lumped together they form an asymmetric pattern across colleges and universities.

Undergraduate selectivity is the basic measure employed by all commercial college handbooks. Literally, selectivity should reflect the percentage of applicants who are selected for admission ("admit rate"). More significant for prospective students, however, is the implicit question, "How hard to get into is college x?" For purposes of institutional prestige this question gets turned around: "How good are the students of college x?" It is generally assumed that the correlation is close among admit rates and student quality, but in fact quality can be elusive to define. Should the quality of the student body be judged by the number of students with superior academic abilities, or by the percentage? Are the abilities of the average student a better measure? Should one use the interquartile range of abilities, which many college guides now report? Or are nonacademic attributes, which loom very large in the admission decisions of the most selective schools, more significant?

The size of an institution clearly has a major impact upon its selectivity ratings in the college guides. The most selective institutions in the country are found among the private liberal arts colleges and private research universities. Although these institutions may on occasion compete for the same students, they represent two segments of the hierarchy. For the top, wealthy liberal arts colleges, the quality of their student body is the primary source of status. For private research universities, a high degree of selectivity is also a source of status, but for them it is complemented by the scholarly prowess of the faculty. Public research universities constitute another segment of the hierarchy. However, with freshmen classes ranging from three thousand to seven thousand students, admission to these institutions is more easily obtained. On all measures of selectivity, they occupy a lower range than their smaller private counterparts.

Among research universities, institutional reputation is based upon faculty contributions to the advancement of knowledge. There is controversy here too over measurement. Dollars of research expenditures is a crude measure, weighted toward the sciences; ratings by academic peers are suspect for being backward-looking and biased; measures of faculty publications and citations carry definitional and operational problems (Goldberger, Maher, and Flattau, 1995; Graham and Diamond, 1997; NSF, 1998). But scholarly reputation is a vitally important institutional characteristic regardless of the imprecision of the pecking order. Here, both public and private universities compete, but not the colleges (McCaughey, 1994).

At the top of the status hierarchy, then, two segments overlap. The most selective institutions are private research universities and a small group of wealthy liberal arts colleges. The leaders in scholarly reputation are private and public research universities. Private research universities may appear to have the best of both worlds—and the leaders certainly do. But the others walk a tightrope: a critical size is needed for high departmental reputation, but university size works against selectivity.

SELECTIVITY AND STATUS IN PRIVATE UNIVERSITIES

To identify prestige as the coin of the realm in higher education markets would seem, at least implicitly, to trivialize university motives. In fact, prestige ought to reflect crucial underlying processes—effectiveness in undergraduate education or in the advancement of knowledge. Moreover, reflectors in this case become predictors as well, helping to determine the effectiveness of an institution's continued performance. A recent study reported strikingly direct evidence of this latter process. A decline in an institution's ranking in the widely followed annual surveys by *U.S. News & World Report* had effects that "[lead] the institution to accept a greater percentage of its applicants; that a smaller percentage of its admitted pool . . . then matriculates; and that its resulting entering class is of lower quality, as measured by average SAT scores." Moreover, although posted tuition prices do not change, declining institutions "offer less visible price discounts . . . in an attempt to attract additional students from their declining pool" (Monks and Ehrenberg, 1999). That the somewhat capricious judgments of a newsmagazine can have such an impact may be both alarming and depressing, but the link between status and selectivity is consistent with recent economic studies.[2]

Since the 1950s, according to Caroline Hoxby, top universities have extended their recruitment to the entire nation, creating a single integrated market. Given a greater range of choice, high-ability students have tended to cluster increasingly at elite institutions. Overall, geographical integration has meant an increasing stratification by ability in American higher education: greater difference in levels of student ability across institutions and less variation in ability within institutions.

High-ability students seem to be attracted chiefly by perceived educational quality, as indicated by the abilities of student peers and the level of educational resources. Since bright fellow students constitute an important educational input, such students have a vested interest in hiving together. Their presence at a given school thus becomes an attraction for others of their ilk. These students are at once an educational asset to their peers and a marketing asset to their institution. They are also apparently attracted to institutions offering the greatest level of educational resources, which can be roughly measured by educational spending.

An institution's desire to attract high-ability students thus encourages it to increase educational spending, as Hoxby (1997) argues. This can be achieved in part by raising tuition, which covers a large portion of educational costs in the private sector. But high prices might also discourage students. Elite private institutions have adapted to this situation in two ways. They have generally sought to increase spending more rapidly than prices (tuition), thereby enlarging the educational subsidy received by each student (Winston, 1997). They have also given direct subsidies to price-sensitive students in the form of need-based financial aid, and increasingly merit-based aid as well (McPherson and Schapiro, 1998). An institution's educational costs (expenditures) are thus met through net tuition revenues (list-price tuition payments minus institutional financial aid) plus subsidies from other sources of income.

Hoxby (1997) validates this general picture with econometric data. It also appears consistent with apparent developments at private universities. Gordon Winston (1999) has termed this a "positional market" in which institutions must spend ever larger sums to maintain, let alone enhance, their relative position. Such a market induces selective institutions, according to Hoxby (1997: 39), "to supply a more expensive education to students of higher ability who receive higher 'wages' [subsidies] for their inputs and pay a higher price for their education." Market leaders are best able to do this, which makes their advantage cumulative—success begets success, or, the rich get richer (Winston, 1999, 2000).

The number of private schools that excel in this market is limited. Perhaps fifty institutions have the luxury of rejecting more than half their applicants. Success in attracting high-ability applicants is closely linked with financial success, and both result in steep hierarchies. Data from Hoxby and Winston extend only to the early years of the 1990s. In the remainder of that decade, this process accelerated markedly (*Chronicle*, 2000). The result has been the growth of dramatic disparities in the levels of educational expenditures among private research universities. At the top of the Ivy League, estimated educational expenditures may exceed forty-five thousand dollars per student, and subsidies equal thirty thousand dollars. At less wealthy research universities, per-student educational expenditures are closer to twenty thousand dollars, and subsidies may be two thousand dollars or less.[3]

SELECTIVITY AND STATUS AT PUBLIC UNIVERSITIES

According to this depiction of the market, public universities should be at a disadvantage in the competition for high-ability students. Compared with their private counterparts, they offer neither the concentration of high-ability peers nor comparable levels of educational expenditures. Indeed, during much of the 1990s public universities struggled financially in contrast to the burgeoning prosperity of the leading privates. As noted above, the prevailing definition of selectivity favors the smaller private institutions over the more inclusive public universities. If a comparison is to be made, a more neutral basis should be used. For this purpose, the absolute number of superior students provides a better standard of comparison for depicting the overall market. Scores on standardized tests are the only feasible means to identify such students, even though scores represent only one dimension of academic "superiority" (Duffy and Goldberg, 1998; Fetter, 1995; Geiger, 2000).[4] These scores are reported in several commercial guides.

Students who score 700 or better on the verbal or mathematical portions of the SAT examination (recentered), or 30 or more on the ACT examination, constitute roughly the top 5 percent of test takers (ACT, 1999; College Board, 1999). The following data (Tables 3.2–4) estimate the theoretical number of students obtaining such scores in the fall 1997 entering freshmen classes of each institution. The number is theoretical because a math 700 and a verbal 700 would each count for a half of a student, even when not the same person. These theoretical students will for convenience henceforth be termed *super students*.[5] Such students are highly sought after and have considerable choice of college. Their matriculation decisions consequently reflect the desirability of an institution irrespective of size, and their distribution indicates the workings of the market for high-ability students.

Tables 3.2 and 3.3 show the number of super students at the top thirty-five private and public universities. For purposes of comparison, Table 3.3 provides the same information for thirty-five highly selective colleges (Barron's, 1999; Peterson's, 1999).[6] Surprisingly, the total is nearly identical for public and private universities. Each set of universi-

TABLE 3.2
Private Universities with the Largest Number of Super Students

Institution	Freshman class	Pct. super students	No. super students	1995 NRC rating
Cornell University	2971	39	1159	3.96
Harvard University	1643	70	1150	4.38
Stanford University	1647	69	1136	4.20
Brigham Young University	4864	23	1118	2.19
University of Pennsylvania	2349	45	1057	3.79
Duke University	1623	53	860	3.56
Yale University	1307	65.5	856	4.08
New York University	3257	25	814	3.37
Brown University	1411	54.7	772	3.40
Princeton University	1175	64.5	758	4.29
MIT	1064	71	755	4.60
Northwestern University	1891	37.5	709	3.58
Boston University	3867	18	696	2.42
Dartmouth College	1093	56.5	618	2.94
University of Notre Dame	1904	29.5	562	2.64
Carnegie Mellon University	1270	44	559	3.56
Georgetown University	1393	38	529	2.71
Columbia University	967	50	484	3.92
Rice University	704	64	451	3.11
University of Southern California	2758	16	441	3.04
University of Chicago	999	42.5	425	4.13
Tufts University	1273	30.5	388	2.75
Johns Hopkins University	945	39	369	3.56
Washington University	1231	28.5	351	3.22
Boston College	2168	16	347	n/a
Vanderbilt University	1506	22.5	339	2.99
Tulane University of Louisiana	1491	22	328	2.09
Emory University	1170	22	257	3.23
Wake Forest University	975	26	254	2.51
University of Rochester	908	26	236	3.23
Saint Louis University	1118	21	235	2.47
Case Western Reserve University	739	31.5	233	2.88
George Washington University	1716	13.5	232	2.09
Brandeis University	794	28	222	3.24
Syracuse University	2587	8	207	2.65

TABLE 3.3
Colleges with the Largest Number of Super Students

College	Freshmen class	Pct. super students	No. super students
Williams	545	52	283
Wesleyan*	701	37	259
Amherst	434	59	256
Middlebury	567	45	255
Swarthmore	373	62	231
Pomona	393	58.5	230
Vassar	650	30	195
Wellesley	597	32.5	194
Carlton	484	38	184
Oberlin	681	27	184
Wheaton	547	28.5	156
Bowdoin	473	32	151
Davidson	472	32	151
Smith	652	23	150
Rose Hulman	386	37.5	145
Grinnell	414	33.5	139
Colgate	716	19	136
Harvey Mudd	183	74.5	136
Haverford	298	43.5	130
Macalester	452	28.5	129
Richmond	777	16.5	128
Reed	325	39	127
Barnard	563	21.5	121
Colorado	629	19	120
Washington and Lee	454	26	118
Bucknell	892	13	116
Furman	747	15.5	116
Bryn Mawr*	342	31	106
St. Olaf	731	14.5	106
Kenyon	441	23.5	104
Claremont McKenna	262	39	102
Colby	504	20	101
Illinois Wesleyan	571	17.5	100
Bates	459	21	96
Holy Cross	728	13	95

*Institution grants doctoral degrees.

ties claims about 30 percent of all super students in the country. The four universities with the largest numbers are all public, but the next five are private. The shape of the distributions across each set of thirty-five universities differs only slightly, with somewhat higher totals found in the top half of the private list and the bottom half of the public list. The ob-

TABLE 3.4
Public Universities with the Largest Number of Super Students

Institution	Freshman class	Pct. super students	No. super students	1995 NRC rating
University of California–Berkeley	3573	37	1322	4.6
University of Illinois–Urbana Champagne	5805	21.3	1238	3.56
University of Michigan–Ann Arbor	5458	22	1201	4.06
University of Wisconsin–Madison	5882	20	1176	3.7
University of Texas–Austin	6945	13	903	3.63
University of Virginia–Main Campus	2903	29.5	856	3.33
University of California–Los Angeles	3810	21	800	3.85
Texas A & M University	6196	9.5	589	2.99
University of North Carolina–Chapel Hill	3413	16	546	3.42
Ohio State University–Main Campus	5852	9.3	544	3.16
Georgia Institute of Technology	1848	29	536	2.92
University of Missouri–Columbia	3514	15	527	2.25
University of Maryland–College Park	3960	13	515	3.04
Penn State University–Main Campus	4244	11.5	488	3.16
University of Florida	3699	13	481	2.92
University of Minnesota–Twin Cities	3895	12.3	480	3.45
Michigan State University	6815	7	477	2.86
University of California–San Diego	3268	14	458	3.93
Iowa State University	3954	11	435	2.81
Rutgers University–New Brunswick	3900	11	429	3.12
Purdue University	6544	6	393	3.31
University of Kansas–Main Campus	3555	11	391	2.61
University of Iowa	3662	10	366	2.97
University of Oklahoma–Norman Campus	2800	13	364	2.22
University of Colorado–Boulder	4349	8.3	362	3.05
University of Washington	4505	8	360	3.60
University of Georgia	4189	8.5	356	2.64
College of William and Mary	1334	26	347	n/a
University of California–Davis	3540	9.5	336	3.18
North Carolina State University–Raleigh	3620	9	326	3.03
Virginia Polytechnic Institute	4460	7.25	323	2.79
Louisiana State University–Baton Rouge	4443	7	311	2.41
Arizona State University	5191	5	260	2.76
University of Nebraska–Lincoln	3200	8	256	2.33
University of Tennessee	3890	6.5	253	2.39

vious conclusion is that public universities attract a large share of the nation's super students.

The Market for Super Students

Super students, as predicted, tend to cluster together. The ten top private universities and the eleven top publics each account for 15 percent of the national total. What factors attract super students to these universities? The economic studies discussed above identify the most relevant factors in the private sector: peer effects due to the concentration of super students, educational quality as indicated by level of educational spending, the subsidy or wage offered to each student, as well as the geographical integration of markets over time. Clearly these same factors ought to be examined in gauging the attractiveness of public universities.

STUDENT PEERS

Theory posits that bright students concentrated together educate each other in ways not possible in more mixed settings. Institutions certainly act as if this were the case, but in truth there is little evidence to document the existence of such positive effects (Goethals, Winston, and Zimmerman, 1999; Pascarella and Terenzini, 1991: 77–83, 133–36). As a result, the exploration of this factor must be somewhat speculative.

There are two questions to consider. First, how do peers actually affect student learning (as opposed, for example, to providing connections for landing a job on Wall Street)? Most likely, there are three pertinent processes at work. A preponderance of high-ability students could have significant *curricular* effects by allowing a more challenging pedagogy—more demanding classes, greater content, and a higher level of sophistication (Braxton, 1993; Braxton and Nordvall, 1985). Bright peers might also have a *direct personal* effect by improving the academic performance of friends or roommates (Sacerdote, 1999; Zimmerman, 1999). A more generalized *cultural* effect should also result from a richer casual environment in which students would acquire from one another knowledge of the world and cultural sophistication.

Second, does the absolute number of bright students—a critical mass—produce positive peer effects, or is the concentration (percentage) all-important? The concentration would seem to be crucial for curricular effects. Moreover, there is research to suggest that a rigorous curriculum has the largest overall effect on student learning (Adelman, 1999). Concentration is also likely to play a major role in the propensity to transmit cultural knowledge. Acculturation of this sort may be impossible to measure, in contrast to cultural literacy, which may also be important (Hirsh, 1987). However, there can be little doubt that it is one of the most valued products of collegiate education. Direct personal effects, on the other hand, ought to be proportional to the absolute number of super students available to influence others.

The top private colleges clearly possess a degree of concentration likely to produce substantial peer effects (Table 3.3). Almost half of the colleges have first-year classes containing 30 percent or more of super students. For others, the pool is only slightly diluted, with concentrations in the range of 20 percent. Near the end of this list, however, the concentration of super students ebbs noticeably and quickly. Altogether, those thirty-five colleges enroll about 8 percent of the super-student total.

Private research universities have both large numbers and high percentages of super students. Eleven universities have enrollments of half or more super students, and another eight have concentrations of 30 to 50 percent. Eleven of these universities have 20 to 30 percent of super students—the range of the top public universities—and five have still less.

In the public sector, seven universities have concentrations of super students greater than one in five. Thus, in addition to large numbers they have a concentration that is comparable to all but the most select private schools. Of the rest, half are above the level of one in ten, which is double the 5 percent weight for all test-takers. How can the public universities compete with their private counterparts in offering a prospective super student positive benefits from peer effects?

The ability of public universities to offer positive peer effects rests upon a high degree of internal differentiation. Their large numbers of super students in fact would be likely to produce critical mass in several areas. Most of these universities have honors colleges, which are also used as a means of recruiting and sponsoring super students (*Chronicle*, 1999).[7] The most important form of internal concentration of talented students nevertheless occurs through choice of major (Pascarella and Terenzini, 1991: 82). Super students studying premed, physics, or electrical engineering, for example, would experience substantial peer effects, especially after the freshman year.[8] In fact, selective public universities appear to be particularly attractive in natural science and engineering, with all having greater numbers of 700 SAT scores in math than in verbal. This predominance of higher math scores is possibly the chief distinction between public and private institutions in the recruitment of super students.

COST, SUBSIDIES, AND PRICE

The level of educational expenditure (costs) is generally used as a reasonable proxy for educational quality. Greater expenditures generally indicate a well-paid faculty, low faculty/student ratio, large libraries, and good facilities. However, in a multipurpose institution like a university the cost of a single function like instruction is difficult to establish with any precision. For that reason, Figure 3.1 employs revenues instead to calculate an implied cost that is comparable across universities. Conceptually, educational costs can be divided into the portion that students pay as tuition, and the amount that their education is subsidized by other sources of income. Such a distinction is represented in Figure 3.1.[9]

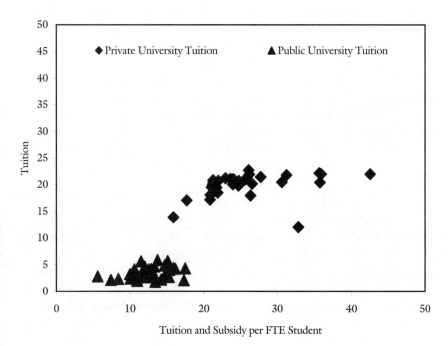

FIG. 3.1. Tuition vs. Implied Costs (Tuition + Subsidy)

The most striking fact about this distribution is that public and private universities represent entirely distinct patterns of costs and subsidies. Among private universities, the implicit cost of a year's education (1995–96) ranged (with a few outliers) from twenty-one to thirty-six thousand dollars. Full tuition for most schools was near twenty thousand dollars, but the subsidy provided by the university's endowment varied from a few hundred to more than twenty thousand dollars. (In Figure 3.1 the vertical distance from the institutional locus to the diagonal indicates the subsidy.) For public universities too there is no relation between tuition and subsidy. Implicit costs at public universities for the most part ranged from ten to sixteen thousand dollars, but most students paid between two and five thousand dollars. Their subsidies from the state and from a generally modest contribution from endowment varied from six to twelve thousand dollars. [10]

In reality, this calculus becomes more complicated. In public universities students from other states pay considerably higher tuition, reducing their subsidy (in some cases below zero) and adding appreciable amounts (again, in some cases) to the educational budget (Geiger, 2001). The private sector is even more variable from the standpoint of individual students. Every university awards substantial amounts of financial aid from their own coffers, producing a situation in which the majority of students pay less than the stated price (tuition discounting). Such differential pricing means that some students receive a greater subsidy, and those paying full price receive a much smaller subsidy, or even pay a premium for the company of talented peers.

The distribution of costs and subsidies (as any parent recently shopping for a high-quality college would know) suggests why super students have gravitated toward the top public as well as private universities. Some students will always have the financial means and the desire to seek "the best that money can buy," or at least the best college that will have them. Indirect evidence would indicate that population has been increasing—the boom in college guides, larger numbers of college visits, students applying to more schools, and increasing use of college counselors (McDonough, 1994; Paul, 2000). However, a high-quality private education carries a high price tag. Most of these students receive some form of financial aid, but such aid invariably includes loans that must be repaid. The private alternative for all but a few requires substantially more out-of-pocket expense.

Expenditure levels in private universities may be twice those of their public counterparts, but it seems unlikely that the relationship between costs and quality is linear—for example, that twice the educational expenditures will produce twice the amount of learning. Moreover, learning is literally subjective, so that different settings will have different advantages for different individuals. For good reason, many top students decide that quality state universities have much to offer at more attractive prices.

A suggestive study of top students who have chosen a public university both corroborates and extends this picture (Bradshaw, Espinosa, and Hausman, 2000). Such students commit to an ambitious educational strategy early, and acutely feel the pressure to attend a high-prestige school. Hence, reputation is an important consideration, which dovetails with a desire to attend with other high-achieving peers. Uppermost on their agenda is the expectation of attending graduate or professional school. They must be assured that the university of their choosing will be a pathway to prestigious postgraduate studies. The stronger state universities have no difficulty providing such assurance, but prospective students deliberately sought it out. The state university's advantage in price also played a role. Looking forward to extended postgraduate studies, these students did not want to incur indebtedness for their undergraduate degree. Merit aid too was a factor. After being deluged with scholarship offers, these students felt entitled to some form of aid. Although the amount of aid was less important, merit aid cemented the decision for many to attend the state university.

GEOGRAPHICAL MARKET INTEGRATION

In Hoxby's (1997) study, market integration is the environmental change that triggers greater quality competition and the concomitant concentration of high-ability students. Indeed, her aggregate data support this argument and lead her to conclude that "public colleges are generally unable to compete in the upper region of quality space." In particular, she predicts: "[P]ublic colleges that were selective in autarky face a particularly difficult transition to geographically integrated markets because more of their students are high demand customers who are likely to be drawn to colleges that are less constrained about raising quality."

However, for the most selective public universities this has not been the case, as is evident in Table 3.4. Two reasons would seem to account for this. First, as just seen, state appropriations to public universities provide a substantial subsidy for state residents. This underpricing of quality education preserves an autarky within the state. Those high-demand students who desire an even higher level of quality must pay substantially more. Thus, individuals face the kind of tradeoff mentioned above, but obviously many choose to attend "Old State."

Second, top state universities are able to offer a level of quality that not only encourages residents to remain but also attracts nonresidents willing to pay the additional tariff. Thus, with the exception of the Universities of California and Illinois, the most selective public universities generally have the largest percentage of out-of-state students. California, of course, is an enormous market in itself, and like some other states imposes caps on the number of nonresident undergraduates. Because of such restrictions, formal or implicit, out-of-state students are often held to higher academic standards and thereby contribute to raising the peer profile. In sum, these universities are able to benefit from both autarky *and* market integration.

CHANGES OVER TIME

Hoxby predicts a loss of share for public universities. Her data show the most selective public universities largely remaining static in terms of average SAT scores. Determining changes in the number of super students is more difficult, however, because of inconsistencies in reporting test scores and the recentering of the SAT in 1996. For most of the universities considered here, a comparison has been possible from the mid-1980s to the mid-1990s. The comparisons are for high-ability students, who are similar but not identical with super students.[11]

For private universities, twenty of twenty-eight universities increased their numbers of these students by 5 percent or more; among public universities, twelve of twenty-six institutions did the same. In the public sector, Berkeley and UCLA registered notable gains, an apparent movement toward quality in the immense, autarkic, California market. The other gainers are almost all from the South. This development may be attributable to the increasing attractiveness of those universities, and perhaps to rising test scores within these states. The other interesting inference comes from the universities not on this list. From the Alleghenies to the Rockies, across the heartland of the country, the flagship state universities (save Wisconsin) show little or no gain in super students.[12] There are few private research universities in this area, but the five located there all registered gains.

It is possible to move these comparisons forward by comparing these data on super students with that for the 1999 entering class. Once again, the data are available for most, but not all, of the institutions monitored here. Two interesting conclusions emerge. First, the increases registered from 1997 to 1999 are of similar magnitude to those estimated for 1984 to 1995. There was a decided increase in the number of 700 + scores, and these students continued to choose mostly the same institutions. This suggests that the trend toward concentration of high-ability students may be accelerating. Second, the pattern of the earlier years appeared to continue, thereby bringing it into clearer focus. Among private universities most institutions registered significant gains, and almost none experienced losses. Among public universities the picture was mixed. The academically stronger institutions tended to register gains. The University of California campuses stood out in this respect, with San Diego and Santa Barbara following Berkeley and UCLA. But Midwestern universities for the most part were fortunate to maintain their share. Academically weaker institutions were the ones generally experiencing losses, when losses occurred. Thus, Hoxby's thesis that public universities are destined to lose high-ability students to higher quality private institutions may be a half-truth, at best. However, the highest quality public universities seem the least vulnerable. Still, many factors affect these results.

Because of the persistence of autarky, state universities operate in quite disparate markets. Some do not seem to have become more attractive for high-ability students, nor do they perceive this as a problem. On the other hand, some states, particularly in the South, have created merit scholarships for their universities in order to prevent talented students from leaving the state (Williams, 2000).

On the private side, a ceiling effect operates at the most selective and national universities, leaving little room for improvement unless they rejigger their multiple criteria for admissions. Below this level, however, universities seem to have been able to increase spending and quality, in part by following the tuition hikes of the leaders. They were also positioned to expand their recruitment areas. This was definitely the case with the premium private universities of the South, all of which improved from the 1980s to the 1990s, and it was probably true for the Midwestern group as well.

ACADEMIC REPUTATION

The distinctive attribute of public universities for large numbers of super students is their reputation for research and scholarship, which is reflected in high ratings of research and graduate programs. The leading private research universities also have stellar ratings, but they also lead in selectivity and educational costs. For the top public research universities, research reputation appears to be a magnet attracting superior undergraduates. Grunig (1997), for example, found that "the amount of research performed by an institution contributes substantially to the reputation of the institution's undergraduate educational program." The seven public universities with the highest numbers of super students are among the most highly rated public universities for research and doctoral education. For the other universities in Table 3.4, any link between research rating and number of super students is probably overshadowed by other factors. These are generally strong research universities with particular eminence in certain areas. Hence, their reputation, especially within their own state, may be higher than the average ratings of their programs. However, if one were to look very far beyond the academically strong public universities, ratings and reputation are low and the number of super students is below the 5 percent norm.[13] Put simply, public research universities with highly rated departments attract super students and those without them do not.

Discussion

This study endeavors to identify and analyze the distribution of the most academically talented students across segments of American higher education that include public universities as well as selective private colleges and universities. The findings correct the misperception that high-ability students disproportionately attend private institutions, but they also raise as many questions as they answer. Three areas are particularly intriguing.

First, the fact that the top thirty-five public universities recruit nearly as many super students as their private counterparts indicates that existing explanations of selectivity, based on peer effects and subsidies in the private sector, do not tell the whole story. The top public universities are able to offer some advantages deriving from peer effects that may be difficult to measure but in all probability are real. However, academic reputation would also seem to be a significant component of status when it comes to attracting super students. Intellectually talented high school seniors in all likelihood respect the intellectual distinction of major research universities. Recognition of this fact has some important implications for the policy dialogue that has enshrouded research universities over the past decade.

Critics of research universities have been quick to dismiss the synergies that exist between undergraduate education and research, typically framing the issue as "teaching versus research." In another version of this critique, lower-rated universities have been attacked for trying to strengthen their research role instead of focusing solely on instruction. But students apparently know better.[14] One means for public universities to enhance their competitiveness for high-ability undergraduates and thereby strengthen undergraduate education may be to enhance their reputation for research. Thus, in the competition for undergraduates, as in internal university policies, the notion that faculty research is somehow inimical to instruction is a harmful shibboleth (ibid.).

Further investigation of the experience of high-ability undergraduates at public research universities is needed. In addition to gauging the importance of research reputation, more needs to be learned about the heterogeneity of experiences within these universities—how internal differentiation influences peer effects and the implicit subsidization of students. In this vein, the role and rationale for honors colleges appears to be a neglected topic that now merits attention.

The second topic that could benefit from further study is the overall market for high-ability students. The admissions directors of individual universities know their respective markets exceedingly well, but, as indicated above, a theoretical understanding of the total market is incomplete. The evidence presented here suggests that within major market segments the distribution of high-ability students exhibits a deeper fine structure. One can recognize elements of autarky and positional markets. Despite the prominence of national markets in competition among the leading private institutions, individual states have preserved autarkies of sorts by charging lower tuition to state residents. Major state research universities thus have a competitive advantage in price over other alternatives, while offering an attractive value in terms of price and subsidy. Thus, many flagship universities with merely strong academic ratings attract a fair number of super students from within their own state. But competition within a state plays a role as well. This factor is most evident in California, where Berkeley and UCLA draw the preponderance of super students from other UC campuses with sterling national academic ratings. A similar phenomenon is visible in Michigan, Virginia, and perhaps Texas, but not in Iowa or Indiana.

The in-state advantage seems to disappear in the Northeast. There, public higher education was historically neglected, although perhaps less so in recent decades. Rutgers and the University of Maryland have boosted their selectivity, but the state universities of New York, Connecticut, and Massachusetts still appear to do poorly in attracting super students. Not only is the private sector most strongly entrenched in those states, but many students have traditionally sought quality in the stronger public universities farther to the West.

A different form of autarky exists in the private sector. Brigham Young is able to draw its students from a loyal community of Mormons. A statistical anomaly in this grouping, it has by far the largest entering class in the entire private sector. Georgetown and Notre Dame similarly benefit from the loyalties of Catholics to achieve high levels of selectivity.

The markedly different performance of outwardly similar institutions is a third curious finding that begs for further study. Although the comparisons over time are crude, they still show some institutions doing far better than others. In the private sector, some universities have jumped places in Gordon Winston's positional market; others have failed to benefit from the workings of market integration. In the public sector, not all universities have translated their academic prowess into enhanced attractiveness for undergraduates. All of this suggests that the measures taken or not taken by individual universities have played a prominent role in mediating environmental forces. Illuminating what those measures might be is a subject for additional investigation.

In the final analysis, students seek status from the university they attend and vice versa. Particularly in the past decade, universities have perceived increasing potential benefit from the recruitment of superior students. These students, in turn, are drawn by connotations of quality that are far less precise than those monitored in this paper. Nevertheless, reputation is crucially important for attracting the initial attention of superior students. When they visit campuses and compare institutions, they become informed in a far more tangible way of the likely stature of student peers, of the level of affluence exuded by the campus ambiance, and of the eminence of the faculty evinced through tales of intellectual accomplishments. Public universities have much to offer superior undergraduates in peer effects and subsidization, but their stature in research is perhaps their chief competitive advantage in the toughest market in higher education.

Notes

1. Aggregate data on enrollments and finance are taken from the *Digest of Education Statistics, 1999* (NCES, 1999).

2. The following discussion draws chiefly upon Hoxby (1997) and utilizes the perspective developed by Winston (1997, 1999, 2000) in the Williams Project on the Economics of Higher Education.

3. Subsidies are defined as educational costs per student minus net tuition revenues per student. These figures, calculated by the author from the NSF CASPAR database, are meant to be representative only. There is no general agreement on the measurement of educational costs. Winston (1995), who has done most to publicize this concept, argues that the implicit costs of capital investments ought to be included. Such capital costs, which are not included here, inflate educational costs by perhaps 30 percent, depending upon interest rate assumptions.

4. Besides SAT or ACT scores, selective colleges place considerable weight on high school academic record—grade point average, class standing, and the rigor of courses taken, especially Advanced Placement. In addition, highly selective institutions place great emphasis on extra-academic factors in choosing among their largely high-ability applicants.

5. Super students are theoretical constructs in another sense, since they are meant to be a proxy for high-ability students for the purpose of this study. No implication that super students form a separate category of applicants or matriculates is intended.

6. These tables contain the universities or colleges with the largest numbers of super students in the fall 1997 freshman class. Data were compiled from *Barron's* (1999) and *Peterson's* (1999). Standardized test scores are from 1997. Reported test scores are neither complete nor consistent, so some estimation was required using triangulation with other sources. Data for individual universities should be considered approximations, but the overall distribution of super students, which is what these tables are meant to show, is believed to be accurate.

7. In 1998, twenty-four public universities sponsored from 30 to a high of 149 National Merit Scholars. See the *Chronicle of Higher Education Almanac* (August 27, 1999): 21.

8. For example, institutional data from a top public research university reveal that graduates with the highest SAT scores majored in bioengineering, electrical engineering/computer science, physics, mechanical engineering, molecular and cellular biology, and mathematics. All averaged well over 700 on the SATM.

9. Implied educational costs per student are defined here as stated tuition plus the subsidy per student from endowment income for private universities and in-state tuition, plus per-student state appropriations and endowment income in public universities. Source: NSF, CASPAR Database, 1995–96.

10. These estimates exclude income from gifts, which is mostly restricted, and from all other sources. They do not attempt to factor in the cost of capital, as

advocated by Winston (1995). Nor are they deflated for Net Tuition Revenue (list-price tuition revenue minus institutional financial aid).

11. A comparison was made of freshmen in 1984 and 1995 who took the SAT tests in 1983 and 1994, respectively. The scores are prior to the recentering that occurred in 1996. The percentage of freshmen with verbal scores of 600+ and math scores of 700+ were compared. More students took the SAT in 1994, and more scored in the indicated ranges (97,996 vs. 140,509). Thus, more *super students* were available in the latter year. Because of the intervals used, more of these students had high verbal scores (66,292 and 89,606) than high math scores (31,704 and 50,903). For this reason, precise comparisons are impossible. These data indicate which universities were attracting increasing numbers of high-ability students and give some indication of the magnitudes. Comparable data were available for fifty-four of the seventy universities in Tables 3.2 and 3.3, twenty-six public and twenty-eight private.

12. For another eight state universities, average ACT scores can be compared for 1984 and 1995. The same pattern is evident: significant improvement for two Southern universities and no meaningful gain for the Midwestern universities.

13. Numbers of super students were calculated for all Research I and II universities, but only the thirty-five with the highest totals are shown in Tables 3.2 and 3.3.

14. Zemsky et al. (1999) take the quixotic position that prospective students do not know what they are doing. In their view, "much of the dysfunctionalism of the educational market today derives from the fact that too many educational consumers remain bad shoppers: too quick to mistake prestige for quality" (p. 108). The other economic studies cited here are predicated on the assumption that student preferences for selective schools are rational.

References

Adelman, Clifford. 1999. *Answers in the Toolbox*. Washington, DC: Office of Educational Research and Improvement.

American College Testing (ACT). 1999. ACT National and State Scores. http://www.act.org/news/99/t1.html.

Barron's Profile of American Colleges. 1999. Great Neck, NY: Barron's Educational Series, Inc.

Birnbaum, Robert. 2000. *Management Fads in Higher Education*. San Francisco: Jossey-Bass.

Bradshaw, George, Suzanne Espinosa, and Charles Hansman. 2000. "The College Decision-making of High Achieving Students." Paper presented at the annual meeting of the Association for the Study of Higher Education, Sacramento, CA.

Braxton, John M. 1993. "Selectivity and Rigor in Research Universities." *Journal of Higher Education* 64: 656–75.

Braxton, John M., and R. C. Nordvall. 1985. "Selective Liberal Arts Colleges: Higher Quality as Well as Higher Prestige?" *Journal of Higher Education* 56: 538–54.

Chronicle of Higher Education Almanac Issue. 1999. (August 27): 46.

Chronicle of Higher Education. 2000. "The Rich Get Richer." *Chronicle of Higher Education* (October 13): A49.

Clotfelter, Charles T. 1999. "The Familiar but Curious Economics of Higher Education: Introduction to a Symposium." *Journal of Economic Perspectives* 13 (1): 3–12.

College Board. 1999. "Profile of College-Bound Seniors." http://www.collegeboard.org/sat/cbsenior/yr1999/NAT/natsdv99.html.

Crenshaw, Albert B. 1999. "Two Sides of the College Coin: Applicants Woo Top Schools; Other Schools Woo Applicants." *Washington Post* (Dec. 19): H02.

Duffy, Elizabeth, and Idana Goldberg. 1998. *Crafting a Class: College Admissions and Financial Aid, 1955–1994.* Princeton: Princeton University Press.

Fetter, Jean H. 1995. *Questions and Admissions: Reflections on 100,000 Admissions Decisions at Stanford.* Stanford: Stanford University Press.

Garvin, David A. 1980. *The Economics of University Behavior.* New York: Academic Press.

Geiger, Roger L. 1993. *Research and Relevant Knowledge: American Research Universities since World War II.* New York: Oxford University Press.

———. 2000. "Markets and History: Selective Admissions and American Higher Education since 1950." *History of Higher Education Annual* 20: 93–108.

———. 2001. "Politics, Markets, and University Costs: Financing Universities in the Current Era." Working paper, Center for Studies in Higher Education, University of California, Berkeley.

———. Forthcoming. *American Universities at the End of the Twentieth Century: Signposts on the Path to Privatization.* American Academy of Arts and Sciences.

Goethals, George, Gordon Winston, and David Zimmerman. 1999. "Students Educating Students: The Emerging Role of Peer Effects in Higher Education." Williams Project on the Economics of Higher Education, Discussion Paper no. 50 (March).

Goldberger, Marvin L., Brendan A. Maher, and Pamela Ebert Flattau. 1995. *Research-Doctorate Programs in the United States: Continuity and Change.* Washington, DC: National Academy Press.

Graham, Hugh Davis, and Nancy Diamond. 1997. *The Rise of American Research Universities: Elites and Challengers in the Postwar Era.* Baltimore: Johns Hopkins University Press.

Grunig, Stephen D. 1997. "Research, Reputation, and Resources: The Effect of Research Activity on Perceptions of Undergraduate Education and Institutional Resource Acquisition." *Journal of Higher Education* 68: 17–52.

Hirsch, Jr., E. D. 1987. *Cultural Literacy: What Every American Needs to Know.* Boston: Houghton-Mifflin.

Hoxby, Caroline M. 1997. *How the Changing Market Structure of U.S. Higher Education Explains College Tuition.* National Bureau of Economic Research, Working Paper 6323. December.

Keller, George. 1983. *Academic Strategy: The Managerial Revolution in American Higher Education.* Baltimore: Johns Hopkins University Press.

McCaughey, Robert A. 1994. *Scholars and Teachers: The Faculties of Select Liberal Arts Colleges and Their Place in American Higher Learning*. New York: Barnard College, Columbia University.

McDonough, Patricia M. 1994. "Buying and Selling Higher Education: The Social Construction of the College Applicant." *Journal of Higher Education* 65: 427–46.

McPherson, Michael S., and Morton Owen Schapiro. 1998. *The Student Aid Game: Meeting Need and Rewarding Talent in American Higher Education*. Princeton: Princeton University Press.

Moll, Richard. 1985. *The Public Ivys: A Guide to America's Best Public Undergraduate Colleges and Universities*. New York: Viking.

Monks, James, and Ronald Ehrenberg. 1999. "*U.S. News & World Report's* College Rankings: Why They So Matter." *Change* (Nov./Dec.): 43–51.

National Center for Educational Statistics (NCES). 1999. *Digest of Education Statistics, 1999*. Washington, DC: NCES.

National Science Foundation (NSF). 1998. *Science and Engineering Indicators*. Washington, DC: National Science Board.

Pascarella, Ernest T., and Patrick T. Terenzini. 1991. *How College Affects Students*. San Francisco: Jossey-Bass.

Paul, Bill. 2000. "Another Roadblock for Equal Access to College: The 'Counselor Advantage.'" *Chronicle of Higher Education* (March 10): B9.

Peterson's Guide to Four Year Colleges. 1999. Lawrenceville, NJ: Peterson's Thomsen Learning.

Sacerdote, Bruce. 1999. "Peer Effects with Random Assignment: Results from Dartmouth Roommates." Unpublished manuscript. Dartmouth College and National Bureau of Economic Research.

Williams, Roger L. 2000. "Southern Research Universities and Their Ambitions for Pre-eminence." Unpublished manuscript. University of Arkansas, Fayetteville, AK (June).

Winston, Gordon C. 1995. "Capital and Capital Service Costs in 2700 U.S. Colleges and Universities." Williams Project on the Economics of Higher Education, Discussion Paper no. 33 (December).

———. 1997. "College Costs: Subsidies, Intuition, and Policy." Williams Project on the Economics of Higher Education, Discussion Paper no. 45.

———. 1999. "Subsidies, Hierarchy, and Peers: The Awkward Economics of Higher Education." *Journal of Economic Perspectives* 13: 13–36.

———. 2000. "The Positional Arms Race in Higher Education." Williams Project on the Economics of Higher Education, Discussion Paper no. 54.

Zemsky, Robert, et al. 1999. "Market, Price, and Margin: Determining the Cost of an Undergraduate Education." Unpublished manuscript. Institute for Research on Higher Education, University of Pennsylvania (January).

Zimmerman, David. 1999. Peer Effects in Academic Outcomes: Evidence from a Natural Experiment. Williams Project on the Economics of Higher Education, Discussion Paper no. 52.

CHAPTER FOUR

The New World of Knowledge Production in the Life Sciences

WALTER W. POWELL AND
JASON OWEN-SMITH

The division of innovative labor in the life sciences was once drawn between academic basic science and more applied, developmental research conducted in industry. This divide was never a clear one, as translational and clinical research often fed back into basic science (Gelijns and Rosenberg, 1994), and some key discoveries were made in industrial laboratories. But with recent fundamental breakthroughs in molecular biology and genetics and the accompanying rise of the biotechnology industry, this old divide has been rendered moot. "Commercial" scientists are at the forefront of research on the human genome, while "star" academic scientists have been closely involved in the creation of small science-based firms (Audretsch and Stephan, 1996; Zucker, Darby, and Brewer, 1998). Consequently, academic and commercial life scientists are now members of a common technological community (Powell and Owen-Smith, 1998).

Universities are becoming major players in this new arena. Their new commercial role is underscored by huge increases in academic patenting (Henderson, Jaffe, and Trajtenberg, 1998; Owen-Smith, 2000), growing revenues from intellectual property licensing (Mowery, Nelson, Sampat, and Ziedonis, 2000), academic forays into venture capital financing (Desruisseaux, 2000), equity ownership of faculty start-up corporations (AUTM, 1998), and even prototype development (Jensen and Thursby, 2001). As the once separate realms of the academy and commerce overlap, both universities and academic scientists face a new constellation of possible challenges and opportunities.

Changes in the availability of research funding (Chubin, 1994; Feller,

1990), expanded possibilities for university scientists to conduct research that crosses disciplinary and institutional boundaries (Powell and Owen-Smith, 1998), and an increasingly fuzzy demarcation between basic and applied biomedical science (Narin, Hamilton, and Olivastro, 1997) have created a new environment for academic work. The traditional view of the university researcher as a dedicated and disinterested, though passionate, searcher for truth is being replaced in the life sciences by a new model of the scientist-entrepreneur who balances university responsibilities and corporate activities in the development of new compounds and devices designed to both improve human health and generate revenues for the investigator, the university, and investors.

This new landscape raises questions about the roles of university faculty and the mission of research universities. Answers, however, are not readily available because these developments constitute new terrain for faculty and their institutions. To be sure, parts of the university have long been deeply engaged in the world of practice. Professional schools of business, education, law, and departments of computer science and engineering have always had a strong orientation toward the arenas of either professional practice or commerce. But circumstances in which fundamental basic discovery has profound and immediate commercial consequences are unusual and pose novel challenges. We have been interviewing faculty at research universities and scientists at commercial firms about the changes in the nature of their work in the life sciences. We selected faculty on the basis of their scholarly prominence and entrepreneurial engagement, and scientists on the basis of their roles as leading figures in the discovery efforts of companies.

Our aim in this chapter is, first, to explain this new world of knowledge production in the life sciences, and, second, to account for the various forces that have given rise to the joint focus on academic and commercial accomplishments. Then we turn to an assessment of the consequences of these developments for faculty, universities, and their commercial partners. We close with thoughts on the extent to which the life sciences have become a general model for entrepreneurialism at universities.

Public and Private Science

Sociologists and economists of science have long recognized that the realms of science and technology are separated more by their social practices and reward structures than by the specific content of the research that is conducted (Dasgupta and David, 1987, 1994; Merton, 1973; see also Rabinow, 1996, for an illustration). But while scientific practice at the bench may be similar across sectors, scientists in industry and the academy operated according to the different rules of their respective games. For academic scientists, priority of discovery was the goal, and publication the means through which new knowledge was shared in a timely fashion (Merton, 1957). The public nature of scientific knowledge encouraged its use by others and in so doing, increased the reputation of the researcher (Merton, 1988; Stephan, 1996). In contrast, patents were the coin of the realm in the world of commercial science, where rewards were pecuniary and the incentive to divulge new information quickly was not as potent.

This separation between public and private science no longer holds in the life sciences, for a variety of reasons. Universities are much more engaged in transferring basic science into commercial development and garnering income in the process. Entrepreneurial faculty start companies to speed the progress of their work, to obtain access to better equipment and resources, and to reap rewards from high-impact science. At the same time, private firms are much more intensively involved in fundamental research. At many smaller, young companies, scientists publish their work with few constraints. Publications in prestigious journals such as *Nature* or *Science* are a clear and valuable signal—to the labor market, as a means to attract talented young scientists; to financial markets, to attract support from investors; and to the technological community, as both a marker of existing capability and an invitation to collaboration. As firms mature, the need for such signals declines somewhat, and companies exercise more control over what is public and private science.

Since 1980 the number of patents assigned to research universities has risen more than 850 percent (Owen-Smith, 2000). Figure 4.1 documents this growth, and shows the percentage of the patents that are pharmaceutically based.[1] Much of the rise in university patenting has been driven by biomedical technologies, which increased by 2,100 percent over this same period (Ganz-Brown, 1999; National Science Board, 2000). Figure 4.2 documents both a significant increase in overall patenting by U.S. universities and an accompanying rise in the proportion of those innovations that are based in life science research. In 1976 just under 18 percent of university patents were related to pharmaceuticals. By 1998 more than 46 percent of research university patents were based in biomedical research. Much of the trend in university patenting, then, appears to be driven by increases in the commercialization of life science research.

F I G. 4.1. Total R₁ Patenting and Percent Pharamceutical Patents

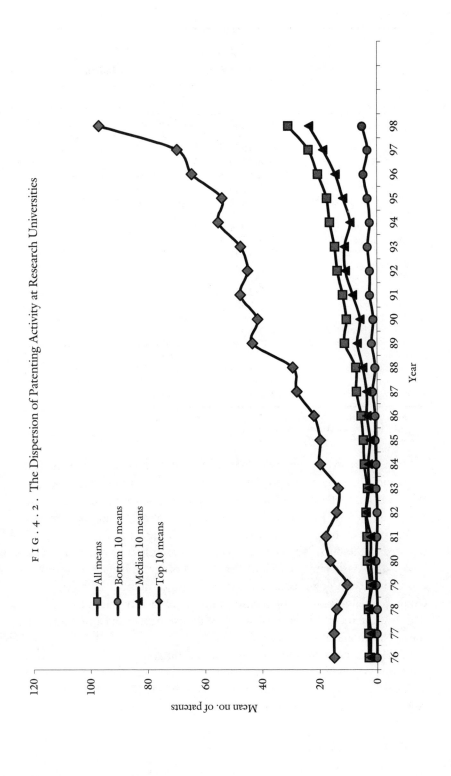

F I G . 4 . 2 . The Dispersion of Patenting Activity at Research Universities

TABLE 4.1

Top 20 Universities by 1998 Adjusted Gross Licensing Income

University	1998 licensing income	1997 income	1997 pct. from life science
UC system	$73,101,000	$67,279,000	66.0%*
Columbia	61,649,002	50,287,528	85.7%*
Florida State	46,642,688	29,901,112	97.0%
Stanford	43,197,379	51,762,090	81.9%*
Yale	33,261,248	13,091,174	98.7%
Carnegie Mellon	30,065,000	13,381,000	1.6%
Michigan State	24,336,872	18,293,388	99.6%
University of Washington	21,299,214	11,510,000	NA
University of Florida	19,144,753	18,156,198	98.8%
MIT	18,046,991	21,211,295	69.9%
WARF/Wisconsin	16,130,000	17,172,808	75.1%
SUNY	12,131,553	7,613,787	95.5%
Harvard	12,089,841	16,489,749	94.9%
Baylor Med	7,521,878	5,024,000	98.4%
University of Pennsylvania	7,246,695	2,136,000	85.3%
University of Michigan	6,811,000	1,780,334	82.1%
Tulane	6,633,181	6,640,800	99.7%
Hopkins	5,615,209	4,686,519	99.7%
Cal Tech	5,500,000	4,056,829	76.4%
Emory	5,410,179	2,800,000	58.2%

SOURCE: Association of University Technology Managers, 1997, 1998.
*1995 figures compiled from Mowery et al. (2000): 107, Table 2.

In addition to a growing volume of patents, American postsecondary institutions have increasingly developed in-house technology transfer and licensing competencies. Whereas only a very small number of the nation's eighty-nine Research 1 universities had internal technology transfer offices in 1980, by 1998 all but two had created new organizational units devoted to the pursuit and management of intellectual property (AUTM, 1998). The Association of University Technology Managers now tracks university technology transfer activities, using a number of metrics, including patents, number of licenses, number of faculty start-ups, and the like. But the most salient measure is, of course, revenues earned through the sale of intellectual property.

Table 4.1 presents the AUTM revenue rankings for 1998 and 1997; the latter year includes the percentage of the income that came from life sciences licenses. Note several features of Table 4.1. First, the most successful universities in terms of licensing revenue are relatively stable from year to year. More interestingly, the list is a diverse one. Both public and private universities appear on the list, as do institutions that span the basic science prestige hierarchy. The most well known campuses for biomedical research (Stanford, Yale, MIT, Harvard, Penn, Johns Hopkins) and less prestigious universities (for example, Michigan State, Florida State, University of Florida) are also garnering significant returns to licensing. Finally, note the extremely skewed distributions of this income within universities. On all but one campus,[2] life science innovations drive revenue earnings, often accounting for nearly 100 percent of overall royalty income. Even at universities known for their strength in engineering and physical science (for example, Stanford, MIT, and Cal Tech) life science revenues account for the lion's share of licensing returns to intellectual property.

A small group of universities are now generating sizable sums of income. The overall amount of income has grown sharply, from a total of $123 million in 1991, the first year reported by AUTM, to $271 million in 1995, to $862 million in 1999. This heightened attention to intellectual property is captured in the remarks of a professor of biology we interviewed: "Patents are much more an issue now. Twenty years ago, the chances that basic research, no matter how beautiful and fundamental, would have recognizable commercial potential were relatively low. That's less true now. Patenting is more on everyone's radar screen. Biotechnology was not an industry 20 years ago. Now it's a huge industry. The number of biotechnology patents has exploded for reasons that have to do as much with the science as with the patents."

While universities are active in commercializing basic science, commercial firms have become important contributors to the stock of basic life science knowledge. Scientific publications by researchers at established biotech firms, such as Chiron, Genzyme, and Genentech, are widely cited, and these organizations routinely appear on rankings of high-impact scientific organizations published by the Institute for Scientific Information. Most established biotech firms have created postdoctoral fellowship programs, and graduates of elite life sciences Ph.D. programs choose careers in firms as readily as university positions (Smith-Doerr, 1999). Among the key reasons for this career choice are the opportunity to publish and the perception that future career mobility into government or university employment is not hindered by experience with a private firm. The autonomy to publish is a critical component of this career calculus. Scott Stern (1999) finds that young scientists are willing to accept less salary to retain this key option. Put differently, if biopharmaceutical firms want to restrict scientists' freedom to publish, they have to pay them higher salaries. Rabinow (1996) provides a detailed portrait of the scientific community at Cetus during its start-up phase, and observes that this commercial firm compared favorably with a university setting in terms of colleagueship, diversity, and research intensity.

It would be incorrect to argue that biotech firms are coming to resemble universities or vice versa. The private firms engaged in basic science still have a foremost concern with commercial success. And licensing revenues at most universities constitute a very small percentage of the overall operating budget.[3] Moreover, these developments are taking place in a rather unusual field. The life sciences are notable precisely because they are different. In other areas of technological innovation, discoveries often start out in government or university laboratories and migrate to the private sector for downstream development. Once this transfer occurs, linkages between universities and firms are usually limited to the employment of students, consulting relations for some faculty, and possible gifts from the firms to the universities. The life sciences are a novel case where basic research continues to play a fundamental role in driving commercial development, integration between basic and clinical research is ongoing, and private firms have a hand in basic science and universities in downstream clinical development. As a result, there are complex linkages between public research organizations and private entities, and careers in the life sciences now routinely involve participation in both types of organizations.

The recent publication of a map of the human genome provides a vivid illustration of the complex interweaving of public and private life science. Two rival groups, referred to as the public and private consortia, were racing to see which group would complete their massive project first. As it turned out, both groups published their maps simultaneously, the private group in the nonprofit U.S. publication *Science*, and the public group in the commercial British journal *Nature*. The map of the private group, led by Celera Genomics founder and former government employee Craig Venter, was authored by more than 270 scientists drawn from for-profit companies and the University of California, Berkeley, as well as Penn State, Case Western Reserve, Johns Hopkins, Rockefeller, Cal Tech, Yale, and Bar-Ilan universities, and public institutes in the United States, Australia, and Spain. The intermingling of public and private continues with respect to access to this data. For the first time in its history, *Science* agreed to publication of an article for which access to the data comes at a cost *if* the request comes from someone at a for-profit organization. The effort, rivalry, and accomplishment of the genome project are a clear marker of this new regime of knowledge production.

Factors Promoting the Commercialization of Knowledge

Clearly, the dominant reason for the shifting boundaries between the realms of science and technology is intellectual. The life sciences have undergone a significant scientific revolution that recasts relationships among different scientific subfields, and generates new connections between biology, genetics, and computer science. Indeed, the story of the extraordinary role of programming and computing power in the human genome project has not been fully told. Thus, the internal dynamics of science have generated new forms of knowledge production, in which greater links across existing disciplines and more collaboration across institutions are key features. These changes in disciplinary and institutional boundaries have occurred in a social and political climate that has channeled the science into much greater contact with commercial application and reward.[4]

GOVERNMENT POLICY

Many analysts point to changes in government legislation as the catalyst for the view that universities should play a larger role in assisting industry and enhancing national competitiveness (Cohen and Noll, 1994; Cole, 1993; Slaughter and Leslie, 1997). There is no doubt that a wide range of legislative changes has enabled universities to engage directly with the private sector in the development and commercialization of new technologies. The purported cornerstone of the "new" federal policy was the 1980 Patent and Trademark Amendments (Public Law 96–517), commonly known as the Bayh-Dole Act. This legislation allowed universities, nonprofit institutes, and small businesses to retain intellectual property rights to inventions developed with federal research support. Other industrial nations have either adopted their own version of Bayh-Dole or are engaged in debates about its merits. Some commentators point to the Bayh-Dole legislation as "prescient" (Cole, 1993), and emphasize its role in spurring universities to take the commercialization of basic science much more seriously. Subsequent legislation expanded Bayh-Dole by allowing universities to assign property rights to others (the 1984 Public Law 98–620), and served to both encourage university technology transfer and facilitate collaboration with industry.[5]

Upsurges in university patenting and licensing, rapid growth in university-industry research centers, and increased university involvement in industrial research consortia have accompanied these legislative changes. The adoption of a competitiveness rationale for science and technology policy is widely shared among U.S. government officials (Slaughter and Rhoades, 1996). But we should be careful about the extent to which we consider legislative changes causal rather than facilitative. Eisenberg (1996) points out that universities were added to the Bayh-Dole bill largely as an afterthought very late in the legislative process. Mowery and colleagues (2000) remind us that those universities most intensively engaged in relationships with new science-based industries (for example, MIT, Stanford, and the University of California) were already active in the 1970s. Legislative efforts, then, are more aptly seen as part of a government mandate to all universities to act more like these early first movers.

BUSINESS STRATEGY

Parallel changes in both small start-up firms and large corporations dovetailed with legislative reform. In many rapidly developing areas of technology, research breakthroughs are so broadly distributed across both disciplines and institutions that no single firm has all the necessary capabilities to keep pace. Consequently, in such fields as biotechnology, information technology, medical devices, nanotechnology, and optics, firms are turning to cooperation with former competitors, and to partnerships with universities and government institutes. Rosenbloom and Spencer (1996) capture these developments nicely: "What was once a race has become more like a rugby match" (p. 70). They anticipate a "diminishing role for corporate laboratories as the wellspring of innovation," and suggest that the "seeds of new technological advance will probably sprout more often in university or government laboratories" (pp. 70–71). The private firms that are best able to exploit such new developments are those with both the most extensive external connections and the strongest internal capabilities for both evaluating the quality of research done elsewhere and contributing to the creation of new knowledge (Powell, Koput, and Smith-Doerr, 1996).

Many observers have noted that this transformation of corporate research is most pronounced in the life sciences, where there is a complex intermingling of government and university research, small-firm initiative, and large-firm development and marketing muscle. Federal research funding has supported much of the basic science underlying the new biotechnology, while top researchers in universities and in the intramural branches of the NIH have made the pioneering discoveries. Science-based small firms, whether spun off from universities or with extensive linkages to public research organizations, have played a key role in new product development. Alliances among universities, small start-ups, and established pharmaceutical corporations have proven to be effective vehicles for the commercialization of new medical treatments.

THE POLITICS OF HIGHER EDUCATION

Often overlooked in more general discussions of the growing commercialization of universities is the extent to which university involvement in creating business opportunities is an important resource for universities, both tangibly and symbolically. Many analysts worry about the importation of business values and methods into not-for-profit organizations. (See the analyses in Weisbrod, 1998.) On the whole, however, these concerns involve the possibly unwise importation of marketing, planning, and budgetary practices common to business firms into activities where there is not a clear bottom-line calculus. But in the eyes of some university administrators, faculty, and members of state legislatures, university-based invention and discovery reverses the flow of influence and highlights the university as "an engine of economic development." Rather than being in a subservient position, in need of modern management tools to run purportedly inefficient operations, the commercialization of university-based knowledge signals the university's role as a driver of the economy. Such a lofty status has much more legitimacy and cachet, and makes it possible for universities, especially public universities, to boast of their success in creating employment opportunities. Seen in this light, universities become both a "resource and a catalyst" to economic innovation (Chubin, 1994: 126).[6]

Moreover, the key role of a handful of universities in contributing to successful technology-based regional economies (such as Silicon Valley; Route 128 in Massachusetts; Austin, Texas; and the Research Triangle in

North Carolina) has changed both the hopes and prospects of nearly all research universities. These new expectations create a feedback loop, whereby universities tout their role in commercial application, and in turn politicians and key supporters adopt these accomplishments as markers of university success. Subsequently, universities expand their roles from "mere" incubators or licensors of new knowledge to a much more active and direct role in commercializing knowledge, reflected in science parks, assistance with faculty start-ups, joint university-industry programs, and equity ownership in firms funded on the basis of research done on campus. These efforts reflect the changing evaluative standards for higher education, as well as more active desire on the part of universities to claim a more significant financial share of the rewards from university-based innovations.

Taken together, changes in the nature of knowledge in the life sciences, combined with legislative efforts, new evaluative standards for universities, and the growing outsourcing of corporate R&D, have created an environment in which the commercialization of basic science has become not just an acceptable activity on university campuses but also a key part of the university's mission. The life sciences are clearly the leading edge of these developments, in part because of the closeness of basic and applied science and the revolutionary nature of recent discoveries in molecular biology and genetics. Seen more broadly in terms of science and technology funding, federal and private research investments in biomedical R&D are now larger than any other sector of the economy. Roughly 56 percent of the total public and private expenditures for R&D at universities went to the life sciences (National Science Board, 2000). In short, there is no prospect of turning back from these trends. The investments are so significant, the scale of discovery so vast, and the reality of and potential for improving human health so considerable that the biomedical engine now drives a key portion of the economies of advanced industrial nations. And universities are highly significant participants in these developments.[7]

We suspect that recent changes in academic and industrial practice are so far-reaching that striking a balance between science and commerce involves managing the simultaneous and overlapping involvements of scientists and universities. Most of the scientists we have interviewed share the general opinion that, for good or ill, the warrants, activities, and standards for success in basic research have changed. The increasingly blurry boundaries between proprietary and scientific approaches to information disclosure have led to a situation where individual scientists, universities, and potentially firms must compete in both the academic and the commercial realm in order to achieve. We turn to a discussion of the consequences of this transformation.

Consequences of the New Regime

Many analysts who study university-industry relations stress the collision of two very different cultures, noting that the open-ended goals of academic inquiry do not sit well with the more proprietary aims of business (Etzkowitz and Webster, 1995; Packer and Webster, 1996). These divergent missions create challenges with respect to intellectual property, secrecy, the exchange of research materials, and conflicts of interest. The latter concern has received the most attention, both by policymakers and researchers. Blumenthal (1992) and his colleagues (Blumenthal et al., 1986, 1996) have done a thorough job of analyzing the circumstances in which research funding comes from industry and faculty have either opportunities for financial gain through private knowledge of research results, private relationships with companies that are developing research results, direct involvement in clinical trials that determine the efficacy of a company's medicine, or experienced pressure to either delay publication or not to publish research results (Campbell, Weissman, Causino, and Blumenthal, 2000). Interestingly, the faculty with whom we spoke downplayed the salience of these ethical issues, noting that a variety of procedures are now in place to mitigate these conflicts, and stressing that more than a decade of experience with such conflicts has produced routines for resolving them.

The faculty members with whom we spoke were much more concerned with difficulties they are encountering in the availability of research tools, a concern seconded by Lita Nelsen (1998), the long-time director of MIT's highly successful Technology Licensing Office. Indeed, some professors now actively patent their research findings as a defensive strategy to protect their field of inquiry from external encroachments. As one biochemist put it:

> If this university holds a patent, they're not going to enforce it in a way that interferes with academic research, whereas a private company might. There is some incentive to disclose to the university to protect academic freedom. If someone else files a patent that conflicts with your work, that could really impair your research. In terms of patenting genes, commercial companies that own broad rights to products can require academic researchers to have

licenses. They will do that if they think the academic research generates knowledge that undermines their proprietary work. My lab generates knowledge that could be of great value to companies. Since it is not done in a company, the knowledge could be viewed as a loss to some firms. But we want to be able to publish it. So the company might have an incentive to restrict or control our research.

This scientist believes that the university can mitigate external threats by gaining and broadly disseminating its own intellectual property, thereby undermining corporate efforts to restrict "basic" science investigations. His proposed solution to the external threat of intellectual property claims by commercial firms may have unintended consequences, however. Heller and Eisenberg (1998) have warned that increased academic patenting may lead to a "tragedy of the anti-commons" where scarce intellectual resources are underutilized because excessive patenting deters inquiry by setting up roadblocks to research.

This turf battle is but one of a number of cases of what we term second- and third-order effects. Put differently, overt conflicts of interests, disputes over property rights, and concerns about secrecy are now issues that are handled directly, on a case-by-case basis, and for which federal, corporate, and university guidelines have been developed. We think the most consequential effects of greater university-industry contacts are likely to be unintended, as changes ramify across a range of activities, from graduate training to career ladders to which fields are "hot" and who is able to collaborate with whom (Owen-Smith and Powell, 2001b).

Consider the question of stratification at both the faculty and the university level. We suggest that rather than see faculty at top research universities dividing into two camps—one group with industry funding and one with government funding—we are finding that government and industry money go hand in hand. This is notable, because as Nelson and colleagues show in their studies of invention disclosure at Columbia University, academic research is not becoming less basic and more applied and attuned to the needs of industry. Instead, federal and corporate dollars combine to pursue basic discovery, and in doing so, create a system of accumulative advantage, illustrating again the "Matthew Effect," the felicitous invocation by Merton (1968) of the biblical adage that "to those that have, more shall be given."

One highly successful younger faculty member, who is both recently tenured and a recipient of a prestigious professional award, as well as founder of an up-and-coming firm, notes that discovery efforts in both academic labs and biotech firms can be complementary: "Only a few months after having started the company, it actually has better technology than my lab. The company is able to move much more quickly. Academics vainly perceive that they are the ultimate producers of knowledge. I think that the tables are turning. My company can produce retroviral technologies faster than my lab can." This professor is capitalizing on the opportunity to translate academic ideas into new medicines for HIV and cancer by engaging commercial partners in the process of drug discovery and development. He believes that collaboration will speed the discovery and development of new therapeutic medicines. And he is very open with his students and postdoctoral fellows, encouraging them to take law and business-school courses on intellectual property and entrepreneurship, and sharing both credit and profits on joint research.

Other faculty observed that commercial involvement is shifting the balance of power, determining the availability of research funds, space, and access to graduate students and research technicians. These resources feed back and leave those who have not pursued such connections behind. One faculty member put these developments bluntly:

> There are different ways you can have advantage. You can have more space, have more grant money, or have more hands working with you. People who get involved in biotech as founders or partners in companies end up with all those advantages. They end up with money in addition to their academic grants. This development is part of the blurring of that line between the two sides of the lab bench. These scientists end up with extra hands. They end up privy to ideas and information that other people can't get because of the proprietary nature of the work done in firms. That is another very important kind of advantage. This trend creates huge differentials between the little operator who has to get by on limited grant money with very few co-workers and somebody who presides over a juggernaut.

Processes of stratification have more subtle effects as well, reshaping which subfields attract scientific interest, in turn altering the career choices of young scientists. One senior neuroscientist commented that:

> My group is doing old-fashioned work. We're doing research on models. We are not doing genomics. I think if you're in those trendy modern areas, you might be seduced into biotech or a high-powered tech transfer academic career. If you're doing our kind of work, you might see handwriting on the wall, and figure I'm better off in a small college where I'm not expected to rake in hundreds of thousands of dollars in research money.

This faculty member worries that few academics will resist the temptations of "high-powered" science and commerce, consequently talented students and younger faculty will be lured away from the university.

> We now have competition between biotech companies and the academy for the same people. So it is not only that faculty are living conflicted lives, there is also a hemorrhage of talent from established faculty and from the pipeline. Industry is skimming off really outstanding people. They tend to be the very best people, the ones who you'd like to see become research leaders at universities, and they're gone. It is so bad that in some areas now you don't even see any qualified graduate students, because they're skimmed off as undergraduates. These forces are changing life within the university and the quality and number of people coming in. These opportunities are changing the career choices people make.

A recent discussion in the *Chronicle of Higher Education* on the revamping of graduate education echoes these comments. The eminent scientist Leroy Hood comments: "When I was a graduate student, there was something really wrong with you if you went into industry. What I see now is some of the very best students are going into industry. They see industry as more compatible with a reasonable life" (Manger, 2000). Hood, who in 1999 left an endowed chair in molecular biotechnology at the University of Washington to head a new institute, the Institute for Systems Biology, sees few negative implications, however. He acknowledges the increasingly central role that industry plays in life science inquiry and embraces the view that industry-based scientists may actually have an advantage in races to discover new findings.

These new linkages between academic and commercial labs have another layer of complexity. Whether in the case of formal affiliations, such as the much-publicized agreement between Novartis and the department of plant biology at Berkeley, or more informal but widely known relationships such as those between Chiron and vaccine researchers at the University of Siena or ophthalmics researchers at New York University, close ties between university researchers and scientific companies change the landscape. Commercial scientists in other companies tell us they feel less willing to collaborate with academic researchers in such departments because they worry that information will pass to their commercial rivals. Universities are becoming the venues through which commercial competition takes place.

At a larger level, a new form of competition has emerged among universities. The race for intellectual property and associated revenues has furthered the process of accumulative advantage. Rankings of the most active universities in terms of patents and licensing income are highly skewed. Recall Table 4.1 and its list of the twenty top universities in terms of licensing income. These twenty universities accounted for 74.3 percent of all licensing revenues in 1998. The upbeat story told about the growth in university patenting masks a stark fact. Owen-Smith (2000) has shown that the great majority of the growth in patenting is generated by a handful of prolific universities. Figure 4.2 illustrates this process clearly; the growth depicted in this figure is driven by patenting at the top ten universities. Success in the new realm of university commercialization, then, is highly skewed both within and across campuses.

At most universities, life science and particularly biomedical research represent the leading edge of commercialization efforts. Across campuses, spectacular and robust success is largely the province of early entrants to the technology transfer game. Those universities, such as MIT and Stanford, that began patenting and licensing activities well in advance of the Bayh-Dole act achieved commercial success in the context of evolving policies and procedures. These early successes, then, effectively created the rules of the university commercialization game. Later academic entrants to technology transfer races may find themselves constrained to strive for commercial accomplishment in a competition whose rules may be ill suited to their situations.

While newcomers struggle to establish conflict of interest policies and avoid the pitfalls of negative publicity in their search for licensing windfalls, the most established players benefit from the very accumulative advantage mechanisms we highlight. Early entry and accomplishment, then, breeds continued success in a world governed by the Matthew Effect. MIT's recent decision to make course materials publicly available via the Internet and Stanford's ban on corporate advertising in campus athletic facilities reflect, in part, flexibility borne of their prior commercial success. As Kathy Ku, the director of Stanford's Technology Licensing Office, noted in an interview, "Stanford can afford to take moral stances." The ability to draw the line at some types of commercial involvement, then, may be a privilege available only to the successful. Struggling newcomers to commercialization must prospect faculty laboratories for blockbuster innovations (such as Florida State's patent on Taxol as a cancer therapeutic, which accounts for all but a meager portion of FSU's overall licensing revenues), or break the rules with aggressive and innovative commercialization strategies that may put them at risk of negative press while raising issues of legitimacy and good taste.

The second- and third-order effects of an accumulative advantage–based stratification system may also be apparent within individual universities. While success is skew distributed across campuses, Table 4.1 demonstrates that it is also skewed across fields within those institutions. We argue that the life sciences represent the leading edge of university commercialization efforts, but this success story masks potential dangers. Life science research is unique in the extent to which Nobel Prize–quality basic science can have immediate commercial payoffs. The blurring boundary between commercial and academic research endeavors is all but non-existent in cutting-edge biomedical research.

Other scientific fields make strikingly different uses of intellectual property (Owen-Smith and Powell, 2001a) than biomedicine. Thus, efforts to tailor campuswide policies to the needs of life science faculty may run the risk of limiting commercial uses of physical science and engineering technologies while alienating faculty inventors in fields other than biomedicine. More important, as university departments are increasingly viewed as cost-centers (Gumport, 2000) and each academic tub comes to rest on its own bottom, the stratified nature of commercial returns to technology transfer may result in unintended alterations to the intellectual organization of the academy. Many of the life science faculty we interviewed bemoaned the homogenizing effects of research commercialization on their field, citing the prevalence of "hot" commercial topics among recent faculty hires, and the tendency of university administrators and federal funding agencies to prioritize commercially viable projects over more traditional investigations in subfields such as ecology and evolutionary biology.

If scientists at work in the most commercially viable academic fields express concerns about intellectual diversity and support for noncommercial research, how might importing standards of success from those fields to other areas of the academy effect the institution as a whole? If commercial achievement becomes the bellwether for academic fields, and if policies and procedures tailored to the life sciences are applied across the university, then the city of the intellect may become a strikingly more homogenous environment as less commercially viable scientific subfields begin to struggle and social science and liberal arts departments feel an increasing need to justify their existence in terms of commercial potential.

The commercial turn in academic R&D is an established fact, but its implications for both inter-university stratification orders, and the internal organization of the academy, have not been sufficiently examined. We suggest that the life sciences offer a model of entrepreneurial success that may increasingly determine university policies and procedures. While we believe commercial accomplishments have come at the expense of significant changes to the culture and organization of the academy, we do not hold that those alterations are necessarily pernicious. Instead, we contend that the transformations at work in the university are complex, and their second- and third-order ramifications have the potential to rework a fundamental institution in surprising and potentially dangerous ways.

The genie is out of the bottle and technology transfer is an increasingly important component of the university's mission. The success of life science researchers in this new arena has been notable, but we caution that at least a portion of that success may be founded on the unique characteristics of contemporary life science research and of the university spawned biotechnology industry. Thus, policies and procedures designed to reflect sources of success characteristic of the life sciences may fit poorly with research and commercialization endeavors in other fields. Moreover, attempts to formulate and implement such policies in the absence of consideration of intra- and inter-university second- and third-order effects may have unintended consequences for the organization and societal role of the academy.

Conclusion

The life sciences are, as we have shown, unusual among academic disciplines in several important ways. Very few university-based fields are likely to have the same potential for commercialization of research. But it is possible to speculate about a future in which the differences between the life sciences and other disciplines are less stark. At the highest levels, the boundaries between industry and academe are already blurred in computer science, finance, engineering, and a few other fields. New multidisciplinary endeavors in areas such as photonics and biomedical engineering have the potential to create opportunities for commercialization similar to those found in contemporary life science fields. Opportunities to patent and license new knowledge in these areas has, however, been limited by the nature of the innovations, industry practices, and, in some cases, by the outlooks of academic researchers. One can imagine a future in which those restraints might be significantly lowered because of the financial strength of universities, or changing legal, technological, or market environments.

Two somewhat different futures can be contemplated along these lines, both of which would lead to the reshaping of the university, as we currently know it. The first is the prospect of university administrators using faculty appointments and incentives to encourage the commercialization of knowledge production and creative activity in the widest possible range of fields—from digital arts to environmental engineering. The other is the prospect of faculty entrepreneurs in those few fields most like the life sciences following their lead in the direction of commercialized knowledge production. The university would take on a different form in either case, with knowledge production tilted toward profitable applications and sharp divisions arising between more and less commercially engaged disciplines.

Before universities and their faculties act on such visions of the future, they need to consider the features that make life sciences unique in the extent to which faculty entrepreneurs have been involved in both basic science and commercial applications. They should consider, too, both the extraordinary intellectual advances and the unintended consequences—restraints on free exchange of ideas, increased inequality, and alterations to the contexts of academic research—that have been associated with the new world of knowledge production in the life sciences.

Notes

We thank Steven Brint for his comments, encouragement, and persistence. This research was supported by the Association for Institutional Research (AIR Grants #99-129-0 and 00-129-0, Jason Owen-Smith, P.I.), the National Science Foundation (NSF Grant #9710729, W. W. Powell and K. W. Koput, Co-P.I.s, and NSF Grant #0097970, W. W. Powell and Jason Owen-Smith, P.I.s), and the Merck Foundation (EPRIS Program).

1. "Pharmaceutical" patents were identified by appeal to the Office of Technology Assessment and Forecasting's published crosswalk between three-digit Standard Industrial Classification (SIC) product codes and U.S. Patent Office subject classifications. We consider patents in the SIC classification "drugs" to be pharmaceutically based. Thus, Figure 4.1 undercounts the number of life science patents issued to universities, as the percentages reported do not include non-drug life science technologies such as medical devices and research tools and materials.

2. Carnegie Mellon, whose extensive communication, software, and information technology portfolio drives its impressive revenue gains.

3. Consider Columbia University, the most successful single campus revenue earner in 1998. While Columbia's licensing endeavors yielded an impressive $73 million in that year, the university spent more than $260 million on R&D. Clearly even the largest university revenue stream is not sufficient to cover research expenditures, let alone operating costs.

4. We lack space to chronicle the ongoing debates and controversies over the privatization of the university. A recent essay in *Science* presents the critical view effectively (Brown, 2000). An interesting contrast to this view is the recent move by MIT, one of the most successful entrepreneurial campuses, to eschew revenues from e-education by offering its complete course catalog free of charge online (Associated Press, 2001).

5. See Lee (1994) for an excellent survey of technology transfer-related federal legislation.

6. Such claims have a double edge, especially if state legislatures move to develop measures of academic impacts on the local economy, or, more menacingly, argue that entrepreneurial universities can or should be self-financing.

7. For a useful discussion of the role that public, university-based science has played in the development of biotechnology, see McMillan, Narin, and Deeds (2000). McMillan and colleagues (ibid.: 6) present a list of the public institutions whose research is most often cited by patents issued to publicly traded biotechnology firms. The list is instructive, as it includes federal labs (notably the National Institutes of Health Complex), elite public and private universities (Stanford, MIT, Harvard, UCSF, University of Washington), and research hospitals (Massachusetts General).

References

Associated Press. 2001. "MIT Course Materials to Be Offered Free over Web." April 4.

Association of University Technology Managers (AUTM). 1998. "Licensing Survey, FY 1997: Full Report."

Audretsch, David B., and Paula E. Stephan. 1996. "Company-Scientist Locational Links: The Case of Biotechnology." *American Economic Review* 86: 641–52.

Blumenthal, David. 1992. "Academic-Industry Relations in the Life Sciences: Extent, Consequences, and Management." *Journal of the American Medical Association* 268: 3344–49.

Blumenthal, David N., Nancyanne Causino, Eric G. Campbell, and Karen Seashore Lewis. 1996. "Relations between Academic Institutions and Industry in the Life Sciences—An Industry Survey." *New England Journal of Medicine* 334: 368–73.

Blumenthal, David, Michael Gluck, Karen S. Lewis, Michael A. Stoto, and David Wise. 1986. "University-Industry Relations in Biotechnology: Implications for the University." *Science* 232: 1361–66.

Brown, James Robert. 2000. " Privatizing the University—The New Tragedy of the Commons." *Science* 290: 1701.

Campbell, Eric G., Joel S. Weissman, Nancyanne Causino, and David Blumenthal. 2000. "Data Withholding in Academic Medicine: Characteristics of Faculty Denied Access to Research Results and Biomaterials." *Research Policy* 29: 303–12.

Chubin, Daryl E. 1994. "How Large an R&D Enterprise?" Pp. 118–44 in D. H. Guston and K. Kenniston (eds.), *The Fragile Contract: University Science and the Federal Government*. Cambridge: MIT Press.

Cohen, Linda R., and Roger G. Noll. 1994. "Privatizing Public Research." *Scientific American* 271: 72–77.

Cole, Jonothan R. 1993. "Balancing Acts: Dilemmas of Choice Facing Research Universities." *Daedalus* 122 (4): 1–36.

Dasgupta, Partha, and Paul David. 1987. "Information Disclosure and the Economics of Science and Technology." Pp. 519–42 in G. R. Feiwel (ed.), *Arrow and the Ascent of Modern Economic Theory*. New York: New York University Press.

———. 1994. "Toward a New Economics of Science." *Research Policy* 23: 487–521.

Desruisseaux, Paul. 2000. "Universities Venture into Venture Capitalism." *Chronicle of Higher Education* (May 26): A44.

Eisenberg, Rebecca S. 1996. "Public Research and Private Development: Patents and Technology Transfer in Government Sponsored Research." *Virginia Law Review* 82: 1663–1710.

Etzkowitz, Henry, and Andrew Webster. 1995. "Science as Intellectual Property." Pp. 480–505 in Sheila Jasanoff, Gerald E. Markle, James C. Petersen, and Trevor Pinch (eds.), *Handbook of Science and Technology Studies*. Thousand Oaks, CA: Sage.

Feller, Irwin. 1990. "Universities as Engines of R&D Based Economic Growth: They Think They Can." *Research Policy* 19: 335–48.

Ganz-Brown, Carol. 1999. "Patent Policies to Fine Tune Commercialization of Government Sponsored University Research." *Science and Public Policy* 26: 403–14.

Gelijns, Annetine, and Nathan Rosenberg. 1994. "The Dynamics of Technological Change in Medicine." *Health Affairs* 13 (3): 28–46.

Gumport, Patricia J. 2000. "Academic Restructuring: Organizational Change and Institutional Imperatives." *Higher Education* 39: 67–91.

Heller, M., and Rebecca S. Eisenberg. 1998. "Can Patents Deter Innovation?: The Anti-commons in Biomedical Research." *Science* 280: 698–701.

Henderson, Rebecca, Adam B. Jaffe, and Manuel Trajtenberg. 1998. "Universities as a Source of Commercial Technology: A Detailed Analysis of University Patenting, 1965–1988." *Review of Economics and Statistics* 80: 119–27.

Jensen, Richard, and Marie Thursby. 2001. "Proofs & Prototypes for Sale: The Licensing of University Innovations." *American Economic Review* 91: 240–59.

Lee, Yong S. 1994. "Technology Transfer and Public Policy in an Age of Global Economic Competition." *Policy Studies Journal* 22: 260–66.

Manger, Denise K. 2000. "Critics Urge Overhaul of Ph.D. Training, but Disagree Sharply on How to Do So." *Chronicle of Higher Education* (April 28).

McMillan, G. Steven, Francis Narin, and David L. Deeds. 2000. "An Analysis of the Critical Role of Public Science in Innovation: The Case of Biotechnology." *Research Policy* 29: 1–8.

Merton, Robert K. 1957. "Priorities in Scientific Discovery: A Chapter in the Sociology of Science." *American Sociological Review* 22: 635–59.

——. 1968. "The Matthew Effect in Science." *Science* 159: 56-63.

——. 1973. "The Normative Structure of Science." Pp. 267–78 in Robert K. Merton, *The Sociology of Science*. Chicago: University of Chicago Press.

——. 1988. "The Matthew Effect in Science II: Cumulative Advantage and the Symbolism of Intellectual Property." *Isis* 79: 606–23.

Mowery, David C., Richard R. Nelson, Bhaven N. Sampat, and Arvids A. Ziedonis. 2000. "The Growth of Patenting and Licensing by U.S. Universities: An Assessment of the Effects of the Bayh-Dole Act of 1980." Working paper. University of California, Berkeley.

Narin, Francis, Kimberly S. Hamilton, and Dominic Olivastro. 1997. "The Increasing Linkage between U.S. Technology and Public Science." *Research Policy* 26: 317–30.

National Science Board. 2000. *Science and Engineering Indicators—2000*. Washington DC: U.S. Government Printing Office.

Nelsen, Lita. 1998. "The Rise of Intellectual Property Protection in the American University." *Science* 279: 1460.

Owen-Smith, Jason. 2000. "Public Science, Private Science: The Causes and Consequences of Patenting by Research One Universities." Unpublished Ph.D. dissertation. Department of Sociology, University of Arizona.

Owen-Smith, Jason, and Walter W. Powell. 2001a. "To Patent or Not: Faculty Decisions and Institutional Success at Technology Transfer." *Journal of Technology Transfer* 26: 99–114.

——. 2001b. "Careers and Contradictions: Faculty Responses to the Transformation of Knowledge and Its Uses in the Life Sciences." Pp 109–40 in Steven P. Vallas (ed.), *The Transformation of Work*. New York: JAI Press.

Packer, Kathryn, and Andrew Webster. 1996. "Patenting Culture in Science: Reinventing the Scientific Wheel of Credibility." *Science, Technology, & Human Values* 21: 427–53.

Powell, Walter W., Kenneth W. Koput, and Laurel Smith-Doerr. 1996. "Interorganizational Collaboration and the Locus of Innovation: Networks of Learning in Biotechnology." *Administrative Science Quarterly* 41: 116–45.

Powell, Walter W., and Jason Owen-Smith. 1998. "Universities and the Market for Intellectual Property in the Life Sciences." *Journal of Policy Analysis and Management* 17: 253–77.

Rabinow, Paul. 1996. *Making PCR: A Story of Biotechnology*. Chicago: University of Chicago Press.

Rosenbloom, Richard S., and William J. Spencer. 1996. "The Transformation of Industrial Research." *Issues in Science and Technology* 12: 323–48.

Slaughter, Sheila, and Larry Leslie. 1997. *Academic Capitalism: Politics, Policies, and the Entrepreneurial University*. Baltimore: Johns Hopkins University Press.

Slaughter, Sheila, and Gary Rhoades. 1996. "The Emergence of a Competitiveness Research and Development Policy Coalition and the Commercialization of Academic Science and Technology." *Science, Technology and Human Values* 21: 303–39.

Smith-Doerr, Laurel. 1999. "Career Paths in the Life Sciences: Process and Outcomes of Organizational Change." Unpublished Ph.D. dissertation. Department of Sociology, University of Arizona.

Stephan, Paula. 1996. "The Economics of Science." *Journal of Economic Literature* 34: 1199–1235.

Stern, Scott. 1999. "Do Scientists Pay to Be Scientists?" National Bureau of Economic Research Working Paper #7410.

Weisbrod, Burton A., ed. 1998. *To Profit or Not to Profit: The Commercial Transformation of the Nonprofit Sector*. New York: Cambridge University Press.

Zucker, Lynne G., Michael R. Darby, and Marilyn B. Brewer. 1998. "Intellectual Human Capital and the Birth of the Biotechnology Industry." *American Economic Review* 88: 290–306.

PART II

Technological Forces of Change

CHAPTER FIVE

Becoming Digital:
The Challenge of Weaving Technology
throughout Higher Education

CAROL TOMLINSON-KEASEY

A recent series of television commercials showed children with mellifluous and exotic voices presenting facts about the Internet and its explosive growth and asking, "Are you ready?" This seems a fitting question for academics considering the future of the university, as the Internet provides a vehicle for the unprecedented availability of information. The global proliferation of the Internet and the increasing speeds of transmission mean that information is available at a click of a mouse, anywhere in the world, at the time and place of one's choice, and in a manner that encourages individual exploration. But calls to use the Internet to overhaul the university's traditional lecture, laboratory, and seminar organization have been encouraged also by the convergence of social and economic pressures. These include the increasing importance of knowledge as a factor of production; the growing size of the market for postsecondary education (and the coming prospect of near-universal postsecondary education); and the increasing cost of higher education. The new technology holds the promise to provide not only greater access but also higher quality learning materials provided to students at a lower cost. These methods and materials will foster the move from the classroom, the library, and the dorm to the Internet, the on-line library, and the chat room.

Are we in the academy ready for the opportunities that the technological revolution offers? Are the promises for increased access, quality, and improved efficiency as great as the Internet's advocates foresee? And, if the revolution occurs, what will be the consequences for the work of teachers and students?

This chapter, which considers the weaving of technology into the curriculum, will begin by examining the pressures within education propelling us toward technological solutions. It will then highlight some of the innovative ways in which these forces are being translated via technology into educational practices. It will conclude by identifying and analyzing the critical sociological and economic issues that emerge from successful uses of technology.

Educational Pressures

The convergence of a number of social forces has encouraged intense debate about how best to use technology in colleges and universities. The call for universal higher education has occurred with increasing frequency (Altbach, Berdahl, and Gumport, 1998; World Conference on Higher Education, 1998) and is accompanied by the recognition that the knowledge explosion and the complexity of society require repeated and more frequent updates of that education (Altbach, Berdahl, and Gumport, 1998; Drucker, 2000) Globally, the population that requires higher education has increased dramatically, but the cost and time required to obtain that education have put it out of the reach of the majority of the population (Daniel, 1997). These forces form the backdrop for the dialogue about technology, knowledge, and education.

THE KNOWLEDGE EXPLOSION

"On an average weekday, the New York Times contains more information than any contemporary of Shakespeare's would have acquired in a lifetime." This anonymous but ubiquitous quotation provides some context for the existing knowledge explosion. Knowledge now doubles every seven years, primed by the ten thousand scientific articles that are published every day (Forman, 1995). Coping with this avalanche of knowledge has spurred universities to new levels of specialization. A valiant effort has been made to absorb all of this new information and bundle it appropriately for student consumption. Still, the incredible pace of knowledge production requires a fundamentally different approach to archiving and disseminating information, as well as a recognition that the knowledge base of professionals must be periodically updated.

THE NEED FOR HIGHER EDUCATION

Peter Drucker's (1995) prophecy about the rise of a knowledge-based society began with the assumption that education would be the centerpiece of the society in the new millennium. He argues that formal knowledge—knowledge learned in higher education—has become the chief resource in our economy and that 40 percent of workers currently depend on acquiring formal knowledge for their livelihoods (Drucker, 2000). As more workers depend on knowledge throughout their careers, knowledge must necessarily be acquired past the traditional age at which schooling ends and often in educational settings outside of traditional classrooms. A conservative estimate is that meeting the needs of "knowledge workers" in traditional settings would require the addition of 250,000 students per year to college and university campuses.

THE INCREASE IN POPULATION

Indeed, population growth around the world is outpacing the capacity of societies to provide a university education for even those who would be considered traditional college-age students. The surge in demand for higher education worldwide, and a job market that continually raises its expectations, exacerbate the problem. In the United States, the children of the baby boomers will hit college campuses over the next decade, leading to an increase of some two million traditional college-age students (Dolence and Norris, 1995). On a global level, the crisis is even more severe. One new campus would need to open every week, somewhere in the world, just to keep participation rates in higher education constant (Daniel, 1997). An educational policy to accommodate this expanding population will require considering alternative delivery modes.

THE INCREASING COST OF EDUCATION

If success in the society is based on knowledge, and a prerequisite for success is an education that goes well beyond high school, then access to that knowledge must be affordable. Sending a child to a public university now consumes 15 percent of a family's income compared to 9 percent just fifteen years ago (ibid.). As tuition and fees have increased, students, especially those from lower income families, are unable to attend a residential college. Globally, public financing of higher education has not kept pace with student need because of declining budgets, increasing populations, and competing national goals (Woodward, 2000).

If we fail to educate our young people, the consequences to society are obvious; however, the specific paths we should follow to deal with this tangle of issues are not.

Contemporary Uses of Technology

Today the majority of college courses use technology primarily to complement traditional instructional methods. Green's (2000) survey of the uses of instructional technology on campus reveals that 60 percent of all college courses now utilize electronic mail as a primary communication link. Almost half of all college courses use Web resources as part of the course syllabus, and a third of all college courses have their own Web page.

At a minimum, then, the Web serves as a repository for information about the class and announces critical dates. This information might be maintained by technical staff or teaching assistants, rather than by the professor. But, however it is organized, it is used primarily to facilitate communication between students and teaching staff. Professors who lecture in the traditional manner are posting their syllabi, problem sets, reference lists, and lectures on the Web as a convenience for students. The annual surveys of the Campus Computing Project suggest a continuing integration of Web-based information with more traditional instructional formats (ibid.)

Variations on this theme include efforts by administrators to assist individual faculty members in redesigning their courses for an on-line environment. At Pennsylvania State University, faculty members are paired with an instructional designer who becomes familiar with the course, the professor's desires, and style of instruction, and then organizes a team to help deliver a course. Initially, each course to be transformed was approached de novo. As experience in transforming courses accumulated, some standardization was achieved to bring down costs and increase efficiency. Still, customization from a basic template is the norm, and the faculty tinker with courses even while they are being created (Carnevale, 2000). These efforts, which incorporate help from an instructional team, continue the dominant tendency in academe to add technology to the curriculum one-course-at-a-time and at the behest of the faculty member.

At the other end of the continuum are complete curricula that consciously incorporate technology to accomplish specific instructional goals. On-line learning is clearly a major force in the area of extension education and midcareer credentialing for professionals and managers. The most recent federal survey of distance education estimated that 1.4 million students were enrolled in college courses for credit. That was several years ago, prompting suggestions that participation is currently several million students (Levinson, 2001). The University of Illinois and the University of Maryland, for example, each offer more than twenty degree or certificate programs over the Internet (Institute for Higher Education Policy, 2000). Thirty-five states offer virtual networks that allow students to participate in on-line learning programs (Instructional Telecommunications Council, 2000). In these distance education efforts, the visual and pedagogical quality of materials varies, but for the time being most can be described as the on-line equivalent of reading a textbook and then taking an exam on the material covered. They are a convenience for people who live far from a campus or are too busy to attend classes at specified times, but they have hardly begun to exploit the potential of the new technology.

This brief overview provides a sense of typical uses of the Internet today and the reach of distance learning efforts, which have become a staple of many institutions. But such an overview fails to address the potential of the new technology to create entirely new environments for teaching and learning. Nor does it help us to understand the factors bearing on whether this potential will be realized.

CAPTURING THE POTENTIAL OF THE NEW TECHNOLOGY

A number of programs have pioneered new teaching and learning strategies that transform education. Some of these programs tackle issues tied to a specific discipline, such as improving math and science instruction or maintaining low enrollment courses. Others respond to increased demand for lifelong learning. Still others create new global classrooms. In selecting several examples of programs to profile here, I have begun with an educational goal and examined the ways in which technology helped achieve that goal.

MEETING INCREASED DEMAND IN MATH
AND SCIENCE

One might expect the wave of new students coming to the university to be spread evenly over the curriculum, requiring all departments to accommodate an equal portion of the increase. In fact, math and science departments must absorb a disproportionate share of the incoming students for basic instruction and then watch as they migrate to engineering, the natural sciences, or social sciences. The demand for graduates in all areas of technology and the expectation of policy-makers that graduates should leave college with greater sophistication in math and science adds to the bottleneck in introductory courses (Center for Science, Mathematics and Engineering Education, 1997).

The initial instruction that college students receive in math and science has also come under heavy criticism (National Science Foundation, 1996, 1998). Seventy-five percent of students surveyed for the 1996 National Science Foundation report perceived their science instruction as "poor." Capable students with strong science backgrounds have been leaving the sciences in droves, citing their dissatisfaction with rote memorization, large lecture classes, and lack of integration between the lectures and labs.

Universities have struggled with how to respond to these challenges. Many students require remedial instruction in order to pass basic math competency tests. In addition, an understanding of basic mathematics and statistics has become a prerequisite to entering and understanding a majority of fields outside the humanities and fine arts. No wonder math departments are reeling under the onslaught.

The Math Emporium. Virginia Tech's Mathematics Emporium has proven to be one of the more innovative ways of meeting the heightened demand for math instruction (Moore, 1999). Located in a renovated warehouse, the Math Emporium consists of five hundred workstations arranged in pods of six computers. On these computers students may take any one of fourteen courses. The Math Emporium is open twenty-four hours a day and seven days a week. Mathematics department professors staff the Math Emporium for eighty hours of the week. By converting professors' teaching assignments from number of courses taught per year to number of hours spent staffing the Math Emporium, the math department has been able to offer mathematical instruction to some sixty-eight hundred students, at a significant savings to the department.

The programmed math courses available at each workstation are set to address the individual needs of the students. Students may work individually, in pairs, or in groups. They receive immediate feedback both from the carefully programmed computer instruction and from staff who are on the floor of the Math Emporium. This allows for self-paced learning. Students' learning is well supported by a versatile instructional staff.

Initial evaluations suggest that students learn as well as or better than, they might in traditional courses. During the first years of operation, approximately 10 percent fewer students received failing grades in courses taught at the Math Emporium than in traditional courses. Reducing the number of students who fail saves money, while reducing the demoralization that accompanies poor performance. It also moves students into more advanced classes, their majors, and through their degree faster.

Given the resources that are now being poured into mathematics instruction, it is not surprising that the Math Emporium concept and the associated redesign of mathematics instruction have been modified and adopted by the University of Alabama, the University of Idaho, and most recently by Riverside Community College (Roberts, 2001).

Studio Courses. An equally innovative science teaching project arose at Rensselaer Polytechnic Institute after their very able first-year students expressed mounting dissatisfaction with large lecture classes (Pipes and Wilson, 1996). Math and science courses were restructured into "studio courses" for forty-eight to sixty-four students that combined lectures, laboratories, and discussion sections in one setting and integrated the three with multimedia and Web-based technology. Students presented with this rich interactive environment began to take control of their learning. Although they could, at any time, listen to a professor's explanation, that quickly became the court of last resort. In the studio courses, lectures were de-emphasized and replaced by minilectures, teacher mentoring, cooperative learning experiences, and much more hands-on learning. Textbooks were augmented by a variety of interactive multimedia materials.

As with the Math Emporium, students began to play a greater role in directing their own learning. To integrate lectures, discussions, and labs, professors were required to structure courses carefully and to provide materials that focused on key learning objectives such as higher-order thinking and problem solving (ibid.).

Evaluations of the studio model showed that student performance and satisfaction rose quickly and attendance soared. Students were in class two hours less per week but learned more in the flexible, carefully organized courses. When asked to evaluate the courses, 90 percent of the students indicated that the studio format would be a positive reason for attending Rensselaer (ibid.). Financially, the studio courses provided more intimate instruction at a lower cost because the separate instructional venues of lecture, lab, and discussion were integrated. Since many traditional discussion sections had been taught by professors, introduction of the studio model reduced the faculty's teaching load.

Not every student enjoyed the studio courses, however; some wanted to revert to the traditional approaches. On the faculty side, professors found that helping students work through problems on the computer required more patience and interpersonal skills than lecturing from the front of the room. The higher level of interaction was more comfortable for some professors than others. In general, professors likened the studio approach to an undergraduate research setting.

Overall, the studio model grabs student interest, enhances their learning, and moves freshman toward higher levels of understanding of science and technology. The Rensselaer experience also demonstrates anew that seat time is not a good measure of learning (Bishop, 1998), and that carefully prepared materials that engage students can produce high-level cognitive skills (Gardner, 1999).

More and more students need to master math and science in order to function in our increasingly technologically oriented society. The innovative approaches to instruction in these traditionally difficult subject areas provide insight into how technologically mediated courses can facilitate student learning while keeping costs in line.

LOW ENROLLMENT COURSES

Classes that traditionally attract few students will be under increased pressure as college and university enrollments continue to climb. It is precisely these classes that maintain higher education's identity, values, and principles as keepers of the universe of knowledge, and separate universities from job shops that teach a single skill. Technology offers the opportunity to maintain enrollments in courses like the less frequently taught languages, classics, and other specialized courses by aggregating student interest regionally or globally (O'Donnell, 1998).

Every dean has wrestled with the question of whether or not to fund courses that attract only a handful of students. Although Classics as a course of study occupy a special place in the history of the academy, these courses do not attract a large number of students and have been disappearing from catalogs at a steady rate. Should deans continue to fund these courses while other departments are turning students away from oversubscribed courses?

One of the early examples of the use of technology to serve the needs of important, but low enrollment, disciplines came from the University of Pennsylvania, where a Classics graduate course on Boethius was adapted to serve students who were interested regardless of their location. Rather than a handful of students, the professor was able to teach a class of several hundred from places as distant as Hong Kong, Europe, Canada, as well as localities around the United States (ibid.).

This example suggests the possibility of using the Internet to pool students from many campuses into courses that do not attract enough students at any single institution to gain or maintain a foothold in the curriculum.

A ten-year initiative by MIT to create public Web sites for its two thousand courses offers another approach to expanding access to higher education. Lecture notes, problem sets, syllabi, exams, simulations, even video lectures will all be available on OpenCourseWare. MIT's initiative will not involve registering students or offering credit from MIT. Rather, the course materials will provide the ingredients for learning that can be combined with teacher-student interaction at a local level (Goldberg, 2001). The intent is not to corner a market or compete with other institutions, but rather to disseminate new knowledge and content quickly and widely.

LIFE-LONG LEARNING

Whether as land grant institutions offering advice on agricultural practices or public universities producing technical expertise for policymakers, universities have long conveyed knowledge to a wider circle than their residential students. Universities have recently begun to take a new form of service seriously—the need to provide updated knowledge to midcareer adults. This work, which will surely intensify in the future, can be accomplished best with a technological assist.

The Michigan Virtual Automotive College was formed in 1996 in a collaborative effort of universities, government, and private firms. It involved the state of Michigan, Michigan State University, the University of Michigan, the state's other colleges and universities, and the major firms in the automobile industry. Today, it is known as the Michigan Virtual Automotive and Manufacturing College, a division of the Michigan Virtual University. It is working to integrate the automotive education and training offerings of Michigan's higher education providers with the support services needed to provide convenient, cost-effective, and high-quality manufacturing education and training. Using a variety of technologies to deliver courses, this college addresses the need to provide ongoing education in a rapidly changing industry. This award-winning program offers courses to Ford employees that are the equivalent of Ford's three-day workshops, but at half the tuition cost and without the expense of travel.

Stanford University's School of Engineering has been collaborating with industry for thirty years to provide the technical expertise that fuels Silicon Valley's continued growth. Currently over 250 industries are part of the collaborative effort by which employees in these companies may earn advanced degrees from Stanford University. The classes are of course offered virtually. Thirty years ago they were offered via videotape. The academic goals are the same; the technology has changed and the scope of the enterprise has been enlarged by the improvements in technology.

Examples like this are multiplying rapidly, especially among the corporate and for-profit sector, because on-line courses enable students to return to class without returning to campus (Collis, this volume). Whether degrees, certificates, or a new set of skills are the goal, universities are expanding their course offerings and using technology to help meet the demands of involved professionals. The market in this area may soon include as much as 40 percent of the workforce (Drucker, 2000), especially if the information these professionals need can be packaged in ways that are accessible, flexible, and convenient (Davis and Botkin, 1995).

GLOBAL EDUCATION

Accessing education is a global problem, and as more countries strive to educate a larger proportion of their population, this problem will increase. The Open University offers an innovative solution. Another aspect of global education entails the interaction and interdependence of countries. Corporations recognize that operating within the global economy requires a broad understanding of international issues and differing cultures. The Global MBA, described below, responds to this issue.

The Open University. Although some American universities have expanded their programs to serve a global audience, the best example of a global university is the Open University in the United Kingdom. In 1997, 25,000 UK students and 150,000 non-UK students enrolled. Currently, 50,000 students in England and 200,000 non-UK students attend. By 2020, administrators expect to be educating 150,000 students in England and 300,000 outside England (Daniel, 1998). Affordability and accessibility are cornerstone concepts of the Open University. The modular credit and the high standards for course materials guarantee that Open University coursework transfers readily to other universities.

The experience of the Open University reinforces the view that education is only as effective as the instructional materials and teaching practices that go into it. Open University courses rely on high-quality materials in many media. Books, pamphlets, videos, and, more recently, Internet materials are all part of the instructional armamentarium. The success of the Open University is attributable as much to the high-quality instruction offered and multiple opportunities for students to interact with instructors as it is to the technology used (Masterson, 1998).

The Global MBA. Duke University's Global MBA program suggests one possible future for business education. By combining on-campus activities, on-line activities, and off-site activities, the program provides students with an international perspective. Students begin the nineteen-month program by attending two weeks of class on the Duke campus. Subsequent residential sessions, each two weeks long, are spaced throughout the course of study. Between these five residential sessions, the faculty use interactive, distance-education technology to complement and extend the classroom experience. Additional residential sections might be offered in Salzburg, Buenos Aires, or Hong Kong, but are designed to cover issues related to global business centers whether in North America,

Europe, Asia, or South America. They also include business issues in emerging and developing countries in case study materials. Student evaluations often focus on the benefits of studying in several countries with classmates from around the world. The flexibility of the curriculum, diversity of the participants, and international focus of the learning experience has led to a waiting list for admissions.

One unexpected result of the Duke program has been to help executives think creatively about the uses of technology. Students, who initially viewed the technology as a means to access their coursework and chat rooms, began to see the possibilities for the use of technology in their businesses. As they gained experience in using technology to bridge distances, creating teams of students working together on a problem, and accessing global information quickly, they began to see how they could use technology more effectively to manage the multinational organizations for which they worked.

The unique structure of this program allows students to work and live anywhere in the world as they pursue their MBA, as long as they can secure access to the Internet. Participants represent a wide array of industries, hold varying job responsibilities and professional backgrounds, and represent diverse cultures and nationalities. The flexibility, the chance to grapple with international problems in an international setting, and a diverse set of colleagues have brought consistently positive reviews from the students and a waiting list for the program.

These examples highlight the dawning of the global education market. Countries must respond to the needs of their citizens to learn and participate in the technological surge of the twenty-first century. Technologically mediated courses offer an economically feasible way for students to acquire needed skills.

Sociological Issues

The examples highlighted above may be harbingers of technological innovations that will sweep over college and university campuses in the next decade. But the variety of approaches used and the successes and failures reported suggest that conclusions drawn too quickly are likely to miss the complexity of the issues surrounding the weaving of technology throughout the curriculum. Many of these issues are sociological. They involve establishing curricula that are appropriate to different categories of students, organizing faculty and student roles to make the most of technological opportunities, and insuring that necessary forms of interaction are not compromised.

DESIGNING APPROPRIATE USES

The higher educational marketplace encompasses precocious teenagers, young adults, professionals climbing job ladders, place-bound learners, and hobbyists. Cognitive skills, motivation, and the context of education in students' lives all must be considered when evaluating the efficacy of technologically mediated instruction. Approaches that work well in corporations because they are efficient, cost-effective, and mesh with a professional's life may not work nearly as well with undergraduate students who are undecided about their life direction and feel that their courses are unrelated and removed from life experiences.

Adult learners who are focused on gaining a very specific set of skills can take full advantage of the flexibility and convenience of the Internet. This is one reason why the corporate education and training market is quickly moving on-line. This is a very large market—$50 billion annually—and companies such as Oracle, Microsoft, and Novell are building extensive infrastructure to deliver professional education over the Internet (Baer, 1998). Some futurists predict that by 2010 high-quality versions of the twenty-five most common college courses will also be widely used on-line. Students who take the courses on-line would then submit their coursework for certification to a degree-granting institution of their choice (Dunn, 2000).

But undergraduates are very different from midcareer adults. They are finding out about themselves and about the world they live in. They develop a sense of identity a few steps at a time, by talking to their peers and puzzling through materials they are reading with their instructors. Analyses that see undergraduate education moving on-line typically jump from corporate educational paradigms to undergraduate education without commenting on the critical differences between those two realms. MIT's OpenCourseWare initiative, which provides direct access to MIT materials as references and sources for curriculum development, may prove more viable in the long run than "all-star faculty" versions of the top twenty-five undergraduate courses.

The content and aspirations of college courses also vary enormously.

Highly structured courses that build sequentially into broad knowledge bases may use technology more effectively than interpretive courses. But technology can play a significant role even in courses that at first glance seem inappropriate. For example, science and engineering courses that involve laboratories have been designed so that on-line students can participate by simulating lab activities.

RETHINKING ACADEMIC ROLES

In the specific cases highlighted in this chapter—at Virginia Tech, Rensselaer, Duke, and the Open University—the programs have involved departments, programs, colleges, and universities and have typically been generated and designed by faculty. Abstracting from these programs, we can see that the roles of both the professors and the students change in the technological environment, and the opportunities for students to interact with other students, their professor, and the material have been altered by technological adaptations.

Professors' Roles. The changing role of the professor in a wide range of technologically mediated courses has been reduced to aphorisms such as "the sage on the stage becomes the guide on the side." While this notion conveys some of the obvious differences between traditional and on-line settings, it does not capture the range of changes that take place. Until recently, faculty on college campuses single-handedly designed, developed, and delivered courses, all the while mediating and evaluating student learning. As classes grew, teaching assistants helped with the student services, but the design, development, and delivery were still largely the province of the faculty member.

The Open University has pioneered the dissection of these faculty functions, using faculty to ensure that the design of the course meets very high standards, but then allowing the development of materials to proceed in teams of curricular specialists under faculty guidance and the delivery of those materials to be undertaken by tutors. Reserving faculty and using their expertise for the design and oversight of courses has allowed the Open University to serve students in unprecedented numbers. As this model is reproduced around the world, mega-universities that serve more than a million students have arisen in China and Turkey, and a dozen countries have at least one university that serves over a hundred thousand students (Daniel, 1997).

At Virginia Tech, faculty roles in the mathematics department were

TABLE 5.1
Teaching Activities at Virginia Tech, 1988 and 1998

Activity	1988	1998
Student contact	40%	20%
Lecturing	25	12
Office hours	20	5
Laboratory hours	0	10
E-mail	0	20
Indirect student contact	5	25
Generating materials	35	50
Administration	20	5

transformed when they designed the Math Emporium. To staff the emporium, a faculty member's teaching load was transformed from courses-per-semester to hours-per-week monitoring the Math Emporium. From 1988 to 1998, a faculty member's teaching time was carved into dramatically different slices.

Not surprisingly, lectures and office hours decreased, because the emporium serves as a substitute for both, but time spent responding to e-mail increased. The total amount of student contact has not changed, but it has switched to a heavier reliance on contacts outside the lecture hall and the office. On the administrative side, testing and grading all but disappear as these functions are woven into the on-line courses and become incorporated into the task of generating materials.

The changes in the role of the college professor will undoubtedly vary by discipline, by course, by educational goals, and by delivery mode. Mathematics may be somewhat atypical, at least at the lower division level, because the coursework often focuses on performing certain mathematical functions. Well-codified knowledge can be captured readily in software, allowing professors to spend the majority of their time designing courses that shepherd students through the foundational concepts.

In other areas, promoting critical analysis of a wealth of material will be a central goal. Professors must help with the synthesis, analysis, and evaluation of the torrent of information that pours daily into these disciplines. In 1982, Naisbett portrayed society as "wallowing in detail" and "drowning in information." His characterization predated electronic databases filled with the equivalent of libraries of information and the World Wide Web with its billions of pages of information. The information is available in dizzying quantities, but the sheer quantity only highlights the central role of college professors—to help students organize this information once it has been amassed—to assimilate it, find meaning in it, and assure its survival for use by generations to come (Gregorian, 1993).

Regardless of discipline, however, professors who weave technology into their courses will likely spend their time where it is needed and move away from a fixed schedule of lectures. If faculty agree on the major goals of education, such as the need to expand students' horizons, expose students to the basic concepts in a field, foster an appreciation for research, and enhance analytical skills, they can then consider how best to allocate their time in meeting these goals.

As the discussion about technologically mediated learning continues, faculty must ask whether students learn as well as, better than, or less well than when information is presented in more traditional formats. Careful evaluations of technologically mediated courses to date have highlighted the need for student support services (Institute for Higher Education Policy, 2000), the lack of persistence in a course if such services are not offered (Phipps and Merisotis, 1999), the initial frustration that students experience if they have been used to sitting passively while the professor lectures (Rossi, 1999), and the insignificance of seat-time as an index of student learning (Bishop, 1998). Successful courses often include faculty involvement in group assignments early in the course; later assignments are designed to gradually wean students from depending on the professor.

Students' Roles. Student roles probably change more dramatically than faculty roles in courses that are delivered on-line. In the new course configurations, students assume increased responsibility, no longer waiting passively for the instructor to entertain, to indicate what is on the exam, or to interpret the readings. The professor will provide the structure for the course and design the materials, but students must negotiate their own way through the lessons.

A careful evaluation of the Math Emporium indicated that students accustomed to a more passive lecture mode were initially uncomfortable with the requirement that they be responsible for their learning. They felt abandoned, wondered why no one was teaching them, and seemed to drift in the coursework (Rossi, 1999). By the end of the course, however, most students had learned to direct their learning in much more efficient ways and could use the professor as a resource. The youngest students seemed to have the most difficulty negotiating this transition and expressed frustration with the course format.

Rensselaer's studio courses proved to be enormously popular with the students. Students enjoyed the course, attended the sessions, and learned more. Although not all students preferred Rensselaer's studio classes, the high level of student satisfaction suggests that these students made the transition to active learning quickly and that the frustration and drifting (ibid.) reported in some on-line classes were minimal.

Once students are comfortable with their role as active learners, the flexibility of technologically mediated coursework increases a student's opportunities. Students will be able to leave campuses to study abroad or pursue an internship, maintaining their contact with their campus via technology. Completing coursework necessary for their major or graduation is no longer a barrier to participating in these life-enhancing experiences.

Timely progress toward a degree suffers when classes are oversubscribed and unavailable. Technologically mediated courses can help overcome these barriers. In fact, more and more campuses are reporting that on-line courses designed for students off-site end up attracting many residential students. The University of Colorado at Denver put courses on-line to boost its adult education classes and found that 80 percent of the students who enrolled were actually matriculated day students (Burdman, 1998). Stanford University and the University of Washington also report that students on campus are attracted to on-line courses. On these campuses, class conflicts, work schedules, transportation issues, practice schedules for sports, and personal preferences led students to sign up for on-line courses even though the more conventional presentation was available. These on-campus students were not about to forsake campus life, but enrolling in an on-line course allowed them to juggle course schedules with other activities. The possibility of incorporating on-line classes into difficult schedules has recently emerged as a factor driving college choice for some students (Associated Press, 2001).

Some students, who initially came to an on-line course reluctantly, soon found that the material is individualized in a way no classroom instruction can be. Students can replay the explanation, turn to an alternative explanation, try another problem, or skip ahead if they have mastered the concept and test themselves on the material. In well-constructed courses, all students can receive a curriculum tailored to their needs, learning style, pace, and profile of mastery (Gardner, 1999).

One of the prized aspects of the academy is providing students the time to reflect on the information being presented and to encourage students to probe and extend ideas presented in the classroom or the text (Mauro, 1999). This shading of knowledge and the development of nuance as students infuse their own perspective into the class lessons can take different and largely uncharted forms when the information is mediated with technology (Moore, 1989). The more successful courses often require students to complete assignments in structured ways to avoid cramming an entire course into a short period and abbreviating the assimilation that turns course material into part of a person's knowledge base.

Of course, student motivation overcomes a variety of sins. Older students, students who otherwise would not have access to such coursework, students needing a particular set of knowledge to progress in their career, and students wanting to change careers are all eager learners who adapt easily to technologically mediated courses. Still, even these students need checkpoints, time-lines, course structures, and monitors who express an interest in their learning (Institute for Higher Education Policy, 2000). These support services maintain interest in the class and keep students moving through the coursework. Part of the Open University's success comes from face-to-face tutorial support that is built into the schedule.

For decades, cognitive psychologists have been lobbying for active participation by students in the learning process (Flavell, 1985). The large lectures that grew up in the last thirty years moved the student away from this ideal and fostered an observer role. Discussion classes, designed to bring the student back into the conversation, often became review sessions. Technologically mediated instruction requires the involvement of the student and flounders when students are passive. The experience of the last several years, as curricula have been revised to require the active participation of students, demonstrates that the cognitive psychologists were leading in the right direction. When done well, learning in a technologically mediated course proceeds at a faster pace, and is characterized by higher levels of student involvement, better retention of the material, and greater student satisfaction (Levin and Waddoups, 2000).

INTERACTION

The ways in which students interact with the professor, other students, and the course content remain an important wild card in on-line courses and technologically mediated programs. Television was supposed to bring universal, high-level expertise into American classrooms, but the predicted benefits were never realized, at least in part because students' interactions with the medium were passive and teachers' engagement with the material during and following telecasts was awkward and cumbersome (Bonham, 1972; Cyrs and Smith, 1990). Lack of interaction with instructors and other students has been a drawback of distance learning courses. When flexible, two-way audio and video communications are added to traditional distance learning technologies, students' attitudes improve, they are more likely to complete their coursework, they perform better on tests, and they retain more of the material (Lister, 1998). The technologically mediated programs profiled in this chapter point to a variety of ways to enhance interaction and underscore some of the issues surrounding interaction in a course mediated by technology.

Student-Content Interaction. Technologically mediated courses rely heavily on student-content interaction. The content must be carefully sequenced, thoughtfully presented, complete, and clear, because students have less access to the usual array of interpretive help. In more traditional courses, students occasionally ignore the reading material and rely on the student-faculty interaction in the class. Or they wait until their study group meets to attempt the assigned problem sets. Research indicates that even students who have thoroughly studied the content often feel vulnerable when asked to apply their knowledge if they have had no interaction with the professor or other students. The interpretations of the professor and students provide feedback, a needed reality check, and serve to bolster confidence about mastery (Moore, 1989). Effective techniques for incorporating student-content interaction include specific but open-ended questions in a text or study guide; essays; project-based learning; and journal activities (Forster, 1998; Morgan, 1993).

Student-Faculty Interaction. The Math Emporium profile provides some examples of how faculty roles change when the professor moves to a technologically mediated model of instruction. But the many subtle changes in the interaction between the professor and the students are not examined. The formality associated with transmitting information using technology blurs many of the subtler cues that heighten the value of interaction. As one critic notes: "The complex and delicate group dynamics of a live class and the rich 'orchestrations' that such a learning group provides aren't reproducible in screen-mediated situations" (Farber, 1998: 807–8).

To date, we have hardly begun to consider, quantify, or evaluate the intangibles involved in classroom instruction (Phipps and Merisotis, 1999). The jokes told before class, the disclosing of personal information that makes the professor real to the students, the quirky way the professor arranges notes on the lectern—all may add to the students' interaction with the material. Professors' asides that mention their involvement in research, their interaction with colleagues, their discipline as a profession, or their community activities are absorbed by students as part of their understanding of the subject and of academic work (Henri and Kaye, 1993). Long after students have forgotten the details of a class, they retain vivid memories of the professor that influenced the way they approach a subject. These intangible parts of a class often serve a silent mentoring role for students who are thinking about majors, graduate school, or careers.

How does one maintain these moments in a more formal technological medium? The use of e-mail, chat rooms, and other vehicles for less formal interaction will not duplicate the classroom interaction, but these new forms of interaction may well prove to add their own richness. E-mail may allow shy students, students who are hesitant because of an accent, and students who are slow to formulate their ideas to participate at much higher levels than in the typical lecture class (Burdman, 1998). E-mail also seems to facilitate discussions of more sensitive topics, because of its relative anonymity as compared to face-to-face interaction (Carr, 2000).

Because faculty-student interaction has been largely tied to the delivery of information in a traditional classroom setting, we have little systematic research documenting the different ways that faculty influence their students. As technologically assisted courses decrease the face-to-face student-faculty interaction, educators will need to find alternative ways to encourage informal exchanges.

MIT's plans to put its courseware on line recognizes these materials as learning resources but does not see them as a substitute for faculty-student or student-student interaction. "We are not providing an MIT education on the Web. We are providing our core materials that are the infrastructure that undergirds an MIT education. Real education requires interaction, the interaction that is part of American teaching" (Vest, 2001).

Student-Student Interactions. Alumni often mention interaction with classmates as a critical part of the undergraduate experience. While there is no way to duplicate the residential experience on-line, creating highly interactive learning environments between and among students is actually easier in an on-line course than in a large lecture. In addition to the ubiquitous chat rooms and e-mail, Levin and Waddoups (2000) recommend a variety of strategies including (a) on-line conferencing, (b) conference call opportunities just for students to communicate among themselves, (c) group assignments that become more challenging as the course progresses, and (d) instructor involvement in group activities, especially in the earlier assignments.

Even in on-campus programs that are mediated by technology, such as the studio courses at Rensselaer and the Math Emporium, minor adjustments can impact student-student interaction. The arrangement of workstations in the Math Emporium to form a pod that fans outward provides the opportunity for many students to consider a problem, play and replay an explanation, track a solution, kibitz as others work, and discuss alternative solutions. The physical settings in the studio courses at Rensselaer were also designed to facilitate student interaction.

Brown and Duguid (2000) offer a cautionary note about technological substitutions for social experiences. They argue that strong communities and institutions are necessary for technologically mediated instruction to work properly. If technology is introduced without these human components, students express frustration and dissatisfaction and dropout rates soar (Henri and Kaye, 1993). Successful examples of technologically mediated instruction, such as Rensselaer's studio courses, provide such faculty and institutional support.

Economic Issues

Embracing technology as a means to increase access and respond to worldwide demand for higher education depends on achieving these goals at a reasonable cost and, if possible, at a savings to institutions. Some proponents of technologically mediated instruction argue that the potential cost savings to institutions are great, but most surveys suggest that technologically mediated courses save neither time nor money. Faculty who pioneered technologically mediated instruction reported spending long hours preparing materials, overcoming technical difficulties, and responding to e-mails. While the early adopters put in these hours as a labor of love, extending the technology to the broader faculty clearly requires additional resources.

As Byron Pipes, a former president of Rensselaer, has observed:

"[T]he cost issue is controversial because skeptics claim that the real driver of change in undergraduate education is the cost-cutting itself, rather than the attempt to improve instruction. . . . In the case of the Studio approach, however, cost savings are an incidental and certainly welcome side-benefit. It really is a rare example of 'having one's cake and eating it, too'" (Pipes and Wilson, 1996).

The more sweeping curricular revisions undertaken by the Open University, Rensselaer, and Virginia Tech have, however, been cost effective. To achieve these economies, the curriculum and its delivery must be entirely rethought. In each case, faculty roles were substantially different in the new configuration. The Open University separated the many activities that faculty had traditionally undertaken as part of their teaching responsibilities and enlisted para-professionals in the delivery of information. The Virginia Tech Math Emporium moved from podium hours to hours spent in the emporium. Rensselaer reduced contact time and maximized the efficiency through their studio courses, thus reducing costs. In economic terms, the successful programs that reduced cost changed the labor/capital mix in some manner (Massy, 1995).

New methods of instruction cannot succeed unless professors embrace these efforts, and they also cannot succeed unless traditional practices are completely rethought. A move away from contact hours and fixed-term courses is probably necessary in most cases to realize the potential of the new technology—and also to save on costs. Unless such rethinking takes place, the technological overlay typically becomes an additional expense, not a cost savings.

Some faculty worry that economic motives will eventually be translated into a single version of large introductory courses taught by a master and will displace faculty at many institutions. Michael Saylor, the CEO of Microstrategy, proposed just such a use of technology and predicted that he could replace ten thousand average professors with an all-star faculty (Loose, 2000). Such a prediction ignores both the differences in students and the many approaches that faculty use to create interest in a subject. Saylor's initiative has stalled, perhaps because colleges and universities understand that courses need to be adapted to learners and that such adaptations are often quite subtle (Institute for Higher Education Policy, 2000). Faculty from California State University found, for example, that even the high quality materials from the United Kingdom's Open University were improved if they were revised to reflect the differing backgrounds and cultures of students in California.

Conclusion

Despite enormous changes and what seems like a rapid deployment of technology, the development and use of technology to facilitate learning has just begun, and issues concerning costs, interaction, and quality are likely to receive increased attention in the next few years. Distinguishing among the full range of technologically mediated courses will become easier. Successful learning strategies will be outlined that encompass students of different ages, those with varying goals, and those who have differing learning styles. Material will be adapted to reflect the purposes and methods of specific disciplines. Small liberal arts schools, global universities, and private corporations will find the combination of interaction and Web-based material that best serves their students and faculty. All of this is likely to be accomplished within an environment of increasing technological sophistication in which streaming video and full, two-way communication are as common and easy to use as telephones.

Adoption of technology without serious consideration of the sociological and economic issues analyzed in this chapter will not work. But intelligent efforts to weave technology throughout the curriculum and to use it to its best advantage do offer the best hope for increasing access for college-aged students, serving the increasing population of working professionals, controlling costs, and meeting the national and global priorities of the City of Intellect.

References

Altbach, Philip G., Robert O. Berdahl, and Patricia J. Gumport. 1998. *American Higher Education in the 21st Century: Social, Political, and Economic Challenges.* Baltimore: Johns Hopkins University Press.

Associated Press. 2001. Online Classes Serve Millions. *New York Times* (January 22): http://www.nytimes.com/.

Baer, Walter S. 1998. "Will the Internet Transform Higher Education?" Pp. 81–108 in Charles Firestone (ed.), *The Emerging Internet: Annual Review of the Institute for Information Studies.* Falls Church, VA: Institute for Information Studies.

Bishop, John H. 1998. *Diplomas for Learning, Not Seat Time: The Impact of the New York State Regents Exam.* Policy Seminar. National Center for Postsecondary Education. Washington, DC. September 30.

Bonham, George W. 1972. "Television: The Unfulfilled Promise." *Change Magazine* 4 (March): 11–13.

Brown, John S., and Paul Duguid. 2000. *The Social Life of Information*. Cambridge: Harvard Business School Press.

Burdman, Pamela. 1998. "Classrooms without Walls: More Students Are Taking College Courses Online." *San Francisco Chronicle* (July 20): 1ff. www.sfgate.com/cgibin/article.cgi?file=/chronicle/archive/1998/07/20/MN87525. DTL.

Carnevale, Dan. 2000. "Turning Traditional Courses into Distance Education." *Chronicle of Higher Education* (August 4): A37.

Carr, Sarah. 2000. "A Professor Finds that His Students Are More Willing to Discuss Personal-Health Issues Online." *Chronicle of Higher Education* (July 19): http://chronicle.com/free/2000/07/2000071901u.htm.

Center for Science, Mathematics and Engineering Education. 1997. *Every Child a Scientist: Achieving Scientific Literacy for All*. Washington, DC: National Academy Press.

Cyrs, Thomas E., and Frank A. Smith. 1990. "Maximizing Interaction during a Telelecture." *Teleclass Teaching: A Resource Guide*. 2d ed. Las Cruces: New Mexico State University.

Daniel, John S. 1997. "Technology Is the Answer: What Was the Question?" *Washington Higher Education Secretariat*. Fall Retreat. November 3.

———. 1998. *Mega-Universities and Knowledge Media: Technology Strategies for Higher Education*. London: Kogan Page.

Davis, Stanley M., and James W. Botkin. 1995. *The Monster under the Bed: How Business Is Mastering the Opportunity of Knowledge for Profit*. New York: Touchstone Books.

Dolence, Michael G., and Donald M. Norris. 1995. *Transforming Higher Education: A Vision for Learning in the 21st Century*. Ann Arbor, MI: Society for College and University Planning.

Drucker, Peter F. 1995. *Managing in a Time of Great Change*. New York: Truman Talley Books.

———. 2000. "Putting More Now into Knowledge." *Forbes Magazine* (May 15): 51–53.

Dunn, Samuel L. 2000. "The Virtualizing of Education." *Futurist* 34 (March–April): 34–38.

Farber, Jerry. 1998. "The Third Circle: On Education and Distance Learning." *Sociological Perspectives* 41: 797–814.

Flavell, John H. 1985. *Cognitive Development*. 2d ed. Englewood Cliffs, NJ: Prentice Hall.

Forman, David C. 1995. "The Use of Multimedia Technology for Training in Business and Industry." *Multimedia Monitor* 13: 22–27.

Forster, Anne. 1998. *Learning at a Distance*. Professional Development Program in Distance Education, Department of Continuing and Vocational Education, University of Wisconsin, Madison.

Gardner, Howard E. 1999. *The Disciplined Mind*. New York: Simon and Schuster.

Goldberg, Carey. 2001. "Auditing Classes at M.I.T., on the Web and Free." *New York Times* (April 4): A1.

Green, Kenneth C. 2000. *Campus Computing 2000: The National Study of Information Technology in American Higher Education*. Encino, CA: Campus Computing Project.

Gregorian, Vartan. 1993. *Technology, Scholarship, and the Humanities: The Implications of Electronic Information*. Summary of Proceedings. American Council of Learned Societies: J. Paul Getty Trust.

Henri, France, and Anthony R. Kaye. 1993. "Problems of Distance Education." Pp. 25–31 in Keith Harry, Magnus John, and Desmond Keegan (eds.), *Distance Education: New Perspectives*. London: Routledge.

Institute for Higher Education Policy. 2000. *Quality on line: Benchmarks for Success in Internet-based Distance Learning*. Washington, DC: Institute for Higher Education Policy.

Instructional Telecommunications Council. (2001). http://www.itcnetwork.org/virtualalliancelist.htm. Washington, DC.

Levin, Sandra R., and Gregory L. Waddoups. 2000. "CTER OnLine: Providing Highly Interactive and Effective Online Learning Environments." http://www.ed.uiuc.edu/people/sandy-levin/site2000.html.

Levinson, Arlene. 2001. "E-classes Serve Millions, Off Campus and On." Associated Press story from the AP Wire. January 20.

Lister, Bradford C. 1998. "Interactive Distance Learning: The Virtual Studio Classroom." *Proceedings of the Third International IEEE Conference on Multimedia, Engineering and Education*. Hong Kong.

Loose, Cindy. 2000. "Billionaire Pitches Cyber-U to Businesses." *Washington Post* (March 19): B2.

Massy, William F. 1995. *Leveraged Learning: Technology's Role in Restructuring Higher Education*. Stanford Forum for Higher Education Futures, Stanford University. April 28–29.

Masterson, Bob. 1998. "The Future of Distance Education." Western Association for Schools and Colleges (WASC) Conference, Huntington Beach, CA. April 16.

Mauro, Tony. 1999. "Ginsburg Critiques E-law School: Ginsburg's Speech Puts Internet Law School in the Spotlight." *Law NewsNetwork.com* http://www.lawnewsnetwork.com/stories/A6062–1999Sep20.html.

Moore, Anne H. 1999. "Virginia Tech's Math Emporium: A Model of Academic Transformation." Paper presented at National Learning Infrastructure Initiative. New Orleans, LA. February 1.

Moore, Michael G. 1989. "Three Types of Interaction." *American Journal of Distance Education* 3 (2): 1–7.

Morgan, Alistair. 1993. *Improving Your Students' Learning: Reflections on the Experience of Study*. London: Kogan-Page.

Naisbett, John. 1982. *Megatrends: Ten New Directions Transforming Our Lives*. New York: Warner Books.

National Science Foundation. 1996. *Shaping the Future: New Expectations for Undergraduate Education in Science, Mathematics, Engineering, and Technology (96–139)*. Washington, DC: National Science Foundation.

————. 1998. *Shaping the Future, Vol. II: Perspectives on Undergraduate Education in Science, Mathematics, Engineering, and Technology (98–128)*. Washington, DC: National Science Foundation.

O'Donnell, James J. 1998. "Tools for Teaching: Personal Encounters in Cyberspace." *Chronicle of Higher Education* (February 13): B7.

Phipps, Ronald A., and Jamie P. Merisotis. 1999. *What's the Difference? A Review of Contemporary Research on the Effectiveness of Distance Learning in Higher Education*. Washington DC: National Education Association.

Pipes, R. Byron, and Jack M. Wilson. 1996. "A Multimedia Model for Undergraduate Education." *Technology In Society* 18: 387–401.

Roberts, Lowell. 2001. "Redesigning Learning Environments." *Pew Learning and Technology Program Newsletter* 3 (March): 1.

Rossi, John F. 1999. "Student Issues Concerning Technology and Active Learning." Paper presented at National Learning Infrastructure Initiative. New Orleans, LA. February 1.

Vest, Charles M. 2001. "MIT to Make Nearly All Course Materials Available Free on the World Wide Web." http://web.mit.edu/newsoffice/nr/2001/ocw.html.

Woodward, Colin. 2000. "Worldwide Tuition Increases Send Students into the Streets." *Chronicle of Higher Education* (May 5): 54–56.

World Conference on Higher Education. 1998. *World Declaration on Higher Education for the Twenty-first Century: Vision and Action*. Paris: UNESCO. October 9.

CHAPTER SIX

The Audit of Virtuality: Universities in the Attention Economy

RICHARD A. LANHAM

> It is not things, but what we think about things, that troubles us.
>
> (Epictetus, *Encheiridion*, c. 5)

Like many other people, I have been trying to think about what it means for my own area of interest, which is the history and theory of rhetoric, when we move from an economy based on physical objects, stuff you can drop on your foot, to one based on information. My reflections on the problem go like this.

Economics, as we all remember from Econ 10, studies the allocation of scarce commodities. Normally, then, we would think that the phrase "information economy," which we hear everywhere nowadays, made some sense. It is not physical stuff that is in short supply but the information about it. But information is not in short supply in the new information economy. We are drowning in it. What we lack is the human attention needed to make sense of it all. Whether you call the raw commodity "data" and the refined and usable one "information," or, as humanists like to think, "information" as the raw data and "wisdom" as the usable refinement, what gets you from raw to cooked is human attention. And, that, in an information society, is what stands in chronic short supply.

It would make it easier to find our place in the new regime if we thought of it as an "economics of attention." Where, I have been asking myself, does what I do fit in *that* scheme of things?

Answering that question puts me in an awkward position, and one that I have not coveted. It makes me—so far as I can see, at least—into an economist. I have spent my scholarly life studying rhetoric, classical and modern. For most of Western history, the word "rhetoric" has meant the body of doctrine that teaches people how to speak and write, and thus act effectively in public life. Usually defined as "The Art of Persuasion," it might just as well have been called "The Economics of Attention." We seem to have an economics of attention already in place, if we are willing to acknowledge it as such.

Since I am not a real economist, I cannot make out quite how far we have moved from stuff to what we think about stuff, or how we might measure travel down this road, determine how disembodied we have actually become. But there is one segment of our current life that constitutes an economics of attention in its pure state. Whether we call it "cyberspace," "virtuality," "computer mediated communication (CMC)," or simply "the Net," out there attention is everything. Sure, there are plenty of signposts back to "real life," but they are just that, ways out of a pure attention economy. Out there, *all* you rent is "eyeballs."

And out there, too, new universities are growing up. If you want to know how the campus-based university will fare in this new economy of attention, you might do worse than look at how the virtual university is shaping up. On-line higher education is still in its cradle, but, like a baby picture just snapped with a Polaroid camera, its outlines are beginning to emerge. We might think of the comparison as a kind of "audit" of the current campus in terms of the attention economy. Such an accounting has never been possible before; there was no other way of doing business, no new ground from which to view the old. Now we can make such a comparison. The audit turns out to be a searching one. The virtual university, a Mars in his cradle though it be, questions the main operating assumptions of its parent. Maybe that is why such a baby dose of it has evoked so much strong feeling.

Ten being a number with biblical numinosity, I have distilled the campus-based university's operating system down into ten assumptions, and then examined each of these from the virtual off-campus campus.

Assumption #1
The ideal education is face-to-face, one-on-one education.

Every college that can muster a favorable teacher/student ratio brags about it. Every dean wants the students taught by real tenure-track faculty members, up close and personal. No place, except perhaps the Oxbridge colleges, can afford one-on-one tutorials, but such remain the unexamined ideal. Next best is a seminar taught "by the Socratic Method," the crackling eristic interchange beloved of humanists. The lecture system, however widely still used, is now considered Wal-Mart educational retailing that we want to abolish as soon as we can afford it. This one-on-one assumption defines a peculiar institution. The university is the only enterprise (at least that I know about) where quality is thought to vary *inversely* with efficiency.

The early reports from on-line make us wonder about this assumption. Some students wither in embarrassment under crackling eristic, however much the instructor may enjoy dealing it out, and shrink from speaking in a large lecture class. But on-line they blossom. They have a lot to say, once they are given time to think about it (to get an "A" in one of Socrates' classes, you had to be a very quick thinker), *and to say it in writing*, in the digital space. The writing that emerges from this new kind of "speech" differs from the old. I spent an educational lifetime reading student writing and almost all of it—good or bad—was forced performance. Its model—and how I urged it upon my students!—was the kind of professional writing professors do. A few students prosper under this regime, but for most it is heavy lifting. The whole tone and spirit of on-line writing frees students from trying to imitate their professors. Written for the class and not the instructor, it is sometimes incorrect and often inelegant, but it has the breath of life. The person who is writing it wants to say something and not simply jump through another hoop. The Socratic instructor that I tried so hard to play, in this view, doesn't come off very well. The teacher/pupil ratio still matters, but in a different way. The early reports from the on-line front indicate that students often feel they learned more on-line than in the classroom, and felt more at ease. The whole idea of the classroom and its rhetoric of performance, written and spoken, has been called into question. Everyone who has taught on-line seems to agree that the role of the instructor changes too, from Socratic wise person to *magister ludi*. The burden of instruction, though not of arrangement, seems to move back onto the student.

We might pause here to remark the university's main response to this new kind of "in person" instruction—the wired classroom. The extremely expensive wiring of the classroom tries to engraft the pedagogical powers emerging from the digital expressive space, and native to it, onto the classroom from which these powers have just escaped. Nothing, finally, misses the point and power of digital expression quite so dramatically as a classroom full of computers. "Why," anyone who understands the logic of digital expression must ask, "Why put computers *there*? That's where the students just escaped from." Digital expression puts the classroom in the computer, not the computer in the classroom.

So—the virtual audit calls into question the classroom and everything that goes with it: the standard papers and examinations, the instructor's role and the student's. This is a profound audit for an auditor still in the cradle.

Assumption #2
Higher education, in its ideal form, proceeds in a setting sequestered in both time and space.

Four years it should take, and in a special place, insulated from the world of "getting and spending" which academics never tire of denigrating. But the sequestration model brings with it a radical imbalance in educational rhythm, one that on-line education, by its very nature, corrects. The four-year model says this: at the beginning of your adult life, take four years off to learn about the world and reflect upon it, and also equip yourself with the knowledge needed to make a living in it. If you emerge in debt, don't worry. The certificate redeems all. Spend four years on theory and the rest of your life on practice. But none of us learn this way; the oscillation between theory and practice does not come in four-year intervals but in much shorter ones. That is why students have always created an extra-curriculum, gotten jobs, sought out internships, and stopped out for a year or two. That is why my students at UCLA usually worked at least half-time and often much more. That's why they take six or seven years to graduate, rather than the canonical four.

Signs stick up all over the landscape telling us that the four-year sequestration pattern should be junked. The community colleges have seen this, and tailor their instruction to the places and times where it is needed. The "universities" that businesses have been forced to develop to train their employees do not observe a semester system into which all educational needs must be fitted, but have courses as long as the particular need requires, supplied when and where the employee needs them. The lean automobile-manufacturing system, invented by Toyota, revolutionized the car business by showing the enormous waste that huge inventories create. There is a gigantic "inventory" problem in higher education, if we had the wit to see it. The four-year pattern, the semester course, the credit hour, all pile up useless inventories of knowledge that is supposed to come in useful later on. And of course it sometimes does. But it is a very wasteful "sometimes."

To compensate for its frozen educational rhythm, the modern university has become a quilt of "training" and "education." It could not have continued otherwise. But the quilt is spread over a Procrustean bed of rigid courses on a frame of four-year sequestration. The bed has long since collapsed in the name of common sense.

What has been the response of universities, public and private, to these pressures? Improve the graduation rate! That is, grasp the four-year pattern to our bosoms as ineluctable reality. Ignore everything that has happened to show us that the sequestered four-year model no longer works, and insist that everyone conform to it. The on-line virtual university, by creating a new model, supplies a searching critique of the campus one.

The virtual university supplies a different kind of sequence altogether. It provides "just-in-time" education. You face a problem and need the help of theory to solve it. You find the education you need for that problem and get on with life. No need to wonder about the "relevance" of it. That comes with the territory. The oscillations between theory and practice can vary widely on-line, depending on what you need and when you need it. But it is always a frequency and wavelength suited to the present circumstance, not a four-year one size fits all rule.

Phoenix University has prompted an almost hysterical response in the university world simply by operating for profit, but we should be paying attention to *how* it makes its profit—by ignoring the four-year pattern and its accompanying physical sequestration. The Open University in the U.K. has been a distance-education institution since it was founded, a "virtual university" in an adumbrated "cyberspace" before there was an Internet to be on-line on. It allows students who cannot afford the four years of sequestration to create an oscillation between theory and practice that suits their own need for knowledge. It has recently expanded its operations worldwide, and has allied itself in the United States with the Western Governors' venture in on-line education to create a greater and more American presence. It constitutes a far greater competitive threat to Campus U. than Phoenix U. will ever be. But, because it is not "for profit," few have paid it any mind. And yet it has, by operating in a pure economics of attention, taught hundreds of thousands of students for the price of tens.

The snobbery upon which the sequestration model is built runs very deep. I read in a recent *Yale Alumni Magazine* the standard Dean's Cliché: "We are not a trade school." It does theory not practice, "education" not "training," gentlepersonly preparation for the business of life, not raw-knuckle plumber's training for a life of business. No cliché surfaces more dependably in the current conversation. Yet its self-contradictions are palpably silly. What is the Law School for? The Medical School? The Business School? The Forestry School? The Engineering School? Indeed, the Graduate School? The Computer Science Department? The Economics Department? Do students study chemistry for the soul enrichment to be found in semimicro quantitative analysis? And on and on. What sustains the "trade-school" cliché is the four-year sequestration pattern, the idea that the purposes and problems of life can be postponed for four years while—in adolescence of all times—we philosophize upon them.

Like the other foundational hypocrisies of university life, its main use is to shut down an embarrassing fundamental debate, the debate about educational sequence. "Knowledge does not keep any better than fish," Alfred North Whitehead remarks in *The Aims of Education*, the best discussion of educational rhythm I know. You can't store it up for four years and then use it for life.

The virtual university construes the problem differently. It accommodates many different oscillations between theory and practice, task-specific "training" and the more general exploration of fundamental principles for which we who do it reserve the name of "education." By supplying knowledge when and where it is needed, it keeps the fish from spoiling. Such education does not ignore theoretical knowledge and general knowledge. How could it? That is where the power comes from. But it is willing to accommodate the oscillation between theory and practice at many different frequencies and wavelengths. In the virtual university, the "theory/practice" distinction that bureaucratized academics so prize simply evaporates.

Viewed from the outside, the most astonishing fact about American higher education is its current division into two camps, based on the "theory/practice" distinction: the "theory" world of colleges and universities which we usually mean when we say "higher education," and the "training" world of business, government, and the military. The division embodies the dangers of the Dean's Cliché. For nearly a decade now the "training" sector has been larger than the "respectable" segment of higher education. It is clearly our main competitor and has been for a long time. Phoenix University is an inconsequential part of an enormous endeavor that is all "for profit." The "training" world has much to teach us about the uses of educational technology, about bringing courses to market fast and teaching them efficiently. And yet most academics *do not even know that it exists*. The Dean's Cliché is apotropaic. Because the ignored segment represents "practice" not "theory," "training" not "education," we can continue to ignore it. The future of the City of Intellect is also being constituted in this "applied" world, and yet not a single representative of it is usually invited to conferences on higher education. Yet it has most to teach us, perhaps, about how to use electronic technology to sustain a virtual university that operates on many different educational rhythms and not simply the four-year sequestration model we now make such efforts to preserve.

Assumption #3

The education that every university offers should be generated in-house by a resident faculty employed full-time for this purpose.

This assumption is so ingrained in us, and in our accreditation boards, that we can hardly imagine things otherwise. But otherwise things once were. The professors who staffed the medieval university were individual entrepreneurs. They lived by fees paid to them by the students for their lectures. If they were famous lecturers, they attracted many students and gained larger incomes. If they were boring lecturers, they had few students, and they experienced the usual companions of deprivation: envy, bitterness, hatred, and poverty. The university provided the hall, and a critical mass of students, but the professor owned the educational product and was free to, and sometimes did, take his (they were all *he's*) show on the road. The virtual university re-creates this pattern. In the electronic expressive space, teaching is now publishable. The logical pattern in cyberspace is the medieval pattern, and it is beginning to reappear. Famous professors can cultivate a worldwide group of students. And professors famous in a narrow field can find the critical mass worldwide that they cannot find at home.

This kind of teaching, at least such as I know about, has been over the Internet, punctuated sometimes by site visits every few weeks. But it need not be so. To cite just one example that I know well, my friend and colleague Robert Winter, of the UCLA music faculty, created four pioneering CD-ROMs, before that substrate suffered a premature eclipse. Each of these took as its subject a famous piece of music (Beethoven's 9th Symphony, one of the Mozart string quartets dedicated to Haydn,

Stravinsky's *Rite of Spring*, and Dvorak's *Symphony from the New World*) and spun out from it a course in the music of that period and, more largely, a beginner's guide to classical music per se. Each disk is self-standing and self-teaching, and even self-examining. They exemplify how a "course" might be published in a digital medium and distributed off-line, simply through the mail. One can imagine a whole "faculty" of such programs, and an excellent education it would provide.

The vital ingredient in all this teaching is the digital medium, not—as seems universally accepted—on-line delivery itself. The Winter programs use the vital center of the digital medium. The many "talking head" video courses simply transport the classroom to the desktop. So do some on-line courses. But all such programs point to the same moral. The professor, in electronic space, needs the university only as a retailer, and sometimes not even as that.

We can also look at this virtual configuration from the employer's, the university's, point of view. For thirty-two years, I taught Chaucer and Shakespeare at least once a year, and often the same course twice in a year. It was, although I could conceive no other way to do it at the time, a dreadful waste of effort.[1] I can certainly argue that I tried to keep my teaching fresh, as most of us do, but once I had figured out what I thought the texts meant and published my thoughts in books and articles, it was mostly repetition. In a virtual university, my course need only be bought once every, say, half a dozen years. It could then be presented to its students when and where they wanted it, and not only TTh 10–12. It would have saved the University of California a lot of money and me a lot of repetition.

For a glimpse of an alternative system in action, we can look at how the Open University in the U.K. develops a course. A team of twenty-five or thirty people—scholars, presentation specialists, and producers—develops a course. It is expected to last half a dozen years but hardly to be immortal. The digital medium allows new mixtures of text, voice, and image that create educational programs of unprecedented power. We do not need to assume, as most practicing academics do, that such courses are inferior to live instruction. As often as not, indeed, one might make the opposite assumption.

A system of this sort, digital in medium and transmission, allows us to see the present system as extraordinarily wasteful, a preindustrial handicraft pattern. The virtue of such a handicraft system, we always assume, is the individual attention that outstanding scholars bestow on students. But just here has been its greatest failure. Universities spend great sums to at-

tract famous names to their faculty only to have those famous names unavailable to their students. The most common solution is pure public relations: the Great Name gives a freshman seminar for a dozen students.
Wow! Are we not making good use of our Nobel Prize winner! She is not
just an ornament in the academic status race! She teaches a freshman seminar to a dozen students once every three years! Such sentimental sops to
"teaching" do not solve the problem but only highlight it. If the Great
Name is worth the Great Salary, some means has to be devised to leverage
that person's teaching, really make it available to a broad spectrum of students. Otherwise, we are still in the rhetoric of ornamental names in which
people of my generation have passed their whole academic lives. What is
needed—*hic et ubique*—is leverage. We have tried the leverage of large lecture halls for going on a thousand years but, compared to more modern
technologies, it doesn't generate much power. Electronic expression is the
only workable alternative leverage in sight.

The management and employment pattern the virtual university implies here—and what a reception such a suggestion will get in the present
climate!—is that of an entertainment production company that develops
talent and markets it. Its real business, like a publishing company in the
digital world, is the acquisition of rights. Can we be sure we have nothing to learn from such organizations?

Assumption #4
The ideal pattern of employment for a university faculty is one that
combines a maximum of narrowness and inflexibility in job
description with a maximum of job security: the tenure system.

The combination of lifetime employment and unchanging job description—you cannot be asked to teach "out of your field" even if that
field is now out in left field and no one wants to play in it—is so un-
workable that it has already broken down, as the part-time phenomenon
attests. Even the Japanese, it turns out, cannot afford guaranteed lifetime
employment, coupled, as it is there, with a maximum of job *flexibility*,
rather than *inflexibility*. The usual criticism of the tenure system, that it
preserves people in a profession they are now too lazy or decrepit to
profess, misses the central point. The danger is not that they can no
longer do the same job but that the *job* will remain the same, whether
they can do it or not. In the tenure debate, it is not the unchangeable
faculty that is the problem but the unchangeable job description.

The tenure system is based on a gigantic one-time judgment of fitness. I spent as much time as any other academic worrying about this system, going through it, and then serving on the endless tribunals of judgment where the saved judge the candidates for salvation. But, until I left the academy and had pondered it from the outside for several years, I had never fully appreciated the gigantic amount of time it requires. (When I left it, my department at UCLA was requiring fifteen outside letters for an action at the full professorial level.) The judgmental process has become monstrous. And its premise—that a job will never change and thus will require only one set of qualifications for the lifetime of its holder, and thus that one irrevocable judgment can be made—has simply evaporated. The one-time permanent tenure judgment assumes a rhythm and sequence the world no longer permits.

The tenure system is usually defended on a different basis, as the agency of academic freedom. The free market of ideas requires it. If so, why are now over a third of the teachers in higher education, the non-tenure-track proletariat, denied its protection? The current epithet of choice, "tenure-track," has less to do with academic freedom than with guaranteeing present academic job descriptions and work practices.

The virtual university has created several new patterns of academic employment and will certainly create many more. These patterns will be many and varied—that is their main virtue—and they will respond to a global educational marketplace. On-line employers do not spend their time devising ever-stricter standards for tenure beatification. Part-time enterprise carries no stigma here. This marketplace approximates more closely a genuine free market of ideas, jostling and chaotic and undisciplined, than the mandarin bureaucracies of formal academia. Just as one example, let me cite the quickness and accuracy with which companies have mounted their own on-line educational programs in response to changing business circumstances. But when I talk to an academic about the ReMax on-line curriculum in real estate practices, the lights dim. *We* have nothing to learn from *ReMax*.

Assumption #5
The purpose of the university administration is to protect the faculty from the outside world.

In the virtual university the difference between the university and the outside world evaporates. The virtual university lives and breathes in the real world. Its alternation of theory and practice, as we have seen, varies with time and place. The sequestration model of the university assumes that the faculty's job is to lead "the theoretical life" and that the university administration should create an "eternal childhood" in which the faculty can do this. I have taken these phrases from Allan Bloom's odious discussion in *The Closing of the American Mind*. In as much as the protection succeeds, it does indeed infantilize the faculty, just as Bloom claimed. However, the view from virtual space suggests that this playpen protection is a bad idea, not a good one. Renunciation of the playpen model does *not* mean that inquiry does not need protected spaces and times, but it *does mean* that a lifetime of protection makes for an eternal childhood.

Assumption #6
University faculties are animated by a purity of motive different from, and superior to, the world of ordinary human work.

If this assumption were not so common in university circles, one could scarcely believe that anyone familiar with university life could hold it. Yet it dominates every conversation about "for profit" arrangements of any sort in academic life. It haunts any effort to suggest to graduate students that nonacademic employment might be compatible with human happiness. It constitutes our root conceit. Other people act for profit; we pursue learning "for its own sake." The "for its own sake" argument has, as its main advantage, that it precludes further discussion. If you say, "Well, yes, but what we do must have *some* purpose we can talk about," it only proves that you do not get it. Like the other assumptions in our list, it results in self-enclosure. The argument can be pursued no further.

Let me pursue it a little further, nevertheless. It will require a short excursus if we are to look at campus life from the virtual point of view, but a needful one.

We can plot human motive on a simple spectrum:

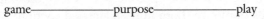

game————————purpose————————play

Under "game" let us enlist all our competitive activity, our Vince Lombardi desire to win. No need to puzzle over this unduly. We are primates and as such hierarchical. What interests us very often in life is where we stand in relation to other people. Since the most common hierarchical counter is money, all hunger for profit clusters under here. But also the aristocratic hunger for fame which goes all the way back to Homer's *Iliad*, where the lust to be first, *aien aristeuin*, is pursued even to death. Under "play" we can assemble all the things we do "just for the hell of it." Our behavioral biology has equipped us for a lot of things that life does not give us a chance to play out "for real" and so we play them out "for play." Here is the domain of hobbies, amateur sports, cars polished within an inch of their lives or made, through the agency of hydraulic cylinders, to dance up and down like mechanical monsters. Here lives the enormous arena of stylistic play, of form for the love of form. In the middle comes the domain of ordinary human purposes: food, shelter, the world from the *Consumer Reports* point of view.

It takes no great perspicacity of mind to see that game and play are the driving sources of human motive. If we are lucky, they are orchestrated to work together and create mature purpose, but we are not primarily purposive creatures at all. No one wants to admit this, of course; we all think ourselves purposive, sensible, and restrained. Everyone, that is, except academics. We academics dwell, we like to think, entirely in the world of play, of behavior "for its own sake." It is knowledge "for its own sake" that justifies the sequestration in time and space, and the freezing of the theory/practice oscillation into the "theory" half of the waveform. Protecting the play space constitutes, as I have just noted, the main theory of management for the university. And because our whole way of life is organized around this motivational purity, we often look down our noses at those whose motives are more obviously mixed. This purity of motive descends, I suppose, from our religious origins.

A spirit of pure play, we argue, drives genuine creativity. Pure research leads to progress; applied research to sordid compromise. At the apogee of this motivational caricature sit the institutes of pure thought where Einsteins sit and think. A purpose, a task, an application: these only disconcert propositional thought.

The virtual university, life in the digital expressive spaces, has from its beginning worked in just the opposite way, from a thorough mixture of all three kinds of motive. Born in play, agitated continually by competition, the original hackers soon noticed that all kinds of work could be done in new ways. The "killer ap" became a holy grail, not a badge of motivational impurity. The extraordinary dynamism of the Internet comes from the continual roiling mixture of motives, of game, purpose, and play. Tim Berners-Lee, all honor to him, has it all wrong in wanting the World Wide Web to remain pure in motive. Its inner dynamic works just the other way. A perfect instance of this mixture is open-source programming. Linux started out as play—my God, is *Windows* the best we can do?—but then enlisted other programming warriors who want to show their stuff in the arena of their peers. Striving to be first. And what comes out but Linux as product, as a new tool in the world of purpose.

Such deeply mixed motives, moving from play to game to purpose in high-frequency oscillation, have not been unknown in the academic world, but they have not come from the institutes of pure thought. They have come from ad hoc groupings with richly mixed motives. It often takes war, alas, to convene such models of mixed motive: the cryptographic establishments at Bletchley Park and Arlington Hall for example, or the Radiation Laboratory at MIT or, most of all I suppose, the Manhattan Project at Los Alamos. The people who were there talk about the heightened sense of life that emerges from such a rich and continually changing motivational mix. This same mixture seems to have generated the explosion of Japanese consumer electronics in the 1960s (see, for example, Johnstone, 1999).

And, of course, when universities really work, they work this way too. Teaching is an intensely purposive activity, and when it has been jammed together with research into one career, as it has in the American university, it has constituted an enormous generative engine. It is hard to bear, maddeningly inconsistent at its heart, certainly, but it is rich in results. It is only when academic life really lives up to its professions of motivational purity that the fire goes out. Purity of motive is a disastrous operating premise, whatever the motive. Pure ambition creates parodies of Achilles. That is why the sixties had to happen. But pure play is a disaster, too. That is why the sixties were a disaster, too. And if you work only for food, well, as was pointed out long ago, humankind does not live by bread alone. It lives by rich motivational mixtures, the kind that have provided the principal propellant for the digital economic explosion. The fear that our motives will be contaminated by contact with this kind of rich mixture is not simply silly and ignorant, it is dead wrong.

Assumption #7
Universities are unique institutions. As such, they cannot be meaningfully compared to any others.

The first response, if you try to talk about "productivity" or "efficiency" or any kind of measured result in academic life, is "the university is not a business." The same recalcitrance is applied to any other kind of comparison. Health care, the most obvious current analogue, is not really like what we do at all. Nor of course can the university learn anything from global distance-learning organizations like the Open University. Nor from the "training sector," which is "for profit." Nor, God forbid, from the educational activities of the military. Again, the assumption is self-sealing. If we cannot compare our organization to any other, then we, by definition, have nothing to learn from anybody else and need pay no attention to anyone else. The "unique institution" argument is the organizational counterpart of the "for its own sake" argument for academic learning. "If the university is not a business," it seems reasonable to ask, "then what kind of organization is it?" If you can rejoin, "It is its own kind of organization and exists for its own sake," then the inquiry comes to a close. You have guaranteed that you will never learn anything from anybody else.

The virtual university constitutes a surprising obverse case. On-line discourse really is unique. There has been nothing like it before. Yet the questions asked of it seek to understand it by trying to find analogues. How does it resemble other mass media? How does it resemble telephony? How does it resemble printed textual communication? What kind of economics is needed to understand it? What does "productivity" mean here? Where and how is the value added? Is it self-managing? If not, how is it to be managed? These are all outward-turning questions, and we can learn from the answers. They provide a striking contrast to the self-sealing moat of uniqueness that university faculties erect around their institution.

Assumption #8
Inefficiency is something to be proud of.

This assumption follows naturally from the previous ones. It proves that one's motives have remained pure. If we are truly a unique institution, then a "bottom line" of any sort travesties our endeavors.

Once in a department personnel meeting, to alleviate the despairing boredom such meetings provoked in me, I tried to end the meeting by using what we might call an *argumentum ad tributum*, an argument from the taxpayers' point of view. We had been debating for two hours whether to give a colleague a fifty dollar/month raise. I did a rough calculation of the amount it was costing the taxpayers of California to keep that group of people in that room for that length of time, and remarked that it was costing far more to debate the case than to grant the raise and go home. On these grounds, I called the question. The argument simply did not register. It was irrelevant even to introduce calculations of this sort.

Of all the assumptions that prevent the university's creating a condign management philosophy for our present economy of attention, this basic assumption is surely the most debilitating. It leads to an accounting system that we might express as a proverb: "Perpetual insolvency sustained by perpetual mendicancy." Bottom lines can be of all sorts, but whatever currency they deal in, they try to measure whether the enterprise is in tone, in good form, as well as whether it has done what it proposed to do. Universities, public or private, do not operate this way, whatever they profess to do, and however often they change "administrator" to "executive." Their only operating plan is to spend all the money they have—the faculty can always think up fresh ways to do this—and then ask for more. Complaining, all the while, of course, about how society no longer values education. Public universities ask for more public money. Private universities invent ever more efficient milking machines for their alumni. But neither sector has ever devised a bottom line condign to the enterprise. To devise one means devising a system of management condign to the enterprise. *Hic opus; hic labor est.*

To repeat: bottom lines need not be always about money. They are about monitoring the power and vigor of an enterprise by measuring how well it has used the resources at its disposal for the purposes intended. If the purposes are vague, unexamined, and infinitely expandable, and if measurement of success never goes beyond the psychology of rumor enshrined in national magazine surveys, then the institution, and the people in it, never grow up. We are back to self-enclosure, back to a theory of management that aims to protect the faculty from "bottom line" reality of all sorts.

The protections afforded higher education against bottom lines, much as we all applaud them, work against the self-knowledge that any complex organization must possess and refine. Consider, for example, the federal student loan program. Who could oppose it? Nobody, so far as I have ever read. Students who cannot afford the costs of a modern higher education are insulated from them. This is wonderful for the institutions because they can keep increasing those costs, rather than controlling them. Loan programs simply pass these increased costs on to the students in the form of a lifetime of debt. That seems fine to the universities and, amazingly enough, to most of the students as well. Yet the net effect is to insulate the university from the kind of cost accounting that tells any enterprise how it is doing. It is no good saying that education is automatically better the more money we spend on it. The bankruptcy of that premise is all too apparent in secondary education, and it ought to be apparent at higher levels as well.

Or we might consider a second sacred cow, alumni giving. The levels that it has attained in the United States are truly extraordinary and testify to the equally extraordinary faith Americans place in education, especially higher education. But the question here, too, is what value the students are getting for their money. For alumni giving is, after all, just another way of passing costs on to students, in this case past students rather than present ones. It is just another form of the mendicancy that has evolved to support a perpetual insolvency. There has to be, at some point, at some time, a real *audit*, an *accounting* of some sort in both the narrow and the wider senses of the word. Without it, there can be no genuine theory of management for higher education, or body of best practices. The need for both is what conferences on the shape of the university in the coming century are finally all about.

Let the virtual university once more audit the bricks and mortar one. One great virtue of virtuality has been that it exists in a marketplace that both admits, and admits to, an accounting system based on solvency. The questions applied to it are, to be sure, often beside the point. It is examined on whether it is doing the traditional tasks better than the traditional university, when it is redefining both those tasks and how they are done. But no matter. From the beginning, the questions that have surrounded it— whatever the answers—are questions of efficiency. How well is it doing? It is indeed a unique institution, but it has never taken refuge in its uniqueness, never argued that it stands above accounting. It has been subject to criticisms from all sides and this is fine, for from it all will emerge a genuine accounting system—one based on solvency, not mendicancy.

Digital teaching methods also provide a means of comparison with bricks and mortar ones. These can no longer claim uniqueness, for there is another kind of university and the results between the two can be compared. Oddly enough, the bricks and mortar world is perfectly willing to apply standards of efficiency to the virtual university that it would never consider applying to itself. Again, no matter. Two systems create a basis of comparison that did not exist before.

Some interesting comparisons result. We might, to take one important instance, consider the difference between Internet time and campus time. The Internet has speeded up the metabolism of thought and decision across the world of work. Everyone feels this, whatever kind of endeavor they pursue. The metamorphosis from an industrial economy to an information economy has been catalytic. The Internet instantiates this fundamental change of pace. Everyone feels this change, that is, except the university. There no metamorphosis has yet occurred. A professor of English at George Mason U. struck precisely the right note apropos some changes in the curriculum proposed by the administration. "If you're talking about a democratic process, it has to be less speedy than an efficiency expert would like. . . . We have time to talk. What's the hurry? We're not going anyplace" (quoted in Manger, 1999: A14).

If you do not know what the hurry is about, you do not know what business you are really in. Does the university? It may realize it is in the information business—it sometimes talks this way—but I don't think so. The business it still thinks itself in is academic landlord: renting space in classrooms to students. The virtual university does not labor under this illusion or think at the old landlord speed.

Assumption #9
The new electronic field of expression does not change what we are doing but only how we are doing it.

We can pivot to this assumption from the last one on the fulcrum of intellectual property. When information is put on the Internet, it gains potential value simply from this act. In the textbook-and-landlord idea of the university, this is not so. It is hard to use information there and you have to come to campus to get it. Anything on the Net can be stolen, and so it is potentially infinitely valuable. Like open-source programming, which may perhaps be the characteristic form of web "property," there is no telling what people may make of it. That introduces Internet time and a market accounting system at the same time. The sequestration model for the university breaks down here too.

The digital medium is not a neutral conduit any more than print was. It creates a different rhetoric that puts words, written and spoken, in new juxtapositions with picture and sound. It would take a day's lecturing to illustrate how this new expressive space works, and any discussion of the future of the City of Intellect really should begin there, since that city will use the new operating system and not its present one of classes and fixed printed texts.[3] The rhetoric of digital expression is already in use across academic life, at least in embryo, and its implications are clear enough and profound. The present disciplinary and departmental boundaries, founded on the divisions of words, images, and sounds, dissolve if these signals become fungible, as they do when they share a common digital code. Electronic text, for example, takes place in a dynamic, three-dimensional space that trespasses into the disciplines of architecture and dance before it has taken half a dozen steps. Conceptual thought undergoes a radical dramatization in the digital medium, dominated as it is by animation. It is not surprising that, in the digital medium, *design*, which works always at the interface between "things" and "what we think about things," should emerge as the central rhetorical—indeed, I should say humanistic—discipline in an attention economy.

These changes cannot be adequately communicated in print but they are the native expression of the virtual university. The audit they apply to the bricks-and-mortar university is deep and wide. From within the rhetoric of digital expression, we can see the present departmental and disciplinary structure, and the career patterns built upon it, as the fossils that they have become. The *how* of academic teaching and inquiry has indeed changed, and this is generally appreciated. That the *what* of teaching and inquiry has changed far more fundamentally has scarcely risen above the horizon of our awareness.

Assumption #10
The university lives in the same kind of economy it has always lived in.

I have been suggesting that we live in a new kind of economy, an attention economy, and that, if we want to glimpse how the university might fit into it, we should look at "the virtual university." There, the economics of attention exists in its pure form. Stuff is derivative; information, fundamental. Not "things," but "what we think about things" stand center stage. This figure/ground shift, we might remind ourselves, signifies a root-level change in how we understand the world: "To the powerful theories of chemistry and physics must be added a late arrival: a theory of information. Nature must be interpreted as matter, energy, and information" (Campbell, 1982: 16). We perceive stuff now as a particular instantiation, a carbon-based printout, of preexistent information. So with DNA and our bodies; so with physical products and the CAD-CAM programs that produce them.

Information as scientific concept and referential metaphor evolved entwined with electronic technologies like a double helix; they are related as breathing in relates to breathing out. The respiration got really intense, though, with the invention of the digital computer, and it is perhaps not a great exaggeration to say that the computer has created the attention economy in which we currently live.

Yes, of course there has always been both stuff and what we think about stuff, and there always will be. Printouts of the DNA code we may be, but also flesh and blood. The economics of stuff and the economics of attention will always coexist and we will, as always, need to oscillate between them. The study of how we allocate human attention has, until recently in Western history, been called "rhetoric." It referred to the training in the spoken and written word that stood at the center of Western education until the devolution of the modern subjects in the nineteenth century. The rhetorician knew how to persuade you to pay attention to X instead of Y, and thus to see the world as he saw it, or would have you see it. As long as the study of the persuasive word, spoken and written, remained central to the Western curriculum, people dwelt in an economics of attention. There was, indeed, stuff and people needed some and wanted much more, but it was a derivative, not the central, reality.

When natural science began to ponder matter and energy, rather than human attention; when industrial enterprise began to dig materials out of the earth's crust and make objects out of them in a really serious way; then figure and ground switched places. At the center stood stuff and an economics of stuff—the modern subject that we now call "economics." And just as rhetoric stood at the center of public debate about the fundamental questions of public and private life, so now economics, the economics of stuff, occupies that place. The serious disciplines were the disciplines that studied matter and energy and how to use the wisdom gained thereby to make stuff. The rest was, well, "just rhetoric," needed, no doubt, since you could not very well do without words, but peripheral to the main event—stuff, and the chemistry and physics that studied it. So began the long whining litany about "the humanities," the subjects which, fanning out from their rhetorical center, studied how attention was allocated in human life. They were pushed out of the center and did not like it. So began, too, the "literacy crisis" which has created a populace that does not read, and hence cannot write, and is currently forgetting even how to speak. If things were the thing, and not words, then words did not really matter. Equations maybe but not words.

Digital technology takes us back to the old, the prescientific and preindustrial economics, to the economics of attention that, in fact, prevailed in the medieval university. Figure and ground, stuff and what we think about stuff, reverse again on the digital screen. That reversal, the return of an economics of attention, constitutes the fundamental cultural change brought about by digital technology. All the issues which now vex the university and prod the foundational assumptions we have been considering—practice muscling in on theory, profit discoloring pure inquiry, volatile job descriptions eroding lifetime employment, teaching turned into publication, even the resentful self-pity of humanists watching new disciplines eat their lunch—all these turn on the economics of attention.

As long as we are made of flesh and blood, we will live in a perpetual oscillation between stuff and what we think about stuff, between "economics" as she is commonly written, and an economics of attention. Our felt life will always mix the two. But this will not occur on the Web. The Internet constitutes a pure economics of attention. The virtual university, the university conducted electronically, is the university in a pure economics of attention. That is why it constitutes so valuable an auditor. How the university fits and fares in this electronic expressive space, in this new rhetoric, provides a litmus test of what it has been, its strengths, weaknesses, and what is to become of it.

The university, by all rights, should feel at home in an economics of attention. That, after all, has always been its business: constructing attention-structures so that students can absorb and use information more efficiently than they could if left on their own. But it still thinks in an economics based on stuff; that is why it still conceives of itself as a classroom landlord. The new management model that the City of Intellect requires must understand the fundamental changes from an economics of stuff to an economics of attention. The sequestration model will no longer serve, because in the attention economy the university moves from the margin to the center of the economy. It deals with the central reality, attention, not the stuff you drop on your foot. The whole balance in its curriculum alters. It is not only—*horresco referens!*—that a new economics replaces the old but that a new disciplinary balance of power replaces the old. The "practical arts" are no longer so practical. The "ornamental" arts which allocate attention—the arts and letters, the law of intellectual property rather than the law of stuff, the biology based on bits and not carbon—are the "practical arts" in an economics of attention. At their core must stand some version of the discipline that for most of Western history supplied the "economics" for the economics of attention: rhetoric. None of the traditional disciplines as yet understands this profound transformation, and I venture to guess that none of them will welcome it when they do.

But if you do not believe such a fundamental change has occurred, just compare the market capitalization of companies that deal in attention with those that deal in stuff.[4] The university's stock should also rise in such an economics, but only when it realizes that its business is not renting seats in classrooms but constructing attention-structures deep inside the world of work. The audit of virtuality is unforgiving. Other enterprises are constructing those attention-structures right now, beginning to build virtual universities. The clock is ticking, and on Internet time, not university time.

Notes

My title is borrowed unabashedly from Correlli Barnett's relentless excavation of the English economy during World War II. See Barnett, 1986.

1. A former student who read this chapter comments at this point: "I didn't think so then and I don't now. I still vividly remember your *Hamlet* lecture and the wonderful way you unpacked the *Troilus*. You can have both." Clearly she is right: we should try for optimal combinations of live instruction and lectures available on-line. And clearly there will be more than one optimal combination.

2. There was, in fact, something somewhat like it, the global military network of the 1950s, which has since metamorphosed into all kinds of reticulations.

3. For a further discussion, see my "A New Operating System for the Humanities" (Rhetoricainc.com; "Lectures").

4. Striking examples: In 1999, Chrysler earned $2.8 billion, with a market capitalization of $27 billion. Microsoft earned $3.8 billion, but the market valued it at $211 billion. Boeing's stock price recently has been so low that its market capitalization fell below its net asset value. Airplanes are not an unpromising business, and Boeing has made them with great success throughout most of the twentieth century, but they are made of stuff and thus the speculative market of the 1990s didn't like the stock. Of course, the market did begin to assess the valuation of "new economy" stocks more realistically at the end of 2000 and in 2001, but it did so without looking back.

References

Barnett, Correlli. 1986. *The Audit of War: The Illusion and Reality of Britain as a Great Nation.* London: Macmillan London.

Bloom, Allan. 1987. *The Closing of the American Mind.* New York: Simon and Schuster.

Campbell, Jeremy. 1982. *Grammatical Man.* Simon and Schuster.

Johnstone, Bob. 1999. *We Were Burning: Japanese Entrepreneurs and the Forging of the Electronic Age.* New York: Basic Books.

Manger, Denise K. 1999. "Battle over Academic Control Pits Faculty against Governing Board at George Mason U." *Chronicle of Higher Education* (June 18): A14.

Whitehead, Alfred North. 1929. *The Aims of Education.* New York: Macmillan.

CHAPTER SEVEN

New Business Models for Higher Education

DAVID J. COLLIS

Venture capitalists have been investing over $100 million every quarter into entrepreneurial Internet educational content companies (Newman, 2000). UNext's Cardean University, visibly and vocally endorsed by three Nobel Laureates and run by former professors from the University of Chicago, started offering business courses in August 2000—after more than $80 million of investment. Kaplan now has the second largest private law school in the United States. Hungry Minds has launched People's U, whose course catalog proudly includes quilting. Of the traditional institutions, Harvard, Columbia, Chicago, Wharton, MIT, LSE, Stanford, Duke, and UNC Chapel-Hill, among many others, have made at least some of their courses available to students who are not formally enrolled in their institution. More broadly, 62 percent of the thirty-six hundred accredited institutions of higher education offered distance learning courses in 2000, and one research firm has suggested that 84 percent will offer distance learning courses (International Data Corporation, 1999).

If, therefore, we take as given the likely occurrence and general thrust of the impending revolution in higher education (see also Collis, 1999, 2001), the interesting question to address becomes the specific and more immediate impact of the underlying changes. I think the best way to capture the most likely of these short-term effects is to consider in more detail the various business models—both of new entrants and incumbents—that are currently being deployed. Understanding what are the current strategies of the players in the new "market space"; why they have been selected; and how they will evolve over time, can shed light on how the revolution will unfold and what sequence of repercussions it may have on universities' and colleges' current business models.

To achieve this objective I will first survey the general trends among both newcomers to, and incumbents in, higher education, and then describe in more detail the current plans of a representative of each—Knowledge Universe's Cardean University, and the Harvard Business School—in order to flesh out the specifics of their strategies. Doing this enables more general implications for higher education to be deduced.

The conclusion from this analysis contains both good news and bad news for universities. First, the bad news: It seems to me that many entrants are better funded and more committed to the market than I had imagined, and are pursuing a fast-growing and attractive market segment. At the same time leading universities, or at least schools or departments within those institutions, are establishing positions that will be hard for other universities and colleges to challenge. Competition, therefore, is going to be tougher than we might have thought.

The good news is that the entry strategies of new players are evolving in such a way as to delay and mitigate their impact on universities. That is not to say we should ignore their potential long run impact. Rather we can be relieved that their strategies, in some ways, allow a little more breathing room than we might have imagined.

Business Models of New Entrants

Many firms are now targeting the higher education market. These include startup enterprises as famous as Knowledge Universe and as unknown as AchieveGlobal.[1] They also include newly established subsidiaries of well-known multinationals, like Thomson Learning, and Pearson Knowledge. Aggregate data on their impact are now available, at least in the form of rough estimates by research firms,[2] and it is these I draw on to describe their strategies.

While it is hard to be precise about the business models and entry strategies being pursued by new entrants (indeed many seem not to know their own strategy, since they believe that "competing on Internet time" makes frequent strategic U-turns desirable), a rough sense of their overall direction can be gleaned from an analysis of 127 firms. These were identified as content providers in research by four brokerages that have studied the higher education industry (First Union Securities, 2000; Hambrecht & Co., 2000; Merrill Lynch, 2000; Piper Jaffray, 1999).[3]

This definition excludes all the firms that are attempting to provide technological infrastructure or platforms for higher education, such as SCT and WebCT; those which are seeking to be student lifestyle or campus portals, such as Campus Pipeline or Student Advantage; commerce related ventures, such as Varsity Books; as well as firms that are targeting markets outside higher education. It does, however, intentionally include those firms that are targeting corporate training.[4] Indeed, if there is one overwhelming conclusion from this analysis, and one that is good news for universities, it is that the primary audience for firms entering postsecondary education is the *corporate* market, not the individual. On reflection this is not unexpected, but it is this entry strategy that provides a temporary respite for universities.

There are many ways to categorize the entry strategies of the new players, from classifying their financial backers to their technology platforms. The five elements I want to focus on are the ones that seem to me to have most repercussions for universities. These are the courses entrants offer; their target customer group; where their content originates; the pedagogy they employ; and their pricing. Data on these five dimensions are by no means available for all 127 firms, so the discussion below is based on what data is accessible.[5] While imprecise, it should nevertheless be a good summary of the overall positioning of entrants.

Courses. Some entrants are already well established in higher education with extensive course catalogs. Hungry Minds is perhaps the extreme, with a reputed twenty thousand offerings, but other entrants— aside from the corporate training companies that offer thousands of courses by including their traditional classroom-based materials—already offer hundreds of courses. University Access, for example, has 450 different courses available.

Those companies acting as "Yellow Pages" that target the adult education/personal interest market, which includes Hungry Minds and eMind, have the largest course catalogs. In contrast, companies that currently or soon want to offer degrees are building their portfolios more slowly in order to ensure the quality of the material. Jones International, for example, offers forty-two courses—although their definition of a course appears to be under some debate.

Examining the course offerings of entrants, one is struck by the predominance of business-related material. Only 25 percent of the companies were focusing on areas other than management, performance improvement, or specific corporate skills, such as IT, and a large fraction of those were offering courses to other professionals, doctors, or lawyers.[6] As their names suggest, RehabMax and Healthstream, for example, focus on continuing education for healthcare professionals. Even when a smaller set of companies, which are explicitly entering the university market, was examined, the percentage offering primarily nonbusiness courses only rose to 40 percent. Concord University—Kaplan's entry into the law school market—Global Education Network's attempt to build a liberal arts program, Fathom's continuing education courses, not Harvard's Barnes and Noble University, or even the National Technological University's MSc offering are relatively rare. Far more typical is Jones International's business orientation for its "first in the US" accredited on-line bachelor's degree, or the MBA offered by Pensare (in collaboration with Duke's Fuqua school).

Indeed, at those firms for which it was possible to determine a definitive content focus, only 6 percent were targeting liberal arts, 8 percent personal interest, 3 percent science, and 14 percent professions other than management. Far more prevalent are the provision of IT certification courses, which the traditional corporate training firms now offer on-line.

The other striking observation is that as many, if not more, firms are offering master's degrees as are offering undergraduate degrees. While by no means all entrants are offering degrees, those that do have begun with graduate level rather than undergraduate level programs.

All of the above facts reflect a very natural progression in an entrepreneurial entry strategy. The most lucrative and most receptive market to enter is for business courses. Liberal arts undergraduate degrees have substantially higher entry barriers—not the least of which is accreditation. One can, therefore, predict an evolution in course offerings as firms build brand names and establish their presence in the market. That evolution will progress from short management certificates and continuing education for any one of the professions; through more general and softer leadership skills and performance improvement; to an MBA or other professional degree; and only finally into undergraduate liberal arts degrees.

The popularity of this entry trajectory does not mean that there will be no direct entry into the undergraduate arena. Some firms, like Global Education Network, will attempt that approach. However, the majority of entrants will take the easy path and begin by offering "business"—defined in the broadest sense—or specific skills training courses.

Customers. Matching the majority orientation to the provision of business courses, the primary customer for new entrants is the corporation. About 60 percent of entrants have identified the corporate market as their first target. For many of these firms it is the international market that is then listed as their secondary market—that is, foreigners who want an American education. Individuals in the United States rank as only the third target for these companies.

Following behind corporations as the primary target are other institutions—that is, universities 6 percent, and the international market 3 percent. Only about 38 percent of companies list individuals as their primary market.[7] Of course, this implies that many entrants, such as Online-learning.net, and Colorado Tech Online, are targeting individuals, but most entrants are first and foremost after the corporate customer. Apart from the corporate training firms that are already serving this market, many of the better-known entrants, UNext, Pensare, Caliber, and Ninth House have gone after these customers.

The reason for this inordinate attention on corporations is obvious. In the first place the corporate training market is very large. At $66 billion, it is one-quarter the size of the entire higher education market (International Data Corporation, 2000). Second, it is growing rapidly—at an estimated 11 percent pa. (Symonds, 2000)—and with all likelihood of continued growth as "knowledge" becomes ever more central to the economy, and firms place emphasis on the lifelong learning of their employees. Motorola, for example, estimates that every dollar spent on training yields thirty dollars in productivity gains within three years (Merrill Lynch, 2000). Third, allocating marketing expenditures toward large corporations, where one sale can result in millions of dollars of revenue, is much easier and more cost effective than trying to establish a consumer brand name and sell directly to thousands of individuals.

In addition, corporate training is the market that is most amenable to the application of the new technologies. Much of corporate training involves short programs that transfer a limited amount of well-specified information. The archetypal course in this regard would be a certificate in C++ programming. In fact, IT training makes up about one-third of corporate training, and it is material that can naturally be translated to the Web (Merrill Lynch, 1999). As a result, while about 72 percent of corporate training is done in the classroom today, it is expected that less than half will be taught this way by 2003 (International Data Corporation, 2000). Instead, on-line training, which is a $1.1 billion market today—between 2 and 5 percent of all corporate training (Credit Suisse

First Boston, 2000)—will have become a $11.4 billion business by 2003, or perhaps 15 percent of all corporate training (International Data Corporation, 2000).

The attraction for companies to switch to on-line training is that these technologies can substantially reduce costs while potentially also improving the quality of the learning experience. The indirect and opportunity costs of traditional classroom education are enormous. One estimate has the indirect costs—mostly travel—at twice the direct costs (*Training Magazine*, 1999). Factoring in the time employees spend training only adds to the expense. Exploiting new technologies that allow for asynchronous training can save a huge portion of these indirect costs (particularly if employees study while flying to "real" business meetings, or on their own time). Cisco estimates that on-line training reduces costs to one-tenth those of an instructor-led class (Merrill Lynch, 1999). A more conservative estimate suggests savings of 50 to 70 percent (*Training Magazine*, 1999). In addition, research appears to demonstrate that self-driven learning has much higher retention rates than classroom education. One study claims that retention rates increase by 25 to 60 percent (Russell, 1999). From the firm's perspective the effectiveness of training can also be improved by monitoring on-line test taking and linking it directly into the company's HR function. Ultimately, using asynchronous technologies for education allows companies to shift from expensive "just in case" training, to productive "just in time" training.

Finally, the corporate market is a natural first target for entrants, since it is already served by for-profit companies. Indeed, a slew of companies that are now providing corporate training are extending their scope of activities from more limited classroom-based training.

This begs the question of why universities should be concerned with this market if it existed previously and was already served by many of these same firms. The answer is, of course, that the technologies they are now adopting remove the constraints under which they traditionally operated. Freed from the classroom and with a marginal cost of serving another customer of essentially zero, in the near future entrants will be looking to leverage their courses into more than just the corporate market, just as they will gradually extend their course offerings from business to liberal arts. Perhaps more important, this market is large, fast-growing, profitable, and demanding. These characteristics mean that successful competitors in this space will be building valuable resources—financial, brand, and expertise with the new pedagogies—that they can then translate to the more traditional higher education market. In many ways, these firms will be exploiting a disruptive technology (Christensen, 1997): using on-line education to target a peripheral market that universities don't currently address, in order to build the skills necessary to compete at a later date in the incumbents' core market.

The evolutionary entry strategy, therefore, appears to follow a hierarchy of customers that begins with the corporation, extends globally, and then turns back to the individual American. It is this sequence of market entry that will ensure a delayed impact on universities, but a no less powerful impact when it does arrive.

Content. From a university's perspective, where the entrants source their content is a vital question. In principle entrants can generate course materials in three different ways.[8] They can hire their own staffs to develop new material and texts in the way that the Open University has done. They can license existing courses from universities or colleges and either rebrand them as their own or use the institutions' own brand on the course, as, for example, Pensare is doing. Or the entrant can cut out the university altogether by contracting directly with individual faculty or other experts for material and courses that have already been developed or to develop new materials—much the same as a traditional book publishing arrangement. University Access, for one, has been actively pursuing this approach, as has Ninth House, which has signed up a number of management "gurus" to translate their books into marketable courses, as also has Corpedia, which signed Peter Drucker.

The interest of the university is very much in keeping the third source of content to a minimum. Indeed, I know that many institutions are now wrestling with faculty over the contentious issue of copyright for course materials. At Harvard, Neil Rudenstine has been vehement in his protection of the university's copyright (*Harvard Magazine*, 2000). Other institutions seem to have been more forgiving (Industry Standard, 2000).[9] At stake, of course, are the potentially very large revenues that courses can now generate, which were not available in the past.

Data suggest that entrants are keeping their options open on sourcing. Indeed, several of the major players appear to be pursuing all three sources of content. Pensare and University Access, for example, are both doing deals with institutions and soliciting material directly from faculty,[10] while each also has its own staffs that convert existing materials for the new pedagogies at substantial cost.[11] Such in-house staffs are also necessary to customize material for corporate customers. Unlike individual students, corporations have the power to demand that course material be adapted to meet their specific needs. As a result, at least 40 percent of training is customized rather than off the shelf, and the continuing requirement for such customization will mean that entrants focusing on the corporate market cannot just rely on licensed material.

While I suspect that entrants would rather deal with individual faculty because that gives them greater bargaining power, the attraction of a university deal is the immediate access to a broad range of courses and the credibility of the university's brand name. However, such deals are not cheap, as the commitment of UNext to pay Columbia University $20 million illustrates (see below), and the long-term trend will probably be for entrants to source more material directly from faculty. The fact that the most prestigious universities will already be involved in deals, only reinforces the need for latecomers to seek to deal individually with faculty who have great reputations or terrific courses—perhaps better than that provided by the brand name institutions.

Pedagogy. As with the source of content, the pedagogical approach of new entrants appears to be broad and eclectic. Clearly they are all introducing Internet-based on-line education, but few are relying exclusively on that technology for their pedagogy.

While Gary Becker can argue that the "Internet has potential to be the first major change in the (educational) process since Socrates,"[12] it is clear that current technology is not yet ideal for education, nor has the educational "killer app" been discovered. Many observers are waiting for the widespread adoption of broadband before expecting the breakthrough. When that happens, perhaps in the year 2005, sufficient bandwidth to the home will exist for streaming two-way video to be realistic. Yet even if that happens, asynchronous technologies may still require support from more traditional pedagogies. One study, for example, found that completion rates for an on-line course were raised from 25 percent without a tutor to 75 percent with a tutor (Russell, 1999). While much research is under way on the relative effectiveness of on-line education, the case that such pedagogy is universally better, and is optimally delivered without support from other pedagogies, has not yet been made convincingly.

The results of current technical inadequacies and the benefits of mixed modes of teaching suggest that entrants are perhaps correct in hedging their pedagogical approaches. Moreover, corporations are looking for a one-stop supplier of their training needs. Since some types of training will always remain best undertaken in the classroom, the pressure for entrants to offer a full range of pedagogies remains. While the Internet's pedagogical advantages are substantial, they are probably best not relied on exclusively.

Prices. Lastly, I want to examine the pricing strategy of the new entrants. It is here that entrants have the greatest potential to disturb the current environment of higher education. One of the great advantages of the new technology is that it allows for very low price courses, since the marginal cost of delivering a course, once the substantial initial investment in developing the material has been sunk, is negligible. In principle, entrants could destroy the price structure that traditional institutions have become accustomed to.

The great news for universities is that this is not happening! What evidence we have on pricing is that for comparable courses, entrants are selling at no more than 30 percent below a state school's price. The going rate appears to be between $300 and $600 per course, with most effectively charging about $500. One entrant, University Access, is even raising prices—charging $90,000 for its global MBA. Of course there are $40 courses on quilting available, and the much maligned correspondence schools will continue to offer degrees for a few thousand dollars, but for serious academic material provided by credible entrants, pricing is not dramatically below the current rate.

There are a number of reasons why entrants are not relying on price competition to get a foothold in the higher education business. In the first place, they do not want to kill the goose that lays the golden egg. Higher education is an attractive business in which to compete, and entrants want to benefit from the price umbrella, not destroy it. Second, entry is expensive, and after the collapse of the Internet bubble in 2000, even dotcom startups need to demonstrate profitability. While none have given up investing, all are striving to demonstrate that their business model can be cash positive sooner rather than later. Third, in the corporate market, which most are targeting, the indirect cost savings of asynchronous technologies are so substantial, that cutting prices for the course itself is unnecessary to make the financial case for companies to switch to the entrants. Merely avoiding classroom attendance saves sufficient travel expense and time on the job to effectively offer a 50 percent discount over traditional programs.

Finally, and perhaps most relevant for the liberal arts colleges, higher education is an experience-based good. Consumers do not know the quality of the education they will receive until after they have received that education. What this means is that the purchase decision involves perceptions and interpretations of signals about quality. One of the most visible signals is price. The assumption is that the higher the price, the better the education. For an entrant that lacks any brand awareness and that has no graduates who can be evaluated or surveyed, price becomes the major signal of quality. While entrants could support a low price strategy, such a strategy would be tarnished with a very negative association. "If it's as cheap as a correspondence school, it must be bad!"

The powerful implication for universities is that extensive price competition is unlikely to occur immediately. This is not to say that peripheral or struggling players will not resort to aggressive pricing, nor that low-cost courses for quilting and such like will not be available, nor that prices won't gradually come down as competition forces prices closer to costs. But what it does suggest is that there will be no sudden collapse of prices as entrants seek to gain market share.

CASE STUDY: CARDEAN UNIVERSITY

How many universities in the United States can boast of three Nobel Laureates on their faculty? By my—rough—calculation only about a dozen. Add a thirteenth—Cardean University.[13] Founded as UNext in 1998, this university now employs over three hundred individuals and is offering courses developed by the faculties at Columbia, Stanford, LSE, Chicago, and Carnegie Mellon, which since June of 2000 can culminate in the granting of an accredited MBA degree. Cardean intends to have invested over $100 million by the time it receives its first tuition revenue—from Barclays, the leading British bank, and yet has reportedly guaranteed a payment of $20 million to its first academic partner, Columbia University.

Cardean is the leading academic business of Knowledge Universe, which was founded by the 1980s financier Michael Milken and Larry Ellison, CEO of Oracle (Collis and Rukstad, 2001). Run by Chicago law professor and erstwhile entrepreneur Andrew Rosenfield,[14] and presided over by J. Gould, a former dean of the University of Chicago Business School, it is perhaps the most visible and best funded of the new players in higher education.

Cardean's strategy gained real momentum in March 1999 when Columbia Business School agreed to become a content provider and an investor. In return for providing courses and the use of the Columbia name (under conditions that Columbia could impose), the company agreed to change the name of the university and for Knowledge Universe to reduce its holding to 20 percent (in order to minimize the connection with Milken); to give Columbia 5 percent of its revenue in cash or stock, with a minimum guarantee of $20 million; and to give the school a board seat. One reason for consummating the deal was that it involved only the dean of the Business School. The agreement was signed without faculty approval.

Having the commitment of one premier institution opened the floodgates, and Cardean has since signed on Chicago, Stanford, LSE, and Carnegie Mellon, although this time with more faculty involvement and disagreement. Students began enrolling in summer 2000, and the company is now a live competitor in higher education.

Courses. The initial twenty-five courses offered by Cardean are all traditional MBA subjects such as accounting and marketing. Each course is divided into relatively short modules, with four or five such modules representing a semester's course. While these courses can culminate in the earning of an MBA degree, students are free to take the individual courses. This means that students are expected already to have undergraduate degrees, and that the material is pitched at the graduate level. Future offerings will include courses in engineering from Stanford and international relations from the London School of Economics. Other courses, including the humanities, are to be offered "later," although some courses have been precluded from the university—medical courses, for example—because of their need for laboratories.

Like many entrants in the business course market, Cardean has found that the preferred course length is very short. Rather than a full semester, or even a quarter-length course, corporations are asking for three- to five-hour "courselets" (or even less). These are designed to be "consumed" at one sitting, and yet to convey the essence of a subject, such as "the Internet."

Customers. Cardean has consciously targeted the corporate, Fortune 1000, market, not the individual market, "because that is where the money is" (Snoody, 2000). Its first large client—the British bank, Barclays—has signed up for one thousand employees. Another large customer is expected to be AT Kearney, the consulting firm. In addition to the reasons advanced above for focusing on corporations, Cardean recognizes that it can exploit employee use of corporate intranets to facilitate the speed of transmission and community building.

Cardean's second target market is the individual in foreign countries. The company is very clear that there is a huge unmet demand from foreigners for a U.S. education. Currently half a million foreign students a year attend American universities and colleges, but Cardean's estimates suggest that three to five times that number would have liked the opportunity to study in the United States. While expense is one barrier, access is even more intimidating for many potential overseas students. Being able to serve large numbers of these customers in their own countries can both open a very large untapped market and reduce the expense that such countries would have in building their own campus-based institutions.

Domestic postgraduates are the third market Cardean intends to pursue, since most of the initial course offerings are at the graduate level. Individuals seeking undergraduate education are not yet specifically targeted, perhaps because there is research that shows they are price sensitive when it comes to choosing distance over campus education.

Content. As its high-profile deals with universities suggests, Cardean is primarily sourcing its course content from existing material and through negotiations with institutions rather than individual faculty. To have the marketing benefit of each university's brand, Cardean appears to be accepting that intellectual copyright vests with institutions. However, the intent is not just to put a lecture-based course on line but also to adapt to a new pedagogy that features learning by doing, or "problem based learning." As a result, faculty at the sponsoring institutions provide the outline of the course content, but Cardean employees design the learning exercises and the Web applications so that the material fits the Cardean learning style. Faculty, however, do have the chance to review those in-house adaptations and developments. It is recognized that there is a unique approach to, and a steep learning curve in, designing courses for the Web, so that permanent employees of Cardean are expected to be the experts in learning psychology, student computer interfaces, and so forth. Course development costs are estimated at up to $1 million per semester-length course, and the company claimed to have already spent $80 million before it opened its doors to students.

Pedagogy. While all the courses are designed to be taken over the Web, they feature a "problem based learning" style and are supported by adjunct faculty—postgraduates hired by Cardean who act as on-line mentors to students, answering e-mails and grading assignments. An important part of the experience is expected to be not just the faculty-student relationship but also, through the use of group work and problems, the establishment of student-student learning that helps build a community on-line. Students will be assessed through on-line assignments and participation in on-line discussions, with some degree of differentiation being made in student performance.

Prices. Tuition costs are designed to be about 80 percent of a traditional university, with a volume discount for corporations. At about forty-five credits for an MBA. this means that courses cost between $500 and $2,000.

With this strategy, Cardean appears to exemplify the logical approach to entering the higher education market. It is following a path that begins by selling business courses to the corporate market, with content outsourced from brand name institutions and priced a little below current market rates. Later steps allow for expanding course content and target markets to additional areas, although, importantly, it is domestic undergraduate programs that appear to be the lowest Cardean priority.

Cardean is distinguished from other entrants in the financial resources it has already committed and can continue to draw on,[15] and by the number and status of its university affiliations. While no guarantee of success, in a business with economics that suggest the "winner takes all," such an early mover with financial resources and brand recognition will be hard to overthrow—if it can deliver a quality product.

TRADITIONAL UNIVERSITIES AND COLLEGES

While there are many experiments and adaptations of the traditional university and college model under way, the set I want to focus on concern the use of technology in courses, both on campus and for distance learning. It is these new approaches that are underpinning the revolution in the institutions themselves. I will not describe the specific pedagogical uses of technology, but rather will concentrate on its strategic deployment by these institutions.

A university campus today is one of the most wired places on earth. Students constitute 24 percent of the adult Web-using population (Merrill Lynch, 2000), since 90 percent of them use the Web (52 percent use it daily, and more than 50 percent have access from their dorm rooms; *Student Monitor*, 1998). Even the notoriously conservative faculty have got on board the technology wagon. Eighty percent of professors use the web for one aspect or another of their activities (Merrill Lynch, 2000). Fifty percent of courses use e-mail (up from 8 percent in 1994). Forty percent use Web resources for their classes (up from 25 percent in 1997), and between 25 and 30 percent of faculty have class Web pages for use in courses (up from 9 percent in 1996).

At the institution level, 62 percent of surveyed universities and colleges offered some form of distance learning in 1998, and 78 percent of those were Internet based (Hamm, 2000). Indeed, there are reputed to be five hundred virtual universities in existence, and six thousand accredited courses are now offered on-line (Merrill Lynch, 2000). The government has even validated distance learning under its experimental provision of financial aid for students attending a group of thirteen universities who are offering such courses. Projections suggest that 84 percent of institutions of higher education will offer distance learning by the end of 2002 (International Data Corporation, 2000).

To support these initiatives, universities and colleges spent $305 million on distance education in 1998 (International Data Corporation, 1999), or $128,000 per institution. The majority of this expenditure was on infrastructure, and only 21 percent was spent on content (which is nevertheless the largest single item of expenditure).

The result of all this activity in terms of current enrollment, is that distributed learning covered 710,000 students in 1998 and is projected to reach 2.2 million students by 2003 (International Data Corporation, 2000). The total on-line higher education market of $1.2 billion in 1999 will reach $7 billion by that same date (Merrill Lynch, 2000). In total it is projected that 5 percent of education will be on-line by 2005 (National Institute of Standards and Technology, quoted in Piper Jaffray, 1999; and OECD, quoted in First Union Securities, 2000).

BUSINESS MODELS AND STRATEGIES

Although I have less data to share about the business models of universities, partly because readers know their own institutions better than I can ever hope to, I would classify the strategies of the incumbent institutions that have produced the numbers described above into four categories.[16] In ascending order of innovation they are:

1. Incremental—Technology is being applied on campus as a complement to the existing classroom experience. In this category are included initiatives like the creation of Web pages for courses, and adding Web sites as reference material into reading lists and curricula.

While enormously beneficial in terms of the educational experience, these initiatives have little influence on the competitive landscape because they are internal to each institution.

2. Distance education—In order to expand the geographic reach of the institution and to make the provision of education more convenient for students, particularly those who are distant from a campus, many schools are entering distance education. Initially this involves offering the most "on-line" courses that are taught on campus—usually computer science related—to students who must also attend some classes. Later it involves the development of course materials that are designed for distance education with minimal physical interaction between the student and the campus. Importantly, the target customer remains the traditional individual student, who is now offered a more convenient alternative for earning a degree.

This approach has been widely adopted by community colleges, which appreciate the ability to expand, at relatively low cost, in accordance with their mission. Indeed, in a number of states, community colleges are collaborating to develop a broader set of on-line courses.[17]

While such moves remove previous geographic constraints on student enrollment and so should increase competition, it seems to me that there are two reasons why they will produce limited immediate impact. Premier institutions that already compete geographically have not yet taken the plunge into offering on-line degrees because they fear brand name dilution. They prefer to earn revenue by partnering with the new entrants. In contrast, most state schools, which would happily expand their number of graduates, appear to be offering distance education within state, to students who have difficulty reaching a campus or other physical facility, rather than competing with each other across state borders. Currently it appears that the distance learning offerings of universities and colleges may well increase the overall market size by better serving a previously underserved market, but do not yet threaten an outbreak of real market competition.

3. Alliances—The next expansion of activity by universities involves entering an alliance that allows a third party to resell an institution's courses more aggressively and into new markets. This is the strategy that most effectively and quickly leverages a university's brand name and existing course content with the least risk, with minimal expenditure of time and money, and with minimal objection from faculty. It also preserves the exclusivity of the institution's own degree, while still earning revenue from its intellectual content.

Because of its attraction a number of leading institutions have pursued this approach. The list now includes, among others, Harvard, Chicago, Stanford, Columbia, Duke, UNC Chapel-Hill, Carnegie Mellon, NYU, London School of Economics, Northwestern, MIT, UCLA, Penn, USC, London Business School, Johns Hopkins, George Mason, and UT Austin. Most of these alliances involve individual schools (unsurprisingly, usually the business school), rather than the entire university, and most ventures have invoked some degree of faculty resistance. Nevertheless their ubiquity suggests how desirable the strategy has become. Columbia now has five on-line partners for its various initiatives (Industry Standard, 2000).

Since the partners for these institutions are initially targeting the corporate and lifelong learning markets, the effect of these moves on the core business of most universities and colleges will again be delayed.

4. Market Entry—The final step, which fewer institutions have yet taken, is to enter the new markets themselves without the benefit of a partner. In this model the university itself bears all the risk and has the task of establishing a new venture itself. So far there have been few of these ventures; Harvard and Columbia have been at the forefront of these activities with HBSi and Morningside Ventures.

As with the private sector entries, these university-generated entries appear to be more directed to the corporate market, again lessening their immediate impact.

The four categories described above are not mutually exclusive, since many institutions, including probably your own, are experimenting with some, if not all, of the above strategies. It is, however, still a useful categorization of approaches because they can be thought of as outlining the evolutionary path that universities and colleges will follow. Just as we can envisage a natural progression to the activities of entrants—from the corporate market to the liberal arts undergraduate degree—so we can expect to observe a sequence in the response of incumbents as they initially adapt technology internally; use it to serve current customers better; then seek the help of others to put their toe into new markets, before finally taking the risk of committing themselves to a new business opportunity.

This evolutionary path is best exemplified by a more detailed look at the Harvard Business School.

CASE STUDY: HARVARD BUSINESS SCHOOL

At Harvard the separate schools sit as "tubs on their own bottoms." This model of decentralized control allows enormous freedom for each school to pursue its own business model. Leading the charge into the new economy, the Harvard Business School has pursued all four of the strategies outlined above over the last five years.

In the core MBA curriculum there has been a heavy emphasis on the use of course technology under the guidance of the current dean, who came from the technology group within the school. All courses are now supported on-line with a standard course platform (developed in-house), although this remains primarily an administrative convenience rather than a pedagogical tool. The school remains wedded to the case method of instruction. Partly as a result, and unlike some other business schools, there has been no effort to extend courses to distance education. The Harvard MBA remains firmly a campus-based degree.[18] To this market—the individual—the school's strategy can be thought of as using technology to supplement (admittedly in limited ways) traditional classroom-based teaching.

In executive education—the corporate market—in addition to the traditional open enrollment courses, the school has introduced and rapidly grown its custom programs for individual corporations. These are designed for the very top of the corporate training market. Courses are explicitly not the rote repetition of specific skills training, but education that contributes to real strategic change in each organization. Harvard now generates over $65 million in annual revenue from such executive programs.

The other innovation in executive education has been the introduction of a global program for managers. This is the school's first real venture into distance learning under its own brand and control, since students spend some time on campus but then work together on-line while back in their individual companies and countries. Note that this initiative is targeted to the corporate market.

With its publishing group, Harvard Business School has always made its content available to other schools and corporations, for them to incorporate into their own courses. While the publishing group has become more sophisticated in its packaging of cases and articles—for example, allowing faculty at other institutions to customize a course packet and then download and print it locally with their own logos, and packaging the same content into multiple media—the shift has been to allow partners, like Pensare, to resell the material as a course. Through an alliance the school can, therefore, capture a revenue stream from the emerging markets while controlling its own brand and not diluting its degree.

Finally, the school is now entering the on-line education market itself with a venture called HBSi, which will be a direct competitor in the corporate market for distance learning (ibid.).

OTHER UNIVERSITIES AND COLLEGES

Harvard Business School is very much pursuing all four strategies, with the notable exception of refusing to offer a degree to anyone who has not had the traditional campus education. Other premier universities and colleges can pursue, and are pursuing, the same strategies, leveraging their brand name and intellectual capital to establish a presence in new markets with willing and aggressive partners.

The issue is, where does that leave most institutions, which lack the brand to appeal to entrants looking for credible partners, and without the expertise or resources to penetrate the most attractive new markets themselves, particularly when their best (course development) faculty are trying to claim copyright and cut independent deals with entrants?

What these universities and colleges are doing is to push into the distance education market for individuals in the United States, most often in their home states. This extends their market with little concern about the exclusivity of the degree. While appropriate, this strategic move raises a question of who will win in the long term. Will it be entrants exploiting the corporate market and then moving into the traditional university market, or institutions that have begun to go after the individual distance learning market?

To me the answer depends on the relative attractiveness of the two markets on a number of dimensions. First, how big and fast growing is each market? This dimension favors the entrants, since projections for on-line corporate training (broadly defined) are higher than for traditional on-line education. As argued above, this is because the benefits to corporations of on-line learning are greater and more obvious than to individuals, so that its adoption will be more rapid. Second is the profitability of the two markets. Here again, I suspect that, for successful entrants, the corporate market is more attractive. Corporations recognize the indirect cost saving of the new pedagogies and are not expecting a huge reduction in tuition prices. Individuals choosing between distance and campus learning are more price-sensitive.[19]

The third and perhaps most important dimension is the technological trajectory that each market will drive. Here again, I think the corporate market is more demanding and so will produce more rapid innovation and developments. While universities basically expect individual faculty to use their own initiative and funding to exploit the new technologies and develop new pedagogies, the entrants are being pushed by demanding and powerful clients to spend the resources to truly exploit the new media. With course development budgets of $1 million directed toward adapting already high quality intellectual content to the new technologies, it seems to me that entrants will be the ones pushing the envelope and learning at a faster rate. As a result, they will be building the capabilities needed to succeed when they enter the traditional university market.

To be blunt, the market that the majority of institutions can go after—individuals through distance learning—is in the short term not the easiest to grow, the most profitable, nor necessarily the best place to learn the skills for competing with the new pedagogies.

For a limited number of top institutions this state of affairs is fine. They can get the best of both worlds, reigning supreme in their own domain while sharing in the benefits of the new markets. However, for the majority, while new entrants do not pose a concern in the short term since competition will be limited and their market will in fact be expanding, in the long term incumbents could be badly hurt by entrants and branded universities whose strategies evolve to the point where they do compete more directly.

Implications and Conclusions

As I indicated at the beginning of the paper, there are two sets of conclusions that I believe can be drawn from these analyses.

First, the direct competitive threat to most of the traditional core offerings of universities and colleges will be delayed. Entrants are coming into the corporate market offering "business" courses and specific skills training at a graduate level and at only slightly lower prices. That is the good news for universities. Institutions have time to prepare for the coming onslaught.

On the other hand, well-funded competitors, often backed by the brand name institutions through an alliance, will be hard to beat once they are established. First mover advantages that they can exploit, particularly the rapid accumulation of the skills needed to harness the new technologies and develop new pedagogies, will put them in good stead as they gradually transition their strategies to compete more directly in the traditional higher education market.

Thus, even if the overall conclusion is that there is a less immediate threat than we might have imagined from new entrants and new technologies, that threat is potentially more insidious because when it becomes obvious the game may already be over. Universities cannot argue that current plans for holding back the water are adequate because the tide is not yet full. By the time the tide arrives, the opportunity to halt it may have passed.

Notes

1. Many of the new start-ups appear to have randomly selected two or three from a list of only about six words—global, network, learning, education, net, mind: as, for example, Global Learning Net.

2. The very fact that research firms as well as many brokerages now cover the higher education arena indicates the degree of private sector interest in the field.

3. Each firm has its own scheme for classifying companies, and I have taken a stricter definition of content than they applied. As a result, the actual number of companies entering higher education is larger than the 127 mentioned above.

4. One brokerage suggested that there are five thousand e-training companies: Hambrecht & Co., 2000.

5. Generally speaking, data were available for over half the firms on any particular dimension. Pricing was the exception, and here the data are somewhat more arbitrary.

6. Percentages are calculated as a share of the total number of institutions. As no revenue numbers are available, it is impossible to calculate a sales weighted distribution. However, 63 percent of the best known and best financed start-ups, such as Cardean, Jones International, Pensare, and Sylvan, have begun with a business content focus.

7. Percentages add to more than 100 since some companies state that they are targeting two primary markets.

8. A fourth source of content is to have no content at all, but merely to be a "Yellow Pages" that lists all the content provided by others. Petersons, for example, follows this strategy.

9. UCLA, for example, asks the permission of its faculty before putting courses on line.

10. Indeed, while UNext was signing up Chicago University, University Access was making deals with individual Chicago faculty.

11. Entrants spend substantial sums on courses even when adapting existing course material. Many are spending at least six figures on each course.

12. This is a quotation that appears to denigrate the importance of the discovery of the printing press.

13. Strictly speaking, the Nobel Laureates are on the board of advisors, not on the faculty.

14. Rosenfield had previously founded Lexecon, a legal consulting firm.

15. No other educational content start-up has yet raised $100 million in venture capital, although subsidiaries of existing corporations, like Thomson and Pearson, potentially have access to more financial resources.

16. These categories are not based on data analysis but represent my interpretation of strategies I have observed.

17. One example is the Virtual College of Texas, a consortium of fifty-one community and technical colleges.

18. Nor has Harvard chosen to internationalize the campus. In contrast, INSEAD, for example, now has a Singapore location, and Chicago offers courses in Barcelona and Singapore.

19. This figure is based on confidential market research for WebCT.

References

Christensen, C. M. 1997. "The Innovator's Dilemma." Boston: Harvard Business School Press.

Collis, D. J. 1999. "When Industries Change: Scenarios for Higher Education." In J. W. Meyerson and M. Devlin (eds.), *Forum Futures, 1999: Forum Strategy Series, Volume 2*. New Haven: Forum for the Future of Higher Education.

———. 2001. "When Industries Change: New Scenarios for Higher Education." Rev. ed. In M. E. Devlin and J. W. Meyerson (eds.), *Forum Futures: Exploring the Future of Higher Education, 2000*. San Francisco: Jossey-Bass.

Collis, D. J., and M. Rukstad. 2001. "UNext.com: Business Education and eLearning." Harvard Business School case #701-014. Cambridge, MA: Harvard Business School.

Credit Suisse First Boston. 2000. "e-Learning: Power for the Knowledge Economy." Boston: Credit Suisse. (March 10).

First Union Securities. 2000. "E-Education Industry." Richmond, VA: First Union Securities. (May 26).

Hambrecht and Co. 2000. "Corporate eLearning: Exploring a New Frontier." San Francisco: Hambrecht and Co. (March).

Hamm, S. 2000. "The Wired Campus." *Business Week* (December 11): (eb)105.

Harvard Magazine. 2000. "Distance Learning @Harvard.edu." (July–Aug.): 74–78.

Industry Standard. 2000. "Grok: Special Reports on the Internet Economy." San Francisco: Standard Media International. (October).

International Data Corporation. 1999a. "Online Distance Learning in Higher Education 1998–2002." Boston: International Data Corporation.

———. 1999b. "Higher Education Institutions Survey." Boston: International Data Corporation.

———. 2000. "The US Corporate eLearning Market Forecast 1998–2003." Boston: International Data Corporation. (January).

Merrill Lynch. 1999. "The Knowledge Web." San Francisco: Merrill Lynch. (May 23).

———. 2000. "The Book of Knowledge." San Francisco: Merrill Lynch. (April 9).

Newman, A. 2000. "Venture Dollars Get Smarter." Boston: Eduventures.com. (September).

Piper Jaffray. 1999. "Helping Investors Climb the eLearning Curve." Minneapolis: U.S. Bancorp Piper Jaffray. (November).

Russell, T. 1999. "The No Significant Difference Phenomenon." Raleigh: North Carolina State University, Office of Instructional Telecommunications.

Snoody, R. 2000. "Nobel Laureates and Junk Bond King Are Backers of the Cardean Philosophy." *Business Week* (July 1): 101.

Student Monitor. 1998. "Computing." Ridgewood, NJ: Student Monitor. (Fall).

Symonds, W. C. 2000. "Education Industry Outlook 2000." *Business Week* (January 10).

Training Magazine. 1999. (October): 26.

PART III

Continuity and Change in
Fields of Knowledge

CHAPTER EIGHT

The Disciplines and the Future

ANDREW ABBOTT

In this chapter I provide a framework for understanding the present status and likely future development of the academic disciplines. There are many who believe that the intellectual world is today in a special ferment, one that will transcend disciplines in ways hitherto unimagined. By contrast, I shall argue that there is little new about current interdisciplinary ferment and that, absent major change in the social structure of the university, there is little likelihood that the disciplinary system will change much. Insofar as the departmental and major structure remains intact, the changing demographics and resource dependencies of the university will have little fundamental impact on the conduct of academic research in the disciplines. By contrast, the long-established strategies of researchers for establishing prominent positions within their specialty fields will continue to have important effects on the conduct of research and the development of the disciplines. For this reason, it is essential to understand the logic of career-building within the context of disciplinary organization.

The first four sections of this chapter establish the theoretical bases for my argument.[1] The final one examines the empirical premises for expecting social structural change that could undermine the system in the future. Here I will focus primarily on the probable consequences of further massification of enrollments and capitalist rationalization of knowledge production.

My argument draws somewhat on theoretical conceptions developed elsewhere, but I shall summarize them here as necessary. I will focus principally on the social sciences and humanities, since these fields share a common position in the larger university. None of them is more than marginally an applied field, and none of them, with the possible exception of economics, is the recipient of the massive infusions of cash that tend to dictate the directions of the natural sciences. I am also more familiar with these disciplines, and in particular with the social sciences.

I begin by underscoring the unusual quality of the American disciplinary system as a social structure. I then examine it as a cultural system, a discussion that leads naturally into a brief comment on the history of interdisciplinarity. On the basis of these analyses, I can assess the overall strengths and weaknesses of the division of labor embodied in disciplines. The chapter then examines conditions, both cultural and social structural, that could lead to serious transformation of the system. This final section of the chapter is speculative, relying in part on interpolation of trends.

The Disciplinary System

For the last century, the list of disciplines has been remarkably constant. The departmental structure of the American university has remained largely unchanged since its creation between 1890 and 1910. Biology, it is true, has fractured into a number of departments, a differentiation produced by the immense resources flowing into biological research. But in the humanities and social sciences, the departmental map has shown only marginal change in the last sixty to eighty years. In the humanities, the only major changes are the astonishingly slow withering of Classics and the intermittent appearance of Linguistics and Comparative Literature. In the social sciences, too, there is little change: merger or separation of some departments at some places and times, the occasional appearance of Statistics and Linguistics among the social sciences, but little else. Moreover, the relative proportions of university faculties in these departments are surprisingly stable, although the steady increase of applied or semiapplied fields—Education, Communication, Business, Accounting, Engineering, and so on—has made the traditional liberal arts and sciences faculty a smaller proportion of the whole (Veysey, 1965).

This enduring social structure of academic labor is internationally unique. The departmental structure within universities appeared only in America, although since midcentury it has gradually spread elsewhere.

Academic disciplines in the American sense—groups of professors with exchangeable credentials collected in strong associations—did not really appear outside the United States until well into the postwar period.

A glance at other systems during the formative epoch of the modern university—the late nineteenth and early twentieth centuries—can help explain why the American system has its peculiar power. In Germany, the professoriat was organized much more individualistically. Universities were divided into faculties, which in turn comprised individual chairs. Most teaching faculty fell under the official control of the few chaired professors. These professors controlled the research institutes, which covered not the broad areas of American disciplines, but areas of particular interest to the chair involved. Germany had many universities, each relatively small and each independent of others. Expansion was slow. Taken together, these ecological and structural facts meant that academic careers advanced through the patronage of chairs, via continuous interuniversity moves seeking higher rank. Rising academics took doctorates in generic fields—doctorates of philosophy or arts rather than of English or Economics, because these allowed broader ranges of opportunity for employment. When moving, professors often changed titular fields even though their research interests might change little or not at all. As a result the German system produced intense research dedication, but nothing resembling the American disciplinary division of turf; Political Economy might mean quite different things at different universities (Jarausch, 1982, 1983; McClelland, 1980. See also Ben-David and Collins, 1966).

In France, as in Germany, chairs tended to have enormous power and impact. But France lacked the research institute structure. Academic careers proceeded by moves around the provinces aiming at ultimate return to Paris. Such careers might traverse universities, lycees, and even other areas in the civil service. Central to career advance were patronage groups or clusters, which like careers tended to cross several organizations. Durkheim's group is an excellent example of such a patronage cluster. Given this clientilism, in France also there was little foundation for disciplines (Suleiman, 1978; Weisz, 1983. See also Clark, 1973).

In England, the great universities were strongly antivocational and, more often than not, antiresearch. They were dominated by the colleges within them, which, like the research institutes in Germany and patronage clusters in France, were intermediate institutions organizing individuals within—and also beyond—the university. Academic careers unfolded within the patronage structure of a particular college, a structure reaching into secondary schools, the various professions, the civil service, the church, and the other colleges of the universities themselves. Such careers involved no formal credentialing until quite recently. The division of labor with respect to knowledge was dictated less by a structure of disciplines than by the content of the undergraduate honors examinations. Since these were not standardized (even between Oxford and Cambridge) and bore little relation to research fields, they provided little foundation for the development of disciplines (Green, 1974; Rothblatt, 1968).

In the United States, a peculiar conjuncture fostered the growth of academic disciplines as social structures. First, as in Germany the universities were numerous and decentralized. Second, throughout the period in which the modern disciplines were formed, faculty employment was expanding rapidly. Third, as part of their own mobility projects, aspiring professions began to view arts and sciences degrees as prerequisites for professional schooling. All these forces together meant that American universities had schools of arts and sciences that were rapidly expanding but that lacked any real internal structure. These were expected to be undergraduate educational institutions on the British model (but on a much larger scale) at the same time as they were to be graduate research institutions on the German model. The dual functions and rapid growth made some sort of internal organization necessary. Since the hierarchy of the European universities was unacceptable to democratic America, American universities compromised by creating departments of equals. The Ph.D. degree, borrowed from Germany, became a Ph.D. "in something." This specific disciplinary degree provided a medium of exchange between particular subunits of different universities. There was thus completed a subsystem of structures and exchanges organizing universities internally while providing for extensive but structured career mobility externally, between institutions. Exactly coincident with this departmentalization of the university was the formation of the national disciplinary societies (Oleson and Voss, 1978; Ross, 1991).

The extraordinary resilience of the American system of academic disciplines lies in its dual institutionalization. On the one hand, the disciplines constitute the macrostructure of the labor market for faculty. Careers remain within discipline much more than within university. On the other hand, the system constitutes the microstructure of each individual university. All arts and sciences faculties contain more or less the same list of departments. This duality means that no university can challenge the disciplinary system as a whole without depriving its Ph.D. graduates of their academic future. Universities can perhaps cancel a department here and there or perhaps merge two departments (like Sociology and Anthropology). But even these minor gestures reflect fluctuations in resources more than willingness to challenge fundamental employment structures. The serious challenges have nearly all failed.

Moreover, the dual structure of disciplines implies that even were all universities somehow to agree to abolish one or another particular discipline, the other disciplines would just fill in the intellectual (and curricular) space that it used to occupy. The system of disciplines, that is, could easily survive the destruction of one or even several of its elements. In reality, even that destruction requires impossible levels of coordination. Universities in fact delegate all hiring decisions to departments. As long as departmental (and hence disciplinary) academics act as the primary hiring agents for universities, they perpetuate the disciplinary system by seeking faculty for their own departments largely from within their own disciplines. Occasionally, differentiation occurs because of immense inflows of money. Sometimes an applied field soaks up disciplinary territory. But absent any radical change in the process of academic hiring, the current social structure of disciplines will endlessly re-create itself.

Also crucial to this immobility is the role of disciplines in American undergraduate education. The most consequential single disciplinary structure—in terms of extent and impact—is not the professional association but the college major. All but a handful of American colleges and universities have majors, and in all but a handful of those that do, disciplinary majors house a large share of undergraduates. The more prestigious the university, the greater this share. And among most students, the arts and science majors remain the most prestigious if not necessarily the most popular.

The system of undergraduate majors spread very quickly at the turn of this century, at exactly the same time as the departmental system. (Pedagogically, majors were thought to be a cure for the perceived excesses of the elective system.) The major system has never since been questioned. Indeed, it has never really been debated, probably because allocating the undergraduate curriculum on some basis other than majors raises unthinkable questions about faculty governance and administration. Most universities use student numbers in majors and in departmentally administered service courses to allocate the most crucial resource of all—faculty positions. There have been occasional attempts to get rid of majors; nearly all have failed (Ellingson, 1995; see also Blumstein, 1990; MacAloon, 1992; McNeill, 1991).

The American system of disciplines thus seems uniquely powerful. Because of their extraordinary ability to organize in one single structure research fields, individual careers, faculty hiring, and undergraduate education, disciplinary departments are the essential and irreplaceable building blocks of American universities.

Disciplines also serve important general cultural functions for academics. (Their more specific cultural characteristics are described in the next section.) The first of these is the Geertzian function of providing academics with a general conception of intellectual existence, a conception of the proper units of knowledge. Disciplines provide dreams and models both of reality and of learning. They give images of coherent discourse. Every academic knows the experience of reading work from outside his or her discipline and knows the unsettling feeling it induces. Disciplines in fact provide a core element of the identity of most intellectuals in modern America.

A second cultural function of disciplines is that of preventing knowledge from becoming too abstract or overwhelming. Disciplines legitimate our necessarily partial knowledge. They define what it is permissible not to know and thereby limit the body of books one must have read. They provide a specific tradition and lineage. They provide common sets of research practices that unify groups with diverse substantive interests. Often, these various limits and canons are quite arbitrary. What matters is not the particular canonical writer or method but rather the legitimation of knowing only the one or the other.

In summary, disciplines as social structures are extremely solid because they are based on an organizational form—the department—that is as essential to the university as it is to the discipline it embodies. The department simultaneously organizes careers and curriculum. Beyond individual departments, disciplines provide crucial supports for and definition of academic and intellectual identity.

Cultural Structure

One of the things disciplines do not do, however, is place many constraints on the kinds of knowledge possible within them. The empirical reality, within the social sciences at least, is that work of nearly every kind is met in nearly all social sciences. Take methodology, for example. All the social sciences have quantitative research communities, although the one in anthropology is quite small. Sociology, psychology, and, surprisingly, economics all have traditions of experimental investigation. Ethnography is done by anthropologists, sociologists, and political scientists. Archival and other historical work is done in every social science but psychology.

Turning to bodies of theory, every social science but psychology has some version of Marxism. Every social science but economics has flirted with psychoanalysis. Every social science but anthropology has some kind of rational choice research tradition. Every social science but economics has a network analysis tradition. And so on. And so on. To be sure, the social science disciplines have axes of unity and characteristic types of work. But these axes are all of different kinds; they are not aligned hierarchically as are those of the natural sciences. Anthropology is largely organized around a method (ethnography), political science around a type of relationship (power), economics around a theory of action (choice under constraint and uncertainty), and sociology around an archipelago of particular subject matters. As a result, there is very little to keep the social sciences out of each other's intellectual hair. The situation is even worse in the humanities with their hazier disciplinary cultures. Indeed, the last twenty years have seen the humanists reinvent a great deal of qualitative social science. The blunt fact is that if we ignore a few markers like standard citations and rhetorical genres, the disciplinary origin of a particular piece of writing is often not very easy to predict.

In addition, there is in the social sciences a set of cultural structures that tend to drive all social sciences into one another's backyards. Much of social science (and of the humanities as well) is organized around a set of basic distinctions. These distinctions are familiar enough: positivism versus interpretation, narrative versus analysis, realism versus constructionism, and so on. What is unusual about them is that they function in a fractal manner. That is, they repeat within themselves at finer and finer levels. So we might think of history as based broadly on a narrative conception of social life and sociology, say, as based on an analytic one. But within each discipline there are both narrative and analytic research traditions, and indeed, within each one of those traditions there are narrative and analytic strands and so on. The positivism versus interpretation fractal that is usually thought to divide quantitative from qualitative sociological work is repeated right down to the bowels of quantitative work, where survey directors argue about questionnaire design with the same positivism-versus-interpretation language that they use in other contexts to divide themselves from the ethnography they deplore. These fractal distinctions are generally quite old. Most of them have been around at least since the celebrated *Methodenstreit* of the German universities in the late nineteenth century. C. P. Snow's "two cultures" argument captures a later instantiation of them. As Snow's title implied, they have usually been construed as either/or dichotomies. This is mistaken. It is precisely their fractal character—their ability to be scaled to any size—that makes them so useful. In negotiating the complexities of social scientific and humanistic knowledge, it is extremely helpful to have a dichotomy like positivism versus interpretation, because it saves our having to remember the exact degree of positivism of any scholarly group. We simply argue with any particular individual about the relative merits of positivism until we figure out exactly where he is placed relative to ourselves in the proliferating fractal tree, just as if we were talking to a distant cousin and figuring out exactly who is the common ancestor and whether we are in the same generation. The indexicality of these distinctions thus encapsulates huge systems of knowledge in compact form. But it also generates endless misunderstandings. For without that extended argument, we read words like "positivism" and "interpretation" as meaning whatever they mean in our local communities, even while the writers who use them may mean quite different things, having in mind quite different communities.

Diachronically, these distinctions reappear endlessly, with quite distinctive consequences. New generations are always using the same old debates to generate "new" paradigms. But these then end up dividing within themselves to produce the same old debates again. This means an immense amount of rediscovery (consider the number of articles entitled "bringing the X back in") and an equally immense (and equally confusing) amount of renaming.

Of course these processes work separately in the several disciplines. But they have a centrifugal tendency. They tend to spread academics out over an extended turf. Moreover, the fact that all the disciplines tend to work with a common heritage of such distinctions means that even starting in very different places and organizing themselves around different principles they have important commonalities. Every single social science discipline has internal debates about positivism/interpretation, narrative/analysis, and so on. The narrative/analytic debate may look very different in economics, anthropology, and English. But underneath all the surface differences it is quite similar.

The endless proliferation of these distinctions within disciplines, coupled with the relatively arbitrary directions and topics around which the disciplines were initially organized, means that most disciplines end up overlapping a great deal in terms of subject matter, theories, and methodologies. Usually overlaps of these varying kinds are not simultaneous, however. So economists and sociologists both write about poverty, but say different kinds of things. The two fields share many methodologies, but apply them to different areas. As a result, to the outsider (certainly to the poor undergraduates sitting in our classes) it seems that there is an immense amount of reciprocal ignorance among the humanities and social sciences; simply imagine what different things one would hear going to classes on poverty in the different disciplines, even though they are all talking about more or less the same phenomenon and using more or less the same underlying fractal distinctions.

In summary, the cultural system of the disciplines has a number of internal forces propelling it toward an extraordinary degree of proliferation and consequent overlap. The disciplinary fixity seen by so many proponents of interdisciplinarity is and long has been a mirage. As cultural systems the disciplines are astonishingly diverse internally, and that diversity so spreads them out into each other that to imagine that there are explicit disciplinary turfs is to make a profound mistake.

Interdisciplinarity

Given the first two pieces of my puzzle, the third should come as no surprise. If the social structure of disciplines appears nearly etched in stone while their cultural structure floats fairly free and flexible, then there should be a long history of concern with relations between disciplines. Why don't they talk more? Why don't they merge? Despite the recent hullabaloo, this issue too is a very old one. Indeed, a serious concern for interdisciplinarity is about as old as the disciplines themselves. The first OED quotation for "interdisciplinarity" is in 1937. But the Social Science Research Council and the Laura Spelman Rockefeller Foundation were already focused on the problem of eliminating barriers between the social sciences by the mid-1920s Thus, in the 1934 ten-year review of the SSRC: "The Council has felt a primary concern with the inter-discipline or interstitial project for the reason that new insights into social phenomena, new problems, new methods leading to advances in the scientific quality of social investigation, cross-fertilization of the social disciplines, were thought more likely to emerge here than from work in the center of established fields where points of view and problems and methodology have become relatively fixed" (Fisher, 1993: 35; SSRC, 1934: 6, 10). At the time that sentence was written (a decade after the foundation of the SSRC), the oldest specialized disciplinary associations in the social sciences—the American Historical Association and American Economic Association—were just two professional generations old, about fifty years. The American Political Science Association, the American Anthropological Association, and the American Sociological Association were all only a single generation old, about thirty years. Nor were any of these, except perhaps the historians, truly stable disciplines—disciplines complete with journals, undergraduate majors, uniformly independent departments, and national disciplinary labor markets—before World War I. In reality, the concern for interdisciplinarity emerged contemporaneously with, not after, the disciplines. There was no long process of ossification; the one bred the other almost immediately.

As it turned out, SSRC-based interdisciplinarity was something of a disappointment. Everyone approved of it, from the sociological purist Louis Wirth to the activist Robert Lynd, but no one really thought it a possibility, particularly not without strong foundations in the disciplines. Nonetheless, interdisciplinarism got another push from the war, which mixed the various social sciences indiscriminately in the OSS and other agencies. Psychology and psychoanalysis provided one of the strong bases for interdisciplinarity in this era (probably because half of American social scientists were in analysis and the other half were reading about it). The "culture and personality" school—reaching its apogee in Ruth Benedict's *Patterns of Culture*—was a product of this era of interdisciplinarity. After the war, in one of the stranger twists of interdisciplinarity, the MIT cybernetics group, with a strong assist from the Macy Foundation, pushed control theory as a unifying interdisciplinary paradigm, plugging into the core of the culture and personality group—Margaret Mead, Lawrence Frank, and Gregory Bateson. Talcott Parsons's general theory of action was yet another totalizing interdisciplinary paradigm of that period.[2]

Nonetheless, the 1950s apparently saw some retreat for interdisciplinarity, perhaps because the extraordinarily rapid expansion of academia in that decade created disciplinary positions for all new Ph.D.s and focused attention on the home disciplines. Elizabeth Bott remarked in *Family and Social Network*: "Ten years ago interdisciplinary research was very much in vogue. But now its value is often questioned, partly because it has proved difficult to coordinate interdisciplinary group projects, partly too because such projects have not always produced the spectacular integration of results that was expected" (Bott, 1957: 36). The 1960s were, however, an interdisciplinary bonanza, as the modernization paradigm swept development studies in anthropology, sociology, economics, and political science. Enormous multidisciplinary teams took on major problems, often the very questions that had driven the first wave of interdisciplinarity at SSRC in the 1920s: population, area studies, agriculture, development, and similar topics. At the same time, moreover, the first glimmerings of social science history appeared, and by the mid-1970s a broad and interdisciplinary "historic turn" was under way throughout the social sciences.[3]

Quantitative measures, so far as we have them, show the same constancy to interdisciplinarity. The frequency of titles including the word "interdisciplinary" in the Social Sciences Citation Index appears to be more or less constant over the last forty years.

Thus, interdisciplinarity has a long and more or less stable history. It has always seemed like a revolution manqué. Everybody always thinks it is a great thing, but nobody has figured out a way to make it work as a formalized, permanent structure.

The Disciplinary Division of Labor

A long historical process has thus resulted in a more or less steady, institutionalized structure in American academia: a social structure of flexibly stable disciplines, to which is attached an extremely complex and loose cultural structure of disciplines, the whole permeated by a perpetual hazy buzz of interdisciplinarity. We must now ask why that system seems so indestructible. As we shall see, the crucial forces involved are of three kinds. There are pressures keeping the disciplines from amalgamating and growing larger. There are also pressures that keep them from subdividing to grow smaller. Finally, there is the comparative weakness of the competitive pressure from other structures serving the same kinds of functions. A first set of preserving forces arise in the general cultural functions of disciplines. For example, I noted that disciplines legitimate partial knowledge, reducing the insufferable welter of learning into comprehensible traditions. The reality is that excessive size would eventually overwhelm scholars' ability to command the material of their fields; there is an obvious problem of overload. This is one consistent cultural force pressing to keep disciplines to a "reasonable" size.

By contrast, the identity functions of disciplines maintain the system because the disciplines are so much better at them than the competition. I have noted that disciplines provide models of learning and images of coherent discourse. Without them, an important sector—probably the most important—of American intellectual life would lose definition and stability. On this argument, disciplines survive because they offer clear and more or less stable career identities to the intellectually ambitious. Of course such an argument explains structures only if alternative structures are lacking or uncompetitive. But there are in truth few alternative sources for these intellectual identities. With the exception of the print and screen media there is no other focal point for intellectual life in America. Like interdisciplinary studies, the media world turns its subjects over much faster than does departmentalized academia, forcing its members to redefine themselves faster than their academic brethren. Moreover, the media world is somewhat smaller, and its denizens have less direct control of their conditions of production than do academics. All of this makes media intellectualism a higher risk matter and defines academic life with its inevitable disciplines as the stable foundation for intellectuals in America. In this sense, disciplines work better than their main competitor, or, put better, they divide the function of supporting intellectual life, providing the larger, low-risk foundation, while direct intellectual work in the media provides a smaller, higher-risk superstructure.

It should be noted too that a surprising amount of media content in elite venues comes in fact from people with some sort of academic appointment. For many such writers, academia represents social structural stability. Because of tenure, academic positions are sinecures: firm positions with but few fixed demands. They permit extraordinary roaming both within and beyond the cultural realm of academia. Thus disciplines combine the solidity of academic appointments with a nearly unlimited cultural purview. Indeed the cultural system of academia, with its perpetual fractal redefinitions, is itself ideally suited to career-building, even within academia alone. The systematic drift of fractals gives to each generation the pleasure of overturning its elders, yet does not in any way fundamentally change the basic repertoire of ideas. Cumulation is deftly avoided by perpetual redefinition, and young people are thus virtually guaranteed successful generational turnover. Yet the foundational tools with which this work is done never change much, so the disciplines retain the best of what they uncover.

The strong overlap between disciplines also means that the disciplines can perpetually renew and challenge each other. They are too big to ignore each other completely, yet too small to overwhelm each other. Career interests again are crucial to this curious linkage. Scholars who may seem to be in the hinterlands or backwaters of their home disciplines are often cheek by jowl with the leaders of other disciplines and hence in a position to borrow from them highly developed techniques that can reroute their own mainstreams. The flood of durational methods through the quantitative social sciences, and of anthropological theory and demographic methods through history, followed this pattern. Disciplines thus rejuvenate each other by a system of reciprocal theft that is facilitated by disciplinary overlap.[4] And this occurs through a system that provides adventurous intellects with a built-in way to excel—as interdisciplinary bricoleurs.

Disciplines also to some extent correct one another's absurdities. Economics and sociology, for example, have a rather curious reciprocal relationship in areas in which they copenetrate, as in studies of labor markets and human capital. Economists are usually clearer and more rigorous about their theories of labor market activity. Sociologists are usually more careful about data. The two criticize each other effectively. A similar reciprocal criticism has developed between anthropology and history for the last two decades. Again this system of correction probably works as well as it does because the disciplines are large but not too large. If they were tiny, they would affect only adjacent groups, and major ideas would take longer to percolate through the system. If they were large, there would not be enough independent bases within which to nurture new ideas.

There are other reasons why disciplines are unlikely to collapse into each other. Central to this separation is what we might call the misalignment of the disciplines. As I noted earlier, each major academic discipline has an axis of cohesion. In the humanities and social sciences, these axes are not aligned as they are in the natural sciences, where they make a natural hierarchy of generality. Quite the contrary. Consider the disciplines interested in culture. The heart of anthropology is its method, ethnography. The heart of cultural studies is the conception of text, which derives from its parent disciplines in literary studies. The political scientists writing about culture are shaped by their discipline's central allegiance to the phenomenon of power. There is thus no naturally "concentric" way for the boundaries of these disciplines to fit together, as would be the case in biochemistry or physical chemistry. They can easily get in each other's way, but they can't merge.

There are thus a large variety of forces keeping the disciplines from becoming too big. There are also a variety of ways in which a disciplinary knowledge system outperforms its most obvious competitors. What remains, however, is to understand why disciplinary knowledge doesn't come apart into smaller units, either through disciplinary specialization or through the problem-oriented structure that is the vision of most proponents of interdisciplinarity.

Of course, the beginnings of an argument against this interdisciplinary restructuring lie in the historical record; if interdisciplinarity were going to reorganize the university it would have done so long ago. Interdisciplinarity correlates not with change in university structure, but with stability. But there is another characteristic of interdisciplinarity that makes it unlikely to drive structural change. Interdisciplinarism has generally been problem-driven, and problems generally have their own life cycles. Most of them come from the political system, with its short-term imagination. Indeed, in the last thirty years the typical problem-driven interdisciplinary enthusiasm has lasted a considerably shorter time than a full academic career. It thus does not provide a good foundation for lifetime training or career building. There is ample evidence that problem-oriented empirical work does not create enduring, self-reproducing communities like disciplines except in areas with stable and strongly institutionalized external clienteles like criminology. Even there, the status differences seem to keep the disciplines in superior power. Criminology departments hire from sociology departments, but seldom vice versa.

Two other factors help prevent problem-driven interdisciplinarity from changing disciplinary structure. First, there is the stability of the academic labor market. It is true that if the academic labor market were completely problem-driven, disciplines might fail. But undergraduate education is generally not problem-driven and it—not graduate education or research—is the driving consideration in the staffing of contemporary American universities. As long as liberal education through majors remains a central goal in American undergraduate education, faculty will be hired to teach within the majors that their disciplines define.

But second, there are far more research problems than there are disciplines—so many, in fact, that a university organized around problems of investigation would be hopelessly balkanized. (Bear in mind, vis-à-vis an earlier argument, that such balkan "disciplines" would be quite able to ignore all but their immediate neighbors.) Furthermore, there do exist bodies of knowledge that can be used to address many different substantive problems. Such problem-portable knowledge is precisely what disciplines generate. To be sure, any particular disciplinary knowledge works better with some problems than with others: hence the practical importance of interdisciplinarity. But an academic system based merely on problems—with Ph.D.s only in fields like women's studies, poverty studies, American studies, urban studies, population studies, criminology, and Asian-American studies—would be hopelessly duplicative and would obviously require far more "interdisciplinarity" than does the current one. The reality is that problem-based knowledge is insufficiently abstract to survive in competition with problem-portable knowledge. As Lynd and others recognized long ago, interdisciplinary studies are ultimately dependent on specialized disciplines to generate new theories and methods. Interdisciplinarity presupposes disciplines.

To all these other forces supporting the continuation of disciplines we may add a final one. No one, in reality, has any serious alternative to the present system. It is true that some universities see the majority of their active intellectual life vanish from departments into centers. This happens in universities with large quantities of intellectually inactive faculty, where the intellectually active have to rearrange their lives locally to make exciting homes for themselves. But even these faculty keep their roots in the departments, and no one—absolutely no one—has a comprehensive model for curriculum that does not involve departments. Pure vocationalism is one such model, as we shall see. But the forces arrayed against it are very strong. The reality is that at present nobody has thought up another organizational structure that can pull as many different pieces together as does the department/discipline/major structure.

In summary, there are many forces conducing to keep the disciplinary system the way it is. The humanities and social science disciplines perform their function of knowledge generation reasonably well. They would get worse at it if they were much larger or much smaller. There is no large and stable foundation for American intellectual life outside of universities, the only real competitor being the higher risk arena of media work and publishing, and disciplinary academics manage in any case to get a fair amount of air time in media venues without the occupational risks involved. A variety of forces—both career structures and cultural ones—keep the disciplines from collapsing into each other, while the dependence of problem-based research on a continuous flow of new theory and methods ensures that the interdisciplinary world cannot survive without first-quality disciplinary training. At present, the system seems to have an extraordinary resilience.

Disciplines in the Future

In order to think about the possibility of radical change in the disciplinary matrix, it is necessary to think about sources for that change. These are of two kinds: internal, intellectual ones and external, social structural ones.

The first are fewer and simpler. The intellectual functions and power of the fractal distinction system that undergirds academic knowledge are so great that it is quite unlikely that change can come internally. Some see such internal change coming from the much-advertised "destruction of the canon." But the destruction of the canon doesn't matter much interdisciplinarily, because, as I have noted, interdisciplinarity is just a standing wave set up by the disciplinary system and coextensive with it. Canon destruction does matter within disciplines, because if students don't learn the repertoire of fractal distinctions they don't have the basic material for career production, and if they don't learn some canon (it doesn't matter what) disciplines lose the historicist cohesion of a set of common references (you are what you read in graduate school, and one discipline reads different things than another). Simply put, if disciplines make no attempt to reproduce themselves culturally, they will not necessarily be reproduced in spite of themselves. But since the "destruction of the canon" debate is itself conducted in completely traditional terms— using the same old fractal distinctions—there seems little danger that the basic repertoire will be lost.

Moreover, for any one canon-less discipline there are large contextual pressures maintaining it in its place. If no one around you vacates his place, it is hard to spread out randomly from your own. In fact, initial canons of some kind are still taught in most departments in most disciplines, and even while their content changes, the intersections between them, across disciplines, do not grow appreciably larger. Cross-disciplinary borrowers themselves have very little interest in disciplinary merging. Quite the contrary. Few of those who sell rational choice outside economics could make it as economists; their self-interest is very much in maintaining disciplinary lands of the blind in which they can be one-eyed men. The same is true for cultural studies scholars peddling second-hand anthropology. Put another way, a social science that had only one or two departments would present many fewer opportunities for ambitious intellects to produce apparent interdisciplinary revolutions.

Another possible source for serious internal change would be a line of research that recast the repertory of distinctions that has driven inquiry for the last century or more. This seems very unlikely. There are unlikely to be profoundly new fractal distinctions. The extensive array of distinctions that we currently have means that there is no major intellectual position that cannot be expressed as a combination of existing distinctions.

To create a fundamental change in the arrangement of disciplines, it would in my view be necessary for someone or some group to destroy some of the foundational ideas—the key fractal distinctions—of late nineteenth century social thought. For example, someone might write a work of Darwinian greatness demonstrating that history really doesn't matter to the fate of the world. Such a demonstration would need to reject all the prior evidence to that effect and at the same time to show that all the phenomena history seems to explain in fact have synchronic origins. Such a work would indeed revolutionize the social sciences, for no single idea is more central to our current tradition of social thought than historicism. The rejection of historicism would redefine at a stroke how the various combinations of fractal positions currently in existence relate to one another. But if one can imagine such a means of revolution, nonetheless it seems in practice very unlikely.

For the present, the disciplines work surprisingly well as a cultural system. They borrow from each other endlessly, but train scholars more or less within consistent lineages. The system turns out both "normal science" disciplinarians and cross-disciplinary borrowers. Fractal cycles within disciplines generate a lot of random motion, resulting in much serendipitous contact between disciplines in odd places over odd things. Incentives for thievery are high; of the major sociologists of the past generation nearly all of the methodological innovators were pirates—Duncan borrowing from biology, Coleman from engineering, White from physics. But overall the system plows along, enduring major cultural fads and vagaries without much deep structural change. At the same time, it produces in individual careers the culturally proper trajectory of youthful greatness followed by responsible maturity.

A final source for change in the cultural structure of disciplines is commodification. By embodying large amounts of disciplinary knowledge in portable form, commodification could strike a serious blow at the disciplinary system, at the least reducing its size and extent. There are many examples. Inferential statistics was turned into a commodity by widely available canned computer programs in the 1960s. By the early 1970s, cutting-edge statistics was widely available to and widely used by professional academics who had fairly marginal understandings of its mathematical and computational foundations. Even those who understood these underpinnings very well were led by the pressure of low-quality competitors to extend their efforts through shop-based divisions of labor, with a consequent loss of control. As new statistical techniques emerged, they made the move from esoteric artisanal status to exoteric commodities much more quickly. As a result of all this, the discipline of statistics is no longer the site of most statistical analysis, a development that has been paralleled in operations research. But while it may have reduced the size and dominance of statistics as a discipline, commodification did not destroy it.

We now face commodification on the qualitative side. New techniques for qualitative data search make the definitive bibliography of this or that topic child's play; librarians used to get master's degrees for such efforts. Here too we have an old example—law reviews. The entire legal reference system was commodified in complete detail by Shephard's and others in the nineteenth century. As a result, it has been possible for nearly one hundred years for a tyro to write an enormously learned but substantively worthless law review article. And, indeed, complaints about the resultant vacuity of law reviews date from the 1930s at least.

But I remain unpersuaded that commodification will really result in much change in disciplinary structure. Commodified knowledge still has to be originated somewhere, which means that a disciplinary system could persist, albeit much smaller than before. Moreover, everything we know from earlier waves of commodification, both in the professions and in academia, suggests that commodification has always ended up extending what knowledge workers can do rather than throwing large numbers of them out of work.

It is much more likely that change in disciplinary systems might come from changes in the underlying social structure of which they are a part. Some of these changes have to do with the immediate experience of everyday academic life, others with broader social trends. Many of them have their roots in technological changes in one way or another.

A first broad family of changes involves transformations of the educational system. Americans are spending longer and longer periods in the educational system. The vast majority of the population completes high school, even within severely deprived demographic groups. Even by comparison with thirty years ago, much less fifty or seventy-five, far larger percentages of students are going on to college and indeed to postgraduate education. These trends have had enormous effects on the university, which has in one century changed from a specialty institution for elites to a mainline institution for the mass. As a result universities are subject to political and economic pressures quite undreamed heretofore.

A consequence of this, and of concomitant changes in the labor force, is that higher education is providing a far larger percentage of skills training than it did before. This change is of course evident in the rise of the community college sector and the expansion of vocational majors throughout the system as a whole. At the same time, the commercial world itself is spending an enormous amount on training in-house, with a budget now surpassing that of higher education. Thus, not only has higher education been forced to become more of a vocational institution, it has also become only one among several sites of vocational education. In part, this is a matter of renaming. The polytechnics and vo-techs and normal schools of bygone years are now all renamed universities. But the elite university sector has not been immune. The drift toward vocationalist majors in elite universities is quite strong. "Pre-med" paved the way, followed by "pre-law" and now economics (= "pre-business").

So one major change in the university in the last fifty years is massification, which has to a considerable extent redefined the university as market-driven service organization. A second broad change is the move of capitalism—and of a capitalistic conception of intellectual property— deep into the academic world. This is of course familiar enough in the sciences, where its roots go back to the beginning of this century. But the social sciences and perhaps even the humanities are now coming under the shadow as well. Like the commons of early modern England, academic knowledge is essentially an enormous public resource that the commercial sector will simply claim as property (because no one else has) or buy up at cheap rates. One might think that interpretations of Locke

and Weber will hardly command such attention, but the rise of commodified Internet-based curriculum will in fact push the process of ownership far into such areas. To be sure, commercialization of academic
knowledge is hardly new. Commodified curriculum has been with us for
centuries in the guise of textbooks, and the managed textbooks that have
become standard in large fields have long been written by marketing. But
there are many textbooks, whereas there are likely to be far fewer versions of multimedia or Net-based courses. So the danger of control is far
greater, and the implications for the disciplinary system perhaps greater.

The higher education system of the United States thus seems rather
likely to divide into two basic parts. There will be a fairly small group of
elite universities and colleges—perhaps forty to fifty, certainly less than
one hundred—providing most graduate education in the humanities and
social sciences and elite undergraduate education in all fields. Some of
these will be the remaining handful of private colleges that continue to
specialize in liberal education, colleges that offer excellent educations,
good social connections, and degrees well known to gatekeepers in postgraduate admissions. Others in this group will be multipurpose state
universities in states wealthy enough to support at least one first-class institution beyond their (more politically important) second- and third-tier
institutions. These first-class state institutions will probably have elite
honors colleges that mimic, to the extent they can, the high-priced private colleges. The rest of this group—probably the majority of it—will
comprise elite private universities, whose rather lackluster efforts at undergraduate education are offset by magnificent student bodies, name
recognition, and social connections. Sheer financial power will give the
elite privates the pick of faculty.

The rest of American higher education, particularly at the undergraduate level, will look quite different. It will employ large amounts of
off-the-shelf screen- and Net-based curriculum, with the local faculty
probably shifting strongly in the direction of more teaching and less research, guiding the students through materials they themselves will not
have prepared. For this and other reasons, faculty will increasingly be
hired by the course or in other nontraditional fashions. The lowered necessity of course-development and lecturing will probably result in
enough shifting of faculty effort to undercut the need for graduate programs in such institutions, which have used graduate programs extensively as peonage teaching operations. (There will thus be less overproduction of academics, which has been a by-product of this method of

buying cheap teaching.) Most of the undergraduate education in this part of the system will be—indeed already is—frankly vocational. Students will still live at such universities—the main purpose of college has after all been social rather than educational for many years—but they will effectively get distance learning once they get there.

In the hard sciences, whose finances are considerably influenced by pork barrel politics and direct industry investment, the differentiation between universities will be less. Indeed, science money will to some extent mitigate the pressures to cut faculty spending that will sweep the system with the spread of high-quality off-the-shelf teaching materials. A glance at current figures on scientific dollars in universities shows that this source of funds buoys many universities of little renown in humanities and social sciences. Indeed, one of the likely outcomes of the growth of direct industry and government investment is a differentiation of universities in terms of their concentration in the sciences (which get such funds) and the humanities and social sciences (which do not).

This differentiation of levels of universities could falter if faculty seize the initiative and use the new curricular materials to generate a new conception of education. This is possible but quite unlikely. Older faculty are stuck in their ways. Younger talent is not heading into academia at anything like the rate that it did in the 1960s, and when it does it follows the lead of its teachers, for whom intellectualism comes before innovative teaching. It is quite possible that all the major innovations in teaching will come from the commercial sector, which will view higher education—as it has already viewed social service, health, and other eleemosynary activities—as a region for easy profit through downsizing and explicit product differentiation. The American higher education outlay is after all a quarter of a trillion dollars a year; the commercial sector has the necessary money, talent, and desire to take it over. It is extremely unlikely that this takeover will be seriously challenged by faculty, in the sense of traditionally educated researchers organized into academic disciplines. Of course individual faculty will play crucial roles. "Great lecturer" tapes already abound, as do various institutional marketing schemes designed to make money from faculty ideas. But, as a whole, faculty will probably do little. As a result, the medical care system is probably our best prediction for the academic future: a small, extremely elite and high-quality sector that looks like the "traditional" system, coupled to a rationalized and decentralized mass sector based on subcontracting, efficiency, and explicit productivity measures.

Disciplines will survive in the elite sector. First, like all commercial idea systems, the new educational/vocational training system will need its ideas to come from somewhere, and there is no obvious better model for generating new ideas—or at least new representations of ideas—than the current elite academic system with its disciplinary foundations. Second, since a large portion of the elite system is private, it is far more controlled by its faculty than is the nonelite system. This too will give faculty resources with which to protect the disciplinary system. Third, and quite curiously, the massification of the whole system has greatly increased the importance of diploma name recognition, with the inevitable dramatic rise in undergraduate applications to the elite schools. This, too, puts those schools in a position of financial, and hence intellectual power. Hence their faculties will be in an even stronger position to lead their disciplines. Finally, at the undergraduate level, the elites focus on general education, which is unmeasurable and hence an unlikely basis for profit. There is thus less attraction for invasion by the commercial sector, with its various threats to disciplines.

The overall consequences of this bifurcation of the academic system for the disciplinary system seem considerable. Outside the elite level, the social structural foundations of disciplines are steadily eroding, both in terms of the employment relation and more importantly in terms of the curriculum. There is a steady pressure from the private sector for a more vocational emphasis, and there will soon be pressure to let the private sector take over the "measurable-outcome," profitable parts of education, just as it has already done in medicine and social service. (Language education is an obvious example—far more efficiently accomplished by professional language instructors than by hag-ridden graduate students interested in literary studies.) There is to be sure an enormous inertia in the mass system: administrative systems in place, tenured faculty with decades of service ahead, and so on. But the same was true of medical care, which has been completely reorganized in two or three decades. It seems inevitable that we will see a much smaller portion of mass educational system under the direct control of disciplinary academics than is now, bearing in mind that the present level has fallen from a high point sometime earlier in the century. Disciplines won't vanish from the mass university, but they could become relatively much less important in it. Discipline faculty in such universities could come to resemble high school teachers more than they do research university faculty. Indeed, in many ways, they already have.

In the elite system, as I have said, there will be less change. The elite system has most of the same inertial factors as the mass one. But even ignoring them, the disciplinary system in elite universities is powerfully ensconced through its dual institutionalization, through its current control of faculty hiring, its proven success in generating new ideas while retaining old ones and in producing both normal and heterodox careers in suitable proportions, and, finally, through the lack of any serious alternative to it. It is quite hard to envision the disciplinary system coming apart in the elite universities. Its weakest point is the undergraduate major, but surprisingly, despite the small attention expended on majors, there seem relatively few forces pushing to abolish them as a curricular structure.[5]

Thus, in fifty years, we will probably have a disciplinary system recognizably descended from the present one. There will undoubtedly be new parallel intellectual worlds outside the disciplines. Certainly one will grow up on the Internet through the adventitious connections that seem to be the Net's most novel product. And another might emerge through organization of the vast structures of training within the commercial world itself, although the growth of firm-based education will ultimately be limited (as it already is to some extent) by the problem that firms cannot recoup their investments without placing impossible restrictions on interfirm mobility. There will thus be continued expansion of intellectual environments outside the university and the disciplines. But the disciplines will remain with us, and the internal organization of universities will continue to have a strong disciplinary basis for at least the next fifty years.

Notes

1. This paper relies heavily on two previous works of mine. The first is "The Context of Disciplines," chapter 5 of the book *Chaos of Disciplines* (Abbott, 2001). The second is "Academic Intellectuals," a piece in an (as-yet-untitled) festschrift for Donald Levine. I have stolen both ideas and, in some cases, text from these pieces.

2. For Wirth's view, see Wirth (1937: 145ff). A roundtable on Social Sciences was part of the tenth anniversary for the Social Science Research Building at the University of Chicago (Wirth, 1940). Also of interest is Ogburn and Goldenweiser (1927), a long compendium of articles covering every possible pairwise combination of the basic social sciences, from "Anthropology and Economics" to "Sociology and Statistics." On the MIT group, see Heims (1993).

3. I do not know of a serious institutional history of the modernization paradigm as it flourished in the 1950s and 1960s. By comparison with modernization, current interdisciplinarity seems tame in both its ambitions and breadth, al-

though perhaps equivalent in its self-confidence. Sherif and Sherif (1969) edited a fine 1960s collection on interdisciplinarism, in which the reader will find the wonderful essay of Donald Campbell, "Ethnocentrism of Disciplines and the Fish-Scale Model of Omniscience" (Campbell, 1969).

4. Nancy Tuma was the lead borrower bringing durational methods from biology and industrial reliability studies to sociology. William Sewell, Jr., was one of the chief importers of anthropology to history, while the much earlier Cambridge School handled the demography importing. Vacancy chains were borrowed from electron hole theory by Harrison White (1970), and network analysis via blockmodels were borrowed by the same author from the renormalization methods aimed at Ising models in physics (White, Boorman, and Breiger, 1976). My own experience is as the importer of alignment algorithms to the social sciences from the pattern-matching literature on DNA patterns and string editing (Abbott and Forrest, 1986; Abbott and Hrycak, 1990).

5. I have not mentioned some other important forces, which again will unfold differently in the elite of the system than they do elsewhere. There are thus a number of changes in academic careers that could seriously damage the current disciplinary system. The most obvious are changes in the reward system. In the present system, academics are rewarded for publication, in particular for quantity of publication. (The forces behind this are numerous, but the important ones are growing university size, decreasing administrative trust in faculty judgment with consequent trust in "objective" [*sic*] measures, expansion of available journal space [see Abbott, 1999: chap. 6], and deliberate credential inflation driven by competitive pressures.) Any force reducing the reward for or possibility of quantity publication would slow the fractal process considerably. A number of such developments or policies are clearly possible: abolition of tenure, award of tenure for teaching alone, or consideration of only a fixed number of pages or items at tenure-time. Another possibility, given the extraordinary ease of publication on the Net, would be the complete ending of all constraints on quantity, so that it would become (more than it is already) obviously meaningless. Another possible, but very unlikely, transformation would come through the ending of the cultural obsession with the new, which would end the need to pretend that old ideas are new. All of these forces could challenge the disciplinary system by challenging either its means of social reproduction (career production) or of cultural reproduction (the fractal system of ideas).

References

Abbott, Andrew. 1999. *Department and Discipline: Chicago Sociology at One Hundred*. Chicago: University of Chicago Press.

———. 2001. *Chaos of Disciplines*. Chicago: University of Chicago Press.

Abbott, Andrew, and John Forrest. 1986. "Optimal Matching Methods for Historical Sequences." *Journal of Interdisciplinary History* 16: 471–94.

Abbott, Andrew, and Alexandra Hrycak. 1990. "Measuring Resemblance in Social Sequences." *American Journal of Sociology* 96: 144–85.

Ben-David, Joseph, and Randall Collins. 1966. "Social Factors in the Origin of a New Science." *American Sociological Review* 31: 451–65.

Blumstein, Sheila. 1990. *The Brown Curriculum Twenty Years Later: Report to the President*. Providence: Brown University.

Bott, Elizabeth. 1971 [1957]. *Family and Social Network*. New York: Free Press.

Campbell, Donald T. 1969. "Ethnocentrism of Disciplines and the Fish-Scale Model of Omniscience." Pp. 328–48 in Muzafer Sherif and Carolyn W. Sherif (eds.), *Interdisciplinary Relationships in the Social Sciences*. Chicago: Aldine.

Clark, Terry Nichols. 1973. *The French University and the Emergence of the Social Sciences*. Cambridge: Harvard University Press.

Ellingson, Steven. 1995. "The Emergence and Institutionalization of the Major-Minor Curriculum, 1870–1910." Unpublished paper. Department of Sociology, University of Chicago.

Fisher, Donald. 1993. *The Fundamental Development of the Social Sciences*. Ann Arbor: University of Michigan Press.

Green, V. H. H. 1974. *A History of Oxford University*. London: Basford.

Heims, Steve J. 1993. *Constructing a Social Science for Postwar America*. Cambridge: MIT Press.

Jarausch, Konrad H. 1982. *Students, Society, and Politics in Imperial Germany*. Princeton: Princeton University Press.

———, ed. 1983. *The Transformation of Higher Learning*. Chicago: University of Chicago Press.

MacAloon, John J. 1992. *General Education in the Social Sciences*. Chicago: University of Chicago Press.

McClelland, Charles. 1980. *State, Society, and University in Germany, 1700–1914*. Cambridge: Cambridge University Press.

McNeill, William H. 1991. *Hutchins' University*. Chicago: University of Chicago Press.

Ogburn, William F., and Alexander Goldenweiser. 1927. *The Social Sciences*. Boston: Houghton Mifflin.

Oleson, Alexandra, and John Voss (eds.). 1979. *The Organization of Knowledge in Modern America*. Baltimore: Johns Hopkins University Press.

Ross, Dorothy. 1991. *The Origins of American Social Science*. Cambridge: Cambridge University Press.

Rothblatt, Sheldon. 1968. *The Revolution of the Dons*. New York: Basic Books.

Sherif, Muzafer, and Carolyn W. Sherif (eds.). 1969. *Interdisciplinary Relationships in the Social Sciences*. Chicago: Aldine.

Social Science Research Council (SSRC). 1934. *Decennial Report, 1923–1933*. New York: SSRC.

Suleiman, Ezra N. 1978. *Elites in French Society*. Princeton: Princeton University Press.

Veysey, Laurence R. 1965. *The Emergence of the American University*. Chicago: University of Chicago Press.

Weisz, George. 1983. *The Emergence of Modern Universities in France*. Princeton: Princeton University Press.

White, Harrison C. 1970. *Chains of Opportunity*. Cambridge: Harvard University Press.

White, Harrison C., Scott A. Boorman, and Ronald L. Breiger. 1976. "Social Structure from Multiple Networks." *American Journal of Sociology* 81: 730–80.

Wirth, Louis. 1937. "Report on the History, Activities, and Policies of the Social Science Research Council." Prepared for the Committee on Review of Council Policy. Typescript, Joseph Regenstein Library, University of Chicago.

———. 1940. *Eleven Twenty-Six*. Chicago: University of Chicago Press.

CHAPTER NINE

The Rise of the "Practical Arts"

STEVEN BRINT

The major interpretations of the development of the American university focus on knowledge production and the service faculty provide to society through the generation of new ideas and expert advice (Geiger, 1986, 1993; Kerr, 1964; Veysey, 1965). More recent interpretations have maintained these emphases, while focusing also on the significance of increasing business influence on knowledge production (see, for example, Slaughter and Leslie, 1997). However, if we shift our attention from the research to the teaching activities of the undergraduate college, a different picture takes shape. That picture is of the gradual shrinking of the old arts and sciences core of the university and the expansion of occupational and professional programs.

Students of the urban economy have shown that functions once considered ancillary to the main economic activity of the city often become part of the economic core at a later period. Thus, light manufacturing, legal services, and financial services in New York all grew initially out of the activities surrounding shipping in and out of the port of New York (Hoover and Vernon, 1959). Something analogous has occurred in the City of Intellect. Activities considered ancillary in an earlier age have moved to the center and have become leading engines of growth.

To be sure, the professional studies university has nowhere cast the arts and sciences university entirely in its shadow. The two coexist—and with many complementarities. Indeed, I will argue that the one of the more surprising outcomes of the rise of the practical arts is not *how much*, but *how little* has changed, at least at the major research universities that are the main focus of this volume. At the same time, the rise of the practical arts has had important consequences for these universities, quite apart from its effects on the distribution of courses and enrollments. Some of these consequences are predictable, others less so. They include: support for the ethos of student utilitarianism, support for faculty entrepreneurship, and support for "social partnership" models of problem solving. These consequences also include migration of arts and sciences faculty toward professional schools and indeed the migration of whole disciplines toward the professional school model, the increased vulnerability of small arts and sciences disciplines, and increased emphases within colleges of arts and sciences on interdisciplinary program development.

A New "Practical Arts" Core?

By the liberal arts, I mean the basic fields of science and scholarship housed in colleges of arts and sciences—physics, chemistry, history, English, political science, and others. By the practical arts, I mean occupational and professional programs often housed in their own schools and colleges—business, engineering, computer science, nursing, education, and other fields oriented to preparing students for careers.

The academic year 1969–70 was the last year in which a majority of American four-year college and university students graduated from arts and sciences fields.[1] Over the next fifteen years, occupational fields gained significantly as compared to arts and sciences fields, with nearly two-thirds of degrees awarded in occupational and professional fields by 1985–86.[2] The liberal arts rebounded from their nadir in the mid-1980s, but a decisive majority of degrees have continued to be awarded in occupational fields; in 1997–98, more than 58 percent of bachelors' degrees were awarded in occupational fields. Occupational and professional degrees have long dominated at the postbaccalaureate level (even if the arts and sciences category is expanded to include all doctorate degrees), but today they dominate to a far greater extent than before. In 1970–71, practical arts fields accounted for approximately two-thirds of all graduate degrees; today they account for nearly 80 percent.

At the undergraduate level, the fastest-growing degree fields include a number that barely existed thirty years ago. Protective services and computer and information systems both experienced a tenfold growth between 1970–71 and 1995–96; fitness, recreation, and leisure studies experienced a fivefold growth; and communications grew three times larger. Protective services involve programs for training police and other security personnel. Fitness, recreation, and leisure studies include a variety of programs training people to work in recreational areas or in travel and tourism. Few people in 1970 would have considered these "true" professional fields. Engineering technology—more a technicians' occupation than engineering itself—has doubled in size since 1970–71, as have degrees in public administration and many health professions. Some of these programs are not intrinsically connected to higher education by virtue of the cognitive skills demanded by their work. Instead, their rapid growth indicates that higher education is deeply involved in monitoring potential markets for educated labor.

The first adopters of new occupational programs are typically second-tier research universities that have both the resources and incentives to reach out to incorporate training for emerging white-collar occupations. Institutions such as Florida State University, Wayne State University, and Syracuse University have been among the leaders in the creation of new fields.[3] These institutions have been attentive to occupations of high market demand and acceptable social status that can be constructed, in collaboration with aspiring groups of practitioners, to include all of the institutional forms of academic professionalism—notably, an abstract vocabulary, scholarly journals, and a curriculum that can be accredited. Once a field has been accepted by as few as fifty institutions, its place in the curriculum leading to the baccalaureate degree is likely to be secure (Hashem, 2002).

As Table 9.1 indicates, over the last three decades the fast-growing fields have been occupational in virtually every case. The fastest growing of all has been business, which now accounts for some one-fifth of all undergraduate degrees—up from one-seventh in 1970–71. As Clifford Adelman (1995: 229) observed, business became in the 1980s the "empirical core curriculum." By contrast, over the period only four liberal arts fields grew relative to other fields. Two of these fields—psychology and life sciences—are closely linked to health occupations. The other two are "liberal/general studies" and "interdisciplinary studies." These latter two—still quite small in numbers of graduates—illustrate one facet of another interesting trend in academe: the slow and still very limited erosion of disciplinary boundaries in the liberal arts.[4] Performing and visual arts, halfway between liberal and occupational fields, have also grown a little relative to other fields.

TABLE 9.1

Growing, Stable, and Declining Degree Fields, 1970–95

A. Bachelor's Degree Fields

A. Growing fields	B. Stable fields	C. Declining fields
I. Fields with Fewer than 1% of BA/BS Degrees in 1995–96		
Law/Legal Studies Transportation-Related Studies	Architecture Area/Ethnic Studies Communications Technology Theology	Library Science Philosophy/Religious Studies
II. Fields with 1–5% of BA/BS Degrees in 1995–96		
Public Admin./Services Visual/Performing Arts Communications Computer/Info Systems Parks/Recreation/Fitness Protective Services Liberal/General Studies Interdisciplinary Studies	Agricultural Science Home Economics	English Literature* Physical Sciences* Mathematics* Foreign Languages/ Literature*
III. Fields with More than 5% of BA/BS Degrees in 1995–96		
Business Health Professions Psychology Biological/Life Sciences	Engineering	Education† Social Science/History†

B. Master's Degree Fields

A. Growing fields	B. Stable fields	C. Declining fields
I. Fields with Fewer than 1% of Master's Degrees in 1995–96		
Communications Tech. Engineering Tech. Law/Legal Studies Liberal Studies Interdisciplinary/Multi- disciplinary Studies Parks/Recreation/Fitness Protective Services	Area/Ethnic Studies Home Economics	Foreign Languages/ Literature Philosophy/Religion
II. Fields with 1–5% of Master's Degrees in 1995–96		
Communications Computer/Information Sciences Psychology	Agriculture/Nat. Resources Theology Visual/Performing Arts Architecture	Biological/Life Sciences English Literature Library Science Mathematics Physical Sciences Social Science/History

TABLE 9.1 — *cont.*

A. Growing fields	B. Stable fields	C. Declining fields
III. Fields with More than 5% of Master's Degrees in 1995–96		
Business Administration Health Professions Public Administration/ Services	Engineering	Education

SOURCE: Computed from NCES, 1998: 282–23.
  *Decline in both absolute and relative terms for all four fields.
  †Decline in both absolute and relative terms for both fields.

Virtually every other liberal arts and sciences field has declined not only in relative but also in absolute terms. It is important to emphasize this point, because the higher education system is now substantially larger than it was in 1970–71. More than 1.1 million students graduated with bachelors' degrees in 2000–2001, compared to about 840,000 in 1970–71. Under these circumstances, it is not easy for a field to decline in absolute terms, however poorly it may fare in competition with other fields. So, let me say again with emphasis: *During a period in which the system grew by 50 percent, almost every field which constituted the old arts and sciences core of the undergraduate college was in absolute decline. This includes not only all of the humanities and social sciences (except psychology and economics) but also the physical sciences and mathematics.* One could say that all of the traditional liberal arts fields, except those closely connected to health and business careers, have a receding profile in today's universities.

By contrast, only two professional fields have experienced relative declines: library science and education. An important source of change in education has been the upgrading of standards for teacher training in several states, including California and Massachusetts, where prospective teachers are required to major in an academic discipline and to take courses in education programs only in their fifth year for purposes of certification. For its part, library science has been losing out to computer science for jurisdiction over the organization and distribution of information.

Broadly similar patterns can be described at the masters' and doctoral levels. The growing fields at the masters' level are occupational and professional—with the exception of psychology and the various "blended" programs (such as liberal studies, interdisciplinary and multidisciplinary studies, and ethnic studies). The declining fields are those in the traditional arts and sciences—this time including biological and life sciences. Business administration now rivals education for the top spot in masters' degree production, and the top seven degree-producing fields are now all occupational; indeed, computer science will soon supplant the combined social sciences as the eighth largest field at the masters' level. Because the growing fields at the undergraduate and masters' levels require faculty to teach them, doctoral production closely parallels production at the bachelors' and masters' levels; the same fields growing at the bachelors' level are also growing at the doctoral level.

Beginning during the depressed college labor market of the early 1970s (Freeman, 1976), shifts in enrollments have been encouraged by a vastly larger number of students vying for a less rapidly growing number of good careers. From these new enrollment patterns arises the prevailing wisdom: "[In] recent decades, students . . . have been oriented chiefly toward gaining useful skills and knowledge rather than to membership in a cultural elite" (Trow, 1998: 1), and the familiar but nevertheless arresting statistic showing that the proportion of college freshmen interested in attending college to develop a "meaningful philosophy of life" dropped by 45 percent in the period between 1967 and 1987, while the proportion interested in attending to "become well off financially" grew by 40 percent over roughly the same period (Astin, 1998).

When specific growth fields are considered, theories of postindustrial society fare relatively well, as do theories emphasizing postmaterialist trends in cultural life. The landscape described by the data show the increasing popularity of business and business service fields; the advent of mass computing; and the growth of health fields, entertainment, and other quality-of-life concerns. But to explain the patterns fully postindustrial and postmaterialist theories would require revision to account for the increasing importance of government social control and administrative activities, and for the extension of higher education deeply into fields previously occupied by less well educated technicians and front-line bureaucrats. Far from fading away, occupational fields connected to the state have grown more important. New fields, which would have been considered semiprofessional at best in earlier generations, have also entered higher education.

Changes in enrollments and curricula do not, of course, simply reflect changes in the occupational structure in a one-to-one correspondence. In the first place, access to many professional and managerial occupations is not tightly controlled by the credentialing system. Although they may help, degrees are not required to obtain jobs in such fields as computer science, business management, communications, or even education during periods of teacher shortage. Courses of study connected to these jobs would be significantly more important within colleges and universities if access to them depended in all cases on credentialing in the relevant occupational specialty. In addition, the demand for courses of study among students differs significantly from the demand for college-educated workers among employers. Colleges and universities create their own organizationally based demand through prescription of general education requirements. Some colleges and universities, particularly the more elite schools, also choose to limit occupational/professional degree programs at the undergraduate level. The demand for courses may also be influenced by the difficulty of the field, the intellectual capacities of students, and the psychic satisfactions associated with particular fields of study. Today many fields high in psychic satisfaction are closely connected to student interests in forms of personal expression. In this regard, it is instructive to compare the fate of engineering and the performing arts over the last thirty years. Enrollments in engineering, a high labor demand field, have remained generally stable, while enrollments in performing and visual arts, low labor demand fields, have grown substantially. Similarly, enrollments in psychology programs greatly exceed the market demand for psychologists, therapists, and counselors, and reflect the personal discovery interests of many students.

Nevertheless, the university's relative autonomy from the occupational class structure—its propensity to operate on a set of compatible but distinct principles involving judgments about culturally significant forms of knowledge—has been substantially reduced over the last thirty years. Administrators, at least those outside the elite institutions, no longer assume the unquestioned centrality of scientific and humanistic culture, and the old triumvirate of the natural sciences, the social sciences, and the humanities have all experienced a declining appeal. From an historical perspective, this is a striking change. Only a generation ago, UC Berkeley Professor T. R. McConnell, a well-known consultant and influential commentator on higher education, observed: "Many of (the) professional schools still do not feel at home in the university, and the university does not feel comfortable with them. . . . When the university and the professional school strengthen and support each other . . . the professional school will not only be 'in the university' but also 'of the university'" (McConnell, Anderson, and Hunter, 1962:

257, 261). Clearly, the "practical arts" have come a long way in a generation—so much so that it is no longer always clear which are the "central and fundamental disciplines" in the eyes of university administrators.

Consequences

Occupational and professional programs have moved closer to the center of academic life partly because they have modeled themselves on the arts and sciences—developing similarly abstract vocabularies, similarly illuminating theoretical perspectives, and similarly rigorous conceptual schemes (see, for example, Schlossman and Sedlak, 1988). If the liberal arts have been dethroned, they have been usurped by a claimant whose principles and bearing show striking similarities to those of the previous rulers.

But have the arts and sciences really been dethroned? Survey data suggest some reasons for skepticism. The majority of arts and sciences faculty at American universities do not portray themselves as alienated. Fewer than one in five say that the phrase "at odds with the administration" is "very descriptive" of circumstances at their institutions, and the great majority consider themselves "satisfied" or "very satisfied" with their jobs (Finkelstein, Seal, and Schuster, 1997: 58–59). At Research I universities, arts and sciences faculty are as satisfied as their colleagues in professional schools, and humanities and social sciences faculty are, rather surprisingly, the most satisfied of all.

One reason may be that employment conditions in the arts and sciences have not suffered as much as one might expect given the changing student enrollment patterns. It is true that the proportion of faculty in the arts and sciences has declined relative to the proportion of faculty in occupational and professional programs. Yet at a time in the later 1980s and early 1990s when three-fifths of undergraduate degrees (and three-quarters of graduate degrees) were awarded in professional programs, almost half of new hires continued to be in arts and sciences fields (ibid.: 22). Moreover, adjusting for inflation, tenure-track faculty salaries in the arts and sciences rose in the 1980s and 1990s (Scott and Bereman, 1992), and faculty in all fields have been more likely in recent years than in the 1970s and 1980s to rate their salaries as "good" or "excellent" (Finkelstein, Seal, and Schuster, 1998: 59). Nor have the work conditions of faculty suffered significantly. At both doctoral-granting and research universities, arts and sciences faculty hired in the late 1980s and early 1990s spent somewhat less time teaching than their more senior colleagues— and they taught less at a comparable stage in their careers than their predecessors of an earlier academic generation (ibid.: 65–67).

DIFFERENCES BY TIER AND SEGMENT

Even so, the answer to the question, Have the arts and sciences been dethroned? depends on where one looks among the large number of universities in the United States. The Carnegie Foundation classification scheme until recently grouped universities into three major categories: Research Universities, Doctoral-granting Universities, and Comprehensive (or master's-granting) Universities. The rise of the practical arts has led to impressive changes at most of the more than six hundred doctoral and comprehensive institutions. Here enrollments have shifted dramatically toward the practical arts, and liberal arts faculty have in many cases become primarily providers of distribution requirements for students in departments and schools of professional studies. Without the protection of distribution requirements, arts and sciences faculty at institutions such as Central Michigan University, San Jose State University, Sam Houston State University, and the University of Massachusetts-Boston would shrink to a small cadre. At these institutions, senior faculty in the arts and sciences do show comparatively high levels of dissatisfaction. This dissatisfaction may reflect, at least in part, a sense of status incongruity among professors who were trained during a period when the arts and sciences formed the undisputed disciplinary core of the system.

The story is different and more complex, however, in the country's research universities, which are the main focus of this volume. Among the research universities, the movement over time has been in one of two directions—either toward a pattern of many relatively equal parts—the multiversity of Clark Kerr's vision—or toward a continued focus on the arts and sciences as the undergraduate core of the university. Multiversities can be distinguished from liberal arts universities by the number of fields—and particularly the number of applied fields—in which baccalaureate degrees are offered.[5]

Harriet Morgan's (1998) analysis of curricular change between 1966 and 1992 indicates a growth in both the multiversity and the liberal arts university categories. Among research universities, multiversities outnumber liberal arts universities by a ratio of approximately two to one.

Multiversities are most common among the public land-grant institutions, particularly those in the Midwest, the mountain states, and the South, and in urban private universities serving upwardly mobile student populations. Thus, the University of Arizona, the University of Nebraska, the University of Florida, Temple University, and the University of Cincinnati are examples of multiversities. By contrast, the liberal arts university model predominates among the most prestigious research universities, including both the elite privates and the flagship campuses of the leading public land-grant institutions. The great majority of the fifty leading research universities fall in this category. Duke, Northwestern, UC-Berkeley, the University of Virginia, and Yale all fall in the liberal arts university group.[6] Occupational and professional training is typically highly restricted for undergraduates at these elite universities. This restriction is a consequence of value commitments linked to status, and it ensures that undergraduates focus their professional aspirations on the graduate level.

Quantitative changes in enrollments are only one measure of changing centrality; the more elusive criterion of prestige is another and frequently far more important measure. Undoubtedly the arts and sciences stand at the highest levels of prestige at liberal arts universities, together with graduate schools of business, law, and medicine. Even at multiversities, however, where student enrollments and faculty appointments have increased the quantitative strength of occupational fields, the arts and sciences colleges often rank highest in prestige.

THE CONTINUING STRENGTH OF THE ARTS AND SCIENCES

Some sources of the continuing strength of the arts and sciences at research universities are obvious enough. The distinctive mission of research universities is to conduct research, and the arts and sciences are the original sources of this mission. Among these universities, membership in prestigious organizations such as the Association of American Universities requires demonstration of a well-balanced scholarly and scientific eminence. The natural sciences are a particularly important source both of prestige and revenues for all research universities because of the grants they generate. Support for them seems secure, regardless of trends in undergraduate enrollments. It should be noted too that, even in multiversities, the arts and sciences are an important element in enrollment management. Arts and sciences faculty offer an indispensable array of service courses for students in all fields. In addition, students who do not perform well in fields where projected incomes are high (or do not have interest in these fields) must have some place to go. Some of these destination fields are in the "soft" humanities and social sciences; others are in the schools of the so-called minor professions, such as communications, education, and social work (Glazer, 1974).

Some less obvious reasons also exist for the continued importance, even centrality, of the arts and sciences in research universities. The most consequential of these have to do with the priority placed by professors in all fields on the more purely intellectual side of academic life, and with the disproportionate influence on university governance exercised by administrators and faculty drawn from the arts and sciences. Because these strengths are not always appreciated by contemporary observers of the "market-driven university," I will discuss them at somewhat greater length.

Cultural Prestige. The university would be a very easy institution to analyze if its only source of strength lay in its connection to high-income occupations. But this is manifestly not the case. The prestige of academic fields reflects their cultural distinction at least as much as their value in the labor market (see Bourdieu, 1984, 1988).

Faculty in the arts and sciences bring attention to the university in ways that are not easily duplicated by faculty in occupational and professional fields. The most prestigious academic bodies are connected to the arts and sciences: the National Academy of Sciences, the American Academy of Arts and Sciences, the American Council of Learned Sciences, the MacArthur and the Guggenheim fellowships. These are the institutions that tend to speak for the values of higher education at the most elite levels. All are dominated by people trained in the arts and sciences. Similarly, studies of intellectual life show that authors of articles in the most prestigious general intellectual periodicals, such as the *New York Review of Books* and the *New York Times Book Review*, are likely to be either journalists or professors in the humanities and social sciences. Faculty in professional fields are not well represented (Brint, 1994: chap. 7). Not surprisingly, while public figures rely on technical experts drawn from a variety of fields to help develop and assess policies, they rely almost exclusively on liberal arts faculty and writers influenced by them to define broader themes and to suggest proper contexts for understanding.

Arts and sciences faculty are the university's experts in fundamental forms of analysis, whether in verbal or mathematical expression. Their theoretical and methodological skills encourage the continuing centrality of the liberal arts within the university. They allow for the creation of new knowledge. And they tend, however unevenly, to influence the conduct of research in the professional schools and occupational programs. Law is a rather self-enclosed system, but even many law professors have adopted approaches that combine case analysis with the tools of the humanities and social sciences. Faculty members in other professional schools remain still more dependent on faculty in basic fields. Professors in business rely overwhelmingly on economists and other social scientists for providing theoretical and methodological tools. Professors in engineering draw on the work of physicists and mathematicians for similar reasons. Professors in education meld practitioner knowledge of schools with the tools of the humanities and the social and behavioral sciences. And clinical faculty members in medical schools rely on the knowledge of biologists, microbiologists, and biochemists, who form their basic science faculties. Because they are less deeply involved, in general, in the fundamental theoretical and methodological questions of their disciplines, faculty in the professional schools may enjoy very high standing outside the university, while remaining mindful of the intellectual status of the arts and sciences disciplines, particularly those most closely connected to their work.

Nor would it be wise to underestimate the university's commitment to encouraging students' intellectual development through study of the liberal arts. Many faculty and administrators, including a great many in professional schools, continue to agree with a traditional justification for the centrality of the arts and sciences in undergraduate studies: that they provide superior opportunities for the development of the thinking abilities that mark a broadly capable, rather than simply a technically proficient, mind. These thinking abilities include the capacities to understand logical relations and abstract languages, to make meaningful discriminations, to develop empathy, to appreciate the interplay between the particular and the general, to understand the rhetoric and structure of arguments, to perceive and evaluate context, and to develop skills in building evidence in support of a position. Roger Geiger's conclusion of two decades ago therefore continues to ring true to many faculty and administrators: "[S]haping the intellectual maturation of young people and widening their cultural horizons has traditionally been the strength and the mission of American undergraduate education. . . . If [this source of strength and mission falls into disfavor], the vitality of intellectual life throughout the broad middle of the academic hierarchy will deteriorate badly" (1980: 54).

Participation in Governance. Participation in governance is another less obvious factor that may help to explain the continuing strength of the arts and sciences. We know that the backgrounds of top executives can influence the climate of the firms they lead (Useem, 1989). If this is true in corporations, is it not likely to be true a fortiori in colleges and universities?

The number of college and university presidents from nonacademic backgrounds has grown significantly over the last thirty years, but these top administrators are still primarily recruited from either the arts and sciences or education (American Council of Education, 2000). Doctoral-granting institutions, including research universities, are far more likely than the rest of higher education to have presidents trained in a liberal arts rather than a professional field.[7] The difference a degree field makes should not be overemphasized. All academic leaders are required to assess overall institutional interests—the opportunities, benefits, and costs of moving in one direction or another relative to the actions of their relevant comparison institutions. Nevertheless, within these constraints, it seems likely that disciplinary backgrounds predispose many, and perhaps most, presidents and provosts to see the particular virtues of the fields and colleges closest to their own (compare Kraatz and Zajac, 1998).

Patterns of faculty involvement in governance may be at least equally important. Although the influence of faculty senates is limited today, participation in the political process on campus remains a factor in shaping agendas and policy decisions. By serving on committees and by taking an active role in the politics of university decision-making, arts and sciences faculty put themselves in a position to interact on collegial grounds with administrators, to protect their priorities, and even to help select new university leaders.

Faculty in the arts and sciences may be more likely than those in professional programs to consider the university "theirs" and to participate in academic senate and other governance activities. As a way to begin to test this proposition, I conducted a study of participation as chairs of academic senate standing committees on seven of the University of California's nine campuses, excluding only the San Francisco campus,

TABLE 9.2

Background of College and University Presidents, 1986 and 1998

(percent)

Field	Public		Private	
	1998	1986	1998	1986
Doctorate-Granting				
Liberal Arts*	52	60	50	57
Education	9	10	6	12
Religion/Theology	0	0	11	9
Other Professional†	39	30	33	22
Master's-Granting				
Liberal Arts*	48	50	41	47
Education	28	37	29	30
Religion/Theology	0	1	12	13
Other Professional†	22	12	19	10
Baccalaureate-Granting				
Liberal Arts*	53	54	44	48
Education	32	26	30	28
Religion/Theology	0	3	10	16
Other Professional†	13	12	17	8

SOURCES: American Council on Education, 1995: 101, 107; American Council on Education, 2000: 67.

*Liberal arts includes biological sciences, physical sciences, social sciences, humanities, and fine arts.

†Other professional programs include agriculture, engineering, medicine, other health professions, law, and nonspecified professional fields.

which is exclusively medical, and the Santa Cruz campus, which has no professional programs. Such a study is only a beginning, but it suggests that the topic deserves further attention. In the three study years (1994–95, 1996–97, and 1998–99), arts and sciences faculty served as chairs on a majority of committees on all seven campuses. These faculty members served as chairs in a significantly higher than expected proportion at four of the seven campuses. On the other campuses, participation was approximately proportionate to the distribution of faculty between liberal arts and professional programs.[8]

NEW PRIORITIES IN THE UNIVERSITY

In spite of the continuing strength of the arts and sciences, it is clear that some important changes have occurred in the purposes and activities of research universities over the last thirty years. These include: (a) the rise of a utilitarian ethos among students; (b) the rise of faculty and university entrepreneurship; and (c) the extension of "social partnership" models in community relations. To what extent might the rise of the practical arts be related to these developments?

The curricular changes discussed in this chapter show a distinct affinity with each of these developments, but they have been by no means their only or primary cause. In some cases, they have not been a direct cause at all. The following developments show a much more direct relationship to these new priorities of the university:

—College attendance has become the norm rather than the exception; two-thirds of students aged eighteen to twenty-four (and an increasing proportion of older adults) now spend some time studying at a college or university.

—Throughout the 1970s and into the 1980s the relative share of state funding of public universities declined, leading to a markedly greater financial dependence on student tuition and fees, and on private gifts.

—Legislation passed in the early 1980s, particularly the Economic Recovery Act of 1981 and the Bayh-Dole Patent and Trademark Act of 1980, provided incentives for both universities and industries to deepen their collaborative involvements in research.

—The role of "big government" came under ideological attack in the 1970s and early 1980s, opening the way for the rise of smaller-scale collaborative solutions to problems of economic and social development.

Because the rise of the practical arts is but one source of support for the new social and economic priorities of the university, my argument in this section will be based on affinities, not on causality. I will argue that students and faculty in occupational and professional programs provide a constituency of support, and a growing one, for key changes in the university's relation to society, but I will not argue that they have been a direct cause of these developments.

The Ethos of Utilitarianism among Students. The ethos of utilitarianism can be defined as the tendency of students to think of higher education primarily as a means to obtain credentials that will be valuable to them in the labor market. Responses to surveys show that students in occupational and professional programs are more likely than those in the arts and sciences to express utilitarian outlooks. As the data in Table 9.3 indicate, freshmen who expect to declare professional majors are 10 percent more likely than those who expect liberal arts majors to say that "being well off financially" is essential to them. They are more than 10

TABLE 9.3

Attitudes and Activities Related to Dimensions of Materialism and Service, University Freshmen and Faculty, by Academic Discipline Categories, 1998

(percent)

A. Freshmen attitudes*	Being very well off financially is essential or very important	Developing a meaningful phi- losophy of life is essential	Taking part in community action is very important or essential	Being a commu- nity leader is very important or es- sential
Expect Professional Major†	39%	14%	22%	35%
Expect Liberal Arts Major‡	29%	25%	29%	27%

B. Faculty attitudes/activities	Being well off financially is essential or very important	Spend one hour or more per week on free-lance con- sulting work	Spend one hour or more per week consulting pa- tients or clients
Professional Disciplines§	45%	46%	29%
LiberalArtsDisciplines‖	33%	32%	10%

SOURCE: Higher Education Research Institute (1998a, 1998b).

All differences by discipline are signficant at p<.05.

*The reported percentages are based on weighting to reflect the distribution of freshmen by expected majors.

†Professional majors include agriculture, business, education, engineering, and health professions.

‡Liberal arts majors include biological sciences, English, history/political science, humanities, fine arts, mathematics/statistics, physical sciences, and social sciences.

§Professional disciplines include all departmental affiliations in agriculture and forestry, business, edu- cation, engineering, health sciences, and "other technical" disciplines.

‖Liberal Arts disciplines include all departmental affiliations in biological sciences, English, humani- ties, fine arts, mathematics and statistics, physical sciences, and social sciences.

percent less likely to say that developing a meaningful philosophy of life is essential.

Faculty members teaching in occupational and professional programs tend to support the practical, job-oriented interests of students. They are much more likely than liberal arts faculty to say, for example, that being well off financially is essential or very important to them. They are also significantly more likely to supplement their incomes with outside con- sulting or consultation with clients and patients.[9]

Entrepreneurial Activities among Faculty. Higher education scholars have used the term "entrepreneurial" in a variety of ways. I will focus on the efforts of universities and individual faculty to capitalize on research discoveries. These efforts to profit from research include partnership ar- rangements with industries for support of potentially profitable research, patent and licensing activity, and the creation of faculty and graduate student spin-off firms.

TABLE 9.4

Disciplines Represented in University-Industry Research Center Research Activities, 1990

	Percent of UIRCs in which discipline is represented in research activities	Number of UIRCs
Natural Science Disciplines		
Chemistry	39	192
Biology	34	169
Physics	24	120
Geology/Earth Sciences	20	91
Mathematics	11	54
Professional Schools/Programs		
Materials Engineering	34	171
Electrical Engineering	32	159
Mechanical Engineering	31	155
Materials Science	29	145
Chemical Engineering	28	137
Computer Science	26	130
Agricultural Sciences	21	106
Civil Engineering	21	103
Medical Sciences	19	93
Industrial Engineering	18	87
Aeronautical/Astronautical Engineering	12	58
Applied Math/Operations Research	12	57
TOTAL N		497

SOURCE: Cohen, Florida, and Goe, 1994: 14.
NOTE: Only disciplines represented in 10 percent or more of the UIRCs are reported in this table.

Walter Powell and Jason Owen-Smith's chapter in this volume indicates how much of the recent activity in patenting and licensing is concentrated in the applied biomedical sciences. Indeed, these disciplines are the center of many forms of entrepreneurial activity in the university. Studies of university faculty engaging in collaborative research with industry show a compatible but slightly different picture. According to the studies of Wesley Cohen and his colleagues, chemistry and biology are the disciplines most likely to be represented in university-industry research centers (UIRCs). However, if one looks at the disciplines represented in at least 10 percent of the UIRCs in Cohen's sample, professional disciplines, such as engineering and agriculture, outnumber basic science disciplines by two to one (Cohen et al., 1998).[10] (See Table 9.4.)

Social Partnerships. Less frequently noted has been the rise of community service and social partnership arrangements on campus (Newman, 1985). These activities include "service learning" opportunities and broader institutional commitments to community development. The University of California, Berkeley, for example, currently lists more than three hundred community-serving activities of various types. These activities include: volunteer and charity work and charitable donations; educational outreach activities; research specifically designated as oriented to public service; and community economic development activities. In many research universities, both public and private, community and civic activity extends from relatively large-scale community development and public research activities to "bite-size" programs, such as computer and furniture donations, the provision of extra street-sweeping and "safety ambassadors" in surrounding neighborhoods, and small-scale job training programs for local residents (Brint and Levy, 1999: 183–85).

According to the most recent survey by Campus Compact, five of the top ten "service-learning" disciplines are professional: education, social work, business, communications, and nursing. Two others — psychology and biology — attract many students planning careers in counseling and the health professions (Campus Compact, 1998: 41, 197). These data may reflect at least a weak affinity between the ethos of professionalism and the growing significance of social partnership activities in academe. The ethos of professionalism, after all, encourages engagement with practical problem-solving in the world, rather than detachment.

Additional support comes from national faculty data. In 1998 university faculty teaching in professional programs were more likely than their colleagues in the liberal arts to say they spent at least one hour per week on community or public service (71 percent of occupational and professional faculty, compared to 60 percent of liberal arts faculty). They were also more likely to agree strongly that colleges should encourage students to participate in community service activities. Business faculty were more likely than humanities faculty to take these positions, and engineering faculty were more likely than natural science faculty to take them. The differences here are not large, but they are at least mildly supportive of the argument that affinities exist between the rise of the practical arts and university-community partnerships.

NEW PRIORITIES AND PRACTICES IN
THE LIBERAL ARTS

Even at the leading research universities, arts and sciences departments often feel themselves to be under-supported. The temptation is great to consider one's own field under special duress, while others thrive. But mathematics does not prosper while English languishes. The pressure is in fact quite general in the arts and sciences disciplines, and it is connected to the growing significance of the practical arts.

This pressure has led to a number of consequences for colleges of arts and sciences. Among the most important of these are: (a) the migration of individual faculty and even whole fields in the direction of professional preparation; (b) the increased vulnerability of the smaller arts and sciences fields; and (c) the growth of interdisciplinary programs in the arts and sciences—a phenomenon likely to become still more important in the future.

Migrations of Faculty and Disciplines. If growth is greater in occupational and professional programs, arts and sciences faculty will have incentives to migrate to those programs, because of the greater number of positions available and sometimes also because of the higher salaries offered. Tables 9.5 and 9.6 examine the academic origins and destinations of faculty in two survey years, 1969 and 1992.[11] The data show that more movement exists in virtually all fields in 1992 than in 1969.

In the earlier academic generation, people trained in the arts and sciences were particularly unlikely to move from their home disciplines. But when they did move, they typically moved into professional programs. Today fewer faculty members trained in the arts and sciences remain in their home disciplines, and the amount of increased movement into professional programs is roughly proportionate to this decline in the proportion of those who stay in their home disciplines. Major changes have also occurred among faculty trained in professional schools. In the previous academic generation, people trained in professional programs were also more likely to remain in their home disciplines than they are today. When they did move, they tended to move into associated disciplines in the arts and sciences. For example, doctorates in engineering sometimes moved into natural science departments, and doctorates in education sometimes moved into the humanities or social sciences. Today the net

TABLE 9.5
Academic Origins and Destinations, 1969 and 1992

(percent)

I. All Full-time Faculty: 1992

Academic origin: professional	Academic destination			
	Same field	Other professional*	Letters and sciences	Other fields†
Agriculture/Home Econ.	59.3	15.0	24.5	1.1
Business	68.6	19.6	10.3	1.5
Education	79.7	8.3	10.9	1.1
Engineering	79.3	8.8	9.7	2.1
Health Sciences	76.3	14.1	8.9	.5
Other Professional	71.2	12.1	15.0	1.7
Academic origin: letters and sciences	Same field	Other letters and sciences	Letters and sciences	Other fields†
Fine Arts	89.8	4.1	4.9	1.2
Humanities	85.3	3.8	10.3	.7
Natural Sciences	83.3	2.0	14.4	.3
Social Sciences	83.1	3.8	12.6	.5

II. All Full-time Faculty: 1969

Academic origin: professional	Academic destination			
	Same field	Other professional*	Letters and sciences	Other fields†
Business	67.3	17.8	13.7	.3
Education	87.9	2.2	9.6	.2
Engineering	83.1	5.5	9.3	–
Health Sciences	82.9	6.3	9.6	.2
Other Professional	81.2	7.5	9.3	.1
Academic origin: letters and sciences	Same field	Other letters and sciences	Letters and sciences	Other fields†
Fine Arts	92.0	2.9	4.2	.1
Humanities	94.1	2.3	3.2	.1
Natural Sciences	90.8	.9	7.8	–
Social Sciences	88.0	3.6	7.8	.2

SOURCES: Carnegie Foundation for the Advancement of Teaching Faculty Survey, 1969; National Survey of Postsecondary Faculty, 1993.

*"Other Professional" includes architecture and environmental design; city, community, and regional planning; interior design; advertising; communications and communications technologies; law; library science; parks and recreation; theology; protective services; public affairs; and science and engineering technologies. Agriculture and home economics are included in this category in 1969 only.

†"Other Fields" includes all fields otherwise uncategorizable. These include many fields that would at one time have been considered preparation for blue collar or lower white collar occupations, such as industrial arts, construction, personal service, repair, precision production, and transportation-related fields.

TABLE 9.6

Professional Migration Ratios

	1992	1969
Agriculture/Home Economics	-9.5	NA
Business	+9.3	+4.1
Education	-2.6	-7.4
Engineering	-.9	-3.8
Health Sciences	+5.2	-3.3
Fine Arts	+.8	+1.3
Humanities	+6.5	+.9
Natural Sciences	+12.4	+6.9
Social Sciences	+8.8	+4.2

SOURCES: See Table 9.6.
  NOTE: Professional Migration Ratio = percentage movement into professional – percentage movement into arts and sciences. A positive ratio indicates net movement into professional programs. A negative ratio indicates net movement into arts and sciences.

movement of doctorates in business and health sciences has been toward other professional programs, while doctorates in education and engineering remain slightly more likely to move into the arts and sciences. But even in the latter cases, the proportion moving into the arts and sciences is now substantially lower than in 1969. Overall, this is a picture of a faculty less anchored to its fields of origin and one that has been increasingly attracted to teaching in occupational and professional programs.[12]

Perhaps more surprising than the migration of individual faculty has been the migration of whole disciplines and specialty areas within disciplines toward professional organization. Perhaps the most notable examples of this trend are psychology and chemistry. Psychology has long been divided between researchers and clinicians, but with the arrival of the licensing of clinical psychologists, the major part of psychology has been transformed into a professional field. Chemists have eschewed occupational licensing, but they increasingly market themselves as a field providing training for positions in chemical-based industries.

Professionalization can also occur through a splitting of tracks within departments and majors. At some institutions economics has become a substitute business major for the great majority of students, while remaining a basic social science field for the minority of students with public policy and academic interests. In sociology, criminology and social welfare tracks are sometimes organized as professional programs, while the major itself remains academic. In political science, public affairs and international relations have become professional tracks at some institutions, while the subdisciplines of political theory, American politics, and comparative politics remain academic.

The Increased Vulnerability of Small Fields. The research thus far on program closings and mergers suggests that the fields most likely to suffer in a competitive environment are those involved in public sector social welfare activities (Gumport, 1993; Morphew, 1998; Slaughter and Silva, 1985). It seems likely that these are not the only fields to face dimmer prospects in an environment in which occupational training programs are increasingly important. Very small fields are likely to be vulnerable, too, unless they are staffed by unusually distinguished faculty or so rare as to be virtually one of a kind.[13] Reliable data do not exist about departmental cutbacks, consolidations, and closings nationwide, but the existing evidence suggests that small departments in area studies and foreign languages have been vulnerable (see, for example, National Council of Area Studies, 1991). The same may be true of some other humanities disciplines. The number of philosophy departments, for example, appears to have declined since the mid-1970s (Philosophy Documentation Center, 1974–95).

In most cases, the issue is not elimination but reduction through attrition and budgetary cutbacks. Administrators can encourage the consolidation of smaller fields by proposing "integrated" majors involving a number of related, small fields. Some small universities with low science enrollments, for example, have adopted integrated natural science majors. Under pressure, scholars in small fields sometimes themselves seek affiliation with larger departments. Thus, archaeologists rarely attempt to make a go of it outside of anthropology departments, and classicists have in some cases transformed themselves into experts in comparative ancient civilizations. Geneticists only rarely attempt to sustain departments separate from other biological sciences (National Center for Educational Statistics, 1998: 285–92).

The Rise of Interdisciplinary Programs. Statistics on degrees awarded indicate a small to moderate increase in the number of interdisciplinary and multidisciplinary degrees awarded in recent years. These statistics do not do justice to the level of interest in interdisciplinary work in contemporary universities. Many universities, such as the University of Rochester and UCLA, have reorganized their general education curriculum to emphasize the contribution of several disciplines to the understanding of multidisciplinary topics. Foundations, such as the Hewlett Foundation, have provided funds for these "cluster courses." Liberal arts deans throughout the country have been promoting new research umbrella groups and the hiring of faculty who "improve two or three fields rather than one." The new model college searches not for replacements to keep up with specialized fields, but for "synergies" across fields.

To a considerable degree, this remarkable interest in interdisciplinary work reflects a sense that the intellectual excitement lies at the boundaries of fields, rather than in the development of existing disciplinary specialties. The shifting intellectual frontiers in the biological and biomedical sciences and the perceived successes of interdisciplinary "cultural studies" programs have helped to fuel this sense of excitement. But budgetary exigencies may ultimately figure at least as prominently in the thinking of university administrators. As Lynn Hunt has observed, intellectual excitement is but one source of interest in interdisciplinary program development. "[I]nterdisciplinarity may only make the case that humanities faculty are all interchangeable and hence that many are expendable. Interdisciplinarity has tended to weaken the argument for . . . coverage . . . and might thereby facilitate downsizing" (Hunt, 1997: 28).

The ideology of interdisciplinary development substitutes coverage of new topics and approaches for coverage of specialized scholarly fields, the ethos of cross-fertilization for the ethos of specialization, and the politics of coalition-building among groups of enterprising faculty and key administrators for the politics of disciplinary authority. Perhaps this is why many believe that interdisciplinary programs are ultimately more likely to satisfy provosts than professors (Menand, 1997: 214). Yet for institutions focusing scarce resources on developing new professional programs, there may be little choice but to make the most of the current wave of enthusiasm for interdisciplinary work.

Conclusion

The sharp shift of student enrollments over the last thirty years from the arts and sciences to occupational programs represents an important change in American higher education. It is reasonable to ask whether these shifts have led the rise of a new "practical arts" core, replacing the old liberal arts and sciences core of the undergraduate college. The answer given in this chapter is that such an outcome is in fact evident at many master's and doctoral-granting institutions, but that the situation is less clear at leading research universities. In these institutions arts and sciences faculty have generally been able to maintain their centrality, due to the cultural prestige of their disciplines and perhaps also their greater propensity to participate in university governance, among other factors.

Nevertheless, some important changes have occurred in the wake of the shift of students toward the practical arts. These include: reinforcement of utilitarianism as the dominant ethos among students; contributions to the acceptability of faculty and university entrepreneurship; and encouragement of collaborative models for the solution of social problems. The rise of the practical arts has also encouraged migrations of faculty and even whole disciplines toward the occupational training fields, created new vulnerabilities among the smaller arts and sciences fields, and intensified interdisciplinary trends in the liberal arts.

As these changes unfold, opinion data suggest that humanists and scientists are more like one another than they are like professional school faculty on some important issues, such as levels of skepticism about administrators' motivations (arts and sciences faculty are more skeptical), support for intellectual over service commitments (arts and sciences faculty are more purely intellectual), and resistance to the ethos of the market (arts and sciences faculty are more resistant). Thus, the division in mentality represented by C. P. Snow's "two cultures" of science and the humanities is now crosscut, in limited but observable ways, by another line of cleavage dividing professors of the liberal and the practical arts. These tensions are one result of a shift in orientation that has allowed the City of Intellect to prosper even as its one-time center has moved to the periphery in some institutions and become but one of several competing nuclei in many others.

Notes

I would like to thank Andrew Abbott, John Barcroft, Michael E. Brint, Roger L. Geiger, Michael Nacht, Francisco O. Ramirez, Judith Wegener, and David Weiman for comments that improved the quality of this paper. I would also like to thank Maria Bertero-Barcelo, William Korn, Charles S. Levy, Shoon Lio, Mandy Liu, Harriet P. Morgan, and Mark Riddle for research assistance.

1. I have classified the visual and performing arts as liberal arts fields, and communications as an occupational field. At the graduate level, I have classified both of these fields as occupational. I have also classified virtually all other fields outside the humanities, social sciences, and natural sciences as occupational. These include such large and familiar fields as business, engineering, and educa-

tion. They also include fields such as agriculture and natural resources, computer and information sciences, and protective services. At the graduate level, I have compared occupational-professional degrees to a combined category of liberal arts and academic research degrees. This comparison makes intuitive sense insofar as we want to look at the hypothesized replacement of the old core of the university, involving basic scholarly and scientific research, with an hypothesized new core of programs preparing students for employment. In the occupational-professional category, I have included all occupationally oriented masters' fields plus all first professional degree programs. In the liberal arts and academic category, I have included all liberal arts masters' fields plus all doctoral fields. The major changes here are adding first professional degree programs—that is, degrees in theology, law, and medical areas—to the occupational-professional category (where they would belong in any event) and placing all research degrees (including those in fields such as business and engineering) as part of the liberal arts-academic research category.

2. I will concentrate on degrees awarded rather than enrollments, because of methodological problems surrounding the use of enrollments for comparing fields and change over time. Comparison of enrollments is particularly difficult because educational programs are organized differently at different schools and across fields. Some institutions begin enrollment in a professional college in freshman year, while others begin to count in the junior year. Typically when a program is organized in a separate school or college, enrollments include students in all four years. When the program is organized in a department or a college of arts and sciences, only the junior and senior years are reported. Enrollments are also less reliably reported to NCES than are degrees awarded. A few institutions fail to report enrollments; therefore, it is necessary to make estimates in order that the totals may take all institutions into account. For a detailed analysis of data on enrollments and degrees from 1970 through 1985, see Bowen and Sosa (1989).

3. Although most new fields begin at nonelite research universities, some new fields with links to prestigious established fields (computer science and legal studies are two examples) begin at more elite institutions (see Hashem, 2002).

4. Note that interdisciplinary studies does not include either area studies or ethnic studies, fields that have remained both small and relatively stable over the twenty-five-year period. Instead, it includes other sorts of interdisciplinary programs, such as Renaissance studies, environmental studies, comparative ancient civilizations, and politics, philosophy, and economics.

5. Based on a cluster analysis of degrees awarded by institution, Morgan (1998: 35–36) defines "multiversities" operationally as institutions offering master's in education and business and law degrees, each of which account for more than 1 percent of degrees granted. In addition, they grant more than 1 percent of baccalaureate degrees in at least twenty-five different fields, eleven of them applied. She defines "liberal arts universities" as institutions granting more than 1 percent of degrees in each of several graduate and professional fields and, with

the exception of graduate-level professional education, granting degrees primarily in traditional arts and sciences fields. I will use this empirically based definition of patterns of differentiation among research universities.

6. I am grateful to Harriet P. Morgan for sharing the detailed results of her dissertation research. This section is drawn from an unpublished file of institutions from her cluster analysis of HEGIS/IPEDS degrees awarded data for the years 1966 to 1992. I have cross-classified her findings by Carnegie classification codes to describe changes in research universities during the period.

7. Even in the doctorate-granting institutions, men and women with doctorates in educational management have gained over the last decade in public institutions, moving from 10 to 18 percent of the total number of presidents sampled by the American Council on Education.

8. One can imagine two possible explanations for these findings. One is that the outward looking norms of professional life lead to a relatively lower level of interest in university governance. Another possibility is that busier faculty, whatever their fields, are less able to participate, and less interested. The particularly low level of participation of medical and business school faculty suggests that the second hypothesis may be closer to the mark.

9. Data exist on only one facet of student consumerism—the interests of students in practical, job-related courses of study. The desire of universities to maintain or improve the size and quality of their applicant pool has also greatly encouraged a buyer's market for college amenities. University funds have consequently been poured into recreation centers, food courts, student services, and building up other amenities of the campus and the areas surrounding the campus. On some campuses, the same level of effort may not attach to maintaining the rigor of educational standards, or even to ensuring that libraries are well stocked with books and journals.

10. The Cohen et al. (1994) data are based on a response rate of under 50 percent. Efforts to determine the representativeness of these data involved contacting a sample of nonresponding UIRCs. In comparing the two samples, Cohen and his colleagues found no significant differences in total annual budget, number of research and development projects, and number of companies providing support. However, UIRCs in the sample tended to dedicate significantly greater effort to research and development activities and less effort to education and training and technology transfer activities. Generalizations about national trends must be understood with these sample characteristics taken into account.

11. When examining field mobility data, it is important to keep in mind the extraordinary changes in the distribution of faculty over a generation. In 1969, some two-thirds of the surveyed faculty taught in arts and sciences departments. In 1992, the overall proportion was below 60 percent, and only 50 percent for faculty with "new" and "mid-level" faculty. These changes in the marginal distributions are not highlighted in Table 9.5, but they are an important context for evaluating the data in the table.

12. A comparison of cohorts in the 1993 data suggests that younger doctorates in the arts and sciences have been more likely to move from their home dis-

ciplines than senior faculty and that their movement has been in the direction of professional programs at roughly the rate that would be expected given their lesser tendency to stay put in their home disciplines. The patterns of movement among cohorts of doctorates from professional programs are more mixed, however, and seem to depend to a considerable degree on when education schools began to recruit faculty trained in business, health sciences, and other popular professional disciplines.

13. To investigate this possibility further, it might be assumed that fields producing fewer than one in a thousand baccalaureates annually are small and therefore vulnerable. These fields include virtually all area studies programs; botany, ecology, genetics, entomology, and physiology in the biological sciences; Chinese language and literature, Japanese language and literature, Eastern European languages and literatures, Scandinavian and Germanic languages and literatures, Middle Eastern languages and literatures, and classics in the humanities; mathematical statistics, astronomy, astrophysics, atmospheric science, oceanography in the physical sciences; archaeology and urban studies in social science; dance, painting, music history, and music theory and composition in the fine arts.

References

Adelman, Clifford. 1995. *A New College Course Map and Transcript Files*. Washington, DC: U.S. Department of Education.

American Council on Education (ACE). 1995. *The American College President: 1995 Edition*. Washington, DC: American Council on Education.

———. 2000. *The American College President: 2000 Edition*. Washington, DC: American Council on Education.

Astin, Alexander W. 1998. "The Changing American College Student: Thirty Year Trends, 1966–1996." *Review of Higher Education* 21: 115–35.

Bourdieu, Pierre. 1984. *Distinction*. Cambridge, MA: Harvard University Press.

———. 1988. *Homo Academicus*. Stanford, CA: Stanford University Press.

Bowen, William G., and Julie Ann Sosa. 1989. *Prospects for Faculty in the Arts and Sciences: A Study of Factors Affecting Demand and Supply, 1987 to 2012*. Princeton, NJ: Princeton University Press.

Brint, Steven. 1994. *In an Age of Experts: The Changing Role of Professionals in Politics and Public Life*. Princeton, NJ: Princeton University Press.

Brint, Steven, and Jerome Karabel. 1989. *The Diverted Dream: Community Colleges and the Promise of Educational Opportunity, 1900–1985*. New York: Oxford University Press.

Brint, Steven, and Charles S. Levy. 1999. "Professions and Civic Engagement: Trends in Rhetoric and Practice, 1875–1995." Pp. 163–210 in Theda Skocpol and Morris Fiorina (eds.), *Civic Engagement in American Democracy*. Washington, DC: Brookings Institution.

Campus Compact. 1998. *Service Matters: Engaging Higher Education in the Renewal of America's Communities and American Democracy*. Edited by Michael Rothman. Providence, RI: Campus Compact.

Cohen, Wesley, Richard Florida, Lucien Randazzese, and John Walsh. 1998. "Industry and the Academy: Uneasy Partners in the Cause of Technological Advance." Pp. 171–200 in Roger Noll (ed.), *Challenges to Research Universities*. Washington, DC: Brookings Institution Press.

Duffy, Elizabeth A., and Idana Goldberg. 1998. *Crafting a Class: College Admissions and Financial Aid, 1955–1994*. Princeton, NJ: Princeton University Press.

Finkelstein, Martin J., Robert K. Seal, and Jack H. Schuster. 1998. *The New Academic Generation: A Profession in Transformation*. Baltimore, MD: Johns Hopkins University Press.

Freeman, Richard. 1976. *The Overeducated American*. New York: Academic Press.

Geiger, Roger L. 1980. "The College Curriculum and the Marketplace." *Change* (November/December): 17–23 ff.

———. 1986. *To Advance Knowledge: The Growth of American Research Universities, 1900–1940*. New York: Oxford University Press.

———. 1993. *Research and Relevant Knowledge: American Research Universities since World War II*. New York: Oxford University Press.

Glazer, Nathan. 1974. "The Schools of the Minor Professions." *Minerva* 12: 346–64.

Gumport, Patricia J. 1993. "The Contested Terrain of Academic Program Reduction." *Journal of Higher Education* 64: 284–311.

Hashem, Mazen. 2002. "Academic Knowledge from Elite Closure to Public Catering: The Rise of New Growth Fields in American Higher Education." Unpublished Ph.D. dissertation, Department of Sociology, University of California, Riverside.

Higher Education Research Institute (HERI). 1998a. *The American College Freshman: National Norms for 1998*. Los Angeles: Higher Education Research Institute.

Higher Education Research Institute (HERI). 1998b. *The American College Teacher: National Norms for the 1998–99 HER.I Faculty Survey*. Los Angeles: Higher Education Research Institute.

Hoover, Edgar M., and Raymond Vernon. 1959. *Anatomy of a Metropolis*. Cambridge, MA: Harvard University Press.

Hunt, Lynn. 1997. "Democratization and Decline? The Consequences of Demographic Change in the Humanities." Pp. 17–31 in Alvin Kernan (ed.), *What's Happened to the Humanities?* Princeton, NJ: Princeton University Press.

Kerr, Clark. 1964. *The Uses of the University*. New York: Harper Torchbooks.

Kraatz, Matthew, and Edward Zajac. 1998. "Executive Migration and Institutional Change." Unpublished paper, Kellogg School of Management, Northwestern University.

McConnell, T. R., G. Lester Anderson, and Pauline Hunter. 1962. "The University and Professional Education." Pp. 254–78 in Nelson Hardy (ed.), *Education for the Professions*. Chicago: University of Chicago Press.

Menand, Louis. 1997. "The Demise of Disciplinary Authority." Pp. 201–19 in Alvin Kernan (ed.), *What's Happened to the Humanities*. Princeton, NJ: Princeton University Press.

Morgan, Harriet. 1998. "Moving Missions: Organizational Change in Liberal Arts Colleges." Unpublished doctoral dissertation, University of Chicago, Department of Sociology.

Morphew, Christopher. 1998. "The Realities of Strategic Planning: Program Termination at East Central University." Unpublished paper, School of Education, University of Kansas.

National Center for Educational Statistics (NCES). 1998. *Digest of Educational Statistics, 1998.* Washington, DC: Government Printing Office.

National Council of Area Studies Associations. 1991. *Report from the National Council of Area Studies Associations.* Stanford, CA: National Council of Area Studies Associations.

Newman, Frank M. 1985. *Higher Education and the American Resurgence.* Princeton, NJ: Carnegie Foundation for the Advancement of Teaching.

Philosophy Documentation Center. 1974–1995. *Directory of American Philosophers.* Bowling Green, IN: Bowling Green State University. Series.

Schlossman, Steven L., and Michael Sedlak. 1988. *The Age of Reform in American Management Education.* Los Angeles: Graduate Management Admissions Council.

Scott, Joyce A., and Nancy A. Bereman. 1992. "Competition versus Collegiality: Academe's Dilemma for the 1990s." *Journal of Higher Education* 63: 684–98.

Slaughter, Sheila, and Larry L. Leslie. 1997. *Academic Capitalism: Politics, Policies, and the Entrepreneurial University.* Baltimore, MD: Johns Hopkins University Press.

Trow, Martin. 1998. "From Mass Higher Education to Universal Access: The American Advantage." Unpublished paper presented at the North American and Western European Colloquium on Challenges Facing Higher Education, Glion sur Montaux, France, May 14–16.

Useem, Michael. 1989. *Liberal Education and the Corporation.* New York: Aldine de Gruyter.

Veysey, Laurence R. 1965. *The Emergence of the American University.* Chicago: University of Chicago Press.

CHAPTER TEN

The Political Economy of Curriculum-Making in American Universities

SHEILA SLAUGHTER

Although higher education is almost inconceivable without curricula, very little has been written about curricular formation and change. Many historians of the academic disciplines tangentially address curricula while focusing on trends and progress in scholarship. Some of these works are hagiographies that concentrate on the research achievements of great men in the discipline (see, for example, Odum, 1927); at best, they carefully examine the intellectual history of the disciplines within the narrow confines of the official organization of the field (see, for example, Coates, 1960; Somit and Tanenhaus, 1967). Work by institutionally oriented higher education scholars often sees the curricula as changing in response to new types of students, ranging from minority students to "nontraditional" or older students (Conrad and Haworth, 1990) or changing in response to new economic conditions. Today an increasingly popular view holds that market forces are the primary influence on curricular formation (see Volk, Slaughter and Thomas, 2001).

Because these conceptions of curricular formation and change represent the views of higher education leaders, I will call them "the dominant narratives."[1] I consider them to be not so much wrong as incomplete. They are incomplete because they do not pay sufficient attention to the interests of social groups and organizations outside of academe. I will argue that studies of the activities of social movements and external resource providers tell us as much about curricula as do studies that concentrate on the research findings of scholars or the search for market advantages by students and academic administrators.[2]

This chapter is organized into three sections. In the first section, I examine the dominant narratives of curriculum and discuss their limitations. In the second, I present a set of alternative narratives that can enrich curriculum studies. Here I focus on the ways that professional class organization, social movements, and external resource providers influence the development of curricula. In the final section, I provide a revised model of curricular formation and change. This revised model retains some of the emphases of the dominant narratives but adds the insights of political and organizational analysis.

Dominant Narratives of Curricular Change

I have chosen examples of dominant perspectives from three sources: (a) published histories of disciplines and fields; (b) analyses by administrators and higher education scholars that appear in major higher education journals or in books reviewed in these journals; and (c) studies specifically concerned with higher education and market forces.

HISTORIES OF THE DISCIPLINES

The stories that historians of the disciplines tell about curricular formation pay more attention to research than course content. According to these narratives, knowledge makes its way into curricula as part of a lengthy but rational and linear process. Researchers discover new knowledge that is incorporated into peer reviewed journals, then into textbooks, finally appearing as curricula in the classroom. Scholarly research and peer review are at the core of this process (Chubin and Hackett, 1990). The content of the discipline, which forms the basis of its curricula, is shaped by scholar-researchers exploring the frontiers of knowledge and reporting their results in peer reviewed academic journals.

Professional understandings of fields of specialization provide the boundaries around which curricula are organized. Course offerings are determined not by the needs of students so much as by course content that professors see as inducting students into the knowledge of their particular fields. The heart of undergraduate student engagement with the curricula is the major. This is where the accepted knowledge of the field is packaged for student consumption.[3]

Historical accounts of the influence of great scientists are, of course, legion. Many histories tell the story of how the work of scientists such as

Newton, Darwin, Einstein, Watson, and Crick (and also many less towering figures) changed their fields forever. Indeed, the tale of the expert-hero was, until recently, one of the most powerful supports for the position of researchers as the authors of curricula. This tale is embodied in such late-nineteenth- and early-twentieth-century works as Sinclair Lewis's *Arrowsmith*, Henrik Ibsen's *Enemy of the People*, and C. P. Snow's *The New Men*. In these works, transforming discoveries are made possible by the scientific method, and the pursuit of knowledge expresses the interests of society at large. A related genre features natural and social scientists working in the public interest against uninformed and sometimes corrupt special interests. In the biological sciences, the public health advances brought about by germ theory are the classic embodiment of this narrative. In the social sciences, Franklin Roosevelt's "Brain Trust" of economists and lawyers developing social and economic policy tools would perhaps be a comparable example.

In recent years, authors in this tradition have added some qualifications to the story of scientific progress; they have recognized that scientific knowledge often develops slowly and that mistakes are sometimes made along the way. They have recognized certain negative consequences of scientific discoveries—for example, the impact of radiation, the unexpected side effects of certain drugs, and the environmental repercussions of some forms of chemical pollution. Some also strive to make the operations of science more encompassing, including, for example, gender, race, and social class, in their accounts of the social organization and consequences of science.

These newer authors have not abandoned commitments to the universalistic principles by which scientific knowledge is thought to cumulate (Ricci, 1984). Like their predecessors, they continue to place disembodied knowledge at center stage, so we see neither the persons who organize knowledge nor the ways that the structures of organized knowledge articulate with the political economy. Although professors are not obviously present in these texts, their presence is taken for granted, because when all is said and done they are the ones who endorse the progress of science and scholarship. These narratives obliquely but powerfully confirm professors' control of knowledge and their authority over the curriculum.

To what extent are scientific and scholarly pioneers truly the authors of curricula? The answer is: to a considerable degree, but they do not act in environments composed solely of other scientists and scholars. The ideas and principles of leading scientists and scholars are in fact often absorbed into curricula. A breakthrough in the understanding of social network structure, for example, may over time become the central part of new courses on network analysis. The empirical investigations of professors, their theories, and their arguments with one another are primary materials out of which curricula grow. Often these are influenced by the discovery of new source material, technological improvements, new research methods, and other forces closely associated with the internal development of idea systems.

But the story is not as simple as it is usually recounted. The interests of faculty are not simply the result of intellectual progress in which the contributions of scientists and scholars are judged solely by other scientists and scholars. Social movements influence the research programs of individual professors, including those that eventually find their way into curricula. The influence of social movements can even at times lead to the creation of whole new fields, such as ethnic studies and women's studies. Other influences come from external resource providers. The work of professors who contribute to new knowledge (and hence to the development of curricula) is usually supported by outside parties and, in that respect, reflects larger structures of power, opportunity, and preference. Even a topic that seems purely "academic," such as network analysis, may be given a material boost by outside groups, such as drug companies interested in the patterns of personal influence that lead to the adoption of new pharmaceutical products. In other cases, the influence of outside interest groups may be even more direct. When a software firm develops an influential new design or analysis tool, it is a safe bet that courses will soon train students in the use of that tool.

In general, accounts of research scholars as the authors of curricula do not recognize that faculty have vested interests in theories and methods that bring them prestige, position, and resources. The faculty may try to express the values of value-free expertise, but they are inevitably also part of a political structure that favors "standard" incremental science within established paradigms (Bloland and Bloland, 1974; Kuhn, 1962), relies heavily on the judgment of professors at the most prestigious institutions (Cole and Cole, 1973), and has been decidedly tilted in its funding patterns toward research connected to the health care and military contracting industries.

INSTITUTIONAL ACCOUNTS OF
HIGHER EDUCATION SCHOLARS

Articles in higher education journals, which are aimed at higher education scholars and academic administrators, also include themes relevant to the study of curricula. When these authors discuss the preservation and extension of knowledge, they often sound very much like the historians of the disciplines discussed above. They too focus on heroes and heroines of research as authors of the curriculum. The major difference is that they tend to include administrative review and approval as part of the process by which old knowledge is preserved and new knowledge is admitted to the academy.

These accounts do, however, also introduce two new themes: (a) the importance of demographic change (Adelman, 1992; Haworth and Conrad, 1990; Levine, 1989, 1993a); and (b) the importance of changing requirements in the economy for new cognitive skills (Levine, 1993b; Rudolph, 1977; Rudy, 1960).

The demographic explanation sees curricular change as an institutional response to the changing composition of the student population (Conrad and Haworth, 1990; Rudolph, 1977; Rudy, 1960). As Conrad and Haworth (1990: 4, 9) state:

> The ethnic composition of American society has diversified markedly over the past decade, a trend that is expected to continue well into the twenty-first century. . . . A chorus of new voices has [therefore] recently been heard in the academy. These stakeholders—although expressing diverse points-of-view—share a single shared perspective in common: the belief that knowledge, as it is currently understood in the undergraduate curriculum, is partial, incomplete, and distorted. Calling for an end to the exclusive dominance of the traditional canon in the undergraduate curriculum, these scholars have argued for an expansion of curricular borders in higher education to include various cultural and theoretical perspectives.

Analyses based on demographic change do provide an approach to mapping curricular development in the twentieth century. Certainly the "agricultural and mechanical classes" to which the Morrill Act of 1862 was directed represented new groups of students who were attracted to a different, more practical kind of higher education. So too the rise of research universities can be partially understood as a response to the growth of a middle class committed to the idea of science, different than either the practical curricula that were initially linked with the land grants or the philosophical/ religious curricula associated with denominational colleges (Brubacher, 1997; Rudolph, 1977).

But precisely how these new groups encouraged faculty to offer new curricula is not explored, leaving a large "black box" between demographic change and institutional response. In fact, I would argue that demographic shifts are usually better interpreted as part of the context of change than as causal factors in their own right. Changing demographics can certainly provide a favorable setting for changes in particular directions; the rise in the number of women and minorities in higher education in the 1960s, for example, created a favorable context for women's and ethnic studies curricula. But demographic change represents at most an inchoate potential for change. Actual changes are based on students, faculty, and administrators interpreting and acting in response to the various pressures and opportunities in their environments. For example, some writers link increasing numbers of working-class students to the rise of new "vocational" curricula in higher education (Cohen and Brawer, 1982). However, if students interpret the meaning of higher education as study of the liberal arts, an increasing number of working-class students will not necessarily lead to new vocational curricula, as evidence from the early junior colleges demonstrates (Brint and Karabel, 1989).

Arguments about the connection between economic change and the need for new cognitive skills (and, therefore, new courses) are also popular in the administrative literature. When looking back at the nineteenth century, for example, these types of accounts draw connections between the industrial revolution and the incorporation of science and engineering in higher education. A recent example often cited in the literature is the connection between information sciences and the development of global markets. Again, these accounts focus on very general affinities, neither locating nor closely examining mechanisms mediating the response of students, faculty, and administrators to economic and technological change. The arguments have an air of plausibility, but they do not provide any concrete sense of the mechanisms involved in translating broad economic trends into curricular responses.[4]

MARKET FORCES

Narratives based on the role of market forces have become so important in recent years that they deserve separate treatment. Several variants of market narratives provide explanations for curricular formation and change. The most important focus on the human capital investments made by students and their families, or on students-as-consumers of educational products. In both cases, students' choices as rational economic actors are the keys to change, together with faculty and institutional responsiveness.

Human capital narratives are particularly influential in public sector higher education, which has long been committed to increasing access. In this narrative, students' economic interests drive curricular change. As students enter college, they assess their possibilities in the job market, and choose curricula accordingly. Thus, in the late 1970s students moved away from disciplines popular in the countercultural 1960s—sociology, history, the humanities, education—and into fields such as business and computer science to take advantage of opportunities in the market for educated labor. In these narratives, students search for careers that will increase their human capital, thereby repaying their investment in higher education (Leslie and Brinkman, 1988).

The student-as-consumer narrative is, by contrast, particularly significant in elite liberal arts colleges. Here higher education is frankly recognized as a costly expenditure, the largest purchase other than a house that a student (or her parents) will likely make. The main choice in question is the choice of a particular college or university to attend. Institutions compete with each other to attract students, catering to their consumer interests with coffee bars, physical fitness centers, and comfortable dormitories with large rooms and even larger closets. The curriculum is another area in which students exercise choice. In these narratives, the boundaries between market and marketing dissolve, and curricula are not so much constructed by scholar-experts as they are "packaged" or "tailored" to meet student interest—for example, through interdisciplinary programs organized around such appealing topics as the environment or popular culture.

Market narratives are important correctives to studies emphasizing pure academic autonomy in matters of curricular creation. Market narratives remind us that curricula have always been related to status, career choices, and markets for expertise. Market narratives provide a valuable perspective, in particular, on the development of new curricula in occupational and professional fields. Undoubtedly, colleges and universities monitor the development of new fields that will employ educated workers. Today environmental engineering and e-commerce are popular new programs on university campuses, precisely because employment in these fields is projected to grow.

At the same time, market narratives tend to overlook the social structures of power and status that shape market influences. The institutionalized power of organizations and the more diffuse power of social classes are among the most important social structures surrounding curricula. It is possible to see the shaping influence of power and status very clearly when two market forces come into conflict. In the allocation of resources to departments, is student demand for more courses in the arts really decisive in institutions that emphasize entrepreneurial science and engineering, or are institutional priorities based on expectations of grants, contracts, and potential alumni contributions more decisive? Market narratives also tend to overlook the extent to which fields are arrayed not just by student demand but also by the social composition of students who have the opportunity to pursue them. Differences in the purchasing power of students from different social classes send most working-class students to proprietary schools and community colleges, most middle-class students to state colleges, and most upper-middle-class students to research universities and independent liberal arts colleges.

Alternative Approaches

The dominant narratives offer plausible, but limited accounts of the causes of curricular change. Scholars of curriculum should consequently ask themselves what other perspectives are available and what those alternative approaches might contribute to an understanding of curricula. There are at least three alternatives that should, I believe, be brought into theories of curricula and curricular change. These are narratives about: (a) professional organization; (b) social movements; and (c) external resource providers.

PROFESSIONAL ORGANIZATION

Behind contemporary views of the faculty as authors of the curriculum lie assumptions about the prerogatives of professional organization. These assumptions should be inspected. It is useful to think of the origins of modern professional organization as an undertheorized middle-class social movement. For all of its contemporary emphasis on inclusiveness and diversity, higher education has historically been tied to the rise of the professional class.

In a sense, professional associations were to middle-class economic organization as labor unions were to the working class. However, the professions' emphasis on "value-free" knowledge, and their commitment to the "public interest" (as defined by the Progressive movement), make it difficult to see the class implications of professional organization (see Bledstein, 1977; Kolko, 1967; Silva and Slaughter, 1984). In the Progressive era, professionals began to secure legal monopolies on practice through higher education and state licensure, to raise their salaries, to attain a modicum of academic freedom, to speak with the authority of professional expertise, and to create the organizational infrastructure of associations that would enable them to sustain and expand these benefits.

Academic professionalism, with its institutionalized guarantees of control by credentialed experts, provides a foundation for the appearance (and the partial reality) of individual experts as authors of the curriculum. Other forms of curricular development—whether through professional consensus, professional committees, cross-disciplinary networks, government agencies, or collaborative societal efforts—can be easily imagined (and all have existed historically). The success of the professional movement installed the individual expert as the primary judge of what should enter and what should not enter the curriculum. It is the success of the ideology of professionalism that encourages inattention to the larger contexts of professional work. It obscures the extent to which professional judgments take place in a context shaped by many forces other than the idea-driven progress of knowledge.

SOCIAL MOVEMENTS

Science itself was able to enter the American university at least in part because it was linked to a social and political movement, the Progressive movement. Until the late nineteenth century, both natural and social science were organized outside the academy—in associations such as the American Statistical Society, the American Physical Society, and the American Social Science Association. Although science had made inroads in the mid-nineteenth century, it was widely incorporated into college and university curricula only following campaigns by coalitions of professionals, aspiring professionals, university managers, businessmen, and philanthropists. Progressivism embraced science as a fundamental force of order and progress. At its peak, Progressivism celebrated all things scientific, from physics to the new "science" of management (Kevles, 1978; Noble, 1977). As befits its importance in the professional movement, advocacy of science was hardly limited to professors in a handful of natural science disciplines. It was the banner under which engineers, social scientists, agriculturalists, and educators all marched.

Science was an expression of middle-class claims to professional authority, a way of staking out space between the industrial working class and corporate capitalism (Perkin, 1989). Specialized curricula that led to credentials with a university imprimatur were building blocks of expertise and authority. Without the Progressive movement and the myriad secondary associations that championed science, the penetration of science into higher education might have been more successfully limited, at least temporarily, by the many groups of clergy, humanists, moral philosophers, and gentry families who opposed its incorporation, because it threatened their conception of higher learning as providing appropriate "furniture for the mind" (Veysey, 1965).

In portraying science as a social movement, I do not wish to discount the valid truth-claims of science. I do, however, want to question the story that is commonly told of depersonalized, disembodied science entering the university simply because it demonstrated superior explanatory power. An examination of the coalitions behind the incorporation of science suggests that the social movements of the 1960s are not necessarily exceptions to normal patterns of curricular formation, but are very likely closer to the rule.

Today writers such as Clifford Conrad and Jennifer Haworth (1990), Clifford Adelman (1992), and Arthur Levine (1993b) see the curriculum changing to meet the needs of the new groups that have become "stakeholders" in higher education. By contrast, I see faculty and administrators as making little effort to accommodate the curricular interests of new groups until student and community activists demanded that knowledge central to these groups be incorporated into the curricula. In other words, institutions did not change the curricula in response to demographic change, but rather in response to social movements originating outside the university.

In the early 1960s, African-American students were overwhelmingly concentrated in segregated institutions (Trent 1991). Black studies programs did not exist in the historically black institutions, nor did they exist at white institutions. In the 1960s, the Black Power and student movements pressed for increased access to white institutions for black students and for curricula that addressed their historical experience (Mc-Adam, 1988). These social movements provided the impetus for the formation of five hundred Black Studies programs by 1971 (Altbach, 1991). Contrary to demographic explanations of curricula, examination of the history of African-Americans in American higher education suggests that African-American students were not automatically or easily included as their numbers increased. Disruptive, popular social movements were the keys to expanded access and to the creation of curricula that spoke to the lives of a group previously excluded from higher education.

Like African-American studies, the institutionalization of women's studies demonstrates the importance of social movements in curricular formation. Women entered the academy in substantial numbers during the late nineteenth and early twentieth centuries. However, women's studies did not emerge as a field, even though large numbers of women made arguments strikingly similar to those that encouraged the growth of women's studies in the 1970s and 1980s. Instead, women were routinely directed into fields associated with women's work, such as education, social work, and nursing (Rosenberg, 1982). If women enrolled in the humanities or social science, their primary goal was assumed to be finding a husband, their secondary goal educating themselves to better educate their families, and a tertiary goal the development of career skills in women's fields so they could better support their families in the event of the death of their husband.

Changing demographics created fertile ground for curricular change— by 1970, women constituted some 42 percent of the student population—but I see the necessary catalyst as the development of a radical feminist movement organized around an analysis of society that saw gender as the central and salient divide (DuBois et al., 1985; Echols, 1989). This analysis, fueled by the civil rights and student movements, was developed outside of the university, and it moved into the academy only after demands and protests by participants in the women's liberation movement. Until women organized around gender issues as a fertile field for inquiry, the academy remained blind to gender as a problematic category and major division in society.[5]

One response to the mobilization of underrepresented minorities and feminists was a countermobilization of conservatives who sought to reverse or at least contain these forces of change. In widely reviewed and well-publicized books, writers such as Allan Bloom (1986), Roger Kimball (1990), and Dinesh D'Sousa (1991) attacked changes in the curriculum that challenged what they construed to be the heritage of Western civilization. They argued that courses on science and Western civilization were being pushed out of the curriculum by required courses on race, gender, and non-Western societies. Appropriating popular democratic themes, they portrayed themselves as bravely confronting the mass of students and "tenured radicals" in the name of academic standards, values, and excellence.[6]

This opposition to curricular change was also a social movement, albeit one funded and led by participants with greater access to power and privilege than most others. Unlike the social movements of the 1960s, the neoconservatives were by and large established professionals, white, male, and sponsored by foundations with a conservative moral and fiscal agenda (Diamond, 1992; Weisberg, 1992). Far from appealing to grassroots conservatives of the "Moral Majority," its natural constituency was members of the National Association of Scholars and other professors threatened by the new approaches to knowledge inspired by the interest of younger scholars in race and gender.

This countermovement may have had its largest impact in helping to create a climate conducive to professional studies, both because of the movement's sympathy for the market as an arbiter of the value of disciplines (at least outside elite institutions) and because of the doubts these writers raised concerning the continued centrality of the humanities and social sciences in an age of contentious cultural politics.

EXTERNAL RESOURCE PROVIDERS

Perhaps the most significant oversight of the dominant narratives is their inattention to the direct linkages between curricula and powerful groups and organizations outside the university. According to those who emphasize market forces, curricula and market are related, but not in any way that would compromise the autonomy, integrity, or authority of faculty as authors of curricula. This is misleading. Professors do have considerable say over what is and is not included in curricula in their fields, but they are far from completely autonomous.

An alternative and more realistic approach is to set disciplines within the context of powerful organizations and social groups. Disciplines are dependent, to a large degree, on the organizations and groups that provide support for them, and these organizations and groups can and do influence curricula. For this reason, critical accounts of curricula provide a valuable complement to studies that focus on the progress of ideas within autonomous and self-regulating scholarly communities.[7]

In most cases, these critical narratives stress the close ties between academic fields and specific sectors of the political economy. Often they focus on industries in military and medical fields and on government mission agencies that have close ties to these industries (see, for example, Braverman, 1975; Domhoff, 1970; O'Connor, 1973; White, 2000). Some studies stress the ties between university departments of science and engineering, the Department of Defense, and defense industries such as aerospace, computers, and electronics (Dickson, 1984; Leslie, 1993; Markusen and Yudkin, 1992; Melman, 1982; Noble, 1984). Other studies describe the ties between university departments of chemistry, bioscience, pharmacy, and medical technology industries (Ehrenreich and Ehrenreich, 1970; Navarro, 1982; Starr, 1982). These studies trace the movement of faculty between corporations and universities, detail consulting and spin-off arrangements, and describe the formation of curricula that directly serve mission agencies and corporations (Leslie, 1993). They suggest that the bulk of academic science funding arises out of the shared interests of faculty researchers, mission agencies, and industries.[8]

Another body of literature shows connections between the social sciences and corporate and government activity. Some studies link the development of engineering and management science, describing these fields' efforts to increase productivity by close surveillance of labor, often through time-and-motion studies that encouraged management control over almost every physical movement made by workers (Baritz, 1960; Larson, 1977; Noble, 1977). Other studies document how Cold War politics and Central Intelligence Agency funding led to the development of whole new fields, such as area studies. Related studies discuss the role agribusiness interests played in shaping curricula in the area of international development and how social science participated in efforts to control popular insurgencies in Third World countries (Horowitz, 1975; Rowen, 1971). Social control has been a theme too in the critical literature on the development of education and social work curricula. This literature emphasizes how students in these fields are provided with means to control the wayward, deviant, and underprivileged who do not share the values and habits of the larger society (see, for example, Apple, 1979; Kunzel, 1994; Piven and Cloward, 1977).

Accounts of the direct connections between curricula and powerful external interests could plausibly be seen as fleshing out the dominant narratives. But the dominant narratives generally find little of value in them. Direct ties between curricula and external organizations raise the possibility of academic knowledge as the servant of power, ministering to special interests at odds with the public good. More problematic still, if curricula are seen as cementing ties to external groups, corporate managers and government officials would become the coauthors of curricula in many concrete instances. Such a change of orientation would challenge conventional views of the autonomy and authority of science and scholarship.

A New Model of Curricular Formation and Change

It is possible to improve on existing models of curricula by adopting the useful features of the dominant narratives, rejecting their less useful features, and adding elements from the alternative theoretical traditions I have discussed above. In this section, I will provide the outlines of a new model of curricular formation and change.

THE CURRICULUM IN CONTEXT

Curricula exist at many levels in academe. At the most macro level, entirely new programs are introduced, as colleges and universities try to keep up with developments in knowledge and opportunities in the market for educated labor. At the institutional level, professors add to programs through the creation of new courses or create new courses of study in their areas of specialization. These courses reflect developments in the field, as influenced both by the internal development of idea systems and by the groups and organizations surrounding the discipline. And, finally, students and faculty negotiate the meaning of courses in the process of their interactions in the classroom. Each of these levels is important; unfortunately, they are rarely, if ever, studied together.

The essential assumption in my model of curriculum making is that knowledge is contested and constructed within a context of competing and cooperating interests. In this respect, I share the presuppositions of the school of cultural studies that is often labeled "social construction-ism." This school argues that cultural ideas and practices do not simply reflect an agreed-upon reality, but are instead constructed by social actors

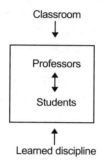

University administration oversight
University curriculum committee
Department and college curriculum committees

FIG. 10.1. Conventional views of social construction of curriculum

as they attempt to advance their interests and understandings in cooperation and conflict with other social actors. Most social constructionists focus on small-scale studies because it is easier to see how interaction influences the construction of common realities in such settings (see, for example, Becker et al. 1961; Fine, 1979; Latour and Woolgar, 1983). I am sympathetic to the outlook of social constructionists, but I must reject their tendency to focus on the micro level, on interactions of a small number of actors in one institutional setting. A more appropriate, expanded form of social constructionism would look not only at the immediate actors—in this case, faculty and students in classrooms—but also at the organizations and groups that impinge on the classroom and the curriculum.

I will show how an expanded social construction approach can enhance understanding of curricular formation by using it to examine the forces at play in curriculum making in physics and women's studies. These fields are often viewed as extremely different on many dimensions, but I will show that the same type of analysis can help to explain the context of curriculum making in both fields.

The organizational framework of a conventional discipline-based view of curricula is shown in Figure 10.1. The focus here is on the classroom. Professors are seen to have links outside the classroom, but usually only to their professional societies. More accurate representations of the organizational landscape for the disciplines of physics and women's studies are provided in Figures 10.2 and 10.3. These figures show that many powerful organizations help to mold curricular formation for the disciplines, thereby strongly influencing departments, majors, and ultimately concrete course offerings. These organizations help to shape curricula through decisions on funding, through influencing the climate of thought in which curricula are developed, through pressing directly for answers to questions that are of significant interest to them, and in other ways.

Physics as an Organizational Structure. Figure 10.2 illustrates the social organization of physics as a disciplinary field. The primary learned association for physics is the American Physical Society (APS),[9] established in the nineteenth century. APS is at the heart of a network of related scientific associations, many of which are subspecialties (such as the American Nuclear Society), others of which are applied (such as the American Institute of Physics), and still others of which are multidisciplinary (such as the American Association of Physics in Medicine). The density of learned associations surrounding physics creates clout in Congress and government agencies, stimulates resource procurement, and encourages membership and commitment among physicists. The nine official APS journals provide outlets for the construction of academic careers through peer-reviewed publication. The costs of publication are usually paid by scientists' grants or by funds from scientists' universities, freeing APS monies for use in other endeavors.

Contrary to narratives about the purity of science and its isolation in ivory towers, the APS actively works with a wide range of nonscience organizations to influence the future of physics. The Association's Public Affairs Committee comments on issues related to physics. Some are technical issues—for example, the official APS position is against renewing the Strategic Defense Initiative if tests fail to prove the technical accuracy of the system—but others aim at lobbying for legislation favorable to physics. For example, the APS Public Affairs Committee advocates the National Research Investment Act of 1998, introduced in the Senate. The APS Congressional Fellows Program is a joint government–learned association program in which academic physicists serve for a year on a congressperson's staff, providing technical information to inform policy relevant to physics.

The APS, like many other physical and life sciences, is represented in the Academy Complex—the National Academy of Science, the National Research Council, the Institute of Medicine, and the National Academy of Engineering. The particular subgroup that represents physics is the

FIG. 10.2. Social Construction of Physics Curricula

GOVERNMENT

MISSION AGENCIES

Department of Defense
Defense Advanced Projects Agency (DARPA)
Strategic Defense Initiative (SDI)
Office of Naval Research
Department of Energy
National Aeronautics and Space Agency (NASA)
National Science Foundation

(selected) LEGISLATION GOVERNING PHYSICS FUNDING

Annual mission agency appropriations,
National Defense Education Act (1956)
Excellence in Mathematics, Science & Education (1990)

DEFENSE CONTRACTORS

General Electric
Westinghouse
AT&T
[list of defense primes–Markusen & Yudkin]

FOUNDATIONS

Carnegie Foundation of Washington
Rockefeller Foundation
Ford Foundation
Mellon Foundation

ACCREDITING AND TESTING ASSOCIATIONS

North Central Accrediting Association, etc.
Educational Testing Service
SAT, GRE

BRIDGE GROUPS (selected)

DOD-University Forum
Business-Higher Education Forum

PROFESSIONAL

LEARNED ASSOCIATIONS

American Physical Society
Related learned associations (selected)

International Union of Pure and Applied Physics
American Institute of Physics
American Association of Physics in Medicine
American Astronomical Society
American Nuclear Society
Federation of Materials Society
International Association of Mathematical Physics

JOURNALS

American Physical Society Journals

Physical Review Online Archive
Physical Review A: Atomic, Molecular & Optical Physics
Physical Review B: Condensed Matter and Material
Physical Review D: Particles, Fields, Gravitation & Cosmology
Physical Review E: Statistical Physics, Plasmas, Fluids
Physical Review Special Topics: Accelerators & Beams
Physical Review Letters
Physical Review Focus
Review of Modern Physics

Related Journals

Applied Physics Letters
Chaos
Computing in Science & Engineering
Journal of Applied Physics
The Journal of Chemical Physics
Journal of Mathematical Physics
Journal of Physical & Chemical Reference Data
Medical Physics

University Administration Oversight
University Curriculum Committee
Department and College Curriculum Committees

CLASSROOM

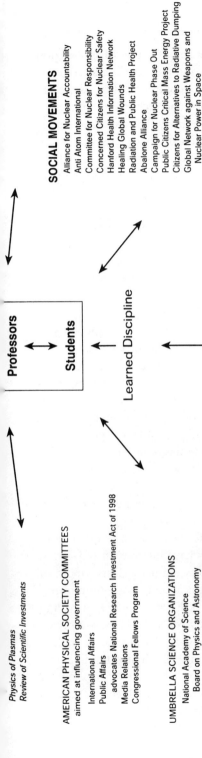

Physics of Plasmas
Review of Scientific Investments

Professors

Students

Learned Discipline

SOCIAL MOVEMENTS

Alliance for Nuclear Accountability
Anti Atom International
Committee for Nuclear Responsibility
Concerned Citizens for Nuclear Safety
Hanford Health Information Network
Healing Global Wounds
Radiation and Public Health Project
Abalone Alliance
Campaign for Nuclear Phase Out
Public Citizens Critical Mass Energy Project
Citizens for Alternatives to Radiative Dumping
Global Network against Weapons and
  Nuclear Power in Space
Grandmothers for Peace International
Physicians for Social Responsibility

AMERICAN PHYSICAL SOCIETY DEVELOPMENT DEPARTMENT

Raises funds for physics research and physics education programs,
bringing together Nobel Laureates and leaders of corporate America

AMERICAN PHYSICAL SOCIETY COMMITTEES
aimed at influencing government

International Affairs
Public Affairs
  advocates National Research Investment Act of 1998
Media Relations
Congressional Fellows Program

UMBRELLA SCIENCE ORGANIZATIONS

National Academy of Science
  Board on Physics and Astronomy
  Government-University-Industry Roundtable
National Research Council
Institute of Medicine
National Academy of Engineering

American Association for the Advancement of Science

CORPORATE ASSOCIATES OF THE AMERICAN INSTITUTE OF PHYSICS

"...serv[ing] the industrial physics community by improving the effectiveness of people and
organizations in advancing corporate goals through the use of physics"

The Aerospace Corporation
Agilent Laboratories
AGR International, Inc.
AIL Systems, Inc.
Bechtel BWXT Idaho, LLC
Corning Incorporated
The Dow Chemical Company
Eastman Kodak Company
Energy Conversion Devices, Inc.
Exxon Research and Engineering Company
Exxon Production Research Company
Ford Motor Company
General Atomics

General Electric Company
General Motors R&D Center
The Goodyear Tire& Rubber Company
Hewlett-Packard Company
HRL Laboratories, LLC
Instruments, SA, Inc.
International Business Machines
Janis Research Company, Inc.
Lake Shore Cryotronics
Libbey-Owens-Ford Company
Lockheed Martin IR Imaging Systems
Lucent Technologies, Bell Laboratories
3M Company

MacroSonix Corporation
MIT Lincoln Laboratory
Monsanto Company
NEC Research Institute, Inc.
Philips Research
Phillips Petroleum Company
Polaroid Corporation
Schlumberger-Doll Research
Shell E&P Technology Company
Springer-Verlag New York Publishers
Texas Instruments
Thomas Jefferson National Accelerator Facility
United Technologies Research Center

Board on Physics and Astronomy. The Academy Complex has a section that deals with Policy for Science. This section has boards and committees that deal with science, technology, and economic policy, as well as analysis and comment on the federal science and technology budget. It also sponsors the Government-University-Industry Research Roundtable (GUIRR), which works with member organizations to cross the boundaries between sectors. GUIRR smoothes out problems in cooperation, which can result from the standards of academe, the regulatory barriers of government, the profit-seeking behavior of corporations, or other sources. GUIRR attempts to build standards and consensus, for example, setting rules for how long graduate students' work can be withheld from public shelving in the library to protect universities' and corporations' patent rights. The GUIRR is an example of bridging organizations that are common in powerful disciplines. (Selected other bridging organizations are listed also in Figure 10.2.)

The APS does not limit its efforts to influencing and encouraging resource flows to physics through government funding. The applied section of APS, the American Institute of Physics, has a corporate associates program, which is committed to "(serving) the industrial physics community by improving the effectiveness of people and organizations in advancing corporate goals through physics" (*www.aps.org*, 2000). A number of the thirty-nine corporate associates are global high-technology corporations noted for their extensive assets and high profits. Corporate associates contribute money to the APS, provide information about careers and research opportunities, serve on a variety of committees, and generally increase the movement between university-based researchers and corporations. The APS also has a development committee that solicits corporate gifts, many of which are used for scholarship programs.

As APS has interests in government, foundations, and other nonprofit organizations, so these organizations have interests in physics. A number of the mission agencies fund physics, with the Department of Defense (DOD) and the National Aeronautical and Space Administration (NASA), followed by the Department of Energy (DOE), providing the largest amounts of money for university research. Physics received more than $1 billion in research funding in 1998, of which $804 million came from federal sources. The vast majority of physics funding was from the federal mission agencies. Sometimes the federal government enacts special legislation relevant to physics, some of which is indicated in Figure 10.2. As noted above, representatives of the physics community, working through associations like the APS, actively work with government in negotiating this legislation.

Many corporations produce products based on physics. Perhaps the best examples are General Electric and Westinghouse, corporations responsible for pioneering nuclear energy. DOD and NASA contractors also draw heavily on physics. These contractors include: McDonnell-Douglas, General Dynamics, Martin-Marietta-Lockheed, Boeing, Rockwell International, TRW, Ford Aerospace and Communications, United Technologies, and many others (Markusen and Yudkin, 1992). As the Cold War ended and nuclear energy generation declined, physicists began to work in materials science, biophysics, and medicine, particularly in the area of medical devices. All of these areas are of great interest to high-technology corporations.

Like other learned associations, APS works with the various accrediting associations to establish what is essential for a "good" physics department. The accrediting associations, along with members of the discipline, measure physics departments by these standards, until all resemble physics departments at research universities funded and shaped by the constellation of organizations in Figure 10.2.

Physics does not interact only with mainstream organizations. Social movements intersect physics and organizations like the APS. The organizations listed under social movements in Figure 10.2 are only some of the organizations concerned with nuclear power. Many other organizations are concerned with different aspects of physics. The line between social organizations and organized academic physics, as represented by organizations like the APS, is not hard and fast. Professors of physics participate in a number of social movements. For example, physics professors led the movement to end Star Wars and continue to monitor the Strategic Defense Initiative. The APS has a task force that deals with SDI and an official statement. The Civil Rights Movement and the Women's Liberation Movement affected physics: the APS helps women and minority applicants access funds and opportunities aimed at encouraging their participation in science. Social movements, however, generally do not occupy as much of APS attention as do mainstream organizations.

The point of Figure 10.2 is analytic rather than descriptive. Curricula are not constructed by scientists whose exclusive interest lies in revealing the inner logic and structure of the subject of their discipline (Latour and Woolgar 1983). The instrumental interests of the organizations with which physicists interact are also important. High-energy physics advances, for example, only so long as governments or universities provide linear accelerators. Laws of nature undoubtedly exist, but the laws of nature are understood in ways shaped by physicists in learned associations and the many organizations with which they interact.

The status of physics as a field is undoubtedly related to its organizational network, its ability to regularly and predictably secure substantial funding, its ties to powerful corporations, its utility in relation to economic development, the career paths it opens for its students, the international prizes and awards available to scholars, and the overhead funds it brings to universities. Physicists are not simply acted upon by external forces; they are part and parcel of governments and corporations. They have successfully connected their knowledge to a wide variety of power and funding sources that allow their field to thrive.

Women's Studies as an Organizational Structure. In contrast to physics, women's studies is located in a relatively sparse network of organizations, and it constructs itself very differently than physics. (See Figure 10.3.) The National Women's Studies Association (NWSA) is the association that represents Women's Studies.[10] NWSA sponsors few journals. Its caucuses, task forces, and interest groups have titles that sound more like social movements than the American Physical Society's International Affairs, Public Affairs, Media Relations and Development units, although both sets of subcommittees aim to influence the environment in which their respective disciplines are lodged. NWSA has no formal ties with corporations, and no long-standing ties with government funding agencies. Its ties to government are to agencies that prohibit discrimination rather than agencies that provide funding.

The National Science Foundation does not fund the humanities, and, among the social sciences, recognizes only psychology, economics, political science, and sociology. Other social science fields are categorized as "all other social science." Women's studies would fall in that category. In 1998, the category of other social sciences received $495 million in research funding, of which $155 million was federal funding. In other words, the field of physics, a single science field, received more than five times as much federal funding as *all* "other social science" fields, which included anthropology, geography, linguistics, cultural studies, American studies, and women's studies.

As in physics, the status of women's studies is related to its organizational networks. Women's studies is able to access only a fraction of the resources for research, including scholarships and fellowships for stu-

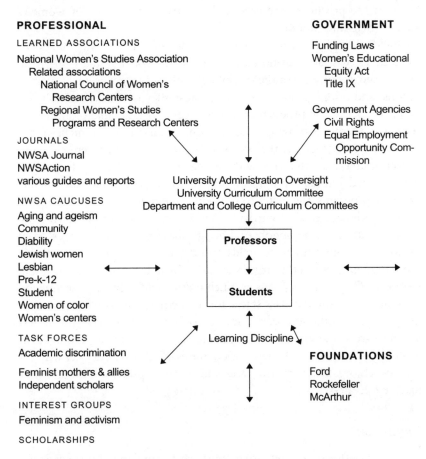

PROFESSIONAL

LEARNED ASSOCIATIONS

National Women's Studies Association
   Related associations
      National Council of Women's
         Research Centers
      Regional Women's Studies
         Programs and Research Centers

JOURNALS

NWSA Journal
NWSAction
various guides and reports

NWSA CAUCUSES

Aging and ageism
Community
Diability
Jewish women
Lesbian
Pre-k-12
Student
Women of color
Women's centers

TASK FORCES

Academic discrimination

Feminist mothers & allies
Independent scholars

INTEREST GROUPS

Feminism and activism

SCHOLARSHIPS

GOVERNMENT

Funding Laws
Women's Educational
   Equity Act
   Title IX

Government Agencies
   Civil Rights
   Equal Employment
      Opportunity Com-
      mission

University Administration Oversight
University Curriculum Committee
Department and College Curriculum Committees

Professors

Students

Learning Discipline

FOUNDATIONS

Ford
Rockefeller
McArthur

FIG. 10.3. Social construction of Women's Studies Curricula. Data for this figure were taken from the National Women's Studies Association homepage (http://www.nwsa.org/).

dents, available to physics, and it has almost no ties to corporations, economic development, or high-technology science. The career lines available to graduates of women's studies programs are unclear. Many graduates work in government or nonprofit organizations, particularly in agencies that deal with social welfare, which disproportionately employ women and minorities (Carnoy and Levin, 1985). Because so many women work in public sector agencies concerned with social welfare, the current emphasis in higher education on market ideology and high-income fields in the private sector erodes the status and prestige of women's studies (Slaughter, 1998).

Fields that promote new curricula—women's studies, African-American studies, Chicano/Latino studies, gay and lesbian studies—often do not see the importance of the discipline's linkages to government, corporations, and bridging organizations, because they have taken established narratives about the production of knowledge by academic pioneers too seriously. Members of new fields, aspiring to find a secure niche in the university, piece together the obvious accoutrements of academic organization: learned associations with annual meetings, heavily footnoted, peer-refereed journals, programs or perhaps departments, and finally, graduate programs, the better to reproduce themselves.

Institutional denial of curricular legitimacy stems not so much from racism, sexism, or homophobia (although these may play a part) as from institutional commitment to fields and departments with close links to those organizations in the larger society with status, power, prestige, and resources. Credibility depends as much on the field's ability to secure and maintain upper-middle-class status for its membership as on its commitment to truth. Although peer review, autonomy, and the individual quest for truth are at the forefront of academic narratives, the background is at least equally important. Unless communities of scholars intersect with resource-rich organizations, they are unlikely to be preferred, though they may be tolerated.[11]

Conclusion

I have outlined an alternative approach to thinking about curricular construction, one I have referred to as an expanded social construction approach. This approach looks beyond immediate actors to the organizations and movements that constitute their broader environment. The approach allows scholars of curricula to take power, organizations, and social classes into account without losing sight of the actions of individual professors in their classrooms.

My analysis suggests that curriculum planners of the future will need to think about more than creating a series of courses, whether these are located on-campus or in virtual classrooms. To implement new curricula successfully, faculty and administrators will have to position programs in the dense web of organizations that surround the disciplines and professions. Although they are in the background in most accounts of curricular formation, the professional associations create and maintain many of the links that connect the academy, the economy, and the state. Strong programs have strong professional associations. For new curricula to become widely institutionalized, curriculum planners must be able to ensure that programs will lead to prestige and resources for faculty and well-paid professional careers for students.

The implications of this approach are important for understanding the trajectory of academic disciplines. In recent years, fewer students have shown an interest in studying physics as a major field. In spite of this decline in enrollments, physics continues to thrive on campus. To some degree, the strength of physics in the face of declining student interest represents a testimony to the field's record of intellectual achievement. But, I would argue, the dense web of powerful and prestigious organizations supporting physics has an even more direct bearing on its continued vitality. By contrast, fields like women's studies are vulnerable because, while they have a record of intellectual achievement, they lack comparable levels of class and organizational support.

Notes

1. I prefer the term "narrative" to the terms "explanation" or "argument," because the term highlights the mix of rhetoric, cultural assumptions, and facts typically involved in accounts of curricular formation and change. I use the term "narrative" in a sense similar to Haraway (1989). I see scholarly and administrative accounts of disciplines and curricula formation as part "of story-telling . . . rule-governed, constrained, [but] historically changing (practices)" (p. 4). These story-telling practices occur among members of (segmented) communities. Narratives that treat curriculum are primarily concerned with interpreting science and professional life within postsecondary education to varied audiences.

2. In some sections, this chapter draws on arguments first developed in Slaughter (1997).

3. Typically, undergraduates take from 30 to 40 credit hours in the major, from 12 to 24 hours in the minor, which is prelude to another field's major, between 40 and 50 hours of general education, and between 25 and 30 hours of electives, for a total of 125 to 130 hours. Roughly 70 to 115 hours of courses taken by undergraduate students are part of a major.

4. The notable exceptions to this treatment of curricula formation occur with regard to the role of the federal government. The work of postsecondary curricula scholars tends to view the role of the federal government as having "turned

from a helping hand to a clenched fist" (Mayville, 1980) through legislation and regulation. This conception sees the state as monolithic and authoritarian a post-secondary education, whether public or private, as separate from the state. This is a rather inaccurate conception that pits "us" (colleges and universities) against "them" (the federal government) and argues that postsecondary institutions, which are often formally part of the state sector, should receive federal monies without oversight or procedures to ensure accountability (Berdahl, 1978; Mayville, 1980). Moreover, this limited conception of the state as regulator overlooks the relationship of the complex interplay of different parts of the state and different parts of the political economy. An understanding of the complex links between the two might reveal a more accurate picture of the curricula formation process (Rhoades and Slaughter, 1991).

5. The civil rights movement, the student movement, and the women's movement were clearly not the only 1960s social movements to shape curricula. The Chicano movement, as embodied in La Raza (Acuna, 1988; Shorris, 1992), the Native American movement, as embodied in the American Indian Movement, as well as lesbian and gay social movements all began outside the university (Bensimon, 1992; D'Emilio, 1983; Kennedy and Davis, 1993). They entered the academy as students who became movement participants, and demonstrated on campus, demanding that curricula and programs treating a wider scope of human experience be developed. The curricula, then, were broadened in response to direct action by social movements and by policies inspired by these movements.

6. As others have noted, the neoconservatives' description of curriculum change is an inversion of the actual situation on most campuses, where there are relatively few minority students, where women are still heavily concentrated in fields according to traditional gender patterns, and where white male professors still hold most senior faculty positions. It also reverses the reality of course-taking patterns among undergraduates. Undergraduate students are at most required to take one class that deals with race, gender, and non-Western societies, and some 80 percent of students still take Western civilization courses (Adelman, 1992; Levine, 1993b).

7. Some post-Marxist approaches, in particular, offer important insights. On the one hand, post-Marxist theory points to the continued and complex interaction between the military, federal mission agencies, civilian technology policy, and large corporations in sustaining high-prestige curricula in the university (Barrow, 1990; Dickson, 1984; Kevles, 1978; Noble, 1984; Slaughter, 1990; Winks, 1987). On the other hand, it underscores the connections between low-prestige fields and the class, race, and gender of faculty and students, as well as the relation of these curricula to (perceived) social welfare functions of the state (Slaughter, 1993; Volk, Slaughter, and Thomas, 2001).

8. Ironically, the physical and biological sciences, which have the closest links to corporations and mission agencies, are those that make the most emphatic claims to objectivity (Anderson, 1990: 135). Perhaps the claim to objectivity is, in part, an effort to distance these fields from sponsors and patrons, strengthening the brittle professional autonomy of scientists.

9. Much of the information for Figure 10.2 was taken from the American Physical Society home page, www.aps.org.

10. The information on NWSA was taken from the NWSA home page, www. nwsa.org.

11. There are some ironies and costs in the quest for legitimacy. The trappings of academic organization may fail to secure legitimacy within the university for fields without strong external support, while at the same time distancing scholars from the culture and aspirations of the communities they intend to represent. Scholars in new fields often undermine their initial purposes by reproducing the signs, symbols, and structures that perforce put distance between themselves and their communities, between their passion and its expression, between their quest for social justice and its realization (Wegman, 2001).

References

Acuna, Rudolfo. 1988. *Occupied America: A History of Chicanos.* New York: Harper and Row.

Adelman, Clifford. 1992. *Tourists in Our Own Land: Cultural Literacies and the College Curriculum.* Washington, DC: U.S. Department of Education.

Altbach, Philip G. 1991. "The Racial Dilemma." Pp. 3–17 in Philip G. Altbach and Kofi Lomotey (eds.), *The Racial Crisis in American Higher Education.* Albany: State University of New York Press.

Anderson, Melissa L. 1990. "Changing Curriculum in Higher Education." Pp. 119–44 in Clifford F. Conrad and Jennifer G. Haworth (eds.), *Curriculum in Transition: Perspectives on the Undergraduate Experience.* Needham Heights, MA: Ginn.

Apple, Michael W. 1979. *Ideology and Curriculum.* London: Routledge and Kegan Paul.

Baritz, Loren. 1960. *The Servants of Power: A History of the Use of Social Science in American Industry.* Freeport, CT: Wesleyan University Press.

Barrow, Clyde W. 1990. *Universities and the Capitalist State: Corporate Liberalism and the Reconstruction of American Higher Education, 1894–1928.* Madison: University of Wisconsin Press.

Becker, Howard S., Blanche Greer, Everett C. Hughes, and Anselm L. Strauss. 1961. *Boys in White.* Chicago: University of Chicago Press.

Bensimon, Estella M. 1992. "Lesbian Existence: The Challenge to Normative Constructions of the Academy." *Journal of Education* 173: 98–113.

Berdahl, Robert O. 1978. *Statewide Coordination and Governance of Postsecondary Education: Quality, Costs and Accountability* (ERIC Education Document no. 202 388).

Bledstein, Burton J. 1977. *The Culture of Professionalism.* New York: Norton.

Bloland, Harland J., and Susan M. Bloland. 1974. *American Learned Societies in Transition: The Impact of Dissent and Recession.* New York: McGraw-Hill.

Bloom, Allan 1987. *The Closing of the American Mind.* New York: Simon and Schuster.

Braverman, Harry. 1975. *Labor and Monopoly Capital: The Degradation of Work in the Twentieth Century.* New York: Monthly Review Press.

Brint, Steven, and Jerome Karabel. 1989. *The Diverted Dream: Community Colleges and the Promise of Educational Opportunity in America, 1900–1985.* New York: Oxford University Press.

Brubacher, John S. 1997. *Higher Education in Transition: A History of American Colleges and Universities.* New Brunswick: Transaction Press.

Carnoy, Martin, and Henry Levin. 1985. *Schooling and Work in the Democratic State.* Stanford, CA: Stanford University Press.

Chubin, Daryl, and Edward Hackett. 1990. *Peerless Science: Peer Review and U.S. Science Policy.* Albany: State University of New York Press.

Coates, Arthur W. 1960. "The First Two Decades of the American Economic Association." *American Economic Review* 50: 555–74.

Cohen, Arthur, and Florence Brawer. 1982. *The American Community College.* San Francisco: Jossey-Bass.

Cole, Jonathan, and Stephen Cole. 1973. *Social Stratification in Science.* Chicago: University of Chicago Press.

Conrad, Clifford F., and Jennifer G. Haworth (eds.), 1990. *Curriculum in Transition: Perspectives on the Undergraduate Experience.* Needham Heights, MA: Ginn.

D'Emilio, John. 1983. *Sexual Politics, Sexual Communities: The Making of a Homosexual Minority in the U.S.* Chicago: University of Chicago Press.

Diamond, Sarah. 1992. "The Funding of the NAS." Pp. 89–96 in Patricia Aufderheide (ed.), *Beyond PC: Toward a Politics of Understanding.* St. Paul, MN: Graywolf.

Dickson, David. 1984. *The New Politics of Science.* New York: Pantheon.

Domhoff, William. 1970. *The Higher Circles: The Governing Class in America.* New York: Random House.

D'Sousa, Dinesh. 1991. *Illiberal Education: The Politics of Race and Sex on Campus.* New York: Free Press.

Dubois, Ellen C., Gail P. Kelly, Elizabeth L. Kennedy, Carolyn W. Korsmeyer, and Lillian S. Robinson. 1985. *Feminist Scholarship: Kindling in the Groves of Academe.* Urbana: University of Illinois Press.

Echols, Ann. 1989. *Daring to Be Bad: Radical Feminism in America, 1967–1975.* Minneapolis: University of Minnesota Press.

Ehrenreich, John, and Barbara Ehrenreich. 1970. *The American Health Empire.* New York: Random House.

Fine, Gary Alan. 1979. "Small Groups and Culture Creation: The Culture of Little League Baseball Teams." *American Sociological Review* 44: 733–45.

Haraway, Donna. 1989. *Primate Visions: Gender, Race and Nature in the World of Modern Science.* New York: Routledge.

Horowitz, Irving Louis (ed.). 1975. *The Use and Abuse of Social Science: Behavioral Research and Policy Making.* New Brunswick, NJ: Transaction.

Kennedy, Elizabeth, and Madeline Davis. 1993. *Boots of Leather, Slippers of Gold: The History of a Lesbian Community.* New York: Routledge.

Kevles, Daniel J. 1978. *The Physicists*. New York: Knopf.

Kimball, Roger. 1990. *Tenured Radicals: How Politics Has Corrupted Our Higher Education*. New York: Harper and Row.

Kolko, Gabriel. 1967. *The Triumph of Conservatism: A Reinterpretation of American History*. Chicago: Quadrangle.

Kuhn, Thomas. 1962. *The Structure of Scientific Revolutions*. Chicago: University of Chicago Press.

Kunzel, Regina G. 1994. *Fallen Women, Problem Girls: Unmarried Mothers and the Professionalization of Social Work*. New Haven: Yale University Press.

Larson, Magali S. 1977. *The Rise of Professionalism: A Sociological Analysis*. Berkeley: University of California Press.

Latour, Bruno, and Steven Woolgar. 1983. *Laboratory Life: The Social Construction of Scientific Facts*. Beverly Hills, CA: Sage.

Leslie, Larry, and P. Brinkman. 1988. *The Economic Value of Higher Education*. New York: American Council on Education/Macmillan.

Leslie, Stuart W. 1993. *The Cold War and American Science: The Military-Industrial-Academic Complex at MIT and Stanford*. New York: Columbia University Press.

Levine, Arthur. 1989. *Shaping Higher Education's Future*. San Francisco: Jossey-Bass.

———. 1993. "Diversity on Campus." Pp. 333–43 in A. Levine (ed.), *The Higher Learning in America: 1980–2000*. Baltimore: Johns Hopkins University Press.

Levine, Arthur (ed.). 1993. *The Higher Learning in America: 1980–2000*. Baltimore: Johns Hopkins University Press.

McAdam, Douglas. 1988. *Freedom Summer*. New York: Oxford University Press, 1988.

Markusen, Ann, and Joel Yudkin. 1992. *Dismantling the Cold War Economy*. New York: Basic Books.

Mayville, William V. 1980. *Federal Influence on Higher Education Curriculum*. Research Report no. 1. Washington, DC: American Association for Higher Education.

Melman, Seymour. 1982. *Profits without Production*. New York: Knopf.

National Center for Educational Statistics (NCES). 1996. *The Condition of Education*. Washington, DC: Government Printing Office.

Navarro, Victor. 1994. *The Politics of Health Policy: The U.S. Reforms, 1980–1994*. Oxford: Blackwell.

Noble, David F. 1977. *America by Design: Science, Technology and the Rise of Corporate Capitalism*. New York: Knopf.

———. 1984. *Forces of Production: A Social History of Industrial Automation*. New York: Knopf.

O'Connor, James. 1973. *The Fiscal Crisis of the State*. New York: St. Martin's.

Odum, Howard. 1927. *American Masters of Social Science*. New York: Holt.

Perkin, Harold J. 1989. *The Rise of Professional Societies in England since 1880*. London: Routledge.

Piven, Frances Fox, and Richard A. Cloward. 1977. *Poor People's Movements: Why They Succeed, How They Fail.* New York: Pantheon.

Rhoades, Gary D., and Sheila Slaughter. 1991. "Professors, Administrators, and Patents: The Negotiation of Technology Transfer." *Sociology of Education* 64: 65–78.

Ricci, David M. 1984. *The Tragedy of American Political Science: Politics, Scholarship and Democracy.* New Haven: Yale University Press.

Rosenberg, Rosalind. 1982. *Beyond Separate Spheres: Intellectual Roots of Modern Feminism.* New Haven: Yale University Press.

Rowen, James. 1971. "Politics of University Research." Pp. 121–34 in Philip G. Altbach, Robert S. Laufer, and Sheila McVey (eds.), *Academic Super Markets.* San Francisco: Jossey-Bass.

Rudolph, Frederick. 1977. *Curriculum: A History of the American Undergraduate Course of Study since 1636.* San Francisco: Jossey-Bass.

Rudy, William. 1960. *The Evolving Liberal Arts Curriculum: A Historical Review of Basic Themes.* New York: Bureau of Publications, Teachers College, Columbia University.

Shorris, Earl. 1992. *Latinos: An Autobiography of a People.* New York: Norton.

Silva, Edward T., and Sheila Slaughter. 1984. *Serving Power: The Making of the American Social Science Expert.* Westport, CT: Greenwood.

Slaughter, Sheila. 1990. *The Higher Learning and High Technology: Dynamics of Higher Education Policy Formation.* Albany: State University of New York Press.

———. 1993. "Retrenchment in the 1980s: The Politics of Prestige and Gender." *Journal of Higher Education* 64: 250–82.

———. 1997. "Class, Race and Gender and the Construction of Post-Secondary Curricula in the United States: Social Movement, Professionalization and Political Economic Theories of Curricular Change." *Journal of Curriculum Studies* 29: 1–30.

———. 1998. "Federal Policy and Supply-Side Institutional Resource Allocation at Public Research Universities." *Review of Higher Education* 21: 209–44.

Somit, Albert, and James Tanenhaus. 1967. *The Development of American Political Science: From Burgess to Behavioralism.* Boston: Allyn and Bacon.

Starr, Paul. 1982. *The Social Transformation of American Medicine.* New York: Basic Books.

Trent, William. 1991. "Student Affirmative Action in Higher Education: Addressing Underrepresentation." Pp. 107–32 in Philip G. Altbach and Kofi Lomotey (eds.), *The Racial Crisis in American Higher Education.* Albany: State University of New York Press.

Veysey, Laurence R. 1965. *The Emergence of the American University.* Chicago: University of Chicago Press.

Volk, Cindy, Sheila Slaughter, and Scott L. Thomas. 2001. "Models of Institutional Resource Allocation: Mission, Market and Gender." *Journal of Higher Education* 72: 387–413.

Wegman, Robin. 2001. *The Future of Women's Studies.* Durham, NC: Duke University Press.

Weisberg, Jacob. 1992. "NAS: Who Are These Guys, Anyway?" Pp. 80–88 in Patricia Aufderheide (ed.), *Beyond PC: Toward a Politics of Understanding*. St. Paul, MN: Graywolf.

Winks, Robin W. 1987. *Cloak and Gown: Scholars in the Secret War*. New York: Morrow.

PART IV

Continuity and Change in
Academic Work and University Governance

CHAPTER ELEVEN

The "Academic Revolution" Revisited

RICHARD CHAIT

A little more than thirty years ago, Jencks and Riesman (1968) announced the arrival of the "academic revolution," a term intended to convey a profound transformation of American higher education. At the heart of the revolution was "the rise to power of the academic profession" (p. xiii), which coincided with the "rise of the university" (p. 13). The ramifications included greater emphasis on scholarly (and funded) research, less attention to undergraduate education, fortification of the disciplines, expansion of the faculty, and the accelerated development of professional schools.

The most fundamental shift was the ascendancy of the faculty to a position of unprecedented power, especially at research universities, now the dominant template for higher education. After decades of scuffles and battles with presidents, trustees, and legislators, the faculty, by Jencks and Riesman's estimation, emerged victorious. "The professors . . . won the war" over curriculum, course content, selection of colleagues and senior administrators, and meritocratic standards for admissions and graduation. "Today faculty control over these matters is rarely challenged" (p. 15). Faculty typically exercised determinative influence over workloads, research agendas, and programmatic emphases.

While Jencks and Riesman were the first to herald and label the "academic revolution," many other scholars of higher education (for example, Clark, 1987; Ladd and Lipset, 1975; Metzger, 1987) also chronicled and interpreted this sea change in the academy. Disagreements were largely a matter of degree, not kind. Differences of opinion focused on the breadth of the revolution, a matter considered shortly. Although mindful of the enormous variation among the nation's colleges and universities, Jencks and Riesman ultimately concluded that "the shape of American higher education is largely a response to the assumptions and demands of the academic professions . . . and the model for the future is the 'university-college.'" There was a convergence of goals pursued by "ever more similar means" (p. 480) across a broad spectrum of institutions.

Despite differences about the extent of the revolution, the central weight of scholarship clearly holds that there was, indeed, a basic shift in the nature of the academy along the lines Jencks and Riesman described. The consensus, captured by the title of Kerr's (1991) account of the period between 1960 and 1980, was that these years marked *The Great Transformation in Higher Education*. In these two decades, colleges and universities suffered "the most substantial shocks to governance mechanisms, with a decline in the comparative influence of boards of trustees and presidents" (p. xiii). The faculty collectively, and most professors individually, gained power from the administration. This power was rooted primarily in knowledge, expertise, and professionalism; control was exercised most forcefully at the departmental level, and considerable influence was wielded, through both formal and informal mechanisms, on a rather broad sweep of issues at higher levels of the organization.

The principal question to be addressed here concerns whether conditions today are materially different and, if so, why? What has changed and what has not? To examine an otherwise boundless topic, we will concentrate on three key and related variables: the institutional landscape of higher education, academic tenure, and shared governance.

The Institutional Landscape

A vast and varied enterprise, higher education allows for few unchallenged generalizations, even by preeminent authorities like Jencks and Riesman. As suggested by the titles, *The Divided Academy* (1975), *The Academic Life: Small World, Different Worlds* (1987), "Many Sectors, Many Professions" (1987), Ladd and Lipset, Clark, and Ruscio, respectively, had a more compartmentalized view of the "revolution" than Jencks and Riesman, one that depended upon the stature and structure of the institution and upon the faculty member's particular discipline. In a chapter on "The Grip of Authority," Clark observed that "the further we move from research universities, strongholds of an entrepreneurial professionalism, the more we encounter milieus that restrict professional status and privilege, leading inexorably, where state law permits, to unionization" (p. 149). "Locals" were less apt to have power than "cosmopolitans." Ladd and Lipset focused more on the effect of disciplines, rather than institutional sponsorship or prestige, on the faculty's self-concept and authority.

For immediate purposes, we do not have to pinpoint the impact of the "academic revolution" by Carnegie classifications so much as to stipulate that in the late 1960s, as well as today, different tiers of the academy displayed different degrees of faculty autonomy. This is a well-established proposition.

> To sum the story on authority: at the top of the institutional hierarchy, faculty influence is well and strong. Many individuals have strong personal bargaining power; departments and professional schools are strong, semi-autonomous units; and all-campus faculty bodies have dominant influence in personnel and curricular decisions. University presidents speak lovingly of the faculty as the core of the institution and walk gently around entrenched faculty prerogatives. As we descend the hierarchy, however, faculty authority weakens and managerialism increases. Top-down command is noticeably stronger in the public comprehensive college. . . . The two-year colleges . . . are quite managerial. Faculty then feel powerless, even severely put upon. (Clark, 1993: 170)

In light of this dispersion of relative power, the perceived vitality of the "academic revolution" depends greatly on shifts in the growth patterns of the various sectors of the academy. Since publication of *The Academic Revolution*, the changes have been dramatic. In 1970, 1,063 community colleges enrolled 2.3 million students, or 27 percent of all students; by 1994, 1,471 two-year institutions enrolled 6.5 million students, or 42 percent of the total, approximately a 40 percent increase in institutions and a 270 percent hike in enrollments. Over the same period, the percentage of students attending doctorate-granting universities slipped from 31 percent to 26 percent, even as the number of institutions grew from 173 to 236. Between 1970 and 1987, the number of comprehensive universities and colleges expanded from 456 to 595, with a concomitant enrollment growth from 2.5 to 3.3 million students. In that same time period, the number of liberal arts colleges dropped from 721 to 572, while enrollments tumbled from 690,000 to 584,000 (Carnegie Foundation, 1994).[1] The greater the number of faculty employed at these institutions, the less certain the "academic revolution" can be considered to have been pervasive and sustained. Hence, major shifts in the distribution of faculty are instructive.

Predictably, changes in faculty labor markets mirrored the trends in student enrollments. Community colleges accounted for 19 percent of full- and part-time faculty in 1970 and 30 percent in 1995, almost a 58 percent increase. Over the same quarter-century, full- and part-time faculty at private institutions dropped from 34 percent to 29.5 percent of the professoriat (National Center for Education Statistics, 1999, Table 225, unpaged). Between 1987 and 1992, the proportion of faculty, full- and part-time, at research and doctoral universities slipped from 36 percent to 30 percent, while community colleges advanced from 26 percent to 30 percent. Most significantly, as discussed below, 90 percent of the faculty growth over these five years occurred within the part-time ranks, which swelled by 122,000. In absolute numbers, the full-time faculty actually *declined* by 23 percent at private research, 6 percent at public doctoral, 3 percent at public comprehensive, and 1 percent at liberal arts institutions. Expressed another way, of the 22,675 new full-time faculty positions added between 1987 and 1992, 13,122 (58 percent) were at community colleges (National Center for Education Statistics, 1997: 18, 65).

Clark (1993: 174) cited public and private comprehensive colleges and especially community colleges as the domains with the weakest professional control by faculty and the strongest "managerialism." For these faculty, Clark commented, "the answer has been unionization. The further down the hierarchy of prestige we go, the more widespread do unions become" (ibid.: 170). Of course, the converse holds true as well, faculty at no selective college, no prestigious university, and very few research universities have unionized. "It is not difficult to understand why the top of the American academic hierarchy should be vigorously resistant to unionization. . . . Aware of their independence and influence, powerfully positioned professors sense they do not need unions" (Clark, 1987: 174).

If the "academic revolution" were prevalent across all sectors, then one would not expect faculty union drives to be either necessary or successful on college campuses. Yet, only four years after the publication of Jencks and Riesman's book, the AAUP voted "to pursue collective bargaining as an additional means of realizing the Association's goals" (Metzger, 1987: 173). This momentous decision contradicts the image of a faculty already sufficiently invested with the power to govern effectively. Even more significantly, there were no faculty members covered by collectively bargained agreements in 1960, 92,300 by 1974 (Garbarino, 1975: 57), and 190,000 by 1985 (Kerr, 1991: xiv). By 1995, nearly a quarter million professors were represented by unions at 481 institutions, 344 at two-year colleges, 137 at four-year colleges (81 public/56 private) (Hurd et al., 1996: 121, 125).[2]

The reconfigured contours of American higher education carry two important implications for the present inquiry. First, the academic revolution may have been confined chiefly to a comparatively small subset of selective colleges and research universities, and thus somewhat overstated. The precepts and the paradigm may have appealed to professors elsewhere, but "tissue rejection" was far more common than successful transplants. Second, the explosion of community colleges and state systems of four-year institutions means that, *even if there were no other changes*, the "academic revolution" will still seem much less pervasive because the segments of the academy farthest removed from the epicenter of the "revolution" now constitute a markedly larger portion of the academy.

Academic Tenure

In the minds of most faculty, the strength and stability of tenure as policy and practice represent a vital indicator of the state of the professoriat and the health of the "academic revolution" because, as McPherson and Shapiro (1999) explain so well, tenure acts as the linchpin of faculty authority. Thus, attacks on tenure are, ipso facto, assaults on the balance of power between the faculty and institutional agents—namely, management and trustees.

> It is useful to think of academic tenure as a set of constraints on the discretion of managers (the "administration") over various aspects of the academic enterprise. The effect of these constraints is to influence the distribution of authority between administration and faculty. . . . [T]enure by no means confers absolute authority on faculty. But the institution of tenure clearly does raise the cost to management of undertaking certain kinds of actions.
>
> Faculty members with tenure will have more independence. Administrators need to rely more on persuasion and less on negative sanctions in influencing the behavior of individual faculty. . . . [T]enure will also influence the structure of decision-making in universities. Tenure increases the ability of faculty collectively to shape institutional decisions, through their actions in departments, colleges, or the institution as a whole. (pp. 92–93)

While the effects of academic tenure on shared governance cannot be precisely measured, Chait, Trower, and Urice (2002) examined the relationship between these two practices at four pairs of independent, liberal arts colleges, as closely matched as possible on key institutional variables, except that one offered tenure and the other did not. Because colleges without tenure, almost without exception, are not selective, affluent, or prestigious, neither were the four institutions with tenure determined to be the best matches to the four sites with contract systems. While broad generalizations from this study are not warranted, the research nonetheless supports the proposition that, at least for this category of colleges, tenure "appears to be a reliable, but not infallible, indicator of greater faculty voice in governance, although it is not clear that tenure *creates* a more powerful faculty. That is, the presence of tenure seems to be a proxy for other attributes, such as more faculty with terminal degrees, more attuned to the dominant professional norms" (emphasis in original).[3] Because the financial, programmatic, and political stakes are high for the faculty and the institution on campuses with tenure, the policy debate has been continuous and contentious. Rather than rehearse the various arguments and evidence delineated elsewhere (for example, Chait and Ford, 1982; Commission on Academic Tenure, 1973; Finkin, 1996; Tierney, 1998), we will focus here on trend data that elucidate the state of the "academic revolution."

Between 1975 and 1997, the proportion of full-time faculty with tenure remained remarkably stable at about 52 percent, with very minor fluctuations—a high of 52.3 percent in 1975 and a low of 50.9 percent in 1991 (Leatherman, 1999: A14). In 1975, 53.5 percent of all white, non-Hispanic males were tenured; twenty years later 54 percent were tenured. For women, the numbers are equally steady: 38.4 percent in 1975, 38.8 percent in 1995 (National Center for Education Statistics, 1998: 2-12). The probability of a favorable decision, among candidates formally considered for tenure, has not varied by institutional type and did not change materially either. The odds were a little better than 7 in 10 in 1974 (Commission on Academic Tenure, 1973) and remained so twenty years later (National Center for Education Statistics, 1996: 18). Contrary to well-publicized faculty fears about diminished prospects for tenure, far fewer respondents to the Carnegie Foundation (1989) survey in 1989, compared to 1975, believed that "Tenure Is More Difficult to Achieve than Five Years Ago," 54 percent versus 73 percent (p. 124). Despite the din among faculty precipitated by constant complaints and intermittent initiatives from trustees and legislators, there has been virtually no change in the tenured core of the full-time faculty. Nor has any university, any selective college, or any state system abolished tenure. Nor have the chances of success dimmed among faculty reviewed for tenure. Nor have post-tenure review policies, preponderantly developmental in nature, resulted in dismissals for incompetence (Licata and Morreale, 1997). We must be careful, therefore, not to confuse rhetoric with action. By the logic of McPherson and Shapiro, faculty authority and the concomitant restraints on management, embedded in academic tenure, remain intact.

That authority, however, now rests with proportionally fewer professors, which could diminish faculty power. In the quest for economy and flexibility, colleges and universities have significantly expanded the numbers of nontenure and part-time faculty. The percentage of full-time faculty off the tenure track soared from 18.6 percent in 1975 to 27 percent in 1995 (National Center for Education Statistics, 1998: 2-8, 2-12). For women, the percentage increased from 25 percent to 36.5 percent, and for minorities from 24.4 percent to 29.6 percent (p. 2-12). At the same time, the fraction of tenure-track faculty slipped from 29 percent to 20 percent. Of full-time faculty appointed in the last six years, fully one-third held nontenure eligible positions (Finkelstein et al., 1998: 56). "This is a trend; this pattern is going to stay," predicted Jay Chronister, coauthor of a forthcoming book on the subject (quoted in Leatherman, 1999: A14).

The growth of part-time faculty has been even more robust. The ratio of full-time to part-time faculty nationwide has shifted from 70:30 in 1975 to 59:41 in 1995, a 36 percent increase in part-timers. In absolute terms, there were 188,000 part-time and 440,000 full-time faculty in 1975, and 381,000 part-time and 551,000 full-time faculty twenty years later (National Center for Education Statistics, 1998: 2-2). While a few universities, such as Pace and Georgia State, have started to systematically convert multiple part-time positions into a single, full-time post, these initiatives are exceptions to the rule. "Based on what we saw," Chronister concluded, "I think the two-tiered system is here to stay" (quoted in Leatherman, 1999: A14). Living on the wrong side of the tenure track, tenure ineligible and part-time academics usually have restricted access to campus governance, a decision typically, and not incidentally, made by the tenured faculty. Doctoral institutions afford nontenure track faculty the fewest opportunities— half permit participation at the department level, only 10 percent at the level of the faculty senate. On the other hand, 94 percent of baccalaureate institutions allow nontenure track faculty to serve on the faculty senate (ibid.: A14). "Part-time faculty have no role in institutional governance at most institutions," and "are sometimes allowed to attend department meetings, committee meetings, or meetings of campus-wide faculty governance bodies," although "their voting rights are typically restricted" (Gappa and Leslie, 1993: 196). Effectively disenfranchised, part-time faculty on some campuses (for example, Kent State) have formed separate unions, and at the University of Central Arkansas and Georgia State, part-timers and nontenure academics have formed a separate faculty senate in an attempt to gain a greater voice in governance.

To the extent that more nontenure track and part-time faculty, with a limited voice and, hence, limited interest in shared governance, populate the academy, the full-time faculty's role in governance could be diluted or fragmented. There are fewer tenured and tenure-track faculty to serve on department, college, and campus committees, and these individuals may represent the interests and concerns of a numerical minority. Under these circumstances, the full-time faculty may not be as forceful a chorus, or even the largest. "The part-timers are marginal in influence; their large numbers weaken the influence of full-time faculty vis-à-vis trustees and administrative staff" (Clark, 1993: 174). Even if the increased number of part-time and nontenure track appointments has an adverse impact on faculty governance, effect and motivation should not be confused. The push by administrators, from department chairs to presidents, to add part-time and nontenure track personnel has been propelled principally by the need to save money and gain flexibility, and not by an ideological animus toward tenure, conspicuous exceptions notwithstanding. Moreover, faculty are not innocent bystanders. "Non-tenured full-timers are often hired to teach introductory or intermediate courses to undergraduates—courses that most tenured and tenure-track professors, caught up in the publish-or-perish world, don't have the energy or inclination to take on" (Leatherman, 1999: A14).

While denunciations of tenure are reflective of the drift toward a new order, one would have to construct quite an elaborate causal chain to conclude that public distaste for tenure (Harvey and Immerwahr, 1995: 12) and internal modifications of traditional tenure have contributed significantly to a rollback of the "academic revolution." Still more dubious would be an assertion that the strength of the "revolution" rests upon the tenure level among full-time faculty. In truth, professors are most autonomous on campuses where tenure percentages are relatively low, while less self-directed colleagues typically work at state colleges and nonselective independent colleges where tenure levels are comparatively high. Viewed over time, the tenure controversy, decidedly punctuated more by fiery words than dramatic actions, seems more symptomatic than causal. In order to understand better the evolution of the "academic revolution," we turn now to the "governance wars" that effect shared authority more directly and more profoundly than the celebrated "tenure wars" (Engstrom, 1998).

Shared Governance

Perhaps more than any other document, the 1966 "Statement on Government of Colleges and Universities" (AAUP, 1995) encapsulated the "academic revolution." Jointly formulated by the American Association of University Professors (AAUP), the American Council on Education (ACE), and the Association of Governing Boards of Universities and Colleges (AGB), the policy constituted a consensus among faculty, presidents, and trustees represented respectively by these three organizations. Based on the touchstones of competence to act and responsibility for results, the statement declared that the faculty has "primary responsibility for such fundamental areas as curriculum, subject matter and methods of instruction, research, faculty status, and those aspects of student life which relate to the educational process" (p. 183). In these arenas, the faculty should have the ability to take action that effectively has the force of legislation. "The governing board and president should, on the questions of faculty status, as in other matters where the faculty has primary responsibility, concur with the faculty judgment except in rare instances and for compelling reasons which should be stated in detail" (p. 184). While the document touted "interdependence," the statement was, in many respects, a declaration of independence that codified the "academic revolution."

Twenty-two years later, AGB had second thoughts. In a "Statement on Institutional Governance (1998)," AGB sounded a different note that stressed the board's "ultimate responsibility," "the authority to determine the mission of the institution" and to establish strategic direction, "the right to question, challenge, and occasionally override decisions or proposals," including academic decisions and proposals to adopt or eliminate academic programs. Whereas the AAUP statement centered on "primary responsibility," the AGB document prescribed that "[b]oards should ensure that no single stakeholder group is given an exclusive franchise in any area of governance."

AGB's pronouncement triggered a vitriolic debate in the "Viewpoint" section of the *Chronicle of Higher Education*. James Richardson (1999), then president of the AAUP, fired the first salvo, arguing that the statement "threatens the very framework that underpins" the ideals of shared governance, and "rewrites the book on institutional governance," all in the name of control and concession to the tyranny of the marketplace (p. B9). A few months later, Cary Nelson (1999), a professor of English at the University of Illinois, characterized AGB's stance as part of "The War against the Faculty," a deplorable retreat from the "academic revolution" that empowered faculty. To the degree that faculty are merely one stakeholder among many, there will be "a slow erosion of faculty influence . . . [when] most faculties are accustomed to having primary control over how academic policy is actually enacted and carried out." Nelson called upon colleagues "to resist the current war." "Only organized resistance" can preserve the values of shared governance (p. B4).

Provoked by these attacks, the president of AGB, Richard T. Ingram (1999), defended the association's statement as an attempt to "clarify the authority delegated to faculty." Moreover, Ingram condemned as "arrogant" the authors' perspective that "the faculty *is* the institution—period." If faculty, in general, agreed with Nelson that institutional missions are determined retrospectively by the board as mission "lurches up from below," based upon the choices faculty make about what and how to teach, then professors should recognize that "this kind of thinking . . . illustrates why many trustees, presidents, academic administrators, legislators and governors believe that many faculty leaders simply don't get it" (p. B4).

The discourse in the *Chronicle* became even more shrill when James Carlin (1999), former chairman of the Massachusetts Board of Higher Education, entered the fray with blunt advice about how to "Restor[e] Sanity to an Academic World Gone Mad." Carlin's take on shared governance was that "[n]obody is in charge." Consequently, colleges suffered from uncontrolled costs, grade inflation, political correctness, and "immoral" lifetime employment of faculty. The solution? Not shared governance, but courageous leadership. "Trustees and administrators must provide bold, innovative solutions—in spite of faculty members' objections, and even if, in the short term, those changes run contrary to the faculty's economic interests" (p. A76).

This bombastic volley demonstrates the passion and fury ignited by attempts to undo or maintain the traditions of shared governance. More substantively, the 1966 AAUP statement and the 1998 AGB statement revealed salient and substantively different notions of governance. If the former epitomized the "academic revolution," then the latter, many faculty worried, trumpeted the "academic counterrevolution" with boards of trustees in command.

THE EMPOWERED BOARD

Reports from many fronts have been filed recently about resurgent boards of trustees. "With heavy-handed politics," the City University of New York board implemented a plan to eliminate remedial education on four-year campuses (Staples, 1998). Trustees of the State University of New York challenged the appropriateness of a lesbian workshop on the Stony Brook campus, and served notice that curriculum was within the board's province. At a 1997 conference coordinated by the National Alumni Forum, described as "political conservatives who urge trustees to be forceful leaders," SUNY regent Candace de Russy advocated, "When we encounter dysfunctional curricula, curricula that are inappropriate, politicized, or trivial, it is my view that we have an obligation as trustees to confront this problem. We should do battle over this" (Healy, 1997: A35). Contrary to faculty recommendations, the Board of Visitors at George Mason University increased the number of academic credits for ROTC and eliminated an experimental college (Benning, 1999: A1). Despite faculty and administrative opposition, the regents of the University of California voted in 1995 to end affirmative action in admissions and employment (Lively, 1995: A26). And, as carefully chronicled in articles on "The Miasma in Minnesota" (Farber, 1997), and "Tenure Wars" (Engstrom, 1998), the board of regents of the University of Minnesota pursued an ultimately unsuccessful reform of the institution's tenure code.[4]

While these events occurred at public institutions, some boards of private colleges have been assertive as well. Mallon (2000) has identified thirteen independent colleges (for example, Bennington, College of the Ozarks, Lindenwood, and Westminster) where, since 1974, the governing board abolished tenure. The trustees of the University of Dubuque in 1998 instigated a lawsuit against the faculty to declare the faculty handbook a "policy statement" and to clarify the board's ultimate authority. "If the board succeeds," one of the faculty's lawyers asserted, "it will put the faculty in a position of having no legal right to have a say about the traditional things that faculty care about" (Wilson, 1998: A12).

Beyond the alarm expressed by advocates of faculty power and beyond the most notorious examples, the origins of trustee activism can be discerned from several scholarly works. Five years after publication of *The Academic Revolution*, Duryea (1973) observed, "The history of university organization in the twentieth century has been an account of the disintegration of the traditional form of government conceived in terms of formal authority granted to governing boards, which have exercised it through the president as executive officer" (p. 14). Presciently, Duryea foresaw a problem as boards of trustees retreated to a less influential role akin to the original concept of visitors or overseers. "What is lacking is a new corporation in the sense of a controlling or managerial council to fill the vacuum." This centrifugal, autonomous arrangement nested in academic departments created "the hole in the centre" (p. 15).

Who filled the void? Levine (1997) believed that "the faculty role in governance is likely to diminish. Boards of trustees will become more active in the management of educational institutions" (p. 5). Likewise, Chait (1995) forecasted: "Whatever the matter at hand, trustees are likely to be less deferential. Policy recommendations . . . will undergo closer inspection. More questions . . . will be asked. . . . More data will be expected. More reservations will be expressed. More revisions may be required. . . . Increasingly, at board meetings one will hear the voices of trustees in animated discussion far more frequently than the rhythmic thump of a rubber stamp" (p. 17).

THE UNEMPOWERED FACULTY?

Based on the evidence presented thus far, one might reasonably assume that the "academic revolution" has been undermined, if not reversed, by emboldened boards of trustees. We must be careful, however, not to overstate the proposition. While there has indisputably been a flurry of aggressiveness by boards of trustees, especially in the public sector, the activity may be just that, a flurry and not a blizzard. Additionally, "board bites faculty" stories captured headlines precisely because these are aberrations. Few newspapers report the thousands of faculty initiatives and recommendations boards routinely approve or entirely delegate. And selective perception leads faculty to be less attentive, for instance, to the boards (Columbia [IL], St. Mary's [MD], Alvernia, and Westbrook)[5] that instituted tenure in the last three years (Mallon, 2000), or the board of Princeton University, which publicly chastised trustee and U.S. presidential candidate Steve Forbes for his assault on the academic freedom of a controversial faculty member.

Moreover, for every lament about the loss of faculty power, one can cite a well-regarded academic concerned that college presidents command too little power and confront unusually severe constraints. Kerr (1991: 211) contended that the faculty "is gaining power from the administration," especially at state colleges, community colleges, and less selective liberal arts, due mainly to unionization. Whereas Gumport (1997) envisaged the "drift of authority upward, especially in large public systems," increased tension between "managerial and academic temperaments" (p. 120), and the further expansion of an administrative bureaucracy, Damrosch (1995) commented that "it is remarkable how little influence the administration exerts on the intellectual direction of the typical university. . . . [B]asic policy is rarely set from the top" (pp. 58–59). In a similar vein, while Richardson and Nelson fretted about the concentration of power in professional, market-minded managers, Donald Kennedy, the former president of Stanford, acknowledged that "the intellectual direction and even the leadership of the divisions is not controlled by the center. Nor is it really *managed* at the local level, where the putative 'line managers' scarcely want to manage at all" (Kennedy, 1994: 91). While presidents and boards, Kennedy stated, may appear to be influential, both "have sharply limited powers. . . . Without faculty support, leadership from the administration building simply does not work" (Kennedy, 1997: 271).

In a now popular metaphor, Cohen and March (1974: 203) attributed to the university president as much control and influence over the institution as the driver of a car skidding on ice. Birnbaum (1991: 202) posited that "presidents and other administrators may not be able to make dramatic changes in their institutions most of the time," and in two studies for AGB, Kerr (1984, 1986) urged that boards invest more power in the president, advice that apparently did not penetrate the "top fifty to one hundred institutions" where, Rosovsky (1990) maintained, tenured faculty members were still very much self-regulated. A "critical virtue of academic life . . . is the absence of a boss. . . . [As] a professor, I recognized no master save peer pressure. . . . No profession guarantees its practitioners such a combination of independence and security as university research and teaching" (pp. 163–64).

While insightful, the assessments by scholars (most former administrators) of presidential and regental power should be supplemented by opinions that probably matter much more—namely, the views of faculty members. Three surveys offered pertinent data about the professoriat's perspective on shared governance and possible clues about the impact of governance on faculty work life.

The first set of surveys (Carnegie Foundation, 1989) painted a rather grim picture of the faculty's attitude toward the administration. In 1989, 64 percent of all respondents rated the administration either "fair" (35 percent) or "poor" (29 percent), a steep rise from 46 percent in 1969 (pp. 107, 123). The percentages at research universities were somewhat higher (39 percent and 34 percent), and the percentages at liberal arts (33 percent and 20 percent) and at two-year colleges (34 percent and 21 percent) somewhat lower (p. 107). Even harsher were responses to the question of whether or not the administration was "autocratic or democratic." Of all faculty, 69 percent rated the administration in 1989 as either "very autocratic" (30 percent) or "somewhat autocratic" (39 percent), an increase from 61 percent in 1975 (pp. 108, 124). Only 6 percent worked with a "very democratic" administration, and only liberal arts colleges approached the level where more than half (47 percent) regarded the administration as either "somewhat" or "very democratic" (p. 108). In all, just less than half (49 percent) agreed that "my institution is a very good place," no change from the 1969 poll.

For 20 percent of the respondents, there were "a lot" of opportunities to influence institutional policies, for 49 percent "some" opportunities, and for 30 percent none. When the first two categories are combined, faculty at liberal arts colleges (87 percent) and, curiously, at two-year colleges (76 percent) enjoyed the most opportunities and, contrary to conventional wisdom, faculty (61 percent) at research universities reported the fewest opportunities. By contrast, at the department level, across all Carnegie classifications, between 94 and 97 percent of the faculty had "a lot of" or "some" opportunity to influence policy (p. 131).

The Carnegie Foundation surveys seem to suggest that faculty power has dwindled at the hands of a very or somewhat autocratic administration that afforded too few opportunities to influence institutional policies. This is not what the "academic revolution" envisioned. The two more recent surveys, however, create a different impression.

The Higher Education Research Institute at UCLA (Astin et al., 1991; Sax et al., 1999) periodically polls a representative sample of some thirty-four thousand full-time faculty at two- and four-year colleges and universities in the United States. In the 1998–99 survey, 86.8 percent of respondents were satisfied with "the autonomy and independence" of their positions (Sax et al., 1999: 38) versus 82.9 percent ten years earlier (Astin et al., 1991: 46), nearly a 5 percent increase. Disaggregated by two-year colleges public and private, research universities public and private, and four-year colleges public, private, nonsectarian, Catholic, and Protestant, no segment experienced a decline between 1989–90 and 1998–99, and none had an overall satisfaction level below 80 percent. Additionally, the more recent survey revealed that slightly fewer faculty (18 percent versus 18.6 percent), compared to ten years earlier, characterized as "very descriptive of the institution," the statement: "The faculty are typically at odds with the administration" (Astin et al., 1991: 46; Sax et al., 1999: 38).[6]

A more recent stratified, representative sample survey (Sanderson et al., 1999) of 1,511 faculty members at two- and four-year colleges, conducted for TIAA-CREF by the National Opinion Research Center at the University of Chicago, also depicted a professoriat quite satisfied with their work conditions.[7] For instance, 87 percent of respondents said they would either definitely (63 percent) or probably (24 percent) pursue an academic career again,[8] and over 90 percent were either very satisfied (40 percent) or satisfied (52 percent) with their current position. There were few significant variations, although public four-year institutions had the lowest level of "very satisfied" faculty members (p. 13). Surprisingly, the highest proportion of "very satisfied" faculty (53.9 percent) was on campuses *without* a tenure system (p. 16). By comparison, 40.8 percent of tenured faculty and 33.9 percent of tenure track faculty were "very satisfied."

Of particular relevance to the state of the "academic revolution," 93 percent of the faculty were "very satisfied" (45.8 percent) or "satisfied" (47.7 percent) with the "opportunity to work independently," the highest level of satisfaction among seventeen different "work and career factors" (p. 24). When asked about institutional policies, "the statement with which faculty members in the aggregate agree the most (45 percent 'strongly agree' and another 34 percent 'somewhat agree') is that 'intrusions on academic freedom by the administration are rare'" (p. 31). Finally, just as the HERI survey disclosed generally harmonious relations between the faculty and the administration, at least half the TIAA respondents regarded "the institution's emphasis" on sixteen different priorities, including "maintaining atmosphere of open expression" to be "just right." Only with regard to "sufficient resources for faculty needs" did most faculty disagree with the current emphasis; 64 percent believed it was "too low," and 34 percent thought it was "just right" (p. 33).

Taken together, the data from HERI and TIAA portray, with a broad stroke, the faculty as generally pleased with the nature and terms and conditions of academic work life, especially the degree of professional autonomy. By and large, day-by-day, faculty had the latitude appropriate and necessary to fulfill their roles and responsibilities. There were problems, disappointments, and irritations—especially at the level of institutional priorities—but the data, unlike the Carnegie surveys, do not indicate that faculty have experienced, at least not yet, a notable decrease in their power and prerogatives to teach and conduct research, the cornerstones of the "academic revolution."

Despite a generally high level of professional satisfaction, especially with respect to professional autonomy, many academics still harbor an opinion that the faculty's power has receded as the influence of the board and the president, as the trustees' agent, has advanced. What accounts for that sentiment? In order to answer this question and explore the vulnerability of the "academic revolution," we need to answer another question: "What awakened boards of trustees in the first place?"

Higher Education Goes to Market

Governing boards were, at one time, primarily honorific and ornamental assemblies of stellar citizens that added legitimacy and luster to institutions of higher education and provided a buffer against economic and political turbulence. While there were, to be sure, newsworthy instances of assertiveness either by individual "mischief makers" or by an agitated board, trustees were, on the whole, acquiescent and deferential. What happened, roughly since the mid-1980s, to arouse boards and provoke a more aggressive stance?

First, trustees have been pressured by the press, students and parents, elected officials, the public at large, hypercritical academics (for example, Anderson, 1992; Huber, 1992), and the courts to address a myriad of charges and complaints, whether accurate or not. The bill of particulars included unchecked costs, self-indulgent faculty, an overemphasis on arcane research to the detriment of undergraduate instruction, compromised curricula, glacial governance systems, political correctness, affirmative action, and preferential admissions. Higher education has become essential to individual financial success and social status, indispensable to the economic welfare of the nation, and relatively expensive for consumers. As a result, customers, corporations, and other constituents now expect and demand that boards "take charge" and solve these problems. In turn, trustees, especially of state-supported institutions, feel more urgency and accountability to act.

Second, board members, especially from business, the background of 37 percent of all public and 42 percent of all private college trustees (Madsen, 1997: 8–9), have "learned" how to govern actively as corporate directors. There has been a direct spillover from the increased forcefulness of corporate boards (Demb and Neubauer, 1992; Lorsch, 1989, 1995), which, ironically, was fueled to no small degree by the activism of large institutional investors, most notably TIAA-CREF. Emblematic of the articles that have appeared for nearly a decade now in the *Harvard Business Review*, a periodical targeted to corporate executives, are these two excerpts:

> Boards should "be proactive—and effective—in the policy making process. . . . Overall, the goal of the reforms is to make the board function not as a distant referee but as part of a team of decision makers." (Pound, 1995: 94–95)

> [E]mpowerment is sweeping corporate boardrooms. Empowerment means that outside directors have the capability and independence to monitor the performance of top management and the company; to influence management to change the strategic direction of the company if its performance does not meet the board's expectations; and, in the most extreme cases, to change corporate leadership. (p. 107)

Many directors have heeded this advice and applied the same principles as college trustees as well, convinced that governance is governance, and that colleges should, in any case, behave more like businesses.

Third, institutions of higher education now, in fact, do act more like businesses (for better or worse). "Colleges and universities," the AGB 1998 Statement (p. 4) declared matter-of-factly, "have many of the characteristics of business enterprises," and these traits become more manifest and accentuated all the time. Differences between the ivory tower and the corporate skyscraper have started to evaporate. A few examples suffice:

—Student recruitment and financial aid have become sophisticated matters of marketing, advertising, positioning, pricing, leveraging, and negotiating;

—School logos and trademarks are licensed for every imaginable product;

—Exclusive "pouring rights" are sold to the highest bidder, usually Pepsi or Coke;

—More than five hundred college websites carry commercial advertisements;

—Naming rights for athletic facilities are sold to the highest bidder; and

—For-profit subsidiaries for executive education or research are commonplace.

In the college boardroom today, trustees discuss cost control, productivity gains, strategic alliances, capital formation, market niches, price elasticity, and customer satisfaction. There are deals to be done, both in research and instruction. MIT alone has joint ventures or profit-sharing arrangements with Microsoft, Nanovation, Merck, Ford, Merrill Lynch, Dupont, and Amgen, to name a few (Howe, 2000). A similar pact has been signed by UNext.com and business schools at Chicago, Stanford, and Columbia; and another by Caliber Learning Network and Johns Hopkins and the University of Pennsylvania. Governor Gray Davis just proposed to spend $75 million a year to build institutes for science and innovation on three University of California campuses, with the proviso that "the university's private-sector business partners . . . spend at least $25 million annually for each center and pay operating costs" (Hardi and Hebel, 2000: A28).

Such transactions and language are the everyday fare of many trustees. The more colleges and universities exhibit these properties, the more familiar the territory, the vocabulary, and the options are to the board, then the more trustees' private-sector expertise and experience become relevant, and the more board members and corporate executives (sometimes one and the same) become influential.

Finally, as the need for resources escalates, the board's influence elevates. Directly or indirectly, trustees are a crucial component of the income stream, as embodied in the adage "give, get, or get off." Nationwide, board members tend to provide 15 to 25 percent (and nearly 40 percent on some campuses) of the total contributions to capital campaigns (Taylor and Massy, 1998: 54, 58). Capital campaigns of $1 billion or more are no longer unusual among public (for example, Minnesota, UCLA, Berkeley, Michigan, Virginia) or private (for example, Harvard, Yale, Stanford, Duke) universities. The goals of independent liberal arts colleges are ambitious too: $165 million at Oberlin, $125 million at St. Olaf, $250 million at Smith, for instance.

The need to raise capital has never been greater for several reasons.

Most notably, universities and colleges have an inherently unquenchable thirst for revenues. As Clotfelter (1996) observed in *Buying the Best*: "[F]eaturing weak central control, a remarkable degree of freedom accorded its faculty, traditions of collegiality in governance, the university lacks any corporate goal other than the pursuit of excellence" (p. 253). Simply stated, this is expensive. To compound the problem, state appropriations to public institutions have declined from 45.6 percent of total current revenues in 1980 to 32.5 percent in 1996 (*Chronicle of Higher Education Almanac*, 1999: 40; Zoghi, 1999: 1).[9] These losses have been replaced "primarily with revenues from market goods and services . . . and private and corporate donations" (Zoghi, 1999: 1). Between 1992 and 1997, voluntary support for higher education increased 64 percent to a total of $18.4 billion, with very little difference in the total amount raised by public and private research universities (*Chronicle of Higher Education Almanac*, 1999: 40).

When colleges and universities launch capital campaigns, the board's views on institutional direction and strategic priorities do assume greater significance, since trustee participation and contributions are vital to success. From time to time, as reported anecdotally, wealthy alumni have attempted to exert control or punish the institution for one "misdeed" or another. In the main, however, such incidents have been rare (Prewitt, 1994). Nevertheless, common sense suggests that a measure of affluence begets a measure of influence.

IMPLICATIONS FOR INSTITUTIONAL GOVERNANCE

The commercialization of higher education will have ramifications for governance beyond augmenting the trustees' role. The greater the emphasis on corporate, as opposed to collegial, models, and the more resource-dependent the institutions, then the more the weight of governance will shift from faculty and a power of expertise to public agents and the power of the purse. Public agents include boards, legislatures, governors, corporations, customers, and donors. Financial capital will trump, or at least steer, intellectual capital.

What power remains on campus will migrate from the administrative center to the entrepreneurial periphery, from core operations, like undergraduate education, to research institutes, laboratories, executive education centers, and multidisciplinary programs. This trend toward "expanding perimeters" and "melting cores" was articulated by Zemsky and

Massy (1995):

> The core of the institution—that part most under presidential purview and historically the champion of the academic calling—was under assault. . . . The distinctions between faculty and professional staff were being blurred, as were the traditional perquisites of academic governance. Those along the perimeter now appeared more often as the owners and managers of enterprises than as venerable citizens of the academy. . . . [T]he power of the perimeter to hold onto its own revenue is a sign of a fundamental and perhaps permanent shift of power within most colleges and universities. (pp. 5–8)

At the organizational level, managers and professors associated with profit centers will emerge as institutional superpowers, especially to the degree that the periphery cross-subsidizes the core. The commonweal of the faculty, a special province of faculty senates, will be more difficult to detect and to protect as *the* faculty further transmutes into the faculties, a trend exacerbated by the movement toward "responsibility center management," which requires that the economics, as well as the academics, be right for collaboration to flourish.

At a personal level, as professors experience commercial success, power will transfer from the faculty collectively to faculty members individually. The power brokers are as likely, if not more likely, to be the professorial rain-makers and deal-makers than the faculty senate officers. Superstars able to generate substantial revenues, whether as researchers or teachers, will wield significant power. And while there has always been competition for preeminent professors, the market imperative to showcase marquee professors, the potential to sell courses on-line worldwide, and the need to attract sizable corporate (and federal) research contracts dramatically ups the ante, and foreshadows, to invoke the metaphor of Arthur Levine, president of Teachers College, the "Hollywoodization of academia" (Carnevale and Young, 1999: A45). If Gregory Mankiw, a Harvard economist, can obtain a $1.4 million advance for a textbook, what might an Internet course command (Schneider, 1997: A12)? With the market power of rock stars and athletes, these "Michael Jordans without the hightops" (Carnevale and Young, 1999: A45) will seek large contracts and a bountiful share of the revenues from sales, royalties, and residuals. If one university refuses, another will readily accept.[10]

The emphasis on technology and profitability may have a second-order effect on faculty governance. As university-corporate partnerships generate "world class" courses available via the Internet, academic programs will become, in all likelihood, more homogenized and, consequently, faculty will have a palpably reduced role in the curriculum and in the classroom. On some campuses, the faculty's chief responsibilities may be to select the curriculum to purchase and to then facilitate discussions and suggest resources, in the manner of a teaching assistant, after the "virtual" class has ended. The traditional control that faculty exert over curriculum design may be largely mooted by off-the-shelf products from brand-name "curriculum factories" like Amherst, Brown, and Williams, all on the precipice of a "deal" to offer courses on-line via Global Educational Networks (Carr, 2000: A43). Such developments would seem to be a logical, though not necessarily laudable, extension of the "winner-take-all" market that already characterizes the student admissions and academic labor markets in higher education (Frank and Cook, 1995).

ONE LOSE, ALL LOSE?

Whether the "academic revolution" has persisted, stalled, reversed, or ended has not been conclusively determined, and probably resists a definitive answer. To listen to the most alarmed professors, the faculty's relative position and the basic tenets of tenure and shared governance have been imperiled to a degree that merits a call to arms. The paradox arises from national surveys and databanks, which indicate that faculty are generally quite satisfied and that tenure systems remain intact. On the other side of the ledger, rhetorical assaults on tenure and noteworthy forays by trustees into the faculty's domain have, in fact, escalated. The paradox here emanates from numerous studies and essays which indicated that neither presidents nor boards feel particularly potent, a condition most often attributed, ironically, to the faculty's power to decide important matters and to thwart central initiatives.

Most likely, all parties are correct. The very nature of shared governance, of course, precludes unilateral action, a condition that Birnbaum (1991) argued ultimately serves the "cybernetic" university well. If the essence of shared governance is distributed power, then why all the ferment and frustration now? In a word, it is because less power remains on campus to distribute. The once almost impenetrable membrane between the campus and the larger society has thinned greatly. There has been seepage as colleges, universities, and, not least, professors have entered the marketplace; however, far more crucially, the market has unsentimentally and even ruthlessly invaded the campus and the "industry" of higher education.

As a result, much power now roosts elsewhere. Corporations, research partners, customers, employers, and donors wield ever more influence. An even larger "gorilla," the federal government, also now "market neutral" (Knight Higher Education Collaborative, 1999: 7), appropriates $24 billion annually (*Chronicle of Higher Education Almanac*, 1999: 40) in student financial aid, research funds, and other appropriations, with enough strings attached to stretch from OSHA to EPA to OCR. Federal and state courts have reviewed and occasionally reversed negative tenure decisions and penalized institutions for salary inequities. The U.S. Supreme Court, as well as some state legislatures (for example, Alaska and Ohio), have opened the formerly confidential files of faculty plaintiffs and the dossiers of so-called comparables. A spate of court decisions, plus public referenda, have outlawed race-based scholarships and ended affirmative action in admissions and employment. And television networks and footwear manufacturers have a near stranglehold on Division I football and basketball programs.

In 1991, Clark Kerr captured the net effect of these tendencies:

> There are more claimants for power than ever before, and there is no more power to be divided. Someone must lose if others gain—a zero sum game. One gainer is the government, state and federal. . . . Less power and less influence on the direction of change now reside on campus; the big losers, particularly in the domain of budget, have been the board and the president.
>
> The faculty is in a less clear position. . . . In some places the faculty will gain power from the administration, often in major ways; but it may also lose to the students, sometimes in major ways. The net effect could possibly be a negative one for the faculty in terms of total power. . . . The two net losers are clearly the board and the president. The board is in an increasingly difficult position. Federal and state agencies make decisions it once made. . . . The president loses to everybody, partly because he or she has had the most to lose originally, but also because there is no firm base of support in the power struggle, no natural constituency. (1991: 210–12)

Remarkably prophetic overall, Kerr probably overestimated the amount of power that would accrue to faculty unions, especially at independent colleges, and to students as activists. Like many others, Kerr, underestimated, in turn, the students' power as consumers because the academy, on the whole, was slow to realize the transformational effects that would flow from the immersion of American colleges and universities in the marketplace.

Enlightened by hindsight, we can now see that higher education "is well into a period of the entrepreneurial institution, an era when each college and university is rather mercilessly cast into competition for survival, for growth, for quality enhancement" (Breneman, 1997: 2). As students became consumers, colleges became vendors, and sacred missions started to yield to viable markets. Industry's dire need for knowledge coincided with the university's desperate need for money and, as never before, a robust market for research formed. Even more importantly with respect to shared governance, Breneman contended that the power of market forces caused colleges and universities to lose "much of the autonomy and independence from the market that they enjoyed in earlier periods" (p. 2).

In sum, the single most dramatic shift from the "academic revolution" declared by Jencks and Riesman in 1968 to the "war against faculty" declared by Nelson in 1999 may not be that the professoriat has lost power, but rather that the university has lost control. Changes in resource dependency, revenue sources, customer expectations, and the competitive landscape—in short, changes in market conditions—have reduced the influence of faculty, administrators, and, to a somewhat lesser degree, lay boards, and augmented the sway of external constituencies. No doubt, all three bodies feel less consequential and less equipped to shape the course of events, especially on major institutional policies and priorities.

This shift of power from on-campus to off-campus agents also suggests that internal conflicts over the contested territories of academic tenure and shared governance are symptoms rather than causes of the "counterrevolution." At worst, such skirmishes will be costly diversions—battles to divide meager provisions while the opposition advances. Certainly that has been the case with respect to tenure. While the brisk, and sometimes brusque, barrage of charges and countercharges preoccupies the protagonists on academic platforms, economic realities fundamentally alter the nature of the professorial workforce. At best, both shared governance and academic tenure might be better discussed in the larger context of the march of market forces, and the debate might more fruitfully center on whether adaptations are wrong-headed and unprincipled concessions that will only worsen matters or prudent, tactical compromises that will stem the tide.

There is reason for optimism. The faculty, on the one hand, and the administration and the board on the other, need not be one another's sworn "enemy." The tenure and governance "wars" may well be the wrong wars with the wrong parties. Inasmuch as all three groups share a loss of influence and recognize that the "net loss" has been to external constituencies, there may be reason to collaborate, as Lazerson (1997), among others, has suggested. There is also ample reason for pessimism. The "enemies," if one chooses to apply that term to the marketplace and to external constituencies, is much stronger than any of these three groups alone, and perhaps stronger than all three together. If the board, the administration, and the faculty do not coalesce, and maybe even if they do, the "market revolution" will supplant the "academic revolution."

Notes

This chapter is not to be reproduced or quoted without the expressed permission of the author, Richard Chait, 456 Gutman Library, Harvard University, Cambridge, MA 02138, email: chaitri@gse.harvard.edu. Cheryl Sternman Rule and Frances L. Shavers provided invaluable contributions as research assistants in writing this paper.

1. Because of changes in Carnegie Classification nomenclature, the data on comprehensive, later renamed master's colleges and universities, and on liberal arts colleges, renamed baccalaureate colleges, are not directly comparable between 1970 and 1994. However, the 1970 and 1987 data are comparable.

2. A 1980 Supreme Court decision severely stunted efforts to unionize private colleges, which means that faculty support for unionization, and a sense of disenfranchisement, on these campuses may be understated, a hypothesis reinforced by a reportedly resurgent interest in unions at these institutions in light of a favorable ruling by the National Labor Relations Board (Leatherman, 2000: A16).

3. For most faculty at the contract sites, shared governance, beyond control of curricula and courses, was of little or no interest (nor was tenure). Interestingly, the absence of shared governance was not a reliable indicator of faculty dissatisfaction. To the contrary, the vast majority of faculty on campuses without tenure described their work environment as collegial and portrayed the administration in largely positive terms, findings that corroborate the TIAA-CREF (2000) survey on satisfaction levels.

4. In the interest of full disclosure, the author served as an advisor to the University of Minnesota Board of Regents on this matter.

5. This was the result of a merger with the University of New England, which had a tenure system in place.

6. There were some minor *increases:* 0.7 percentage point at private universities, 0.2 at public four-year colleges, 0.5 at private four-year colleges.

7. In the interest of full disclosure, the author served as a member of the advisory board for the poll.

8. A survey by Finkelstein et al. (1998: 62) reported very similar numbers: 89.1 percent "would do it again" and 84.2 percent are "somewhat or very satisfied."

9. At more than $40 billion in 1995–96, state appropriations are hardly paltry.

10. For accounts of the bidding wars for "academic stars" and the commercial pursuits of "superstar teachers," see, respectively, Schneider, 1998; and Magner, 1998.

References

American Association of University Professors (AAUP). 1995. *Policy Documents & Reports, 1995 Edition.* Washington, DC: AAUP.

Anderson, Martin. 1992. *Impostors in the Temple: American Intellectuals Are Destroying Our Universities and Cheating Our Students of Their Future.* New York: Simon and Schuster.

Association of Governing Boards of Universities and Colleges. 1986. *Composition of Governing Boards, 1985.* Washington, DC: AGB.

———. 1998. *AGB Statement on Institutional Governance.* www.agb.org/governance.cfm.

Astin, Alexander W., W. S. Korn, and E. L. Dey. 1991. *The American College Teacher: National Norms for the 1989–90 HERI Faculty Survey.* Los Angeles: Higher Education Research Institute, UCLA.

Baldwin, Roger, and Jay Chronister. 2001. *Teaching without Tenure: Policies and Practices for a New Era.* Baltimore, MD: Johns Hopkins University Press.

Benning, Victoria. 1999. "Faculty, Board Clash at George Mason." *Washington Post* (May 21): A1.

Birnbaum, Robert. 1991. *How Colleges Work: The Cybernetics of Academic Organization and Leadership.* San Francisco: Jossey-Bass Publishers.

Breneman, David W. 1997. *Alternatives to Tenure for the Next Generation of Academics.* Washington, DC: American Association for Higher Education.

Carlin, James F. 1999. "Restoring Sanity to an Academic World Gone Mad." *Chronicle of Higher Education* (Nov. 5): A76.

Carnegie Foundation for the Advancement of Teaching. 1989. *The Condition of the Professoriate: Attitudes and Trends.* Princeton: Carnegie Foundation.

———. 1970, 1987, 1994. *Institutions of Higher Education by Type and Control.* www.carnegiefoundation.org/cihe/uni_of_institut.htm.

Carnevale, Dan, and Jeffrey R. Young. 1999. "Who Owns On-Line Courses? Colleges and Professors Start to Sort It Out." *Chronicle of Higher Education* (Dec. 17): A45.

Carr, Sarah. 2000. "Distance-Education Company Woos Bastions of the Liberal Arts." *Chronicle of Higher Education* (Jan. 28): A45.

Chait, Richard P. 1995. "The New Activism of Corporate Boards and the Implications for Campus Governance." Washington, DC: Association of Governing Boards.

Chait, Richard P., and Andrew T. Ford. 1982. *Beyond Traditional Tenure.* San Francisco: Jossey-Bass Publishers.

Chait, Richard P., Cathy Trower, and John K. Urice. 2002. "What Difference

Does Tenure Make in Campus Governance?" In R. Chait (ed.), *The Questions of Tenure*. Cambridge: Harvard University Press.

Chronicle of Higher Education Almanac. 1995. Vol. 42, no.1 (Sept. 1).

Chronicle of Higher Education Almanac. 1999. Vol. 46, no.1 (Aug. 27).

Clark, Burton. 1987. *The Academic Life: Small Worlds, Different Worlds.* Princeton: Carnegie Foundation for the Advancement of Teaching.

———. 1993. "Faculty: Differentiation and Dispersion." In A. Levine (ed.), *Higher Learning in America, 1980–2000.* Baltimore: Johns Hopkins University Press.

Clotfelter, Charles T. 1996. *Buying the Best: Cost Escalation in Higher Education.* Princeton: Princeton University Press.

Cohen, Michael D., and James G. March. 1974. *Leadership and Ambiguity: The American College President.* New York: McGraw-Hill.

Commission on Academic Tenure. 1973. *Faculty Tenure: A Report and Recommendations by the Commission on Academic Tenure in Higher Education.* San Francisco: Jossey-Bass Publishers.

Damrosch, David. 1995. *We Scholars: Changing the Culture of the University.* Cambridge: Harvard University Press.

Demb, Ada, and F.-Friedrich Neubauer. 1992. *The Corporate Board: Confronting the Paradoxes.* New York: Oxford University Press.

Duryea, E. D. 1973. "The Evolution of University Organization." In J. Perkins (ed.), *The University as an Organization.* New York: McGraw-Hill. Reprinted in M. Peterson (ed.). 1991. *Organization and Governance in Higher Education.* 4th ed. Needham Heights, MA: Simon and Schuster.

Engstrom, Gary. 1998. "Tenure Wars." *American Behavioral Scientist* 41: 607–26.

Farber, Daniel A. 1997. "The Miasma in Minnesota." *Trusteeship* (May/June): 6–10.

Finkelstein, Martin J., Robert K. Seal, and Jack H. Schuster. 1998. *The New Academic Generation: A Profession in Transformation.* Baltimore: Johns Hopkins University Press.

Finkin, Matthew W. (ed.). 1996. *The Case for Tenure.* Ithaca: Cornell University Press.

Frank, Robert H., and Philip J. Cook. 1995. *The Winner-Take-All Society.* New York: Penguin Books.

Gappa, Judith M., and David W. Leslie. 1993. *The Invisible Faculty: Improving the Status of Part-Timers in Higher Education.* San Francisco: Jossey-Bass Publishers.

Garbarino, Joseph W. 1975. *Faculty Bargaining: Change and Conflict.* New York: McGraw-Hill.

Gumport, Patricia J. 1997. "Public Universities as Academic Workplaces." *Daedalus* 126: 113–36.

Hardi, Joel, and Sara Hebel. 2000. "California Governor Seeks a Big Budget Increase for Higher Education." *Chronicle of Higher Education* (Jan. 21): A28.

Harvey, James, and John Immerwahr. 1995. *The Fragile Coalition: Public Support for Higher Education in the 1990s.* Washington, DC: American Council on Education.

Healy, Patrick. 1997. "Virginia Board Members Urged to Become Activists." *Chronicle of Higher Education* (Mar. 21): A35.

Howe, Peter J. 2000. "MIT, Miami Firm in $90m Optical Networking Venture." *Boston Globe* (Jan. 21): C3.

Huber, Richard M. 1992. *How Professors Play the Cat Guarding the Cream: Why We're Paying More and Getting Less in Higher Education.* Fairfax, VA: George Mason University Press.

Hurd, Richard, Amy Foerster, with Beth Hillman Johnson. 1996. *The Directory of Faculty Contracts and Bargaining Agreements in Institutions of Higher Education, 1996–97.* Vol. 22. New York: City University of New York, Baruch College.

Ingram, Richard T. 1999. "Faculty Angst and the Search for a Common Enemy." *Chronicle of Higher Education* (May 14): B10.

Jencks, Christopher, and David Riesman. 1968. *The Academic Revolution.* New York: Doubleday and Company.

Kennedy, Donald. 1994. "Making Choices in the Research University." In Jonathon R. Cole, Clinor G. Barber, and Stephen R. Graubard (eds.), *The Research University in a Time of Discontent.* Baltimore: Johns Hopkins University Press.

———. 1997. *Academic Duty.* Cambridge: Harvard University Press.

Kerr, Clark. 1984. *Presidents Make a Difference: Strengthening Leadership in Colleges and Universities.* Washington, DC: Association of Governing Boards.

———. 1986. *The Many Lives of Academic Presidents.* Washington, DC: Association of Governing Boards.

———. 1991. *The Great Transformation in Higher Education, 1960–1980.* Albany: State University of New York Press.

Knight Higher Education Collaborative. 1999. "The Third Imperative." *Policy Perspectives* 9 (1).

Lazerson, Marvin. 1997. "Who Owns Higher Education? The Changing Face of Governance." *Change Magazine* (Mar./Apr.): 10–15.

Leatherman, Courtney. 1999. "Growth in Positions off the Tenure Track Is a Trend that's Here to Stay, Study Finds." *Chronicle of Higher Education* (Apr. 9): A14.

———. 2000. "Union Movement at Private Colleges Awakens after a 20-Year Slumber." *Chronicle of Higher Education* (Jan. 21).

Levine, Arthur. 1997. "How the Academic Profession Is Changing." *Daedalus* 126: 1–20.

Licata, Christine M., and Joseph C. Morreale. 1997. *Post-Tenure Review Policies, Practices, and Precautions.* Washington, DC: American Association for Higher Education.

Lively, Kit. 1995. "University of California Ends Race-Based Hirings, Admissions." *Chronicle of Higher Education* (July 28): A26.

Lorsch, Jay W. 1989. *Pawns and Potentates: The Reality of America's Corporate Boards.* Boston: Harvard Business School Press.

———. 1995. "Empowering the Board." *Harvard Business Review* (Jan.–Feb.): 107–17.

Madsen, Holly. 1997. "Composition of Governing Boards of Public Colleges and Universities," and "Composition of Governing Boards of Independent Colleges and Universities." Occasional Paper Series no. 36 and no.37. Washington, DC: Association of Governing Boards.

Magner, Denise. 1998. "A Stable of 'Superstar' Teachers Performs before the Camera." *Chronicle of Higher Education* (Nov. 6): A16.

Mallon, William T. 2001. *Tenure on Trial: Case Studies of Change in Faculty Employment Policies*. New York: RoutledgeFarmer.

McPherson, Michael S., and Morton Owen Shapiro. 1999. "Tenure Issues in Higher Education." *Journal of Economic Perspectives* 13: 85–98.

Metzger, Walter. 1987. "The Academic Profession in the United States." Pp. 123–208 in Burton Clark (ed.), *The Academic Profession*. Berkeley: University of California Press.

National Center for Education Statistics. 1996. *1993 National Study of Postsecondary Faculty, Institutional Policies and Practices Regarding Faculty in Higher Education*. Washington, DC: U.S. Department of Education.

———. 1997. *1993 National Study of Postsecondary Faculty, Instructional Faculty and Staff in Higher Education Institutions: Fall 1987 and Fall 1992*. Washington, DC: U.S. Department of Education.

———. 1998. *Fall Staff in Postsecondary Institutions, 1995*. Washington, DC: U.S. Department of Education.

———. 1999. *Postsecondary Education Digest of Education Statistics*. Washington, DC: U.S. Department of Education.

Nelson, Cary T. 1999. "The War against the Faculty." *Chronicle of Higher Education* (Apr. 16): B4.

Pound, John. 1995. "The Promise of the Governed Corporation." *Harvard Business Review* (Mar.–Apr.): 89–98.

Prewitt, Kenneth. 1994. "America's Research University under Public Scrutiny." In Jonathon R. Cole, Clinor G. Barber, and Stephen R. Graubard (eds.), *The Research University in a Time of Discontent*. Baltimore: Johns Hopkins University Press.

Richardson, James T. 1999. "Centralizing Governance Isn't Simply Wrong; It's Bad Business, Too." *Chronicle of Higher Education* (Feb. 12): B9.

Rosovsky, Henry. 1990. *The University: An Owner's Manual*. New York: W. W. Norton.

Ruscio, Kenneth P. 1987. "Many Sectors, Many Professions." In Burton Clark (ed.), *The Academic Profession*. Berkeley: University of California Press.

Sanderson, Allen, Voon Chin Phua, and David Herda. 1999. *The American Faculty Poll: Final Report*. New York: TIAA-CREF.

Sax, Linda J., A. W. Astin, W. S. Korn, and S. K. Gilmartin. 1999. *The American College Teacher: National Norms for the 1998–99 HERI Faculty Survey*. Los Angeles: Higher Education Research Institute, UCLA.

Schneider, Alison. 1997. "A Harvard Economist Hits the Jackpot with a $1.4 Million Advance for a Textbook." *Chronicle of Higher Education* (Oct. 10): A12.

———. 1998. "Recruiting Academic Stars: New Tactics in an Old Game." *Chronicle of Higher Education* (May 29): A12.

Staples, Brent. 1998. "The Politics of Remedial Education at CUNY." *New York Times* (Sept. 7): A16.

Taylor, Barbara E., and William F. Massy. 1998. *Strategic Indicators for Higher Education, 1996*. Princeton: Peterson's.

Tierney, William G. (ed.). 1998. "Tenure Matters: Rethinking Faculty Roles and Rewards." *American Behavioral Scientist* 41 (5).

Wilson, Robin. 1998. "U. of Dubuque Board of Trustees Take Faculty to Court." *Chronicle of Higher Education* (June 19): A12.

Zemsky, Robert, and William F. Massy. 1995. "Expanding Perimeters, Melting Cores, and Sticky Functions: Toward an Understanding of Current Predicaments." Unpublished paper. The Cost of Undergraduate Education Project, CUE–1, University of Pennsylvania.

Zoghi, Cindy. 1999. "Why Have Public University Professors Done So Badly?" Unpublished paper. Austin: University of Texas, Department of Economics.

CHAPTER TWELVE

University Transformation: Primary Pathways to University Autonomy and Achievement

BURTON R. CLARK

Universities today are facing enormous pressures for change. These pressures can lead to loss of direction and vulnerability, or they can lead to continued effectiveness and achievement. Based on research in European systems of higher education, but with American universities never far from view, I specify in this chapter some modern pathways of university transformation that can promote greater university autonomy and bolster university achievement in these turbulent times. These interacting pathways, largely entrepreneurial in character, can also serve to reaffirm traditional university values.

The Rapid Growth of Demand Overload

We must begin, however, by understanding why the current university structure is facing enormous pressures for change. Four converging trends spell out the magnitude of what is happening.

First, demands for participation are changing student entry into postsecondary education from elite to mass to universal (Clark, 2000; Trow, 1974). A growing entitlement of young people to receive more education after secondary school leads onward to a lifelong entitlement for both repeated professional upgrading and cultural enrichment that extends into the retirement years. Universal expectations that bracket the young and the old dictate long-term continuing growth in number and type of students. This one channel of demand itself, if left unanswered—as in open-door universities on the European continent, where qualification is determined upon graduation from the secondary school—can badly over-load the response capabilities of individual institutions, stretching them beyond all sensible limits in size and scope. And it is organizationally penetrating: it flows into, through, and out of universities as applicants become participants for two, four, six, or more years, only to again nego-tiate passage as adult students in continuing education.

Second, more segments of the labor force demand university gradu-ates trained for highly specialized occupations. At different degree levels, graduates expect qualification in diverse specialties. Graduates also need retraining throughout their professional careers. Thus the training re-quirements for the labor force become virtually endless. This demand in itself can badly overload universities when answers have not been found to control demand and bolster response capabilities. Again, a seemingly "environmental" demand does not merely knock at the door. Rather, a dispersion of future work careers is expressed through the organization of students into separate training tracks and specialized student careers. Output boundaries are increasingly permeable.

Third, patrons in government and the private sector increasingly ex-hort universities to assist in solving societal problems as broad as poverty and poor health and as specific as city charter reform and local traffic control. Here special emphasis is placed on speeding economic and tech-nological progress for state and nation. The competitive strength of the economy and nation becomes a university problem. Universities, par-ticularly public ones, are increasingly not able to turn their backs on such calls for relevant problem solving. With a growing chorus of interest groups repeatedly expressing their voices, accountability extends in many directions. This stream of demand also becomes virtually endless.

Fourth, knowledge outruns resources. This knowledge acceleration is the most troubling trend of all, for it rattles the university at its very foundations. As such, it merits a more extensive discussion.

THE KNOWLEDGE EXPLOSION

In a prodigious essay written in the late 1980s, the historian Walter Metzger provided an overview of how new disciplines emerged in American higher education during the course of the nineteenth and early twentieth centuries—a rich story that he conceptualized as "substantive growth," in contrast to "reactive growth," in which growth of faculty and curricula stems more from student growth and growth in labor force demands (1987). Metzger showed how time and again growth stemmed from faculty pursuing both individual and group advantage, and altruistic "advancement of knowledge." He identified four processes that led to this form of growth: *subject parturition*, in which new fields are born out of older ones; *program affiliation* and *subject dignification*, in which formerly excluded fields are admitted to the family of legitimate subjects, as exemplified in the American system by the professional fields of medicine and law becoming affiliated and such previously low-rated fields as modern languages and technology becoming fully dignified; and *subject dispersion* (or *subject imperialism*, we might also call it), in which, for example, the field of history constantly expands its scope to cover more societal sectors, more time periods, and more geographic locales, producing such three-way specialties as the history of science in Japan during the nineteenth century.

The processes of substantive growth have sped up remarkably during the twentieth century: the gestation period for new subjects has become shorter and shorter; subject dignification has run rampant; and subject dispersion increasingly becomes virtually a genetic form of discipline aggrandizement. Economics, for example, is willing to attempt to explain any and all societal sectors and social practices, including an economics of the family, an economics of love, and even a very chancy economics of hedge funds.

Examples of the current magnitude of substantive growth at the discipline level may be readily noted. A set of large "medical sciences" have grown up as a separate group of academic fields (pharmacology, epidemiology, and immunology are among them) along side of, rather than subsumed under, the biological sciences. The fast-growing engineering sciences (including aeronautical, chemical, and materials engineering) have taken up residence outside the physical sciences. Turning to internal features of specific disciplines: the burgeoning field of mathematics publishes over 200,000 new theorems each year; its journals exceed one thousand in number; its review journals classify over forty-five hundred subtopics arranged under sixty-two major topics (Madison, 1992). Psychology is now huge and extensively fragmented; the American Psychological Association exhibits a structure of over forty major specialties. One of these specialties, social psychology, claims seventeen subspecialty fields (Hewstone, 1992; Leary, 1992).

We have let the dimensions of this substantive growth escape us. Fortunately, the basic information with which to begin to grasp this primary form of university and system development is never far away. Subject differentiation in the twentieth century can be found in old university catalogs. It can be found in the readily available data of such counting houses as the Institute for Scientific Information (ISI) that monitor the production and citation of scientific literature. The ISI reported at the end of the 1980s that it was able to track more than "8,200 currently active specialty areas in science" (ISI newsletter, *Science Watch*). Knowledge growth can be traced in the changing range and depth of encyclopedias. A forthcoming encyclopedia of the social sciences has required fifty section editors to pull together materials in twenty-six volumes on twenty major fields, and some interdisciplinary subjects. This compares to the half-dozen major fields seen as basic four decades ago. Now such major fields as economics and psychology insist on two hundred articles or more with which to explain what they are about (*International Encyclopedia of the Social & Behavioral Sciences,* 2001). A new encyclopedia devoted to the field of philosophy has attempted to cover the waterfront and sort out the complexity of this ambiguous subject in ten volumes containing over fifteen hundred articles assembled by over thirty section editors (*Routledge Encyclopedia of Philosophy,* 1998). The current extreme of knowledge fragmentation is apparently revealed in a new seven-hundred-page *Encyclopedia of Semiotics* (the study of "signs"!), which renders chaos chaotically: an entry on "text" but not on "context"; "space" but not "time"; "apartheid" but not "fascism"; "Buddhism" but not "Christianity"; "baseball" but not "cricket" or "rugby" or even "chess" (*Encyclopedia of Semiotics,* 2000; Harris, 2000).

The international growth and dispersion of knowledge has been driven throughout the twentieth century by the increasing universality of scientific disciplines. It is now spurred in a virtual quantum leap by the globalization inherent in computer-age technology. Because the differentiation of knowledge is proceeding at a rapid pace, would-be "renaissance scholars," broad in their command of scholarship, are more than ever an endangered species. Departments cannot cover and keep up with the spreading waterfront of knowledge in particular disciplines. The common secret of university departments is that they all specialize to the second power, covering only some of the areas found in their specialized field. And in coverage of the growing array of deserving subjects and specialty fields, entire universities, no matter how rich, cannot do it all. To conceptually capture this awesome change, our vocabulary shifts from knowledge growth to knowledge acceleration to knowledge explosion—

or perhaps continuous knowledge eruption. Internationally, no one controls the production, reformulation, and distribution of knowledge. Never ceasing, rampaging knowledge has no stopping place. Fields of knowledge are the ultimate uncontrollable force that can readily leave universities running a losing race.

The differentiation of academic specialty fields within the knowledge foundation of higher education has gotten well ahead of our imagination, let alone our grasp. Subject fragmentation has arguably become *the* source of ever-growing system complexity. It is a source more powerful and extensive in its effects than the expanded inputs of students and the more varied outputs to the general labor force on which analysts commonly concentrate when they observe the scale and scope of modern universities and national systems of higher education. Many universities are able to cap their size and to limit their training lines, but they cannot control the national and international growth in knowledge. The differentiation of knowledge fractures the foundation of the university into a thousand pieces: a major American research university mounts over four thousand courses; even a small liberal arts college offers five hundred.

Research production and related specialization also turn cognitive fragmentation into extremely complicated forms of *institutional* differentiation. Two examples illustrate. First, in a penetrating analysis of graduate training in U.S. higher education, Peter Syverson has revealed that the 125 "research-intensive" universities listed in the Research I and Research II categories of the Carnegie classification actually enroll just 44 percent of all graduate students and 59 percent of students in science and engineering. Another 800 institutions spread throughout seven other Carnegie categories are also involved in the graduate education enterprise, accounting for the converse figures of 56 percent of all graduate students and 41 percent in science and engineering. These other institutions include doctoral-granting universities that are more teaching-led than research-led, master's level universities, bachelor's level colleges that have some graduate programs, and a miscellany of "specialized institutions"—detached medical schools, business schools, engineering schools, all accredited, which do not fit readily into any of the other categories. This extended assortment of an additional 800 institutions, operating beyond the 125 positioned "at the top of the academic food chain," granted in 1997 more than 230,000 master's degrees and 9,000 doctoral degrees (Syverson, 1999). In short, even the graduate level of the American system is extremely diversified in its institutional locations, and it

steadily becomes more so. The many locations differ enormously in resources, faculty, student peers, and programs (Gumport, 1993).

Following the contours of unplanned change in and among disciplines, and of simple imitation among institutions, this spectacular process of knowledge addition and knowledge recasting encourages both disciplinary and institutional drift. Such drift has long served well, keeping
inquiry open and adapting organizational structures. It will continue to
be necessary. But its costs in financial and human resources have been
rising sharply, heightening the need for tough choices and deepening the
importance of who decides and how they go about doing it. From department to faculty or school to university as a whole, what perspectives,
topics, specialties, and disciplines must be included, and which excluded?
Or, on a more practical continuum, which are to be highlighted, which
are to be maintained well above the line of acceptable competence, which
are to be maintained even below that line, which should suffer death by a
thousand cuts during the next decade, and which should be and can be
eliminated tomorrow?

RESPONSES

In the face of demand overload, universities find themselves short of
response capabilities. Resource needs become constant when traditional
funding sources indicate they will pay for only a decreasing share of present and future costs. Traditional infrastructure, if left in customary form,
becomes a major constraint on the possibilities of response: central direction ranges between soft and soggy; elaborate collegial authority adds to
sluggish decision-making as dozens of committees express their right to
study, delay, and veto; enlarged departments and faculties tend to go
their own way, turning the university into a confederation in which major and minor parts barely relate to one another. And even if everyone
becomes cooperative, rational, and willing, in what directions should we
commit our limited resources—and how can we go about doing it? Uncertainty increases about what is most essential now, and especially
about what will be particularly crucial in the future. This uncertainty is
pervasive; it applies to undergraduate education and graduate education
and the balance between the two; to the contents of each of the disciplinary departments, interdisciplinary programs, and applications-generated
research centers; to the attraction and accommodation of new types of
students; to tenure commitments to faculty in different parts of the uni-

versity. A philosophical search for a single, defined best way is not profitable. Too much can be defined as basic, too much can readily be deemed necessary by the academic tribes who serve as the carrying vehicles for the many cognitive territories.

The new circumstances have inspired a variety of prescriptions. University strategists have variously counseled presidents and chancellors to build to their institution's strengths, to concentrate on their core missions, to look ahead to the professional labor market of the future, to find distinctive niches within the ecology of comparable institutions, and to get ahead of the curve by embracing the interdisciplinary and multidisciplinary future. This advice, even where it may be valuable, does not address the key issues facing universities in the future: How can they compose themselves to be more adaptable, while remaining true to their essential traditions of self-management and intellectual achievement?

As universities, individually and in new alliances, seek ways of responding to what is now a flood of converging demands, we seem to have entered a new era of university transformation that necessitates more conscious local steering. Sheer overload forces individual universities to take stock of what matters most, given their particular heritage, internal capabilities, and environmental possibilities. Successful universities will be those able to work their way across decades of uncertainty by defining who they are and what they will and will not do. To become more proactive, they are likely to experiment with entrepreneurial activities appropriate for the underlying disciplinary character of universities.

The Entrepreneurial Reinvention of Autonomy and Achievement in the University

The question is how. How do universities build a systematic capability to be more self-reliant, to be able to take care of themselves come what may in turbulent times? I had the opportunity to seek some answers from a small group of proactive universities in Europe—places that had broken the cake of custom in their own national and cultural settings—in a research study carried out between 1994 and 1997 (Clark, 1998a, 2000). The institutions selected for intensive investigation were chosen because they had been hard at work for some ten years or more (roughly 1980 to 1995) to try to change their own overall character—a period long enough to ascertain how much and in what lasting ways these institutions had actually accomplished major institutional change.

The universities differed greatly in their educational profiles and cultural settings. The University of Warwick in the English Midlands was a relatively new "green fields" nationally oriented university from the 1960s that offered selective comprehensive coverage of the basic disciplines; the University of Joensuu in rural Finland, also new in the 1960s, emerged from a teachers' college background to become a small comprehensive regional university; the University of Twente in the eastern part of Holland, also relatively young, was initiated as a technological university in a depressed region and then soon built a distinguishing posture of coupling applied science with applied social science; the University of Strathclyde in Glasgow, Scotland, was both old and young: it celebrated a bicentennial in 1996 but was only "raised" to university standing in the 1950s, then spread its wings from a purely technological posture to a broader five-faculty structure; and Chalmers University of Technology in Gothenburg, Sweden, could trace its lineage back 150 years as a specialized university that had experienced both private and public control and was currently evolving from pure state university to a new semiprivate status.

Even though these five institutions were variously located and obviously quite different, I was able to tease out some common elements of how they were changing. I identified these features as pathways of transformation, used them to frame case-by-case developmental accounts, and concluded that together they constituted "an entrepreneurial response" to the growing demands of the late twentieth century. By and large, European universities were becoming increasingly strained by the set of demands identified above, but these five institutions had become more adaptive in ways that seemed favorable for long-term viability.

The five pathways were highly interactive and mutually supportive. Although they can be presented in any order, I list them here roughly in their primacy of appearance as the institutional transformation unfolded.

A STRENGTHENED STEERING CORE

The institutions I examined exhibited a greater capacity to steer themselves in 1995 than they had possessed ten to fifteen years earlier. That capability could be organized in a relatively centralized or decentralized way. Sometimes, a strong-minded leader, such as tough rector, initiated new mechanisms; in other cases, they evolved through the work of committees. But over the years, personal leadership, if present, was supplemented by, and generally encapsulated within, collegial forms of leadership. As stronger line authority developed in the positions of rector, faculty dean, and department head, stronger decision-making groups of administrators and faculty were also created at these major levels, with one or more such groups at the university center becoming decisive.

Whatever its specific shape, the strengthened steering core consisted of groups that worked diligently to develop the other four identified pathways. The groups promoted new infrastructure units that reached across old university boundaries to link up more readily than traditional departments with outside establishments (the second element below); they sought diverse streams of income (the third element); and turned to multiple patrons instead of waiting passively for "the government to come to its senses" and rescue the institution from unacceptable resource constraint.

A strengthened steering core is finally fully formed when it is able to cross-subsidize from pooled resources. Newly legitimated central groups tax rich fields to aid less fortunate ones that otherwise would be relegated to the margins or even eliminated because "they cannot pay their way." A vigorous all-university steering core seeks not only to subsidize some new experiments and activities but also to enhance old valuable programs in the academic heartland (pathway four below); an example would be to strengthen departments in the humanities and "soft" social sciences. Several institutions in my study have in effect become international models of how to make this difficult process work, particularly Warwick and Strathclyde in the much-troubled British system and Twente in the Netherlands. Strathclyde has presented a particularly clear model in its central University Management Group (UMG), developed through tough struggle between 1982 and 1987. It has become the place where decisions can be made relatively quickly, a place where the institution can "get up and go." The faculty is heavily represented in the UMG by elected and selected faculty members and particularly through the participation of elected deans who serve in a crucial dual capacity of representing the entire university while also representing their own faculties (as in Faculty of Science).

The concept of a steering core can serve as a useful replacement for the old muddled concept of "leadership," which has been worn out by a thousand definitions overly centered on the characteristics of individuals. It includes the leading role played by groups as well as individuals. It stresses that the formulation and execution of important decisions in universities, characterized as they are by commitments to disciplines, which lead to a bottom-heavy structure, require the regular involvement of many participants from top to bottom. It fits the enduring values of faculty expressed in the ideas of shared governance and due process. And it leads toward the larger idea that entrepreneurship becomes a good fit for universities when it is heavily collegial in its operation.

AN ENHANCED DEVELOPMENTAL PERIPHERY

The five varied institutions in my study also exhibited in 1995, compared to 1980, a larger, more complex set of units operating on the periphery of the traditional structure, reaching across old boundaries to link up with outside interests. Although these units took different specific forms, they can be grouped in two main categories: administrative offices that promote outreach—particularly industrial liaison, technology transfer, consultancy, and continuing professional education; and, most important, multi- or transdisciplinary academic units operating as basic units parallel to disciplinary departments. The latter centers and programs may be closely or loosely linked to the traditional operating base.

Some peripheral units, while using the name and sponsorship of the university, may be so loosely integrated with it that they operate much like mediating institutions situated at the interface between the university and outside organizations. An example is the operationally autonomous Warwick Science Park (sponsored by city, county, and university), where research arms of firms and new start-ups encamp. No one way exists, no one model to emulate, no magic formula to find. The possibilities on the old periphery are made into new realities as they are worked out locally.

The key point is that an enhanced periphery gives the university a dual operating structure: departmental "specialist groups" are complemented by "project groups" (in matrix terminology) that admit external definitions of research problems and needed education and training. The project groups cross old lines of authority and promote environmental linkages in daily practice. They develop new competencies in the university and useful problem solving: the University of Joensuu in rural Finland, for example, has developed a valuable expertise in sustainable forestry, one with worldwide utility, which flows outward through linkage to two outside applied research centers, one occupying shared space at the university; and Chalmers in Sweden has sought to develop a number of new useful "competencies," including one in pollution control pursued by a university-industry group centered on auto exhaust emission. Here knowledge clearly becomes more "applications-generated" and knowledge transfer flows two ways, from outside enterprise to university as well as from university to outside. And of course such units help generate income that can be spent in such valuable ways as supporting graduate students.

The developmental periphery is a place for experimentation. It can have temporary units, serving as agents of exploration, which operate under three- or five- or ten-year sunset provisions and are renewed only if they continue to prove their value. Interdisciplinary centers and teaching programs are generally easier to terminate or transform than are departments, especially those under new ground rules for their existence. An array of such units can serve as a portfolio of small experimental steps; the institution need not stake everything on one grand new investment.

The great danger in the development of peripheral units is that they may move an institution toward the character of a shopping mall. This did not happen in the universities I studied, since the members of the steering core, together with the heartland departments discussed below, saw to it that academic values encircled managerial and budgetary interests. As the British describe it, new units had to help the university go "up-market" in academic esteem and public reputation. And off in rural Finland as much as in the sentiments of British academics, the phrase "this is a university" was voiced to call attention to the need to bring academic standards to bear in establishing a line between proper and improper practices in the gray areas of much enlarged boundaries.

An extended periphery adds considerably to the organizational complexity of a university. It does not make life simpler. But since traditional departments and administrative offices cannot by themselves actuate all the flexible links to a fast-changing environment that universities now need, the enlarged periphery becomes an essential element for lessening the imbalance between environmental demands and response capacity. It gives the university more tools, more flexible tools, for self-development.

A DIVERSIFIED FUNDING BASE

Student growth and knowledge growth together increase enormously the costs of higher education to governments. What was once a minor item in governmental budgets has become a major expenditure, a big-ticket item thrown into direct competition with other primary interests, from military to welfare. Even in good times, governments now seek to control higher education costs. In bad times they insist on major cuts. Some even develop the habit of calling yearly for "efficiency gains"— more work for less money—which can readily become operationally a form of death by a thousand cuts.

As governments become less willing to pay all the costs of these seemingly expensive places, traditional public universities come to a fork in the financial road. They can fall in line and undergo parallel financial increases and decreases as the government specifies, hoping the government will always do better some time soon. Or institutions can choose to become proactive, to seek to develop dependable lines of income from other sources. Worldwide, university ambition encourages this second choice; increasing competition virtually demands it.

The institutions I studied in Europe welcomed the chance to escape from complete dependence on a single patron, commonly a government ministry. Warwick reduced its dependence between 1980 and 1995 from 70 to 38 percent of total income; Strathclyde from 64 to 45 percent; Chalmers from 67 to 55 percent; Joensuu from 96 to 66 percent; and Twente from 96 to 76 percent. Country context mattered considerably in judging how far and fast to push this change. But the trend away from single-source dependency has spread internationally. Science and technology departments, in my group of institutions, generally exceeded the institutionwide change, moving to two-thirds or more of income from "other sources."

A diversified funding base enhances university discretion. It not only increases total resources but also allows an institution to roll with the punches, replacing a loss here with a gain there. Universities can build reserves they can then use to take innovative steps: the University of Warwick offered a striking example in the early 1990s when amid the almost nasty financial stringency of the British nationalized system it used accumulated surpluses from "earned income" to help fund a new research fellowship scheme for junior faculty, which attracted outstanding applicants from around the world. Warwick has made good use of the formulation that if old "hard money" has turned soft, with the government now an undependable patron, "soft money," in its totality, can become relatively hard.

Diversity in university financing has become virtually a prerequisite for adaptability and autonomy. It appears that universities throughout the world are finally latching onto the insight offered by Homer D. Babbidge and Robert Rosenzweig back in the early 1960s, when they stressed that "a workable twentieth century definition of institutional autonomy [is] the absence of dependence upon a single or narrow base of support" (1962: 158).

A STIMULATED ACADEMIC HEARTLAND

A strongly proactive university, as it develops, depends on the acceptance of a new evolving posture by the traditional discipline-led departments that serve as the academic heartland. They have to accept the overall need for more enterprising activities and to learn in many cases how to engage in such action themselves.

This shift is typically made in an uneven fashion. Science and technology departments commonly become entrepreneurial first and most fully. They are more accustomed to competing for extra funds and working with external organizations; generally they already have funds from multiple patrons and have learned how to distribute them internally from pools of amassed resources. Social science departments find the shift more difficult, but led by economics and business they tend to be the next major segment of the traditional structure to find more virtue than vice in melding basic and applied orientations, discipline-led and applications-led activity.

Humanities and arts departments have good reason at first to be resisting laggards. New money does not readily flow their way from either governmental or nongovernmental patrons. Deliberate effort to offer new services with income in mind may seem particularly out of place. It is demeaning to be a poor relative, living off heavier teaching loads or money skimmed from the top of the funds brought in by the rich departments. As the poorer fields slide down past the salt at the table of departmental income, resentment and disarray are likely to increase.

Since departmental adoption of entrepreneurial practices will normally vary by discipline, a university engaged in a transforming effort may soon find itself in a somewhat schizophrenic state, entrepreneurial on the one side and traditional on the other. Administrators and faculties at the five universities I studied rejected this option; a schizophrenic character suggested a split that would mean endless, bitter contention. If that were the outcome, the effort might be more trouble than it was worth; the doubters at other institutions would be right.

The heartland departments in my case studies, after much deliberation, by and large bought into entrepreneurial change for themselves, despite its difficulty. Social science and humanities departments found educational as well as economic value in becoming more enterprising, engaging, for instance, in paid policy analysis for departments of state and national government. It was impressive to discover at little, isolated Joensuu that several students in folklore, wise in the ways of computers, had worked for three years to fashion a CD-ROM entitled "Hyper Kalevala," gathering and integrating a thousand photographs and oral history recordings on the classic epic poem of the country. They figured out how to organize a small company and get the disc to market for use in the schools and for the enjoyment and education of adults. Sometimes students show the way. And however they respond in orienting their own departments, professors in the humanities and social sciences come to realize, after a few years of entrepreneurial effort by a university, that their own departments are better off with some additional cross-subsidy from other departments. Outreach efforts that bring new funds can be put to work across the institution. Monies earned or privately raised then become as legitimate as public funds, especially when there is never enough of the latter.

Whatever the specific combinations of departmental involvement, the roles played by heartland departments in institutional innovation cannot be overlooked. These departments are the bedrock keepers of academic norms. These norms are the basis for judgment, field-by-field and institutionwide, of whether proposed changes and newly installed activities are aimed up- or down-market. Departmental entrepreneurship that leads to "shoddy goods," as defined by academics and the general public, can set in motion a vicious circle of declining reputation and a more difficult recruitment of staff and students. Departments as well as the entire university have to make clear that they are not willing to respond opportunistically to all demands placed upon them—from students, industrial firms, professional associations, or governmental departments. If they are to take charge of their own destiny, while stepping out to forge new connections, they have to select and therefore to focus. When carried out effectively, a widespread embodiment of entrepreneurship in a university strengthens selective growth in its basic units, as part of strengthening the unity of the whole.

AN EMBRACING ENTREPRENEURIAL CULTURE

The four elements of change described thus far are largely structural: new groups and positions of authority, new administrative offices and outreach centers, categories of income and budgeting, and traditional departments and their practices. As such, they do not focus on the more symbolic side of organizational life. They do not capture the role played by ideas and beliefs.

Respondents repeatedly referred to new beliefs and institutional symbols in their involved answers to my open-ended questions. At Chalmers in Sweden, for example, professors and administrators pointed to the student culture as a key part of an overall organizational culture: student leaders who had come to believe in entrepreneurship through certain campus involvements went on to become alumni leaders, connected to one another and to the institution for years to come. They had, in effect, become true believers. Clearly, a fifth element—symbolic and cultural in nature—had to be brought into my explanatory scheme; this led me to trace how a belief system, or culture, centered on an "entrepreneurial spirit" comes about.

In each of my five institutions, the culture I found in 1995 had not emerged as a full-blown fact at the very beginning of change in the early or mid-1980s. It was not the product of an initial strategic plan (least of all, a mission statement!), or of a clear grand idea introduced by a powerful executive. Instead, at the outset of entrepreneurial change, the defining ideas were fragile, amounting to tentative, symbolic thrusts in the art of the possible. They had to be tested, worked out, and reformulated within contexts of changing internal capabilities and environmental possibilities. They had to avoid the Scylla of utopianism, where they would become counterproductive wishful thinking, and the Charybdis of opportunism, in which any adjustment would do, where they would provide little guidance.

This cultural element, interacting with the structural ones, developed over time from idea to belief to culture to saga. Cultural transformation at the University of Warwick, for example, started out in the early 1980s with the fledgling idea that since the government would not be putting up enough money—indeed it would be slashing support—the institution would try to "earn" its way. Over time and with growing success, the "earned income" idea became a sturdy set of related beliefs: that Warwick was an unusual British university, marked by new sources of income, new patterns of steerage, and new relationships with the outside world, all to the benefit of a growing capacity to be an outstanding university.

True believers in what Warwick was doing dominated the steering core and the developing periphery and gradually became more numerous in the departments: we can say the beliefs became an embracing culture. Outsiders took special note and heaped praise on what the institution had done; soon Warwick was a "national model." The university thus became symbolically strong, enough so that it could celebrate its achievements in the early 1990s with an enriched story of "the Warwick way." The idea that had turned into a belief system and then into a still wider culture had in the space of a decade become a saga of successful institution building in a harsh environment. (On the concept of organizational saga, see Clark, 1998b.)

A second example: the University of Twente in the Netherlands started its transformation in the early 1980s with a loud, almost defiant assertion that it would become "the entrepreneurial university." It then had to discover what the term could possibly mean! As the university developed a stronger steering capacity and a lively set of outreach activities, the idea became an explicit set of related beliefs: Twente was "the two-core university," a place that uniquely linked applied science and applied social science; it was "the campus university," uncommon for Holland, that allowed students and some faculty and staff to live and work together on a single integrated site; and a university that was also at once focused, flexible, without frontiers, and responsible to its local and national environments. Heartland departments became part of this embracing culture.

Twente in 1995 could claim a rugged identity formed out of a recent history of successful struggle. It too offered up a saga, a richly embellished and emotional account of achievement and identity. It believed in its distinctive ways enough to make vigorous efforts to spread the gospel to other institutions. Twente became in 1996 the headquarters for a new European Consortium of Innovative Universities (ECIU).

COMPLEMENTARY DEVELOPMENTS IN
THE UNITED STATES

Throughout the study, I worked inductively from European case studies. Absent American cases, I avoided any effort to generalize to the

American scene. But after formulating the five pathways of transformation, and placing them in a demand-response framework, it became clear from the observations and comments of others that the American scene was alive with entrepreneurial responses amid much sluggishness in the system at large, especially in the public sectors of many states. Powerful instances of a strong steering core and an extended developmental periphery can be found among American private universities: at Stanford and the Massachusetts Institute of Technology (MIT), for example. Many flagship state universities have moved strongly into income diversification; the universities of Michigan, Virginia, and California at Los Angeles (UCLA) are among them. UCLA income figures for 1998–99 showed that just 22 percent of total income came from the state of California, while 20 percent came from "contracts, grants, and gifts," 29 percent from the work of the "teaching hospital," and 9 percent from "student tuition and fees" (UCLA, 1998–99: 1).

Also, by the mid-1990s, such insightful university presidents as Charles Vest at MIT were noting crisply that universities generally had become "overextended, under-focused; overstressed, underfunded" (Vest, 1995). Donald Kennedy, former president of Stanford, noted the need for a new collegial approach, arguing that the questions to be asked in reform efforts "will not be answered by academic fiat from the center, nor will they yield to the embedded mechanisms of faculty decision-making. They require a new coalition" (Kennedy, 1993). David Leslie and E. K. Fretwell, Jr., researchers who had pursued site visits at over a dozen colleges and universities, reported a "broad recognition that missions had become too loose, that too many different programs were being offered, and that scarce resources were being spread too thin across too many activities," necessitating better steering and more focus (1996: xiv).

American universities, from rich to poor, large to small, comprehensive to specialized, seemed to be seeking integrated entrepreneurial responses, as institutional strain was now seen as systematically different from periods of stress in the past. In a competitive national system, and with a deepening sense of growing international competition, they are a restless lot, searching for a new organizational footing for autonomy and achievement. Much research is needed, close to practice.

Conclusion: A Summing Up

The modern university is an organization based on a wide array of discrete subjects or disciplines that are intimately a part of widespread fields of knowledge. The connection of basic departments to their own larger disciplines (including interdisciplinary fields) reduces the weight of organizational hierarchy, flattens the organizational structure, and leaves the university bottom heavy in the location of authority and centers of initiative. We understand the continuities of action in universities when we grasp that the many departments, functioning as arms of larger fields, are individual going concerns. Thus we learn to ask not just whither the university, but whither the humanities, whither the social sciences, whither the other major clusters of subjects, and whither the many specific fields within each of the major groupings. We are then not at all surprised to learn that the medical school is indeed on a different trajectory than the history department, that the business school is a quite different operation than the department of chemistry.

Universities have long been under the sway of subject multiplication and segmentation. This long-term trend of differentiation, between and within universities, is increasingly spurred by access demands, labor force demands, governmental and economic demands for relevant advice, and especially by the explosive growth of knowledge, which in a self-accelerating fashion follows from the research activity of universities and other knowledge-producing institutions. Differentiation turns universities into extremely complicated organizations. Who else would try to group folklore and biochemistry, philosophy and nursing, classics and mathematics, and pretend it is an organization? Universities operate somewhere on the far side of loose coupling.

The emerging organizational dilemma in many universities around the world can be portrayed in a demand-response equation. Response capability lags behind the build-up of demand. Constrained funding and fixed organizational structure lead to intolerable demand overload. In these early decades of the twenty-first century, new forms of organization are needed to help universities right the balance; we need to come up with a broader array of organizational tools and a stricter capacity to select among demands.

What is emerging in more and more universities is an entrepreneurial response that currently can be depicted in five middle-range categories: a strengthened steering core; an enhanced developmental periphery; a diversified income base; a stimulated academic heartland; and a wrap-around culture emphasizing entrepreneurial activity. For this response to develop well and to endure for more than a few years, it needs to be worked out in a collegial fashion that fits the way universities are distinctively put together. The professionally guarded disciplinary base, long shaped ideologically by such faculty-based ideas as shared governance and due process, dictates that entrepreneurship in universities will take more collegial forms than those expected from the application of business models. The faculty must become owners of change by being deeply involved in the processes that lead to new response capabilities. Business-based models (the commanding CEO, for example) brought from commerce to higher education commonly do not take hold. They turn into fads that come and go.

Business models are seriously flawed: they promote a conception of the university as largely a tool of economic utility. Reform becomes centered on hierarchical accountability, year-by-year assessment, and improved efficiency. A counternarrative stresses the long-term value of the autonomous university that uses a collegial form of entrepreneurial activity to become more flexible and adaptable and thereby is better equipped to face the open-ended challenges of the coming decades. We then seek to learn how universities take care of themselves in an environment of constant change and growing uncertainty. Since no one really knows what the tomorrow of 2010 and 2020 will bring for different sectors of higher education, prudent institutions make their way by means of their own experimentation and close attention to what other successful universities are doing. The best way to predict the future is to make it yourself.

"The university" is not driven by "globalization" to move decisively in a certain direction, nor by "economic forces," nor by "demographic trends," not even by "state policy." Instead, utilizing an inside-out perspective, we come to see that the active university is mainly driven by the responses it makes, responses that are the sum of reactions in its many parts. There is no automatic stimulus-response: the university is not an infant in a self-contained Skinner box, nor is it an assembly of toothless workers who must passively accept a fate determined by others. University responses are rooted in traditional tendencies, ongoing self-interests, and especially in the will of faculty based in a range of academic professions and of administrators devoted to the welfare of particular institutions. Between demand and response, human volition is the crux of the matter. The new entrepreneurial autonomy, toward which my analysis points, supports a strong universitywide volition that builds upon encompassing interests and capacities. University achievement is then neither state-led nor market-dictated. It finds its propulsion in the agency of those inside the university whose actions decide what actually gets done.

Note

I wish to thank my wife, Adele Clark, for in-depth editing of this paper. The paper draws heavily on Clark (1998a) and Clark (2000).

References

Babbidge, Homer D., and Robert Rosenzweig. 1962. *The Federal Interest in Higher Education*. New York: McGraw-Hill.

Clark, Burton R. 1998a. *Creating Entrepreneurial Universities: Organizational Pathways of Transformation*. Oxford: Pergamon-Elsevier Science.

———. 1998b. "The Organizational Saga in Higher Education." In J. V. Van Maanen (ed), *Qualitative Studies of Organizations*. The Administrative Science Quarterly Series in Organizational Behavior and Theory. Thousand Oaks, CA: Sage Publications. Originally published in the *Administrative Science Quarterly* 17 (2): 178–84.

———. 2000. "Collegial Entrepreneurialism in Proactive Universities: Lessons from Europe." *Change* (Jan./Feb.): 2–19.

Encyclopedia of Semiotics. 2000. Edited by Paul Bouissac. Oxford: Oxford University Press.

Gumport, Patricia J. 1993. "Graduate Education and Research Imperatives." Pp. 261–93 in Burton R. Clark (ed.), *The Research Foundations of Graduate Education: Germany, Britain, France, United States, Japan*. Berkeley and Los Angeles: University of California Press.

Harris, Roy. 2000. "Book Review of *Encyclopedia of Semiotics*." *Times Higher Education Supplement* (Feb. 11): 28.

Hewstone, M. 1992. "Social Psychology." Pp. 2150–63 in Burton R. Clark and Guy Neave (eds.), *The Encyclopedia of Higher Education*. Oxford: Pergamon Press.

International Encyclopedia of the Social & Behavioral Sciences. 2001. Edited by Neil J. Smelser and Paul B. Baltes. Amsterdam: Elsevier Science.

Kennedy, Donald. 1993. "Making Choices in the Research University." Pp. 85–114 in Jonathan R. Cole, Elinor G. Barber, and Stephen R. Graubard (eds.), *The University in a Time of Discontent*. Baltimore: Johns Hopkins Press.

Leary, D. E. 1992. "Psychology." Pp. 2136–50 in Burton R. Clark and Guy Neave (eds.), *The Encyclopedia of Higher Education*. Oxford: Pergamon Press.

Leslie, David W., and E. K. Fretwell, Jr. 1996. *Wise Moves in Hard Times: Creating and Managing Resilient Colleges & Universities*. San Francisco: Jossey-Bass.

Madison, B. L. 1992. "Mathematics and Statistics." Pp. 2372–88 in Burton R. Clark and Guy Neave (eds.), *The Encyclopedia of Higher Education*. Oxford: Pergamon Press.

Metzger, Walter. 1987. "The Academic Profession in the United States." Pp. 123–208 in Burton R. Clark (ed.), *The Academic Profession: National, Disciplinary, and Institutional Settings*. Berkeley and Los Angeles: University of California Press.

The Routledge Encyclopedia of Philosophy. 1998. Edited by Edward Craig. London: Routledge. Ten Volumes.

Syverson, Peter D. 1999. "Forty Percent of the System: The Contribution of DMOS [Doctorate, Master's, and Other Specialized] Institutions to Diversity in Science and Engineering Graduate Education." *Council of Graduate Schools Communicator* 32 (6): 8–10.

Trow, Martin. 1974. "Problems in the Transition from Elite to Mass Higher Education." Pp. 51–101 in *Policies for Higher Education*. Paris: Organisation for Economic Co-operation and Development.

University of California, Los Angeles (UCLA). 1998–99. *Annual Financial Report*. Los Angeles: UCLA.

Vest, Charles M. 1995. "Research Universities: Overextended, Underfocused; Overstressed, Underfunded." Unpublished paper presented at the Cornell Symposium on the American University, May 22, 1995. Boston: Massachusetts Institute of Technology.

Index

In this index an "f" after a number indicates a separate reference on the next page, and an "ff" indicates separate references on the next two pages. A continuous discussion over two or more pages is indicated by a span of page numbers, e.g., "57–59." *Passim* is used for a cluster of references in close but not consecutive sequence.